THE TEOTIHUACAN TRINITY

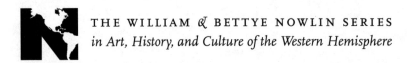

THE WILLIAM & BETTYE NOWLIN SERIES
in Art, History, and Culture of the Western Hemisphere

ANNABETH HEADRICK

THE TEOTIHUACAN TRINITY
THE SOCIOPOLITICAL STRUCTURE OF AN ANCIENT MESOAMERICAN CITY

University of Texas Press *Austin*

Photographs not otherwise credited are courtesy of the
author.

Requests for permission to reproduce material from this
work should be sent to:
    Permissions
    University of Texas Press
    P.O. Box 7819
    Austin, TX 78713-7819
    www.utexas.edu/utpress/about/bpermission.html

♾ The paper used in this book meets the minimum
requirements of ANSI/NISO Z39.481992 (R1997) (Permanence of Paper).

LIBRARY OF CONGRESS CATALOGING-IN-PUBLICATION DATA

Headrick, Annabeth.
The Teotihuacan trinity : the sociopolitical structure of an
ancient Mesoamerican city / Annabeth Headrick. — 1st ed.
        p.   cm. — (The William and Bettye Nowlin Series
in Art, History, and Culture of the Western Hemisphere)
Includes bibliographical references and index.
ISBN 978-0-292-71665-0 (cloth : alk. paper)
1. Teotihuacan Site (San Juan Teotihuacan, Mexico)
2. Aztecs—Mexico—San Juan Teotihuacan—Politics
and government.   3. Aztecs—Mexico—San Juan
Teotihuacan—Rites and ceremonies.   4. Aztecs—
Mexico—San Juan Teotihuacan—Antiquities.
5. Excavations (Archaeology)—Mexico—San Juan
Teotihuacan.   6. San Juan Teotihuacan (Mexico)—
Antiquities.   I. Title.
F1219.1.T27H43   2007
972—dc22
                                        2007008231

For Kurt Otto (K. O.) Headrick
and all that you might have done

The mountains were his masters. They rimmed in life. They were the cup of reality, beyond growth, beyond struggle and death. They were his absolute unity in the midst of eternal change.

THOMAS WOLFE, *LOOK HOMEWARD, ANGEL*

CONTENTS

LIST OF ILLUSTRATIONS

PREFACE

On my first visit to Teotihuacan I was wholly unimpressed. Though this thought now causes me much chagrin, at the time I had been seduced by the florid art and tree-sheltered architecture of the Maya. In fact, my initial view of the city was through the small window of a camper on a pickup truck while making my way home from excavations in Belize. Through this small window, the incredible size of Teotihuacan's pyramids initially elicited some degree of awe, but as I walked the main avenue, the city struck me as charmless and brash. The architecture's repetitive nature and oppressive scale seemed to have none of the finesse of Maya cities. The traces of painting on the surfaces of the walls certainly intrigued me, but the comparative absence of sculpture disturbed my then Maya-centric mind. Teotihuacan appeared to me like a large hulking gorilla devoid of any grace.

My rehabilitation began during another field season in the Maya area. Dolf Widmer engaged me in a series of conversations that summer and pressed me to define the topic of my dissertation. At the time the Terminal Classic city of Chichen Itza was the leading candidate, but then Dolf threw down a gauntlet I could not ignore. He questioned how I could work on the Terminal Classic when I had no deep understanding of Classic period Teotihuacan, the city whose collapse had so radically transformed the Mesoamerica that followed. Gradually, I became persuaded, and I set my sights on Teotihuacan. Thus, ironically, I began working on one of the largest preindustrial cities in the world not for a love of the city itself, but as an exercise to better comprehend a radically smaller and decidedly more short-lived city to the south.

The transformation in my attitude towards Teotihuacan could not be more complete, for now I fully appreciate the strategies behind the scale that at first so oppressed me. Likewise, I have spent considerably more time moving through the maze of side streets, exploring the copious murals and losing my longing for a sculptural emphasis. I now have a passion for the city and extol the cunning agendas crystallized in the painted facades. Teotihuacan is a remarkable place that can be aptly described as unique.

Although Dolf was the pivotal force that pointed me in this direction, he is only one of many who have accompanied me on this journey. I am eternally grateful that a community of supportive individuals typifies Mesoamerican research. Kent Flannery (1976b:2–3) best characterized the devotion of Mesoamericanists to their craft when he painted a vivid picture of an archaeologist easily goaded into throwing his sherds on a table for discussion. While Flannery's hypothetical "Real Mesoamerican Archaeologist" was meant as a scathing critique of research methodology, he nonetheless described a collegiality that epitomizes this field. This spirit of openly sharing information has astounded me through the years.

Chief among those willing to share their knowledge is George Cowgill, one of the most engaged and responsive people in the field of Mesoamerican research. Any inquiry to George is invariably met with a response, and his intellectual rigor and intricate knowledge of Teotihuacan is amply matched by his generous assistance. He has read numerous versions of this text, and though I diverge from his guidance with some proposals, this book is more accurate and complex because of the dialogue we have shared. George Cowgill also orchestrated my introduction to the larger world of Teotihuacan scholars. During my research, he opened the doors and resources of the Teotihuacan Mapping Project facilities, where I met many colleagues who contributed to my work. Included in this group are Saburo Sugiyama, Kim Jilote, Alejandro Sarabia, Ian Robertson, Oralia Cabrera, Cynthia Conides, and Warren Barbour. Rubén Cabrera Castro deserves special acknowledgment: he freely shared unpublished materials with me, facilitated visits to newly excavated locations, and provided critical insight as we visited and walked together through the city's remains.

The impact that Linda Schele has made on my life is inestimable. Her joyous infatuation with Mesoamerica was contagious, and it was Linda who first introduced me into the community of Mesoamerican scholars. Linda contributed to this sense of community by encouraging her students to work collectively but also recognizing each of us as a contributing specialist. Linda not only provided the foundation of knowledge, but also crafted an environment where I could learn from those around me as we evolved from fellow students to colleagues. These include Kent Reilly, Rex Koontz, Heather Orr, Khristaan Villela, Matthew Looper, Julia Guernsey, and those who went before me, Andrea Stone and Dorie Reents-Budet. Two others, Marilyn Masson and Kathryn Reese-Taylor, have been invaluable through the years by inviting me into the field of anthropology, as have David Freidel, Karl Taube, Patricia McAnany, Art Joyce, Rebecca Storey, and John Clark. Likewise, my colleagues in the Vanderbilt Anthropology Department— significantly John Janusek and Edward Fischer— have tirelessly fielded my anthropological inquiries and pushed my interpretations through intellectual debate. My students, both graduate and undergraduate, have also been a remarkable resource. On countless occasions a provocative question or downright challenge has caused me to view the material in a new light. In particular, Virginia Walker deserves special thanks for her dedicated work as my research assistant.

Financial support for the initial research came from a University of Texas Continuing University Fellowship, and the Foundation for the Advancement of Mesoamerican Studies, Inc., provided funds for further research and the production of illustrations for this book. As any art historian knows, obtaining the illustrations for a text can be more onerous than any other task, and I am deeply indebted to artists Jenni Bongard, L. F. (Guicho) Luin, Mareike Sattler, and Christopher Wray. Their attention to detail and tremendous flexibility made this book possible. Kirvin Hodges deserves great credit for assistance with digitization and production of images, and I also thank Susan Toby Evans, Esther Pasztory, Miriam Doutriaux of Dumbarton Oaks, and Sylvia Perrine of FAMSI for their help with information and illustrations at the critical conclusion of this project. In addition, I am indebted to the many editors of the University of Texas Press, including Theresa May, Allison Faust, and freelancer Alexis Mills, who have provided a nurturing environment and countless hours of assistance. Upon every request, they have been wonderfully accommodating.

My intellectual foundations were definitely built upon the fertile and solid ground that my family has prepared and maintained. My parents not only embraced my research, but directed me towards this path. Their travels in the Maya area and insistence that I take "just one" course with Linda Schele exemplify a parent's responsibility to expose their children to new experiences. My dear, beloved husband, Ross, has made all things possible. He is an equal partner and loving father who daily offers his own precious time and emotional support so that I can be both scholar and mother. Finally, there are my own "Hero Twins," Otto and Ballard, who have been so good about sharing their mommy with this thing called Mesoamerica. There is nothing more rejuvenating than coming home to the hugs of warm little boys.

THE TEOTIHUACAN TRINITY

CHAPTER 1

APPROACHING THE CITY

Whether it be A.D. 400 or today in the twenty-first century, the Avenue of the Dead profoundly overwhelms any visitor to the ancient Mexican city of Teotihuacan. In an almost indescribable manner this broad street orchestrates the space around it, incorporating the visitor into the careful integration of architecture and natural landscape (Figure 1.1). The avenue once stretched for three miles, a singularly long, straight route to the very heart of the city center. Large platforms, once capped by towering temples, still line the avenue, dwarfing the visitor and promoting a message of individual human insignificance. Yet it is not simply the scale that so influences the visitor, but the manner in which the design of the street seems to literally pull you forward, enticing you into the web of the city of Teotihuacan.

The avenue does this by capitalizing on the natural environment that surrounds the city. At the north end of the Teotihuacan Valley sits Cerro Gordo, an extinct volcano with a cleft at its summit. The massive mountain imposes itself upon the landscape, and those who designed Teotihuacan recognized this and incorporated its bulk into the city planning. They positioned the avenue on a north-south axis so that the street ran directly toward the colossal mountain. The preferred manner of entering Teotihuacan had to be from the south where the full splendor of the city stretched out before the visitor. As you walk up the avenue from the south, the dominant feeling is one of being drawn toward the mountain, for it looms in the distance like a treasured goal. The sensation is much like the experience of entering a medieval cathedral where the halo of stained glass behind the altar moves the visitor from the back of a dark, deep building toward the light at the other end. For the visitor walking

FIGURE 1.1. View looking north up the Avenue of the Dead towards the Moon Pyramid and Cerro Gordo, Teotihuacan.

have a large structure at their center, forcing one off a central path in order to circumnavigate it. Furthermore, these courtyards work in tandem with another feature of the avenue. The walk is not only a directional one, but a vertical climb as well. The southern section of the Avenue of the Dead is lower in elevation than the northern portion, which not only enhances the visual prominence of the Moon Pyramid and Cerro Gordo, but also means that the visitor constantly moves uphill. In concert with the courtyards, the effect is, for the modern visitor, somewhat like going through a set of locks, where each courtyard raises the pedestrian one more level. The walk up the avenue constantly takes one closer to more elevated and sacred ground.

Although the Moon Pyramid and the mountain of Cerro Gordo serve as the focal point of the walk, the architecture lining the Avenue of the Dead greatly contributes to the whole majestic effect. To the south one passes the imposing walls of the Ciudadela, an enclosed compound where the rulers of Teotihuacan may have lived (Figures 1.2, 1.4b). Smaller, yet still prominent temples once ringed the walls of the Ciudadela, and a broad, grand staircase led from the avenue to the inner compound, both serving as unmistakable markers of the structure's regal importance. Inside this compound is a vast plaza that may have been large enough to hold the entire adult population of Teotihuacan, and to the rear of the plaza is the stunning Pyramid of the Feathered Serpent (Cowgill 1983:322). Richly decorated with elaborately carved stone imagery that inspired its current name, the temple has domestic structures on either side that may have served as the royal habitation (Cabrera et al. 1989:52; Cowgill 1983, 1996:267, 1997:151–152; Pasztory 1993:50–51). Across the street was another immense enclosure called the Great Compound. Formed by two enormous low platforms, the unencumbered open space at its center may have been the location of the city's main market, a place where vendors could display their wares.[1]

Progressing ever closer to the Moon Pyramid, one eventually arrives at another enclosed compound accessed by a set of grand stairs. Yet there is no surprise as to what lies beyond, for the massive volume of the city's largest pyramid, the Sun Pyramid, protrudes over walls that do

up the avenue at Teotihuacan, the allure of Cerro Gordo is simply all powerful; it manipulates your actions and shapes your experience.

The Teotihuacanos further enhanced the effect of the natural landscape by artfully positioning their architecture. Directly in front of the mountain, they built the large Moon Pyramid, which echoes the shape of Cerro Gordo. If the singular bulk of Cerro Gordo were not enough to dictate its centrality, the pyramid serves as a not so subtle reminder. The attraction of the natural mountain and its manmade counterpart is additionally heightened by the surrounding architecture, which skillfully channels visitors onto a unidirectional path, making it seem as if there is only one route to pursue. As you walk from south to north, a series of architectural facades lines the northern half of the avenue, creating walls that effectively contain the visitor. Like the blinders on a racehorse, the architectural walls dictate a concerted focus on Cerro Gordo at the end of the avenue.

The sensation of containment is further amplified by the manner in which the Avenue of the Dead was built. Although the overall effect is of one long road stretching forward, in actual fact, a number of enclosed courtyards punctuate the street. Periodically as one walks up the avenue, a set of stairs blocks the route, forcing the traveler to climb up the stairs, cross over a moderately wide platform, and subsequently descend another set of stairs on the other side. The steps deposit the visitor into courtyards which sometimes

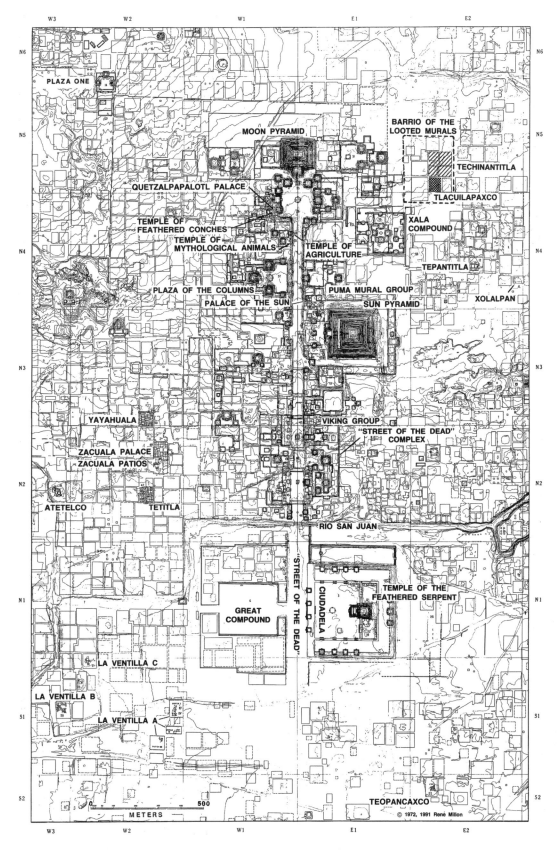

FIGURE 1.2. Map of central Teotihuacan. Copyright © 1972, 1991, René Millon; courtesy of René Millon.

FIGURE 1.3. View of the Sun Pyramid, Teotihuacan.

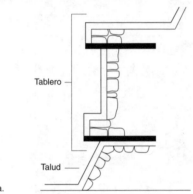

Tablero

Talud

a.

b.

FIGURE 1.4. *Talud-tablero: a*) drawing showing its construction; *b*) view of *talud-tablero* architecture on the Ciudadela along the Avenue of the Dead, Teotihuacan. Drawing by Jenni Bongard after Matos and López 1993:Figure 3.

little to contain it (Figure 1.3).[2] In an interesting paradoxical twist, the Sun Pyramid may be the oldest site of religious pilgrimage at Teotihuacan, and its size certainly makes it one of the city's most prominent features; however, the Moon Pyramid's position on the avenue still designates it as the terminus of the journey.[3] Although the Moon Pyramid is smaller, its integration with Cerro Gordo results in a visual arrangement that manages to de-emphasize even the massive Sun Pyramid.

While the larger structures initially capture one's attention, the splendor of the city did not rest solely with the main pyramids. The design of the street itself forcibly enters one's consciousness. Though broken in places, the walls lining the avenue have a continuous effect, directing but perhaps trapping the visitor at the same time. In a consistent manner, the walls were constructed in the distinctive Teotihuacan architectural style of *talud-tablero* (Figure 1.4). Comprised of a sloping element surmounted by a rectangular platform, the monotonous use of this architecture makes it instantly recognizable as Teotihuacano and constantly impresses the city's identity upon the visitor. Even as the high walls define the street, staircases on the east and west sides of the avenue frequently interrupt the architecture. Some of these stairs lead to the inner courtyards of palaces, while others lead to platforms that probably held temples of a modest size. Although the superstructures of these temples no longer survive, the quantity of temple platforms framing both sides of the street is dazzling. Thus it is not only the size of some temples that overwhelms the visitor, but also the sheer number of religious structures erected by the Teotihuacanos. The walk up the avenue may have once been like passing through a gauntlet of prestigious residences and their temples.

Ultimately, the walk up the avenue ends as the visitor enters a large plaza framing the crown jewel of the city, the Moon Pyramid. After moving up the long avenue, one feels the structure is finally within reach. The pyramid's soaring stairs serve as a focal point, remarkable in their steepness and ability to transport an individual to a supernatural plane. Like a set of enfolding arms, a series of mid-sized temples on stacked platforms once circled the rest of the plaza. The enclosed space is broken only by a large altar and another ritual structure, testament to the various ceremonies that must have taken place here. As in every public area at Teotihuacan, the feeling one has while standing in the Plaza of the Moon is that of being in an enormous space that is, nevertheless, enclosed.

The sense of vastness along the avenue must have been all the more potent before the rest of the city fell into ruin. Many of Teotihuacan's residents once lived in multiroomed structures that housed several families, referred to today as apartment compounds (Figure 1.5). Prior to A.D. 150, most of the construction at Teotihuacan concentrated on the grand pyramids along the main avenue, but during the end of the Miccaotli and the beginning of the Tlamimilolpa periods (A.D. 200–250) an era of urban renewal focusing on domestic architecture swept through the city (Figure 1.6).[4] The domestic building campaign accelerated during the following period (Tlamimilolpa period, A.D. 225–350), when many of the approximately 2,000 apartment compounds were built (Cowgill 1997:155, 2003a:41). These residential structures are roughly rectangular or square and had high windowless walls around their perimeters (Manzanilla 1993b:92; R. Millon

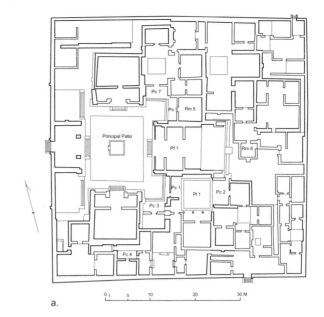

a.

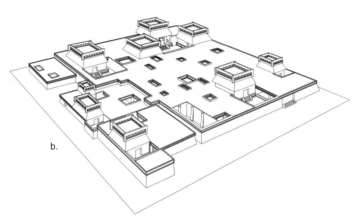

b.

FIGURE 1.5. Views of apartment compounds: *a*) plan of the Yayahuala apartment compound; *b*) perspective reconstruction of the Tetitla apartment compound, Teotihuacan. Drawings by Jenni Bongard: *a*) after Miller 1973:Plan X; *b*) after Séjourné 1966b:Figure 85.

CERAMIC PERIODS OF TEOTIHUACAN	
PERIOD	**DATE**
Tzacualli	A.D. 50-150
Miccaotli	A.D. 150-225
Early Tlamimilolpa	A.D. 225-300
Late Tlamimilolpa	A.D. 300-350
Early Xolalpan	A.D. 350-450
Late Xolalpan	A.D. 450-550
Metepec	A.D. 550-650

FIGURE 1.6. A chronological chart of the ceramically defined phases of Teotihuacan (based on Braswell 2003b and Cowgill 1997, 2003b).

1993:19). A grid of narrow streets separated each compound, some with a walkway that may have served as an elevated sidewalk or bench above the contaminating drainage on the street.[5] Entrance to the compounds could be restricted by one grand door leading to an atrium or reception space, while other compounds had several doors with a more functional and less ostentatious flavor.

The compounds were only one-story high, but inside was a maze of rooms and patios where much of Teotihuacan's population slept, cooked, and went about their daily activities. Individual apartments within the compounds generally consist of several rooms fronted by porticos that surround a central patio (Cowgill 2003a:41). Larger apartments may also have a cluster of additional rooms and smaller patios, and the various arrangements suggest that compounds sheltered two or more households. Smaller apartment compounds may have held 12 to 20 people, and larger ones 60 to 100 individuals. Thus, at its height, Teotihuacan may have had a population of roughly 125,000.[6] Surroundings could be quite lavish, with lime-plastered walls and murals covering almost every surface, or modest homes whose residents resorted to painting on mud-plastered walls.[7] The numerous patios served a vital role, for above them the roof was pierced so that sunlight and air could circulate through the otherwise sealed structure. The light in these areas must have made them prime locations for working. The open roofs naturally let in rain as well, but the Teotihuacanos diverted the water by constructing shallow basins in the middle of the floor. Even though these basins look much like the *impluviums* in ancient Roman households, the Teotihuacan versions did not hold standing water. Holes drilled in the basins led to impressive drain networks in the apartment compound substructures. In this ingenious manner, Teotihuacanos channeled all of the rainfall out of the structures and into the street.

In each apartment compound, one patio is larger and more architecturally elaborate. Commonly called ritual or principal patios, these patios generally have three (but at least one) larger and more elaborate structures that face onto the open area. A small altar, frequently styled to look like a miniature temple, often sits in the center of the patio. Though it is clear that residents used these patios for ritual events, many mundane activities also must have occurred within these spaces (Cowgill 2003a:45). The less restrictive space, better lighting, and comforting breezes on a stifling day would have made the principal patio a choice location for food preparation or craft production whenever the gods had not commandeered the space for themselves.

As an architectural unit, the apartment compounds combine impenetrable outer walls with pleasant open patios to address the discomforts of urban dwelling. The walls would have limited human access and softened the cacophony of sound common to city life (Manzanilla 1993b:92; R. Millon 1993). Concentrating a great number of people within the city boundaries while still providing a measure of privacy was one of the great innovations of Teotihuacan housing. Not coincidentally, during the period of apartment compound construction, there was a simultaneous increase in obsidian working at Teotihuacan and the appearance of the Teotihuacan state outside the Valley of Mexico. This suggests that the manufacture and trade of obsidian were at least partially responsible for an increased population, which stimulated the need for the apartment compounds (R. Millon 1981:209). As René Millon (1976:215) described Teotihuacan of the Tlamimilolpa phase (A.D. 225–350),

. . . the Teotihuacan apartment compound seems to have been designed for urban life, for life in a city that was becoming increasingly crowded, perhaps approaching the chaotic, as obsidian working and other crafts grew more and more rapidly, and as more people came into the city.

Modern-day experiences of living in an urban setting offer insight into the realities of life at Teotihuacan. Perhaps from continuity and not chance, houses in the Central Highlands today have some characteristics reminiscent of the Teotihuacan apartment compound. Houses in Mexico City and the modern towns ringing ancient Teotihuacan are insulated by high walls, and behind the locked gates, gardens and a variety of structures provide for the needs of the family as well as separating them from the commotion outside. Paralleling other great cities, Teotihuacan attracted a cosmopolitan population, in this case from all over Mesoamerica.[8] The privacy of apartment compounds would have helped to defuse the tensions resulting from the mixing of peoples with diverse cultural traditions. Teotihuacanos could freely interact and conduct their business in the large public spaces of the ceremonial center, but they could get respite from this mass of humanity within the sheltered environment of the apartment compound.

The apartment compounds along both sides of the avenue contained a dense population, and the small streets winding through these rectangular boxes surely produced a rather confusing, maze-like means of navigating the city. It is irresistible to imagine what it might have been like to meander along these narrow paths only to emerge on the broad expanse of the Avenue of the Dead. This contrast between the more restrictive passageways of the residential areas and the openness of the public space would have heightened the avenue's prestigious effect and further beckoned the population to the city center.

Furthermore, our imaginations cannot neglect to people the city, which seems so empty today despite the hundreds of tourists climbing its pyramids. Even if the Great Compound once was a marketplace, one wonders if merchants spread out their multicolored blankets along the street to sell the brilliant Thin Orange pottery so loved at Teotihuacan. Because it was a cosmopolitan city, Zapotecs and Maya may have moved through the crowds of local inhabitants. The smells of food and ritual incense would have filled the air, and the general noisiness of a large city would have activated the space. The famous pyramids would have elicited a reverential sensation for those on a pilgrimage, but depending on one's status, certain structures may have been off-limits.

Serving as the center of Mesoamerica's largest city, the Avenue of the Dead surely was the locus of many activities. Religion, commerce, governance, and social events all must have contributed to the life of the avenue. It was a place to meet, conduct business, celebrate civic rituals, and organize the city's disparate peoples. In sum, the Avenue of the Dead was the Mall in Washington, the Champs-Elysées, and Red Square—it was both a symbol of the city and its vital functioning organ. Clearly, the Avenue of the Dead

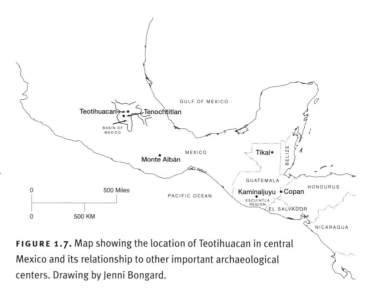

FIGURE 1.7. Map showing the location of Teotihuacan in central Mexico and its relationship to other important archaeological centers. Drawing by Jenni Bongard.

was built to be the symbol of the city, a statement to visitors and its own inhabitants of what the city represented, its very identity. But it was not a hollow symbol, for the people and events that converged on this street were the elements that bound the city together and contributed to its success.

Because the Avenue of the Dead came to represent the city, this book will look to this majestic public space for clues to Teotihuacan's success. The architecture, art, and archaeology centered on the avenue offer information as to what unified the city, resulting in arguably Mesoamerica's grandest city. Yet this study will also repeatedly step away from the avenue and wander in the crowded neighborhoods of the apartment compounds, where we will look at the painting that decorated more private spaces or the pottery used in domestic rituals. But we will always return to the Avenue of the Dead, where multifarious forces coalesced into a multihued amalgamation, a great international city. And indeed, Teotihuacan was a city like no other in Mesoamerica.

It seems as though nothing was done on a small scale at Teotihuacan. The two prominent pyramids, the Sun and the Moon, are staggeringly big. The larger Sun Pyramid is approximately 215 by 215 meters at its base and rises 64 meters (Millon and Drewitt 1995:268). Covering 20 square kilometers, the ancient city sat regally within the Teotihuacan Valley (Figure 1.7). Smaller settlements with Teotihuacan traits permeated the Valley of Mexico and beyond, creating a state that is estimated to have covered approximately 25,000 square kilometers.[9] Teotihuacan was the clear political and religious center of the region.

Teotihuacan's power was expressed not only in physical size, but also in the appearance of the Teotihuacan artistic style abroad, which indicates that it engaged in activities well beyond its immediate boundaries and participated in the arena of Mesoamerican international relations (Bernal 1965, 1966; Braswell 2003a; Hirth and Swezey 1976; Paddock 1972). At Monte Albán, one of the enormous platforms in the ceremonial center features carved images of Teotihuacan visitors in an artistic program that may document the inauguration of a Zapotec king (Marcus and Flannery 1996:217–221). The Oaxacans, in turn, sent some of their own to reside at Teotihuacan, and it appears that they stayed for several generations (Flannery and Marcus 1983b; Marcus 1983b; R. Millon 1973:42; Rattray and Ruiz 1980; Spence 1989). In the Maya area, the city's long tentacles spread to Kaminaljuyu, where Teotihuacan-inspired pottery and architecture indicate a lengthy period of sustained contact (Kidder et al. 1946). Recent epigraphic, iconographic, and archaeological work suggests that Teotihuacan's interaction with Tikal in the late fourth century A.D. was direct and disruptive, so much so that David Stuart (2000), building on ideas proposed by Tatiana Proskouriakoff (1993), posited that a foreigner aligned with a Teotihuacan king

may have killed Chak Tok Ich'aak I, the king of Tikal, and installed a new king with Teotihuacan affiliations. Alternative interpretations of Tikal-Teotihuacan interactions have emerged, but all theories must contend with the overt use of Teotihuacan iconographic elements by the late fourth and early fifth century Tikal kings, Yax Nuun Ayiin I and Siyaj Chan K'awiil II.[10] At Copan, the royal Maya claimed Teotihuacan ancestry and embellished their art with Teotihuacan imagery hundreds of years after the central Mexican city had collapsed and been reduced to ruin (Fash and Fash 2000; Stuart 2000). These claims to a Teotihuacan ancestry may have been fictive or indirect, but rhetorical alliances with the site seem to have been an effective political strategy (Sharer 2003). All told, the extensive nature of contact reveals that other cultures in Mesoamerica believed that Teotihuacan was important and worthy of emulation.

Inevitably, discussion of Teotihuacan's great size and foreign interactions leads to the conclusion that the city was surely an important participant in Mesoamerica. A long history of archaeological investigation offers data that overwhelmingly support the notion that Teotihuacan was indeed a significant political force in the period of its florescence. Embracing that view, one can probe the nature of the city's influence on its neighbors and its distant relations. This has been done and spawned hearty debate, but the assumption also begs a more internal investigation. If Teotihuacan was an influential political entity, then what was the nature of its own political, social, and religious structure? The answer to this question is the focus of this book.

On this point, however, Teotihuacan has been elusive. It yields its secrets with a parsimony that frustrates and baffles those who attempt to discover its past. Despite all the evidence of the city's prominence in Mesoamerica, the political structure of this great power lies mainly in the dark. This situation is not due to a lack of effort on the part of Teotihuacan scholars. The city received early and extensive attention, but the data always seem incomplete and lack the specifics found in other Mesoamerican cultures.[11]

The recent excavation of the Feathered Serpent Pyramid stands as a case in point (Figure 1.8). Between 1980 and 1989, projects headed by

FIGURE 1.8. The Feathered Serpent Pyramid, Teotihuacan.

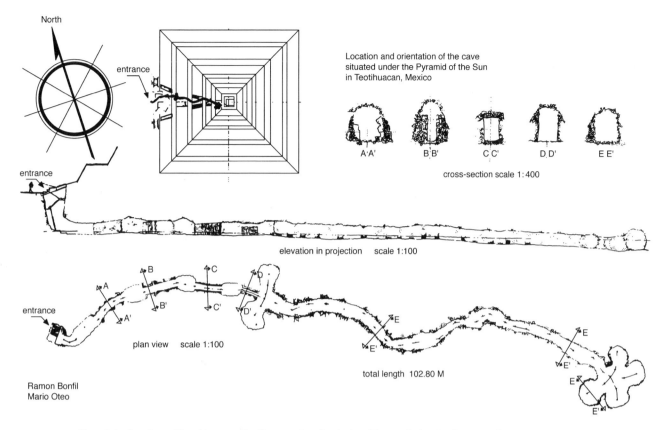

North

entrance

Location and orientation of the cave situated under the Pyramid of the Sun in Teotihuacan, Mexico

A A'   B B'   C C'   D D'   E E'

cross-section scale 1:400

entrance

elevation in projection   scale 1:100

entrance

plan view   scale 1:100

total length 102.80 M

Ramon Bonfil
Mario Oteo

FIGURE 1.9. Plan of the Sun Pyramid and its cave, Teotihuacan. Drawing by Jenni Bongard after Heyden 1981:Figure 1.

Rubén Cabrera, George Cowgill, and Saburo Sugiyama undertook extensive excavations of this temple. In the pattern of earlier excavations by Gamio (1920), Dosal (1925), and Caso and Pérez (see Rubín de la Borbolla 1947), the pyramid yielded evidence of elaborate dedicatory practices. Massive graves that may have held 200 or more people ringed the temple, and some of these contained sacrificed soldiers who seemed to protect a great ruler buried inside (Cabrera 1993; Cabrera and Cabrera 1993:295; Cabrera et al. 1989; Sugiyama 1989a, 2005). Yet when the excavators finally reached the interior of the mound, the evidence they encountered was far from conclusive. At the exact center was a group burial of high-status sacrificial victims. A sizable pit nearby was largely empty, and a looters' tunnel to this pit remained as evidence of an ancient crime (Cabrera and Cowgill 1990; Sugiyama 1991, 1992, 2005:26). Some of the items left by the looters point toward the royal status of the original principal occupant. Cabrera (1993:104) suggested that a wooden staff carved with the head of a serpent, a staff similar to the scep-

ters of other Mesoamerican rulers, may indicate that this was the burial of a Teotihuacan ruler.[12] Because the staff appeared in disturbed fill, separated from the one intact skeleton in the tomb, archaeologists cannot definitively determine whether this belonged to the primary occupant of the tomb, a royal retainer sent to accompany a king to the Otherworld, or even if there actually was a burial of a king associated with this structure.[13]

The largest pyramid, the Sun Pyramid, has left researchers with its own set of similar ambiguities. During excavations directed by Acosta (1971), archaeologists discovered the entrance to a cave at the base of the *adosada,* a large porchlike structure attached to the front of the pyramid. After removing large quantities of fill, they found that the cave had a long shaft terminating in a four-lobed chamber (Figure 1.9). Once again, however, the joy in finding this cave was tempered by a frustrating lack of evidence. Ancient looters had been here too and largely cleaned the cave of its contents. They had broken through adobe walls that formed chambers within the cave, and only a few fragments of mirrors and fish bones remained on the floors beneath the sooty walls (Heyden 1981:3; R. Millon 1981:234, 1992:385, 1993:22).[14] The cave still helped in understanding the worldview of the Teotihuacanos by revealing that caves were a conceptual part of their architectural landscape, but it gave the modern world no ancient kings, no rulers buried at the heart of the pyramid (Heyden 1975, 1981; Taube 1986). The Sun Pyramid may yet yield the tomb of a king, and burials found underneath the Moon Pyramid may shed some light on the city's power structure, yet it is possible that we already have the evidence we need to hypothesize about the sociopolitical structure of Teotihuacan.[15]

PREVIOUS MODELS OF TEOTIHUACAN'S SOCIOPOLITICAL STRUCTURE

ARCHITECTURAL MODELS

Early in Teotihuacan's scholastic history, Kubler (1962:29, 328) viewed the site as a ceremonial center devoid of year-round habitational occupation. He believed that religious pilgrims organized by a faceless sect of priests used the site. Insufficient data and early techniques of archaeological recovery spawned such ideas, but with more excavation, and above all, detailed surface survey, the data showed that this was a large city with permanent residents who exhibited social and cultural variety (R. Millon 1970:1079).

Subsequent reconstructions of Teotihuacan's political structure concede that powerful rulers probably directed the city's growth prior to the Late Tlamimilolpa period (A.D. 300–350). The three largest pyramids—the Sun, Moon, and Feathered Serpent—are thought to represent massive public works constructed in honor of strong individual rulers (Cabrera et al. 1989; Cowgill 1983, 1993a; R. Millon 1992, 1993). Though archaeological evidence is not conclusive, these structures may cover the tombs of the rulers who commissioned them (Cabrera 1993; Cabrera and Cabrera 1993:295; Cabrera et al. 1989; R. Millon 1992; Millon et al. 1965; Sugiyama 1989a, 2005). Cowgill (1983) was the first to suggest that the Ciudadela was the conception

of an individual ruler. He argued that the structure may have served as the residence of the king and his immediate family and also as a monument to the office of the king, yet, ironically, the Feathered Serpent Pyramid inside the Ciudadela may have marked the decline of powerful individual rule at the site.

In the years following construction of the Feathered Serpent Pyramid, the erection of massive pyramids in public spaces diminished.[16] Although the Teotihuacanos substantially enlarged many of the existing pyramids and platforms along the avenue, the energy formerly expended on large monuments for personal glorification largely shifted to construction of the apartment compounds for the city's inhabitants. Cowgill (1983, 1993a:567, 1996:281, 1997:155) and René Millon (1992:396–397, 1993) interpreted this as evidence for political change at Teotihuacan. Perhaps disillusioned by the abuses of kings, the Teotihuacanos checked the power of their monarchs, lacing around their necks a bureaucratic yoke that restrained personal initiative. Cowgill (1983, 1996:280, 1997:152) cited the planned nature of the city as evidence of an organized central power, and he identified the Street of the Dead Complex as a possible administrative center that housed the bureaucratic bodies necessary to orchestrate such a city.

STYLISTIC MODELS

It is in the art of Teotihuacan that scholars have found the greatest confirmation for theories of collective leadership. Historically, it seems, Teotihuacan art has been viewed through lenses developed for other Mesoamerican cultures. There has been a tendency to compare the site, especially to those of the Maya, and to explain it through its differences rather than its own characteristics. Those who ruled Teotihuacan did not erect the stelae of their Maya contemporaries or comparable historical monuments with dynastic information (Figure 1.10). Stelae visually isolate the human actors and provide the modern world with easily decoded royal portraiture. These vertical stones, with their primary focus on a standing individual, make it much easier to proclaim the existence of kings. On stelae as well as on more private art such as ceramic

FIGURE 1.10. Stela 16, Dos Pilas, Maya, A.D. 735. Drawing by Linda Schele, © David Schele, courtesy of the Foundation for the Advancement of Mesoamerican Studies, Inc., www.famsi.org.

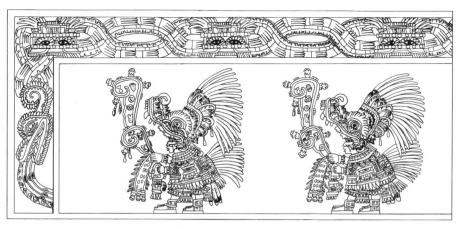

a.

b.

FIGURE 1.11. A comparison of Teotihuacan and Maya figural styles: *a*) mural with processing figures, Room 2, Mural 3, Tepantitla, Teotihuacan; *b*) the god Chak from a Maya vessel at the Metropolitan Museum of Art, New York. Drawings: *a*) by Jenni Bongard after Miller 1973:Figure 173; *b*) by Linda Schele, © David Schele, courtesy of the Foundation for the Advancement of Meso-american Studies, Inc., www.famsi.org.

vessels, Maya kings recorded their personal biographies and exploits along with royal titles in their own words. In comparison, the hieroglyphs at Teotihuacan seem to have a different character than their Maya counterparts. Increasingly, it is becoming clear that there is much more writing at Teotihuacan than previously acknowledged (Taube 2000b, 2003). Particularly among the mural and ceramic art, images previously thought to be clusters of symbols now appear to be hieroglyphs. Yet when glyphs do appear at Teotihuacan, they are solitary and generally not in large clusters, implying that they are nouns without complex syntax.[17] Teotihuacan kings

simply did not proclaim themselves in the same manner as their Maya contemporaries.

The style of Teotihuacan art has also been viewed as particularly idiosyncratic when compared to other Mesoamerican cultures. Because the Olmec and Maya created true portraiture, we question its absence at Teotihuacan. The flattened broad nose of a colossal San Lorenzo head or the droopy lip of K'inich Kan B'alam II of Palenque has no counterparts at Teotihuacan. There is a generic quality to the facial features and body types seen in Teotihuacan figural imagery (Figure 1.11). In a given mural the faces are all identical, and each person is the same height.

FIGURE 1.12. Mural with jaguar approaching a temple, Room 12, Tetitla, Teotihuacan. Drawing by Jenni Bongard.

The figures exhibit similar squat proportions that disclose an interest in recording the concept of a human much more than anatomical realities or variances. Teotihuacan counters the shapely curves and idealized proportions of the Maya god Chak with blocky calves and compact bodies. If one seeks naturalism akin to Classical Greece, Teotihuacan is certainly not the place to look.

The depiction of three-dimensional space is also not a factor of much importance in Teotihuacan art. Arthur Miller best described the flat qualities of the Teotihuacan mural tradition.

A remarkable stylistic feature of Teotihuacan murals is the flatness of the images in the painting. The motifs represented in any Teotihuacan mural are invariably shown in an attitude which emphasizes the two-dimensionality of the motif, i.e., the broadest aspect of it which has height and width. . . . It is as if all the motifs represented in the murals are pushed forward, compressed, flattened out against the picture plane by some invisible force behind the images in the painting. (Miller 1973:24)

In contrast, the Maya tackled problems of space in a manner more akin to Western traditions. On rare but still important occasions, attempts at foreshortening appear in Maya art, and in vase painting, the inclusion of curtains and cushions in a Maya king's throne room offers a more convincing sense of space than ever demonstrated in Teotihuacan art.[18] Often, Teotihuacan figures float in space without any rationalizing props, and when the artist did include background details such as a structural facade, the decorative

patterning of the vacant space reduces the three-dimensional effect (Figure 1.12).

In Miller's discussion of the flatness in Teotihuacan murals, he additionally noted a similarity between the painting style and paper.

If one were to draw a ground plan of the images in a Teotihuacán mural, the space would be as thin as a piece of paper. In fact, the paper analogy is particularly appropriate here because much of Teotihuacán painting looks as if it were composed of motifs which are paper cutouts pasted on a flat surface. (Miller 1973:24)

This "pasted" quality of the images may be due to the fact that Teotihuacan muralists used patterns while designing their wall surfaces. Evidence for the patterns comes from punctations that Miller observed in the plaster, yet he also notes that subtle variations in the design indicate that the painters did not strictly follow the patterns (Miller 1973:32). Although some figures rigidly adhere to the pattern and are arbitrarily cut off at corners or frames, others vary the size to adapt to the given space (Figure 1.13).[19] Furthermore, while the painters followed preparatory drawings made on the plaster, the individual hands of the different painters working on a wall resulted in some variation in the final work (Miller 1973:34–35).

Regardless of the painting technique, it is important to accept the validity of the Teotihuacan style for itself with as few biases as possible from our own cultural expectations. As Westerners, our own aesthetics are firmly rooted in

FIGURE 1.13. Detail showing random cropping of figures, Portico 2, White Patio, Atetelco, Teotihuacan.

the legacy of Classical Greece and the subsequent Renaissance, and the Teotihuacanos' rejection of naturalism can be particularly difficult to accept, especially when their Maya contemporaries had a taste for the realism often favored in our cultural tradition. Pasztory (1990–1991) has been the greatest champion of the Teotihuacan aesthetic, pointing out that abstraction reflects a conscious choice rather than an inability to produce a more naturalistic art form. To combat preferences for realism, she reminded readers that Medieval art and Modernism represent two great abstract traditions in the otherwise naturalistic tradition of the West. In these examples, as at Teotihuacan, style has meaning; that is, it assists the iconography in conveying information.

In an effort to explain Teotihuacan's stylistic differences from some Mesoamerican traditions, Pasztory (1990–1991:114) identified two stylistic categories. Teotihuacan typifies the first category, which she labeled *conceptual.* This type incorporates imagery with less obvious references to the natural world and especially art that moves towards abstraction. The second category, *perceptual,* includes the art of the Maya and Olmec. Perceptual art employs conventions that make the image look real, and thus the art appears to depict the third dimension and frequently exhibits a strong portraiture tradition. Pasztory carefully acknowledged that in actuality these conventions are distinct from the natural world; therefore, while the imagery on a painted flat surface may look as though it recedes beyond the wall surface, it never truly escapes its two-dimensional reality. She explained that all art is conceptual, but some art attempts to achieve the perceptual by giving the illusion of reality.

Such distinctions are necessary in an explanation of Teotihuacan art for they stress that style is not a function of skill but a vehicle for meaning. Looking farther afield, the animals painted in Europe's Paleolithic caves forcefully emphasize the relationship between style and meaning. The elegant and graceful bulls with their naturalistic style appear in direct association with a set of highly abstracted signs. The same cultural tradition produced art falling into both of Pasztory's categories, yet it is clear that both styles carried meaning. The naturalism in animal depiction most likely reflects the pre-

occupations of a culture of hunter-gatherers, and the abstract symbols may record the geometric phenomena seen during hallucinatory trancing (Lewis-Williams 1984; Lewis-Williams and Dowson 1993; Lewis-Williams et al. 1973). In short, style is not a function of ability; instead, it reflects a conscious choice on the part of the artist.

Recognizing the intentionality that drives style, Pasztory (1990–1991:115) emphasized that specific reasons lie behind the conceptual trend in Teotihuacan art. One motivation stemmed from the city's desire to distinguish itself from other cultural groups within Mesoamerica (Pasztory 1990–1991:115, 1992a). The differentiation provided a sense of cultural identity to the Teotihuacanos, thereby reinforcing the connection of the individual to the city as a whole.

Pasztory (1990–1991:115) then extended this argument for differentiation into a comparative analysis of Teotihuacan and other Mesoamerican traditions in which style serves as an indicator of political structure. Among the Maya, a substantial number of the surviving hieroglyphic texts expound upon dynastic information, and a portraiture tradition developed within their art recorded the particularities of the rulers. The art style is effective because the individuality of portraiture augments a system centered on dynastic rule, which invests power in the individual. By comparison, the Teotihuacanos left us with a series of repetitive figures, each seemingly shaped by the same cookie cutter. They march in groups wearing virtually identical costumes, and their squat proportions vary slightly. The aggregation of carbon copies denies the search for portraiture and seemingly the possibility of identifying particular individuals amongst the masses. Elites certainly appear in Teotihuacan art, but they seem depersonalized because they are depicted in multiples that are decidedly similar.[20]

Within the literature on Teotihuacan, the absence of individualized portraiture becomes evidence that the Teotihuacanos' primary concern was integrating society. Pasztory reasoned that because Teotihuacan was cosmopolitan and attracted people from distant regions, the state felt the need to emphasize the inclusiveness of the whole more than the identity of the individual. Teotihuacan art, in this model, did not

FIGURE 1.14. Mural of the mountain-tree with approaching priests, Portico 2, Tepantitla, Teotihuacan. Drawing by Jenni Bongard after the reproduction by Villagra in the Teotihuacan Hall, Museo Nacional de Antropología, Mexico City.

exalt individual rulers through portraiture or inscriptions because it chose to promote a collective ideology (Pasztory 1990:182, 1990–1991:131). As she stated of her theory,

I am going to suggest that Teotihuacan was a culture with a utopian view of the world, in which the individual was de-emphasized for the sake of the group, but in which the citizen members enjoyed high status and material benefits as a part of the group. Teotihuacan, in my view, was a Mesoamerican social and religious experiment in the creation of a society that did not glorify a divine king and warrior aristocracy above a farming people. The Teotihuacan concept of the utopian city included the entire population living in the same type of dwellings all within view of the great pyramids. (Pasztory 1992a:288)

This model for a corporate ideology at Teotihuacan suggests that the Teotihuacanos avoided any emphasis on the individual. The similarities of the individuals were emphasized, and their membership in the group far outstripped attempts at personal glorification. Teotihuacanos celebrated

their city, their gods, and their role in belonging. Not unlike the theoretical principles of a socialist state, everyone worked for the benefit of the state, and through this route all prospered. In turn, the ideology softened the divisive effects of the truly heterogeneous society by using imagery to create reality.

Murals from Tepantitla and Teopancaxco seemingly support this argument (Figures 1.14, 1.15). In these murals, two profile figures approach a central motif, in one case a personified mountain crowned by a sprouting tree and in the other a circular device on a platform.[21] The priests are identical, with no emphasis on their facial features but considerable attention to their costume elements. The specificity of their headdresses, garments, and ceremonial bags stresses their office or membership in a group far more than their individual participation in the ritual event. The mountain-tree and the circular device hold the central positions. Their frontal viewpoint coupled with the profile procession of the figures emphasizes their paramount importance.

FIGURE 1.15. Mural of two figures approaching an altar, Teopancaxco, Teotihuacan. Drawing by Jenni Bongard after Villagra 1971:Figure 6.

The human figures sprinkle precious offerings, and at Tepantitla, the personified mountain returns the favor. Verdant vegetation sprouts from the peak of the mountain, and water drips from the hands that miraculously emerge on either side. Female qualities might be attributed to this mountain as water gushes forth from a womb-like vaginal opening. Below the image, the irrigated fields of Teotihuacan receive the precious water, and the people frolic in the joys of their bounteous situation. The message is clear. Proper propitiation of the mountain performed by the collective body of the city ensures the prosperity of all. Or so it seems.

DIRECTIONS FOR THIS STUDY

It is undeniable that Teotihuacan kings did not employ the same self-promotion in their art as did the Maya; however, the artistic tradition of Teotihuacan is far from unique in Mesoamerica. Similar squat proportions and generic facial features appear in the Mixtec codices and the art of the Aztec (Figure 1.16). In these two traditions accompanying glyphs negate the lack of portraiture to indicate that the imagery concerns historic individuals. In the codices, when hieroglyphs are missing, costume elements still allow the viewer to identify individuals and the particular religious or political offices they held.

The Mixtecs and the Aztecs indicate that portraiture need not be a prerequisite to identifiable individuals.

In her discussion of the corporate model Pasztory did recognize that different groups are identifiable within the marching masses of Teotihuacan, but she argued that "there is an emphasis on the corporate nature of the city which is made up of separate, different, but, in many ways, similar units" (Pasztory 1990–1991:131). René Millon (1992:340, 1993:38) added to this model the observation that examples of hierarchical relationships between groups or individuals are lacking at Teotihuacan.

There are many richly attired individuals in Teotihuacan art but they are not shown in positions of domination over others. . . . A principle of indirection was at work. Much of the subject matter of Teotihuacan art is represented obliquely, particularly social interaction — hierarchical relationships, domination, human sacrifice — everything that is harsh. (R. Millon 1993:38)

Both Millon and Pasztory envisioned a Teotihuacan where the residents shunned difference and engendered a philosophy that all of the disparate parts were equal. Evidence on their side includes the generic faces and body types seen in Teotihuacan figural imagery; however, notable exceptions to this collective interpretation of Teotihuacan's art exist.

FIGURE 1.16. Lord 8 Deer from the Codex Nuttall demonstrating proportions and generic features comparable to Teotihuacan art, manuscript illustration, Postclassic. Note name glyph above the figure. Drawing by Jenni Bongard after Nuttall 1975:49.

Particularly challenging to these ideas is the recent work on hieroglyphic writing at Teotihuacan which proposes that imagery formerly thought of as signs are actually hieroglyphs.[22] Consider for a moment the symbols painted on a portico at Tetitla (Figure 1.17). If these abstract designs are hieroglyphs, their repetitive nature suggests that they represent a noun, perhaps the name of an individual. How different our interpretation of Teotihuacan's political structure would be if these large hieroglyphs boldly proclaimed the name of a ruler. The size of the hypothesized words is so large that they are suggestive of shouting, and perhaps they repeatedly scream the ruler's name or the principal occupant of the apartment compound. Naturally,

such ideas await the decipherment of these symbols, but the case illustrates just how tenuous our understanding of Teotihuacan is and just how perilous it is to argue that the Teotihuacanos de-emphasized the individual.

More transparent examples of name glyphs accompanying individuals in Teotihuacan art include two exemplary instances: the murals from the Techinantitla apartment compound and the Las Colinas vessel (Figures 1.18, 1.19). In the murals an abstracted assemblage of images, surely functioning as glyphic writing, sits directly in front of a single individual, while an animal or

FIGURE 1.17. Possible hieroglyphs, Portico 14, Tetitla, Teotihuacan. Drawing by Jenni Bongard after Miller 1973:Figure 291.

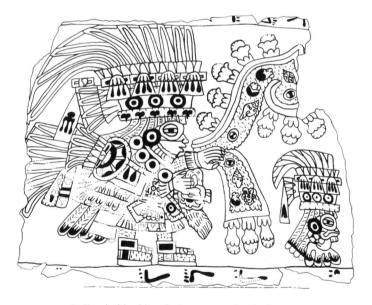

FIGURE 1.18. Mural with a hieroglyph accompanying the figure, Techinantitla, Teotihuacan. Drawing by Jenni Bongard after C. Millon 1988c:Figure V.4.

FIGURE 1.19. The Las Colinas vessel, ceramic, from a Teotihuacan site near Calpulalpan, Tlaxcala. Drawing by Jenni Bongard after C. Millon 1988c:Figure V.14.

headdress accompanies the figures on the Las Colinas vessel. Because these signs have yet to be deciphered, it is unclear whether they represent names of particular individuals or groups, although Clara Millon (1973, 1988c) has made a strong case that the glyphs indicate membership in military units. Although I will refrain from committing myself as to whether the Techinantitla glyphs identify individuals or groups until the glyphs have been deciphered, I do believe that Clara Millon is correct that Teotihuacan art consistently depicts social or military groups. In keeping with this model, I will identify such groups in the iconography of Teotihuacan's art. The recognition of such groups has import, for they indicate that identification with a group was a powerful motivation at Teotihuacan.

The presence of named military associations at Teotihuacan does not necessarily contradict arguments for a collective emphasis in Teotihuacan art. Naming military groups or ranks still highlights corporateness and is significantly different from naming individuals. On the other hand, identification of named groups challenges Pasztory's position. Promoting a collective ideology of the city as a whole is quite different than celebrating collective membership in one of many groups. The corporate model does not explain why so much of the art focuses on the clear delineation of the various parts, and an argu-

ment could be made that this elevates the status of those parts, emphasizing their independence, or, at the very least, their prominent role in the structure of the whole.

In the following chapters I hope to seize upon this distinction. The corporate model for Teotihuacan stresses a unified vision of the site, a vision most likely promoted by the group or groups who held the greatest power in the Teotihuacan state. This model, however, obscures the impact of other groups with their own agendas who may or may not have agreed with the larger vision of the state. If we identify subdivisions within Teotihuacan, then we must consider the relationships between those groups. The dynamics among these groups, whether competitive or harmonious, or the fluctuation between these two extremes, would have shaped the course of Teotihuacan's history. By considering the architectural arrangement of particular murals, I will challenge contentions that Teotihuacan artists downplayed the hierarchical relationships between various social components.

A number of different entities will be discussed, but each of these will fall into one of three grand categories whose interaction seems to have determined, to a large degree, the sociopolitical climate of Teotihuacan. The three upon which this study will focus—the three comprising the Teotihuacan trinity—are the ruler, lineages, and military sodalities. In a city this large, there certainly were other factions who shaped Teotihuacan's history. Groups of foreigners, merchants, and priests all must have played significant roles and exerted power for their own interests, but the three to be considered here seem to have held extraordinary sway over the tenor of Teotihuacan politics. They are all visually prominent in the art, architecture, and general residue of the material culture. Their story was one sung very loudly.

Only after exploring the nature of these three groups and gaining an understanding of their foundations can we return to the overarching agenda of the state and see possible models for the integration of the groups within the state. Although much attention will be given to the friction between the various factions, and the resulting tensions that could have had a destabilizing impact, the evidence for unification will also be considered. The success of Teotihuacan was that its inhabitants found ways to integrate the numerous components, to build bonds between disparate groups, and to fashion an overarching identity that competing factions could share. The following chapters will show how ritual events incorporated propagandistic messages that appealed to state ideology and suggest that even architectural style was coded with meaning that promulgated proper civic behavior.

Because style has been so pivotal to corporate models, I will also reanalyze the meaning of Teotihuacan art style. I will show that it was not the identification with the city as a whole that stimulated the creation of the Teotihuacan art style, but it was the very factionalism or conflict between these groups that led to the development of an art that de-emphasized the individual. The corporate argument will subtly shift, showing that it was identification with one of several groups that was of supreme importance. A model will be developed that continues to see the effects of corporate ideology, but instead of one single corporate entity, the model will include several smaller corporate entities. I will show that much of Teotihuacan art was concerned with expressing the relationships between these smaller corporate groups. Both style and imagery were tools in this endeavor.

Just as this study will reinterpret style and imagery, so it will reconsider some of the most vexing aspects of Teotihuacan. The site teases archaeologists and art historians alike with its empty tombs and cleaned out caves, yet once the frustration passes, scholars can use this as evidence about Teotihuacan's political structure. Instead of bemoaning the lack of conclusive evidence, I hope to show that this missing evidence can be used as signs of Teotihuacan practices that concerned the most sacred elements of their society and world. Surely, the absence of material artifacts falls under the category of negative evidence, which is tenuous and has an unsettling effect in our scientific society. It lacks the solidity of hard facts, and we find that our arguments may not hold with further investigation. This is, ultimately, the nature of the social sciences and humanities, and even when properly understood, of the so-called hard sciences themselves. The relationship of the data with the argument is inexact, and we must always be willing to modify and alter our views as we learn more about our target societies. As for Teotihuacan, I hope to argue that comparison with the cultural practices of other Mesoamerican groups offers clues to the missing materials; that is, by reconstructing the actions, it is also possible to hypothetically reassemble the artifacts used in those activities.

Much of the theoretical basis for this argument will rely heavily on the principle of continuity, and the pendulum for and against continuity has swung both directions in Teotihuacan scholarship. The latest work by Pasztory (1988, 1992a, 1997) and René Millon (1992) expressed reluctance to use other Mesoamerican cultures to approach problems of Teotihuacan. This caution is largely a legacy of early efforts by Seler (1915), who was unaware of the temporal distance between Teotihuacan and the Aztecs and freely applied Postclassic Aztec deity names to the imagery of Classic Teotihuacan.

Kubler (1948, 1961, 1967, 1970, 1972, 1973) was perhaps the most outspoken opponent of continuity. When asked to write on Precolumbian survivals in the Colonial period, he acted as coroner, pronouncing the Precolumbian, "a corpse of a civilization" (Kubler 1961:14). In his most sardonic version he compared possible Precolumbian survivals of the conquest to a piece of embryonic chicken heart kept alive in a vial for years in New York City (Kubler 1961:22). His discussion of Teotihuacan likened the application of Aztec ethnohistories to Panofsky's example of Orpheus and the Good Shepherd (Kubler 1967). In both cases, he argued, similar imagery could obscure cultural change and shifts in meaning. Kubler provided a much needed correction to the field after the work of Seler; however, the absolutism of his condemnation of continuity pushed the pendulum much too far toward the other extreme and forbade the use of vast resources of potentially valuable information. If taken literally, it means ignoring ethnohistoric and ethnographic materials as well as denying the relevance of comparative information from other temporal periods and cultural groups in Mesoamerica.

Much recent work has demonstrated that, with cautionary reins, Mesoamericanists can only gain by culling these resources. Heyden (1975, 1981, 1989) consistently assumed that written documents and oral traditions of the Aztecs preserved core mythologies that were pan-Mesoamerican and argued that central Mexican traditions extend back to the Classic period. Berlo (1983b, 1989) argued that our own religious symbols have survived comparable periods of time and demonstrated that precedents for central Mexican writing systems may be found at Teotihuacan. In a similar manner, Cowgill (1992b, 1996:258, 1997) suggested that Postclassic Nahuatl songs may provide insight into glyphs found in the Teotihuacan murals and has generally counseled that using Postclassic and Post-conquest sources is a challenging but justifiable endeavor. Most synthetic of all, Taube (1983, 1986, 1992a, 2000a, 2003) used not only Mesoamerican but also Native North American traditions to elucidate Teotihuacan's iconography.

This study will follow in the spirit of these latter scholars who have acknowledged that Teotihuacan did indeed exist in Mesoamerica and therefore may hold much in common with other manifestations of this cultural tradition. Comparison, especially to the Maya, has revealed differences that sometimes separated Teotihuacan from the rest of Mesoamerica, but, ironically, this comparison which has so differentiated the city can also serve to reincorporate it back into the Mesoamerican tradition. Teotihuacan need

not be dealt with in isolation, for comparison can offer new insight into the iconography and political structure of this decidedly individual, but nevertheless Mesoamerican, site.

The work of Marshall Sahlins (1981) offers an eloquent validation for a comparative approach. The opening chapter to his study of Captain Cook's demise in the Hawaiian Islands provides a reflective look at structural theory (Sahlins 1981:3–8). He recognized that structural approaches had failed to significantly incorporate the effects of two major factors: history and change. According to Sahlins the clumping aspect of structural theory tends to leave out individuals, specific temporal events, and particularities of environment and culture.

Yet Sahlins did not abandon structural theory so much as refine it. Sahlins asserted that cultures are selective in the things they recognize; that is, perception is culturally based. This, Sahlins suggested, provides the basis for structures, because events produce a recognizable and expected grid, a structure. As he said of Polynesian cosmology, "Hawaiian history often repeats itself, since only the second time is it an event" (Sahlins 1981). In other words, only through reproduction is the event recognizable. Where Sahlins hoped to alter structural theory is in the recognition that these structures change because of history.

The great challenge to an historical anthropology is not merely to know how events are ordered by culture, but how, in that process, the culture is reordered. How does the reproduction of a structure become its transformation? (Sahlins 1981:8)

This recognition that the particularities of the individuals and their circumstances modify the structure allows students of the past to form a more complete image.

Freidel and Schele (1988b) adopted a similar approach in their efforts to understand the alteration of structures. They identified moments of significant change as "thresholds," or situations where "the content of reified models of reality must be revised to accommodate actual social conditions" (Freidel and Schele 1988b:89). As an example, they discussed the Late Formative transition among the Maya from a self-effacing tradition to portraiture. Where previously the art focused on images of deities, there now appeared historical personages. Myth, they contended, was manipulated and differentially stressed to accommodate new social strategies, which in this case included the increasing gulf between elites and non-elites. Freidel and Schele, as well as Sahlins, stressed the importance of two primary characteristics: the patterns and the idiosyncrasies. The following analysis will progress in this vein.

Not only will I look for structures that traverse time and geography, but I will also identify patterns that are culturally distinct. Motifs at Teotihuacan will be weighed in association with one another, looking for groupings that suggest similarities. Those versed in the history of Teotihuacan scholarship will note that this analysis forgoes the groupings established by previous scholars of Teotihuacan art. In 1967, Kubler published a succinct but extremely influential essay on the nature of iconographic identification at Teotihuacan. A notable contribution of the paper was his identification of iconographic "clusters" (Kubler 1967:9–10). Kubler separated the iconography into five groups of related motifs which he argued were associated with different cults at Teotihuacan. Examples of these included the butterfly cluster, which encompassed death and the afterlife, and bird imagery of owls and quetzals, which he suggested concerned war and dynastic agendas.

While Kubler's study was brief, Hasso von Winning's (1987) contribution represents the most comprehensive inquiry to date. Building upon Kubler's clusters, von Winning identified two complexes based on associated meanings. He suggested that disparate motifs like mountains, shells, and droplets all relate to the qualities of water, and, in turn, they are all associated with the deity of water and lightning. Like this water complex, a parallel fire complex contains the symbols which he contended pertain to the god of this element.

I am neither convinced that these deities eclipsed the importance of other supernaturals at Teotihuacan, nor am I persuaded that the Teotihuacanos separated these natural forces into such rigorous categories. Deities in Mesoamerica are notoriously slippery, accumulating diverse attributes depending on the particular message to be delivered. While some attributes may remain consistent with a particular deity, that deity may also appropriate numerous guises with layers of other attributes when the need arises. Thus Tlaloc may appear as an earthly entity when featuring his association with underground water, but he can surface as a celestial being when characterized as a rainmaker.[23] The indistinct boundaries of supernaturals probably reveal a strategy to differentially stress related aspects of the sacred world. The lack of distinction reflects the indescribable qualities of the metaphysical. Through the analysis that follows, I hope to demonstrate that we can assign iconographic meaning to motifs, but the meaning of one motif may be related to the meaning of another motif, and the groupings of these motifs may not pattern into a few complexes so much as to a continuum that created the whole of Teotihuacan religion and worldview. In an effort to avoid the biases posed by previous categorizations of Teotihuacan's iconographic motifs, this study will not, therefore, refer to these complexes but will allow those associations that survive a Mesoamerican approach to stand, and let those who fail to fall aside.

In using data sources outside of Teotihuacan, the researcher of today has information not available to previous scholars. Advancements in the decipherment of Maya hieroglyphic texts and new analysis of both pre- and postconquest mythology offer insight into Mesoamerican concepts. Though these pertain to cultures other than Teotihuacan, the similarities between various Mesoamerican traditions argue for core conceptual beliefs that can, in turn, be applied to the art of Teotihuacan. This Mesoamerican approach does not ignore Kubler's (1967) warnings against continuity, for it avoids reliance on one single culture. Rather than looking only toward the Aztecs, this study searches for concepts inherent in all Mesoamerican cultures; that is, ways of perceiving the world that transcend cultural, geographic, and temporal boundaries. Continuities among the diverse cultural groups of Mesoamerica are not dissimilar to the homogeneous characteristics of Christianity. Though the various branches of Christianity exhibit distinct differences, there are fundamental tenets which all Christians accept. Whether Catholic or Baptist, the Renaissance or the present, the cross and Christ were and are universally recognized symbols. Each branch of Christianity and indeed each Christian may offer subtle differences of interpretation, but such symbols are, nevertheless, consistently identifiable on at least a fundamental level. So it goes with Mesoamerican iconography. Each culture, each site, and each time period constantly reinterpreted the core mythology, but in Sahlins' terms the reproduction and transformation of a structure does not render the structure unrecognizable.

CHAPTER 2

THE INVISIBLE KINGS

Though many have looked for the rulers of Teotihuacan, the search for those who orchestrated the massive building campaigns and designed the city's organized layout has been a perplexing one. The picture is not clear, and any proposals on the issue seem to be tenuous arguments that lack solidity. To the modern researcher, the Teotihuacan rulers simply do not announce their presence with the straightforwardness that Mesoamerican scholars have come to expect. Although their monuments stand in all their glory, we have difficulty making the individual players come into focus. Yet, as is so often the case, the city's original residents had no problem recognizing the imagery of their rulers, reminding us that the opaque nature of the issue is a modern one inherent in reconstructing the past. In consequence, it may be that present-day expectations have obscured our ability to perceive the evidence for Teotihuacan's rulers.

It would be so much easier for modern scholars to identify Teotihuacan's kings had they erected stelae like their Maya contemporaries. However, because they did not, the search for Teotihuacan's kings has been a creative one. Indeed, rather than referring to direct evidence such as tombs or portraits, researchers have often looked instead at the architecture of the city for indications that Teotihuacan did have rulers.

The pyramids, of course, provide the most prominent evidence of Teotihuacan kings. Throughout Mesoamerica, rulers erected pyramids as large-scale public works to celebrate their reigns. At Palenque the Maya king K'inich Kan B'alam II sponsored the Group of the Cross, which consisted of three temples, each decorated with carved panels justifying his claim to power. Each of the great Aztec kings of Tenoch-titlan put his mark on the city by enlarging the central temple, the Templo Mayor. Presumably, as the temple got larger with each addition, so too did the perceived authority of each king increase. Numerous Maya pyramids primarily served to enshrine the holy bones of deceased kings; thus, on Tikal's North Acropolis, new temples continually sprouted up as members of the royal family passed to the supernatural realm. This pattern of building pyramids over tombs led Michael Coe to suggest that the primary function of Maya pyramids was to house the tomb of a ruler or other elite. By extension, a Maya acropolis may be fundamentally viewed as a necropolis.[1]

With such patterns of behavior elsewhere in Mesoamerica, Teotihuacan's prominent pyramids—those of the Sun, Moon, and Feathered Serpent—have been viewed as evidence of the presence of kings. Scholars have reasoned that these large structures were built under the direction of specific rulers as symbols of their rule.[2] The Feathered Serpent Pyramid, in particular, has been the focus of much investigation and speculation on the existence of Teotihuacan kings. Because it is the most completely excavated of all the pyramids, we have more detailed information about this structure than the other two. In excavations spanning the years from 1980 to 1989, archaeologists found numerous burials that may total 260 sacrificial victims should the structure be fully excavated (Cabrera 1993:106; Cabrera and Cabrera 1993:295). The colossal scale of the sacrifice has been interpreted as the expression of power by a single ruler who tried to establish a Maya-style dynastic rule (Cowgill 1983:335, 1996:280–281; R. Millon 1992:396). Pasztory (1993:51) wonders if the feathered serpent sculpted on the structure's facade was a title of rulership or the name of a dynasty that proclaimed this individual's political assertions. Thus, she, along with Millon and Cowgill, sees the destruction of the facade and subsequent covering of the pyramid front by an *adosada* as a movement to quell any future attempts by Teotihuacan kings to concentrate power in any one individual. It is much noted that in the approximately 300 years that followed the construction of the Feathered Serpent Pyramid, no other large-scale pyra-

mid was constructed at Teotihuacan (Millon 1992:396–397).

Archaeologists have also tried to identify rulers in the burial remains of Teotihuacan, but as of yet, these attempts have offered inconclusive evidence at best. With the royal burial patterns of other Mesoamerican cultures in mind, archaeologists have conjectured that the bodies of these rulers would be found in tombs inside the pyramids. In the case of the Sun Pyramid, archaeologists exploring the Noguera tunnel found a sloping fill that might indicate the presence of a pit or tomb near the structure's center, but additional excavations have not been conducted to resolve this question.[3] Recent excavations of the Feathered Serpent and Moon Pyramids have been exemplary in their thorough, scientific nature, but unfortunately, earlier archaeologists and the Teotihuacanos themselves may have obscured the picture somewhat.

The Feathered Serpent Pyramid has two possible candidates that may have once held the body of a ruler. Located near the center of the structure, Grave 13 contained the wooden serpent staff that led Rubén Cabrera (1993:104) to argue that this chamber once held a ruler. The assumption is that this individual was the one who ordered the massive sacrifices in an effort to increase dynastic power. However, Teotihuacan looters ransacked this burial, perhaps as punishment for his pretensions to power; thus the primary occupant seems to be missing, leaving the interpretation of this burial rather troubling. Sugiyama (1992:220–221, 2005:235), on the other hand, believes that a burial under the temple staircase, looted during construction of the *adosada,* is another possible location of the Teotihuacan ruler's tomb. In either case, however, the body was indeed missing, thereby hampering our ability to easily identify a ruler.

The earlier Moon Pyramid is even more perplexing for those expecting to find the simple tomb of a ruler buried inside. When archaeologists tunneled under it, they found two chambers that seem more sacrificial than royal in nature. Burial 2, associated with the Moon Pyramid's fourth construction stage, contained one human occupant who had his hands tied behind his back, clear evidence of a sacrificial and unwilling victim (Cabrera and Sugiyama

1999:29; Sugiyama and Cabrera 2000:167; Sugiyama 2005:205). Upon the next enlargement of the pyramid, a chamber was cut into the *tepetate,* and four humans were placed inside. Like the earlier burial, they all had their hands behind their backs, and none emerged as the primary occupant. Instead of housing the tomb of a ruler, the Pyramid of the Moon records the importance of sacrifice in Teotihuacan's civic rituals.[4]

The missing bodies and multiple burials make Teotihuacan scholars long for the comparatively simple format of the Maya stelae. These stone monuments not only have clear portraits of solitary rulers, but they also include hieroglyphic text. The writing focuses on the personal histories of Maya rulers, recording their military exploits, their marital connections, and significant events such as births, accessions to the throne, and death. Because of the Maya calendar's sophisticated nature, the stelae position these events within a temporal order; therefore, the story of Maya dynasties is that of a true history where events are locked into time and the actors are identifiable individuals. In contrast, distinguishing the writing of Teotihuacan has been a more difficult endeavor, but growing evidence suggests that writing did exist at Teotihuacan and conveyed important political information.

James Langley (1986, 1992, 1993) provided an extensive catalogue of Teotihuacan's symbolic system, but he was hesitant to use the term *glyph* and preferred only to identify "notational signs." A bit bolder with her use of the term, Clara Millon (1988c) studied the Techinantitla murals and recognized the hieroglyphs placed before the marching celebrants (Figures 1.18, 2.1). She did not determine whether the glyphs named individuals or social units, but her analysis demonstrated the unmistakable presence of writing at the site. Looking to the same apartment compound, George Cowgill (1992b) directed our attention to a series of trees painted below a feathered serpent. Each tree has a distinct glyphic compound positioned near its base, and Cowgill noted that some of these Teotihuacan glyphs represent objects described by words in sixteenth-century, colonial Nahuatl texts.

A critical discovery confirming that Teotihuacan had a hieroglyphic tradition occurred during the 1992–1994 field seasons in an area of the city called La Ventilla (Cabrera 1995). In an apartment compound plaza subsequently named the Plaza of the Glyphs, archaeologists found forty-two images painted in red that have the decided appearance of hieroglyphic writing (Figure 2.2). Dating to around A.D. 450, the glyphs are mostly painted on the plaza floor, with a few on the walls and small altar at the center of the plaza. Most of the glyphs are isolated by red boxes. This is important because the arrangement does not suggest sentences with syntax. Instead, each glyph seems to exist separately, indicating that each functions grammatically as a noun. One possibility is that the glyphs represent personal names, titles, or place-names. On the south side of the plaza, however, the glyphs cluster into groups of three, suggesting that there may be syntax in some of these texts. Although still undeciphered, the glyphs in this plaza make the existence of writing at Teotihuacan undeniable.

Groundbreaking work on Teotihuacan writing has also been done by Karl Taube (2000b, 2003), who has suggested that writing is much more common at the city than previously thought. He posits that Teotihuacan scholars often have not recognized the hieroglyphs and largely considered them to be symbols rather than writing. In the murals of the Tepantitla apartment compound, he points to speech scrolls issuing from the mouths of various figures. Near some of the

FIGURE 2.1. Mural including a figure with "tassel headdress–bird claw" hieroglyph before him, Techinantitla, Teotihuacan. Drawing by Jenni Bongard after C. Millon 1988c:V.7.

FIGURE 2.2. Hieroglyphs painted on the floor of the Plaza of the Glyphs, La Ventilla 1992–1994, Teotihuacan. Drawing by Jenni Bongard after Cabrera 1996:Figures 6 and 11.

speech scrolls are images that Taube identifies as glyphs, consisting of things such as a centipede, the head of an old man, or a mouth with emanations coming from it. Taube makes a powerful argument that these represent the words of the people in the mural. Much like the text in our own comic strips, the speech scroll shows that a figure is speaking, and the glyph indicates what is being said.

Taube goes even further to suggest, with a good deal of humor, that some writing at Teotihuacan is so large that researchers had difficulty recognizing its import. For instance, throughout the mural art of Teotihuacan, odd assemblages of multiple symbols appear (Figure 1.17). These often repeat on the wall, again suggesting the absence of syntax. It seems that the Teotihuacanos preferred to record nouns, names, or titles rather than full sentences.

In the search for Teotihuacan's missing rulers, these observations on writing are of critical importance. In the past, it was thought that writing was largely absent at Teotihuacan. Thus, the assumption has been that writing was not an important political tool for Teotihuacan rulers. If, hypothetically, these odd assemblages of symbols represent the names of political officials, even the names of Teotihuacan rulers, then the picture of the city is a very different one. These large hieroglyphs then function more like billboards, advertising rulers' names. Of course, this is pure conjecture until epigraphers decipher the hieroglyphs, for we have no idea whether the glyphs proclaim the name of a person, designate a particular place, or record a historic act. At this time,

the important point is that hieroglyphs did exist at Teotihuacan and our inability to recognize and read them severely hampers our interpretation of the city. It is a cautionary lesson that underscores all research on the site.

Another natural location to find evidence of Teotihuacan's rulers is in the city's art, yet the artistic style preferred at Teotihuacan poses challenges. The idea of conveying portraiture through the physiognomy of the body seems totally missing at Teotihuacan. In murals, figures appear in two dominant styles of painting. As exhibited in the lower walls of the Tepantitla apartment compound, one style is remarkably animated, with arms and legs in action (Figure 2.3). These figures may kick a ball or gesture to one another, but their faces follow a standard format, barring this as a route to identifying individuals. Yet it must be noted that the hairstyles and headdresses of these figures exhibit much variety, and these visuals may provide a useful avenue for future scholars seeking to identify social positions or names. This style of mural has one additional feature that makes this category an unlikely place to locate evidence of the city's rulers. In the murals the different figures engage in a spectacular number of activities, but there is no central focus on one individual or group of individuals. If the ruler were present, one would expect some focus upon him.

The other and more recognizable style of Teotihuacan art includes people with short, stocky proportions (Figure 1.11a). Shown in profile, meticulously elaborated costumes cover most of their bodies, and the only anatomy displayed is a foot, bit of calf, the hands, and the part of the face not hidden by a large headdress. The facial features that do surface are generalized without idiosyncratic characteristics. Commonly these figures appear in processions with identical or near identical costume elements, once again defying attempts to isolate a central figure. Instead of marching toward an individual on a throne, these processions often converge on the image of a god or cult symbol (Kubler 1967). As has been noted, the images suggest a collective mentality that seems to eschew the celebration of an individual (Pasztory 1990, 1990–1991, 1992a).

Thus far the search for Teotihuacan rulers has had rather gloomy prospects, with looted tombs,

FIGURE 2.3. Detail of the Water Talud mural from the lower wall, Portico 2, Tepantitla, Teotihuacan.

undeciphered hieroglyphs, and a generalized art style, but the picture is not as bleak as it seems. Although Teotihuacan artists did not pay much attention to portraiture, they placed an enormous emphasis on the figures' apparel. Their short bodies are almost as wide as they are tall, suggesting that the artists manipulated the body to include as much costume information as possible. Wanting to fully depict objects that would be partially hidden from view, the painters placed devices worn on the back or the chest in a frontal view. Necklaces made of shell or jade appear flattened to make their parts recognizable, and clothing reveals the fine details of the weaving. Bags carried in the hand as well as headdresses are carefully delineated to identify at least the wearers' roles or status, if not their identities. It is in this area, the interest in costume, where Teoti-

huacan artists may have left clues to the identity of their rulers.

In 1995, Linda Schele (1995:110–112) identified two images that may represent a Teotihuacan ruler. The first appears in a mural that probably dates to A.D. 300–400; that is, after the burials in the Pyramid of the Feathered Serpent.[5] The image comes from a program of murals within the principal patio of an apartment compound called Atetelco (Figure 2.4). Consisting of three buildings that are comparatively larger than surrounding rooms, each of the structures has an open air portico that faces onto the patio, with each portico featuring a different subject. The central portico, called Portico 2, opens to the west and is slightly larger and more elevated than the other two, which indicates that this space eclipsed the others in symbolic importance. An

FIGURE 2.4. The White Patio, Atetelco, Teotihuacan.

interlaced pattern, probably depicting serpentine cords of blood, organizes the space of the upper walls (Figure 1.13).[6] In the interstices of the cords, the artists inserted the same figure repeatedly. To the modern eye the mural is reminiscent of wall paper because the artist simply cropped off the figure when the mural encountered a corner or other boundary. The effect is a decorative one in which the overall design dominates the integrity of the individual figure. Nevertheless, it is this figure, confined to the spaces between the interlacing cords, that may be an image of a Teotihuacan ruler.

Schele (1995) built her case from a Mesoamerican approach by establishing that throughout Mesoamerica the iconography of rulership connects rulers with the imagery of trees that symbolically represent the *axis mundi*. For the Olmec, the tree appears as a caiman whose tail becomes a cleft mountain from which corn grows. On other occasions the Olmec eliminated the caiman imagery, and the tree simply sprouts from a mountain with a cave underneath it. The clearest representation of this is on an incised tablet from the Dallas Museum of Art that depicts a U-shaped cave opening below a stepped mountain (Figure 2.5). From the summit of this mountain a cruciform tree grows, replete with leafy vegetation on its branches. In turn, Olmec kings co-opted this imagery and showed themselves carrying the sprouts of the caiman mountain-tree and wearing cleft headdresses that sprouted vegetation. Among the Maya, such imagery continued and developed into the well-known tree on K'inich Janaab' Pakal I's sarcophagus lid (Figure 2.6). This tree similarly emerges from a U-shaped cave opening and has a bird perched in its branches. Like their Olmec predecessors, Maya kings adopted the tree imagery, positioning themselves as trees and wearing birds in their headdresses.

With the pattern established, Schele proceeded to demonstrate how the Portico 2 figure functions in the same manner. At Teotihuacan, the tree also appears on a mountain, closely mirroring the Olmec tablet. The most complete expression of the mountain-tree may be found in the murals of the Tepantitla apartment compound (Figures 1.14, 2.7). Historically, this image has been identified as a deity called the

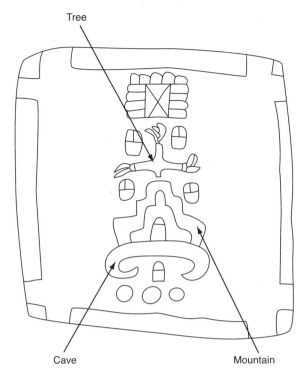

Tree

Cave   Mountain

FIGURE 2.5. An incised tablet from the Dallas Museum of Art, greenstone, Olmec, 900–500 B.C. Drawing by Jenni Bongard after Schele 1995:Figure 11a.

"Great Goddess," but the existence of this all-encompassing female deity has lately been called into question.[7] Therefore, this study will aim at a more neutral descriptive identification. The mountain is personified and faces the viewer in a fully frontal position. In this image the mountain wears earflares that frame odd, triangular-shaped eyes. Just below the eyes is a distinctive fanged noseplaque from which streams of liquid pour. Hands that stretch out to either side echo this watery aspect by sprinkling water down upon the earth. On the summit of the mountain, twisting tree branches rise from a headdress containing the bird that so often graces Meso-american trees. In addition, small birds flitter around the branches of the tree. Although the bird in the headdress symbolizes the celestial realm, the lower body ties this entity to the underworld. A down-turned U-shape represents both a cave and the vaginal opening of the personified mountain, and fittingly, the waters of the world flow from the opening in fertile lush-ness. Collectively, the Tepantitla mountain-tree and the Olmec and Maya cave-mountain-tree assemblages link the celestial and underworld

realms (Pasztory 1974, 1997:85–94). In essence, Teotihuacan shares in the grand tradition seen throughout Mesoamerica of envisioning a central cosmic tree that serves as an expression of the three levels of the universe.

The Tepantitla mountain-tree appears on several walls surrounding a room. On each wall the image of the personified mountain domi-nates the upper section, while the lower portion depicts numerous small figures engaged in vari-ous activities. On one wall the image below the personified mountain has a naturalistic moun-tain that sits directly below its counterpart in the upper mural. Apart from a Mesoamerican comparative approach, this vertical alignment provides the best evidence that the upper image in the Tepantitla mural is indeed a mountain. The lower, naturalistic mountain has a tube in its

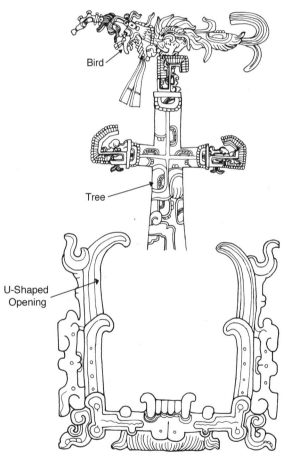

Bird

Tree

U-Shaped
Opening

FIGURE 2.6. Details of K'inich Janaab' Pakal I's sarcophagus lid, Temple of Inscriptions, Palenque, limestone, A.D. 684. Drawing by Linda Schele, © David Schele, courtesy of the Foundation for the Advancement of Mesoamerican Studies, Inc., www.famsi.org.

a.

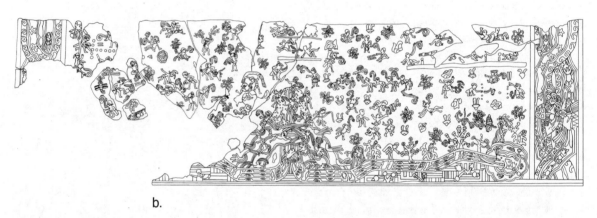

b.

FIGURE 2.7. Details of Portico 2, Tepantitla, Teotihuacan, showing *a*) the personified mountain-tree in the upper mural and *b*) the natural mountain directly below in the lower mural. Drawings by Jenni Bongard: *a*) after the reproduction by Villagra in the Teotihuacan Hall, Museo Nacional de Antropología, Mexico City; *b*) after Schele 1995:Figure 18.

upper section like a volcano, and a human figure emerges from the top. Below this is a cave from which people and, more importantly, water pour out onto the agricultural fields. The water flowing from this mountain is a direct cognate for the water streaming from the personified mountain. This visual juxtaposition of the personified and natural mountains indicates that the Teotihuacan *axis mundi* was not only conceptualized as a tree, but also as a mountain: specifically, a cleft volcanic mountain that spouts a tree above and releases water below. Remembering the cleft

mountain behind the Moon Pyramid, it is an easy conceptual leap to recognize that Cerro Gordo was Teotihuacan's archetypal *axis mundi,* whether it appeared as a mountain or a personified being.[8]

The central figure of the White Patio at Atetelco clearly wears the accoutrements of the mountain-tree (Figure 2.8). His profile headdress has the face and beak of the bird projecting over his forehead, and the distinctive fangs of the noseplaque appear below his nose. Just like the Olmec and Maya kings, the Portico 2 individual wears the imagery of the great tree or *axis mundi;* therefore, in Mesoamerican tradition, this individual claims the centrality and authority of rulership.

The objects prominently held in the figure's hands serve as additional implements of power. Mesoamerican parallels, specifically from Oaxaca, clarify the function of the articles held in the ruler's hands. The shell being carried at the ruler's waist is greatly enlarged to emphasize its importance, and speech scrolls floating from both openings imply the sound produced by the shell. In Prehispanic Mesoamerica, conch shells were important musical instruments that were blown to announce the presence of the gods (Sahagún 1950–1982:I:29). Because Aztec kings or generals often signaled their troops to attack with conch shell trumpets, shells may also symbolize military authority (Hassig 1988:96). Of the Period I (500–200 B.C.) tombs found at Monte Alban, Tomb 43 was the most elaborate. The ten conch shell effigies found inside led Flannery and Marcus to argue that conch shell trumpets were associated with public office among the Zapotec (Flannery 1976a:335; Flannery and Marcus 1983a:90). In addition, Reilly suggested that the conch shell trumpet may derive from the so-called knuckle-dusters commonly held by Olmec kings as an instrument of their office.[9] The knuckle-dusters, like the trumpets, were probably made of the *Strombus costatus.*

The staff held in the other hand consists of

FIGURE 2.9. Zapotec ruler with a staff, Stela 1, Monte Albán. Drawing by Jenni Bongard after Marcus and Flannery 1996:Figure 258.

four elements.[10] The circular portion is a mirror with a petaled flower at its center. This is explained by Taube's (1992a:184) observation that Teotihuacanos often conflated flowers with mirrors. Above the mirror is a horizontal knot binding an eccentric flint to the top of the staff. Von Winning (1987:20–21) identified the volute shape of this flint as flames; however, in this case the knot below the volute indicates that this is a projectile point bound to the pole below.[11] The final component is a tassel that swings from the circular mirror. Explanation of this staff comes from Oaxaca, where similar staffs appear in the iconography of rulers. Most prominently, on Stela 1 from Monte Albán a seated ruler in a jaguar costume holds a staff (Figure 2.9). Although the Oaxacan staff has two mirrors, the corresponding hafted point and tassel are easily visible. Winter (1990:131–132) suggested that the object on Stela 1 was a staff of office and a symbol of power for the Zapotec.

The meaning of the Portico 2 mural staff is manifold. The projectile point on the long shaft clearly designates the staff as a spear, even though it may be more ceremonial than practical. Tassels or swaths of feathers frequently decorate spears, particularly on Maya ceramics.[12] As a spear, the staff conveys the status of a warrior upon the

FIGURE 2.8. Possible image of a ruler from the Portico 2 mural, Atetelco, Teotihuacan. Drawing by Jenni Bongard after Séjourné 1966b:Figure 80.

FIGURE 2.10. Possible sculpture of a Teotihuacan ruler, West Plaza Complex, Teotihuacan. Drawing by Linda Schele, © David Schele, courtesy of the Foundation for the Advancement of Mesoamerican Studies, Inc., www.famsi.org.

king. The mirror, functioning as a device for imaging the supernatural world, may project the ruler's abilities to interface with the gods, therefore advertising his identity as a shaman. The staff's proclamation of the individual as both military ruler and shamanic priest fits well with other traditions because these are consistent traits of rulers throughout Mesoamerica.

A second possible image of the ruler was discovered closer to the political heart of the city in a palace called the West Plaza Complex located on the Avenue of the Dead. Sculpted on a number of stone blocks fitted together, this frontal portrayal makes the noseplaque over the mouth highly visible (Figure 2.10). The headdress arrangement is slightly different from the one in the White Patio: in this case there are two birds just underneath the fan of feathers arching over the headdress, and two profile serpents sitting below. In combination, the bird headdress and noseplaque indicate that this individual also identifies with the personified mountain-tree. The staffs in this figure's hands are different from the one in the Atetelco mural, but they still fit in with Mesoamerican royal iconography. As Schele (1995) pointed out, these staffs are remarkably similar to the bundled vegetation frequently held by Olmec rulers, which associates the ruler with agricultural fertility.[13]

Another possible but decidedly problematic image of a ruler comes from the murals of the Tetitla apartment compound (Figure 2.11).[14] This figure faces the viewer frontally and sprinkles water and precious objects from his hands, just as his Tepantitla counterpart does. His broad,

feathered headdress has the diagnostic bird at its center, although it also has prominent references to sacrifice: hearts removed by extraction decorate the sides of the headdress, and the bird has a vertebral column in its beak. Compared to the Tepantitla image, the eyes in this mural are more human; nevertheless, the same fanged noseplaque hangs over the mouth. Because the figure wears the bird headdress and fanged noseplaque, this image could arguably depict a ruler dressed in the accoutrements of the personified mountain-tree. However, the characteristics of the mural's lower portion somewhat jeopardize this interpretation. Underneath the collar of his garment, the lower body is missing as he rises from a bowl with an outflaring rim. The absence of a lower body is consequential because of arguments that deities may appear in partial form in Teotihuacan art (Berlo 1992; Pasztory 1997:210–219). The bowl, in particular, provides critical information because it reveals that this figure has been conjured or called out from the supernatural world. The bowl is a divining vessel, and the figure emerges from the bowl presumably through the actions of some undepicted priest (Taube 1992a:186–189). Ultimately, the bowl signals the figure's supernatural origins, making it more likely that this image depicts a deceased ruler who has been brought temporarily to the human realm through ritual.

FIGURE 2.11. Mural of a possible deceased ruler emerging from a bowl, Portico 11, Tetitla, Teotihuacan. Drawing by Jenni Bongard after Villagra 1971:Figure 14.

Together, these images present a vision of a ruler that mirrors royal imagery elsewhere in Mesoamerica and is consistent with iconography internal to Teotihuacan itself. With the bird in his headdress and the fanged noseplaque, the ruler associates himself with the costume elements of the personified mountain-tree. Because the mountain-tree manifests the world tree or *axis mundi,* the ruler assumes the symbolism of being the central social element and advertises his contact with the three cosmic levels. The conch shell trumpet and bifurcated staff both have military associations, and the staff may have also embodied the ruler's shamanic abilities to view the supernatural realm. Because the severed hearts in the Tetitla image probably refer to sacrifice associated with warfare, this mural further confirms the ruler's military role. Finally, on occasions when the ruler carries bundled vegetation, he declares his function in maintaining agricultural bounty, an association clearly echoed in the fertile waters flowing in the Tepantitla mural.

Thus far, these identifications of the king have been grounded on the principle that Mesoamerican rulers adopt the imagery of the *axis mundi,* and the pairing of the bird headdress and fanged noseplaque seems to be the Teotihuacan version of this strategy. Yet if we allow for another common royal practice, three other rather speculative candidates emerge as potential depictions of Teotihuacan rulers. The penchant of Maya kings, and indeed the inclination of rulers throughout all human history, to erect stone portraits of themselves leads to a consideration of the city's colossal stone sculptures. One of the most famous is an enormous stone monument that now resides in the Museo Nacional in Mexico City (Figure 2.12). Standing at almost 4 m, the Museo sculpture dwarfs the viewer and epitomizes the grand and commanding scale witnessed in much Teotihuacan public sculpture. Equally typical is the blocky form that incessantly recalls the rectangular stone from which the sculpture was carved. This characteristic reminds the observer of the heavy, massive properties of stone, thereby transferring these qualities onto the figure itself. The flat headdress on top contributes greatly to the overall geometric sense of the body.

Large earflares frame the sculpture's decidedly symmetrical and shallowly carved face, of which the cheeks are flat planes that hardly integrate with the projecting nose. The mouth and eyes are simple raised ovals, and the eyes in particular have little depth. Below the curve of the chin is a large beaded necklace that is partially interrupted by a hole drilled in the chest. The figure, which has its hands drawn in towards its chest, wears the female dress of a cape-like *quechquemitl* and, below a netted skirt with a fringe of beads at the bottom, tasseled sandals. There is no evidence of a loincloth over the skirt, and this, along with the cape or *quechquemitl,* offers the strongest evidence that the figure is female. Rosemary Joyce (1992:64–65) contended that netted skirts are a diagnostic marker of female attire connoting the horizontal, feminine earth, an observation in harmony with an identification of the sculpture as a goddess. Nevertheless, the issue is clouded because men may also have worn capes at Teotihuacan, and the sculpture's short skirt is more typical of those worn by men.[15]

Consistently, this sculpture has been identified as an image of the "Great Goddess," a singular goddess with numerous aspects whose primary attributes are identified as the fanged noseplaque and bird headdress seen in the Tepantitla mural.[16] The rationale for this identification is based on a system of classification that has tended to cluster imagery rather than separate it into smaller components. For instance, the Tepantitla mountain-tree has been interpreted as the goddess, and because this entity sprinkles water from its hands, there has been a tendency to view disembodied hands, even when they are not accompanied by other obvious goddess attributes, as the hands of the goddess.[17] Furthermore, sculptures with nothing more than a *quechquemitl* or a rectangular noseplaque have been invoked as sculptures of the "Great Goddess" despite the fact that the noseplaque does not have fangs or the *quechquemitl* is not on a figure with the bird headdress (Berlo 1992:134–143). Admittedly, the sculpture in the Museo Nacional has decidedly few attributes that associate it with the goddess or, for that matter, any other entity; therefore, it cannot qualify as an image of the ruler posing as the *axis mundi.* While the *quechquemitl* and missing loincloth may identify the individual as female, the sculpture has neither the bird headdress nor fanged noseplaque. Overall, the sculpture

FIGURE 2.12. Colossal Museo Nacional sculpture found in a courtyard behind the pyramids of the southwest corner of the Moon Plaza, Teotihuacan.

is bereft of iconographic elements that clearly identify it as a singular entity.

Apart from the cape or *quechquemitl,* the headdress on the sculpture induces an identification that is somewhat compelling. The rectangular headdress includes a small cleft at the very top. This indentation mimics clefts frequently seen in the heads or headdresses of Olmec kings. For the Olmec, the cleft headdress associated the ruler with the cleft mountain, a point made clear by the sprout or tree commonly emerging from the split in the ruler's head. If the Teotihuacanos inherited this earlier symbolic tradition, then the indentation at the top of the Museo Nacional sculpture could refer to the cleft mountain of Cerro Gordo, the natural form that inspired the mountain-tree of Tepantitla. Thus, this simple cleft in the headdress may associate the figure with the cleft mountain from which corn sprouts and water flows.

While I agree that the sculpture may embody, at least partially, the volcanic cleft mountain of Cerro Gordo, I also maintain that the association of this sculpture with this mountain may have been overemphasized in the past. Within the literature on Teotihuacan, the most common way of identifying the original location of the Museo Nacional sculpture is that it was found near the Moon Pyramid (Cowgill 1997:149; Pasztory 1997:99). Pasztory even suggests that it may have been paired with another colossal sculpture to form a gateway to the Moon Pyramid, the structure that symbolized Cerro Gordo.[18] Although it is true that the Museo Nacional sculpture was found near the Moon Pyramid, this may be only relatively correct. Unfortunately, when the sculpture was moved to Mexico City, its precise original location was not documented by any publication; consequently, we must rely on early visitors to the site who recorded their experiences in ways that were different than our modern scientific approaches. On the matter of the Museo Nacional sculpture, the earliest reference is that of Brantz Mayer (1844:223–224), who provided an inverted drawing of the sculpture and plotted it on a rudimentary map (Figure 2.13). Marked *c* on the map, the sculpture is behind a row of mounds on the west side of the Moon Plaza. Other accounts written soon after this publication confirm that the

sculpture was not in the Moon Plaza proper, but enclosed within smaller mounds just off the plaza. Waddy Thompson (1847:140) reported that he saw the stone "in a secluded spot, shut in by two small hillocks," and in a later publication, Mayer (1852:282) stated that the sculpture was in a "semicircular enclosure among the tumuli." Some years later, W. H. Holmes (1897) provided an even more detailed view of the unexcavated city (Figure 2.14), and he placed the sculpture off the plaza behind the two southernmost temples on the west side of the Moon Plaza. Leaving no room for doubt, he wrote, "on the west side of the court, behind the first line of mounds, was found the large idol recently removed to the Museo Nacional."[19]

Because the Museo Nacional sculpture is in pristine condition, these accounts must accurately plot the original location of the sculpture in a smaller courtyard behind the temples on the west side of the Moon Plaza. Considering the large size of Teotihuacan, this does position the sculpture near the Moon Pyramid, but

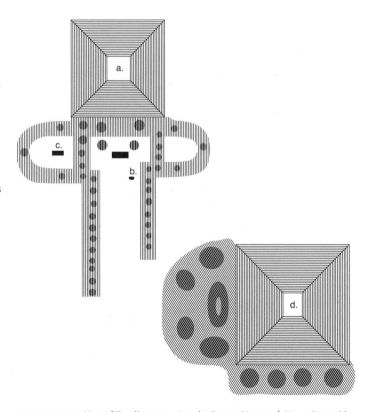

FIGURE 2.13. Map of Teotihuacan, 1842, by Brantz Mayer: *a)* Moon Pyramid; *b)* damaged colossal sculpture; *c)* Museo Nacional colossal sculpture; *d)* Sun Pyramid. Drawing by Jenni Bongard after Mayer 1844.

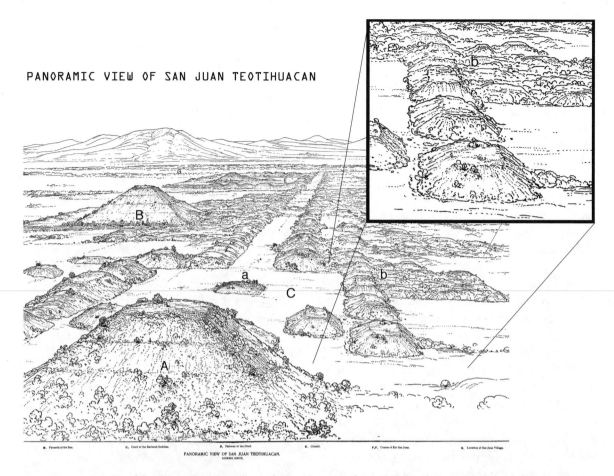

B. Pyramid of the Sun.　　　C. Court of the Battered Goddess.　　　D. Pathway of the Dead.　　　E. Citadel.　　　F.F. Course of Rio San Juan.　　　G. Location of San Juan Village.

PANORAMIC VIEW OF SAN JUAN TEOTIHUACAN.
LOOKING SOUTH.

FIGURE 2.14. Drawing of Teotihuacan by W. H. Holmes: *A)* Moon Pyramid; *B)* Sun Pyramid; *C)* Plaza of the Moon; *a)* damaged sculpture; *b)* original location of the Museo Nacional sculpture. Adapted by Kirvin Hodges after Holmes 1897:Plate XLIX, reproduced by permission of the Field Museum Press.

I would urge future studies to investigate the more private nature of the sculpture's original location. Instead of functioning as part of the most public space in the city, the sculpture had a more restricted audience. A courtyard such as this probably served some of the highest elites of the city. As such, the sculpture certainly could project broad, civic ideals, but it could also speak to the objectives of a specific audience.

A final feature of this sculpture, the hole just below the necklace, may have once reduced the generic iconography of this sculpture and furnished it with a more narrow symbolic purpose. Because the hole is empty, one is left to speculate on its original purpose, but similar sculptural elements in Aztec art offer one possibility. Before remodeling and enlarging the Templo Mayor, the Aztecs placed several sculptures depicting standing humans at the base of the temple stairs

(Figure 2.15). The sculptures probably represented elite captives because some wore the Aztec crown of kings but their only clothing was a simple loincloth. They have holes in their raised hands so that they could hold the banners that were probably captured from these very same individuals. Like the Museo Nacional sculpture, the figures also had holes drilled into their chests, but these holes held pieces of greenstone (Beyer 1965a:423; Matos Moctezuma 1987:32). In the case of the standard bearers, the greenstone probably referred to the heart sacrifice conducted on these captives; however, there is little about the Museo sculpture to suggest that it represents a captive.

Another, more compelling explanation arises from the corpus of Teotihuacan ceramic figurines. There are many examples of figures with a round mirror or shield just below the head where the chest would be (Figure 2.16).[20] A number of figurines exhibit a circular disk prominently displayed on the chest, and some of these are embossed with imagery. Two notable examples are a pair of ceramic figurines that have round shields on their chests decorated with an owl and spear points that were used with a spearthrower, or atlatl (Figure 2.16a). These figurines have received considerable attention since David Stuart (2000) found reference among the hieroglyphic texts of Tikal to a ruler named Spearthrower Owl, who he believes may be the Teotihuacan king who orchestrated the overthrow of the Tikal dynasty at this Maya site. With this argument in mind, the shields worn on the chests of the figurines may indicate the name of this particular king. If the spears represent the atlatl, then the figurines could be portraits of Spearthrower Owl himself. The resulting impact of this interpretation is profound, for if the hole in the colossal sculpture once held the tenon for a similar shield, this shield might tell us the figure's identity. The

seemingly generic features of the face would have lost their anonymity if the sculpture once wore its name upon its chest.

Even if the hole did function as a tenon, a circular disk mounted on the sculpture's chest would not necessarily have incorporated a glyphic component: a number of such disks on Teotihuacan figurines are quite devoid of decoration (Figures 2.16b, 3.11). The greater Mesoamerican figurine tradition may elucidate the plain disks on Teotihuacan figurines. Beginning in the Olmec period, disks of mica and obsidian frequently decorate the chests of figurines, and these miniature mirrors are thought to convey the wearer's shamanic abilities to gaze into the supernatural realm.

The possible presence of a mirror on the sculpture's breast is especially interesting in light of eighteenth-century accounts of Teotihuacan sculpture. Both Gemelli Carreri (1995) and Clavigero (1979) wrote that a gold disk decorated a sculpture on the Sun Pyramid. This claim is ques-

FIGURE 2.15. Aztec standard bearers from the Templo Mayor stairs, stone, Stage III, Tenochtitlan, A.D. 1441.

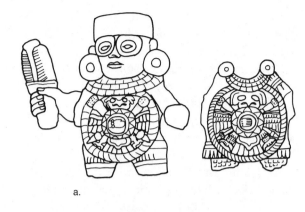

FIGURE 2.16. Teotihuacan figurines with disks on their chests: *a*) figurines with Atlatl-Owl disks; *b*) figurine with blank disk. Drawings: *a*) by Linda Schele, © David Schele, courtesy of the Foundation for the Advancement of Mesoamerican Studies, Inc., www.famsi.org; *b*) by Jenni Bongard after von Winning 1987:58, Figure 2f.

tionable because neither man actually saw the gold disk; instead, both reported the secondhand information of conquistadors. The fact that gold was not a typical Classic period material poses further challenges to the veracity of these historic chronicles, although Aztec pilgrims could have left gold offerings when they visited the site. More likely the Spanish lust for gold led Gemelli Carreri's and Clavigero's sources to mistake another shiny material for this rare metal.

At Teotihuacan mica, or iron pyrite, was one of the most common reflective embellishments for sculpture and ceremonial objects. Bits of reflective mica fill miniature mirrors on censers, and stone masks bear evidence of pyrite inlays.[21] A huge cache of unworked pyrite under the floors of the Viking Group attests to its treasured sacredness, but its most common use was on mosaic mirrors.[22] Warriors wore mosaic mica mirrors at the small of their backs, mirrors appear in headdresses, and figures position mirrors at their chests (Taube 1992a). If the hole in the Museo Nacional sculpture functioned as a tenon for a mirror, the sculpture would easily fit within the greater Teotihuacan tradition. Furthermore, as mirrors represented a view into the supernatural, who better than a goddess or ruler to wield it.

How then do we interpret this colossal sculpture found in a patio off the Moon Plaza? Because it wears a *quechquemitl,* it may indeed depict a goddess, and the cleft headdress could serve as a basis for associating it with Cerro Gordo. Within the private courtyard, it would have served as an object of devotion for the inhabitants of that particular elite space. On the other hand, we must leave open the possibility that the sculpture depicts a person, and that person may be wearing the costume of a female, perhaps a goddess. If a disk with a name originally fitted into the hole in the chest, the sculpture could have revealed whether that individual was biologically female or a male gendered as a female. The name would have afforded historic specificity to the sculpture. If Mesoamerican parallels have any merit, the cleft headdress would associate the individual with the sprouting mountain, and an individual who dressed in the guise of the *axis mundi* would be the ruler of Teotihuacan. In either case, the large scale of the sculpture would be appropriate. Whether an enormous sculpture of a goddess or a large portrait of a ruler who wanted to leave an image behind for posterity, the sculpture projected a suggestion of grandeur that reflected the aspirations of those in the courtyard.

It is certainly acceptable that a group of Teotihuacanos would have made a sculpture of a deity for private devotional purposes. However, the proposal that the sculpture depicts a ruler is rather compelling, especially because this sculpture may not have been unique. Another similar sculpture actually does sit within the Plaza of the Moon. Currently it is near the southeast corner of an altar in that plaza, but it probably once stood atop that altar (Figures 2.14, 2.17). It has been heavily battered and is only a fragment of its former glory. Despite its marred condition, it is still possible to identify some iconography and plausibly suggest its subject.

Pasztory (1997:99) argued that the sculpture depicts the "Great Goddess" by comparing it to the Museo Nacional sculpture (Figure 2.12). Even if the identification is open to question, Pasztory's comparison is valid because the surviving sculpted portions of the battered sculpture are in accord with the Museo Nacional sculpture. A wide nose emerges from a cheek that looks to be similarly flat and abstracted, and to either side of the nose traces of the oval rings around the eyes still exist. Just as with the better preserved sculpture, the facial features are shallow and regularized. Below this, the surface of the chin area is quite marred, but the distinctive form of a jutting curve is present, and it projects out over the same beaded necklace. Quite tellingly, there is a hole under the necklace, the identical location of the hole on the Museo Nacional sculpture.

FIGURE 2.17. Damaged sculpture in the Plaza of the Moon, Teotihuacan.

The rest of the sculpture has suffered the most damage; however, bulges on each side of the hole are in the same location as the hands of the other sculpture. Even though the definition of the fingers is now lost, we can assume that this figure also pulled its hands in toward the chest. In its present state, the sculpture is only 169 cm, yet its shorter stature may be due to the heavy battering seen at the bottom. The massive features of the Moon Plaza sculpture still manage to convey a sense of its original colossal size.

The strong congruencies between these two sculptures imply that they both depicted similar entities. Without knowing the original purpose of the holes in the chests, it is difficult to determine whether they portrayed goddesses or rulers. The standardized facial features fit with either attribution, as they typify the Teotihuacan art style. Only if the holes once held glyphic names or titles would the individual personae of these possible rulers emerge. It is a seemingly telling circumstance that the sculpture in the more private space off the plaza survived intact, while the sculpture in the midst of the public plaza was violently attacked. Although overzealous Spaniards may have committed this act of violence, it may also have occurred upon the fall of Teotihuacan when many temples were burned.[23] In the latter case, the sculpture may have represented a powerful ruler or deity associated with the city, and the marauders may have smashed the image to symbolize the utter defeat of Teotihuacan's government.

A final sculpture may be all that remains of a third ruler's even grander attempt to record his image in stone. George Cowgill (1997) suggested that the Colossus of Coatlinchan (Figure 2.18) might reflect a ruler's unrealized efforts towards "personal glorification." The sculpture is over 7 m tall and was found unfinished in a quarry southwest of Texcoco (Berlo 1992:138). It now stands near the entrance to the Museo Nacional in Mexico City. Like the other two sculptures, the Colossus of Coatlinchan is commonly thought to be female, but Cowgill questioned this interpretation, stating that the gender of the clothing was "ambiguous." A trapezoidal piece of fabric falling over the skirt of this sculpture could be construed as a loincloth, and the rudimentary drillings of a noseplaque, possibly a fanged

FIGURE 2.18. Colossus of Coatlinchan, found in a quarry southwest of Texcoco.

noseplaque, may have been started in the area of the mouth. Because it was never finished, Cowgill speculated that carving on the Colossus ceased at the same time the Feathered Serpent Pyramid was burned, smashed, and covered—a time when Teotihuacan may have moved away from individual rule to a more collective form of government. The sculpture might be one additional monument preserving the uneasy balance between rulers who wanted to glorify their personal position and a society that was wary of such unchecked power.

Because each of these sculptures exhibits varying degrees of gender ambiguity, the existence of female rulers at Teotihuacan should be entertained. The *quechquemitl* on the Museo Nacional sculpture mirrors the capes worn by the priests in the Tepantitla mural. This garment was a strong marker of female dress in the later Postclassic period, suggesting that the sculpture could depict a female ruler. Although not as common in Mesoamerica, women such as Lady Yohl Ik'nal of Palenque and the Mixtec queen Lady 6 Monkey did rise to power and rule in their own right. Others, such as the militant Lady Six Sky of Naranjo, effectively governed as regents, erecting monuments virtually indistinguishable from those of reigning kings (Martin and Grube 2000).

The intriguing proposition that female rulers existed at Teotihuacan is bolstered by archaeological remains from the Epiclassic period (A.D. 650–850), which immediately followed the collapse of Teotihuacan. Mari Carmen Serra Puche (2001) argues for female rulers at the central Mexican site of Xochitecatl, citing a preponderance of female imagery, including figurines depicting enthroned women holding shields and scepters. The figurines also wear serpent headdresses, a feature commonly seen elsewhere on militant elite males, and have *quechquemitls* about their shoulders.

Furthermore, murals at the neighboring site of Cacaxtla include a captured military captain wearing a *quechquemitl,* and although the traces of paint are faint, McCafferty and McCafferty (1994a) argue that the figure may have a female breast. As they point out, there are several possibilities for the female imagery of the captain. The captain could be biologically female, de-

picting a warrior queen in the mode of Lady 6 Monkey and Lady Six Sky. Alternatively, the female garb may signal an office like that of the Aztec *cihuacoatl,* a military position named for a goddess but held by a male. Taken together, the archaeological remains of Xochitecatl and Cacaxtla indicate that central Mexican women likely held powerful military and political positions during the Epiclassic. Given that the colossal sculptures of Teotihuacan have varying degrees of female costume, we must leave open the possibility that some of Teotihuacan's rulers may have been queens. This proposition also suggests that the phenomenon of Epiclassic female rulers may have had its origins in the Classic period.

If one or all of these massive sculptures portrayed individual rulers, they would function much like Maya stelae, answering the nagging question of why Teotihuacan rulers did not place their portraits on large public monuments. Viewing these sculptures as the portraits of particular rulers would suggest that they did. The Teotihuacan rulers would look more normal if they proclaimed their power in such a political manner and memorialized that power through the enduring medium of stone. Furthermore, the fact that one sculpture was brutally smashed and another never completed may stand as testament that authority vested in one individual person was not a system that typified all of Teotihuacan's history.

The difficulty of determining the identity of these sculptures mirrors one of the most troubling aspects of the Atetelco White Patio mural. In the Portico 2 mural (Figures 1.13 and 2.8) the hypothetical ruler appears repeatedly, suggesting a procession of many instead of a focus on one individual. While the costume elements may clearly identify the figure as a ruler, one wonders why his features are generalized and why the image seems mechanically stamped out. Similarly, the facial features of the colossal sculptures are simplified with no references to idiosyncratic traits. These elements could reveal that the Teotihuacanos frequently emphasized office over the individual. By eliminating portraiture, the exact person who holds the office seems less important; likewise, by repeating the image, the individual comes to look more like a part of a social machine instead of an independent actor with personal powers.

The multiplicity in royal imagery may also lead to another conclusion: that authority did not lie with one individual at Teotihuacan but instead the city had a system of joint rulership. A return to the Tepantitla murals does much to clarify this proposition. The upper walls of the Tepantitla murals are quite damaged, but enough evidence remains to decipher that two human figures existed on either side of the mountain-tree (Figure 1.14). The figures walk in profile towards the mountain, sprinkling offerings on the ground in thanks for the water that it gives. These individuals have often been referred to as priests because of their activity, yet a close look at their clothing reveals that they dress in costume elements of the mountain-tree between them (Pasztory 1976:117–120). They wear the short skirt of Teotihuacan males, but a short cape or *quechquemitl* covers their upper bodies. The most diagnostic element is the headdress that the processing figures wear. It is the same headdress crowning the mountain before them with the bird and its beak projecting out over their foreheads. Clearly the figures are dressed as the personified mountain, and if the arguments made here are valid, this would indicate that these priests are also the rulers of the city. It seems inevitable that we should consider the possibility that Teotihuacan had a system of co-rulership in which two people may have shared the highest political office.

While most of Mesoamerica invested royal power in one individual, the Aztec political structure contained elements of joint rulership. The Aztec system was in keeping with the rest of Mesoamerica in that it had one supreme ruler who held the title of *tlatoani,* but at some point they added the *cihuacoatl,* a position that was primarily a military role. Technically under the *tlatoani,* the office of the *cihuacoatl* at times became so powerful that aspects of co-rulership emerged. During the reign of Motecuhzoma I, Tlacaelel held the military position, and a rhetoric entwining the two men emerged. Motecuhzoma I and Tlacaelel were spoken of as twins, and it appears that the latter held significant political power (Gillespie 1989:62–63, 132–133). While time-depth between the Aztec and Teotihuacan

is vast, the repetitive nature of Teotihuacan royal imagery may imply that the Aztecs derived their system from previous traditions of shared power.

The specter of joint rulership at Teotihuacan may do much to further explain the apparent anonymity of the city's art. Emphasis on costume and the exaltation of the office over the individual would nicely fit with a political system that had more than one ruler. For comparison, the Roman Empire instituted shared rule during a period in its history. In the second half of the third century the Roman Empire had been wracked by chronic wars, invasions, and the frequent assassination of its emperors (L'Orange 1965:39–40). To combat the chaos, Diocletian elevated Maximian to *Augustus,* and the two jointly ruled the large empire, with Diocletian overseeing the east, and Maximian the west. Each of the *Augusti* had a *Caesar* directly underneath him, and after twenty years of rule, the *Augusti* were to step down, and the *Caesares* were to become the new *Augusti.* This tetrarchic form of government was instituted to regularize inheritance by addressing the problem of usurpation that had troubled the empire. Concomitant with the system was rhetoric that deemphasized the differences among the four rulers. Real and fictitious family links were forged, and the *Augusti* suppressed their own personae to celebrate their official birthdays on the same day. In art they also appeared as twins, as in the famous tetrarch sculptures in the Vatican and Venice. The sculptures eschew the portraiture so common in the Republican and Imperial periods, resulting in modest sculptures of stubby men in identical clothing hugging one another. The *similitudo* underscores the interchangeability of each individual. Ultimately, the Roman attempt at co-rulership failed, for the human tendency to strive for absolute power and personal glorification defeated efforts to establish a stable transfer of power. A year after the new *Augusti* came to power, one of them, Constantius Chlorus, died, and the army in Britain declared Constantine the new emperor. After a number of deaths and the elimination of rivals through several military victories, Constantine became the singular ruler of the Roman Empire (Le Glay 2001:407–411).

The failure of the Romans to secure a long-lived system of joint rulership might offer a cautionary note regarding the assumption that Teotihuacan managed to establish such a system for very long. The course of human history is often one of individuals because the quest for power seems so ingrained in our very being. Furthermore, the emerging evidence that Teotihuacan rulers may not have been as anonymous as previously thought must frame our view of its art. If some of the imagery long considered to be symbols actually represents writing, then historical figures may emerge from this iconography. While we should certainly entertain the possibility of systems other than that of power invested in a single individual, we should also recognize that there is much about Teotihuacan art that is not understood. Certainly they may have avoided portraiture, but they may have inserted personal identification in ways not recognized at present. Regardless of the number of rulers at Teotihuacan, there is evidence that the power of these individuals did not go unchecked. Instead of viewing them as absolute kings, we are better off seeing them as figures bounded by social constraints that forced them to share power with other social entities at Teotihuacan.

CHAPTER 3

ANCESTRAL FOUNDATIONS

The nature of Teotihuacan art implies that the rulers of this city contended for power with a variety of social entities. As images of the king gradually become more visible to modern eyes, he appears not as a completely submerged personality, but still as an institution that featured the office much more than the individual. Even when the surviving texts of the city are read, it is rather unlikely that we will find much about the personal history of particular rulers. There may be declarative statements of identity, but little about the writing resembles narrative. Visually, the rulers commissioned portraits of themselves without idiosyncratic physical characteristics, and artists used the same canon of squat proportions on every figure be they king or warrior. In public art the rulers seem to yield to the popular norm and conform with the masses. They are recognizable, but their assertions are somewhat tempered. The impetus for this deferential strategy may lie in the very foundations of Teotihuacan. Buried beneath the walls is evidence of a deeply rooted system of ancestor worship, and the familiarly related groups that developed around these ancestors may have been one social aspect that weakened the office of the ruler.

The housing type of choice for most Teotihuacanos was the apartment compound, and it is here that the archaeology reveals a pattern of reckoning ancestral ties and revering familial forbearers. Determining just what factors governed membership in an apartment compound is still something that requires attention, but the evidence available today indicates that familial ties were a primary determinant. In one of the few studies to address this issue, Michael Spence (1974) demonstrated that skeletal traits of males were generally closer than those of females, and concluded that there were kinship ties amongst

residents of apartment compounds. Further research needs to be conducted in this area, but
burial patterns in the apartment compounds do
support Spence's conclusion that the compounds
were lineage based. On the most fundamental
of levels, Cowgill (2003a:42) pointed to the preponderance of burials underneath the floors of
apartment compound rooms and patios, suggesting that this reveals compound residents
who expected to inhabit the spaces and maintain
access to their ancestors well into the future.[1]

DOMESTIC FOUNDERS

Martha Sempowski's (1992) study of mortuary
practices established that the early construction phase of compounds often has a particularly
high-status burial. One such burial from the Xolalpan compound indicates strong connections
between an important ancestor and the construction of an apartment compound. Linné (1934:54–
59) encountered Burial 1 in a stone tomb whose
south wall functioned as the base of a compound
wall. The tomb was part of the compound's initial construction and perhaps an integral aspect
of the structure's conceptual underpinnings. In
this case the founder buried inside the tomb
epitomized his title in real terms as he was a part
of the structure; the founder literally became the
foundation of the residential space. This burial
prompted René Millon (1981:209) to propose
that "Founder's burials may also be associated
with the building of a compound and thus serve
as a clue to the particular circumstances under
which specific compounds came to be built." In
other words, the instigation of a new apartment
compound may have necessitated the bones of a
revered ancestor, and this would imply that the
residents of the compound claimed descent from
that ancestor.

Another burial pattern furthers the argument
for lineage ties and can, moreover, help illuminate the function of the principal patios found in
the compounds. In some cases the most elaborate
burial of a compound is associated with the altar
of the principal patio (Figure 3.1). In excavations
north of the Moon Pyramid, Monzon (1987:157–
164) reported that the richest burial recovered,
Burial 129, was a female located in Patio I, which

FIGURE 3.1. Altar in the Tetitla principal patio, Teotihuacan.

also contained the remains of an altar, marking
it as the main patio of the compound. At Tlajinga 33, burials with the most impressive grave
goods were concentrated near a shrine room at
the center of an Early Tlamimilolpa (A.D. 225–
300) principal patio (Widmer 1987). There were
two high-status burials in association with the
Tlajinga 33 shrine room. The earlier Burial 56 included an impressive thirty vessels. Subsequently,
the compound residents razed the shrine room,
and the placement of Burial 57 followed. This
was the highest-status burial at the compound,
with the individual buried in a robe made of
10,000 olivella shells and a headdress of carved
shell serpents. Likewise, when Evelyn Rattray
investigated several residential structures in an
area of Teotihuacan called the Merchants' Barrio, she excavated five altars and all contained
burials, prompting her to speculate that the altars
were ancestral shrines (Rattray 1992:78). Indeed,
the patio altar was a popular location for burials, making it likely that rituals conducted in
the patio included ancestor veneration (Sánchez
Alaniz 1991:173).

Storey's (1987:100) analysis of the altar shrines
at Tlajinga 33 warrants attention, for she confirmed the ancestral association of these structures and exposed another interesting burial
practice.[2] The compound had three successive
courtyards, each with a central altar or shrine
room. The first dates to the Early Tlamimilolpa period (A.D. 225–300) and contained a
shrine room with the above-mentioned high-

status Burials 56 and 57. In the final Late Xo-lalpan period (A.D. 450–550) the central patio had an altar instead of a shrine room, but it still exhibited some consistency in the burial pattern. Archaeologists encountered the remains of five adults in a shaft tomb underneath the altar (Storey 1992:61). The shaft tomb resembles the earlier burials by establishing the central patio structure as a locus of burial activity. Yet between these two phases, there was a transformation in the burial pattern under the altar. During the Late Tlamimilolpa/Early Xolalpan period (A.D. 300–450) the inhabitants of Tlajinga 33 interred two juveniles and three perinatals under the altar; thus young children claimed the location earlier reserved for the highest-status adult individuals. The incongruency in behavior pattern demands an explanation.

THE YOUNGEST ANCESTORS

The practice of placing young children under principal patio altars is not restricted to Tlajinga 33. In fact, fetal burials inside ceramic vessels frequently appear in association with altars at Teotihuacan, prompting much speculation as to why there is such a high number of infant burials at Teotihuacan (Sánchez Alaniz 1989:154, 1991:174). Burials excavated by Vidarte (1964) at La Ventilla B could indicate that sacrificial customs were a contributing factor (Rattray and Ruiz 1980:107; Rattray 1992:12). Of the five altars at La Ventilla B, four had infant burials associated with their construction, including Altar II, which had five fetal burials. Serrano and Lagunas (1975) noted that infants accounted for 20 percent of the bodies recovered and contended that this high infant mortality arose from both natural and artificially induced abortions. However, Storey (1985:531) countered that poor nutrition and disease alone can account for the high mortality of perinatals. Taking a global perspective, she compared the mortality statistics of Tlajinga 33 to particular Native North American sites and found Teotihuacan infant mortality only slightly higher. She then compared Teotihuacan to preindustrial cities of Europe and suggested that urban population pressures may explain the elevation in infant mortality. Higher population density

may have contributed to the spread of disease and created more fluctuation in food supplies.

The ethnographic record indicates that all of these positions may be at least partially correct. Accounts of the Aztecs document that child sacrifice was sometimes a Mesoamerican practice. In ritual context, they killed a significant number of young children in a feast during the first month of the year, *atl caualo* (Sahagún 1950–1982:II:1–2, 42–44). They called the children "human paper streamers" because they symbolically represented sacrificial paper banners. In a parallel fashion, Maya rituals may also corroborate such practices. Taube (1994) reasoned that the modern Zinacanteco practice of sacrificing a chicken during house dedication rituals may have involved the sacrifice of a baby in the Classic period.

When it comes to infanticide, however, nature is humanity's accomplice. The disease that Storey reported for ancient Teotihuacan is still a major factor in modern day Mexico. Hugo Nutini graphically reported that child mortality was a common reality in modern central Mexico.

Given the extremely high rate of infant mortality in rural Tlaxcala until the early 1960s, an inordinate number of deaths fall into this category. In some communities, as many as 50 percent of all children die before the age of five, and the most critical period falls between birth and the age of two and a half. The sheer weight of numbers makes this category of the dead extremely important, for there is no other stage in the life cycle of rural Tlaxcalans that exhibits such a high concentration of mortality. The importance of the cult of dead infants is enhanced by the position that infants (and children generally) have as especially effective mediators between man and the supernatural. (Nutini 1988:133)

Regrettably, due to rampant disease in preindustrial societies and poverty in the modern world, there seems to have always been an ample supply of deceased children. Regardless of the source, whether the children died of natural or human causes, there was an inclination at Teotihuacan to bury perinatals or children near the altar of the principal patio in apartment compounds. Because children can in no way be construed as important founding ancestors, this pattern would seem to undermine the association of the patios with ancestor veneration. However, this threat subsides with an examination of the most important ancestral ritual in Mexico today.

Every year during the end of October and the beginning of November, contemporary Mexicans celebrate *los Días de Muertos,* the Days of the Dead. During this holiday, lasting two to five days, many Mexicans pay homage to their ancestral dead. The number of days varies between communities, and each day honors a different category of the dead. One day might honor those killed in accidents, while another is dedicated to unbaptized children; nevertheless, one feature always typifies the categories.[3] No matter how many days a community celebrates, at least one day venerates children, called *angelitos,* and another memorializes adult dead (Foster 1948:219; Scheffler 1976:94). Those who celebrate the Days of the Dead consistently make this age distinction.

It is often speculated that the Days of the Dead have their roots in Precolumbian rituals, and the altar burials at Teotihuacan support this position.[4] The altars at Teotihuacan have the same age-based division; they were either dedicated to very young children or adults. This distinction is most explicitly expressed in the sequence of altar burials at Tlajinga 33, where the burials under the central altar fluctuated between adults and children.[5] In a parallel manner, Postclassic Aztec rituals included the same age distinction. A festival called Miccailhuitontli, the Little Feast of the Dead, celebrated young children, and Hueymic-caylhuitl, the Great Feast of the Dead, celebrated the adult dead (Nutini 1988:59–60; Carmichael and Sayer 1991:28). The customs surrounding the Days of the Dead demonstrate that children are an integral part of family rituals for the dead and recognized as legitimate and even significant members of the family despite their short earthly lives. Furthermore, Mexican rituals dedicated to the dead confirm a long tradition of dividing the deceased into the categories of children and adults.

Hugo Nutini's (1988) study of the cult of the dead amongst the Tlaxcalans does much to clarify the special role played by the youngest ancestors, the *angelitos.* Rural Tlaxcalans classify children who cannot yet speak clearly as infants, and the funeral of an infant has unique characteristics. Although the infant's parents may be grieving,

most of the people around them are happy and relieved that the child will not have to suffer in this world. The night before the burial, a festive wake is held with much drinking, feasting, and game playing. The custom is surprising because one expects to find only sorrow, but the festivities surrounding *angelito* burial are quite jubilant. Nutini effectively clarified this paradox by illuminating the unique role that young children play in the supernatural realm.

. . . what explains its content [the exuberant celebration upon an infant's death] is the deeply ingrained pre-Hispanic belief that children, especially infants, are the best intermediaries and conveyors of the supplications addressed by humans to the supernatural. Thus, when an infant dies of natural causes the people rejoice collectively insofar as they regard the dead infant's soul as one more link in the communication chain between the earthly and the supernatural, an addition to the corps of supernatural advocates that they must have for successful approaches to higher supernatural powers. (Nutini 1988:135–136)

Or as one of Nutini's collaborators said,

I have always believed that the (souls of dead) infants and children are the best advocates we have where it counts, and thus, we must keep them happy and pray to them a lot. (Nutini 1988:136)

Hence children, in this tradition, are especially adept mediators between the world of the living and that of the gods. It is as though their short-lived stay never allowed the children to shed the qualities of the supernatural realm from which they recently came, and because of this, they never fully assimilated into the human world. In rural Tlaxcalan belief, children and, in particular, infants left the supernatural realm only briefly to enter this world, so their return is far easier than that of adults who have lived in the earthly realm for many years. Their eternal existence in a liminal zone benefits their relations, who are able to use these messengers to communicate with the gods. It is their usefulness to the living that explains the joyous send-off the children receive at their interment.

Such explanations illuminate the Teotihuacan practice of placing infants and young children under their altars. If the Tlaxcalans inherited their concept of *angelitos* from earlier traditions in Mexico, perhaps the Teotihuacanos also saw the infants as figures comfortably existing simultaneously on two planes, the supernatural and the human. Their deaths, while tragic on the emotional level, could be rationalized into a positive event by recognizing their ability to communicate with the gods on behalf of the family. The altar itself would serve as a focus of prayer and ritual activities, and the children sealed under the altars would receive those supplications and transport them to the deities. Most likely, the perinatals of Teotihuacan were mediators, and as such, they were valued members of the family. By playing such a vital role in the family, the deceased infants of Teotihuacan were, despite their age, probably considered ancestors.[6]

The Postclassic and modern worlds also indicate just what type of prayers the Teotihuacanos may have uttered as they gathered around their altars. The Aztecs sacrificed children on mountaintops in honor of the Tlalocs, the mountain deities who controlled rain, hail, and lightning (Sahagún 1950–1982:II:1–2, 42–44). Participants encouraged the children to cry because their tears were thought to mirror the rain the Aztecs hoped to bring. With a similar agricultural emphasis, Nutini observed that contemporary Tlaxcalan beliefs and actions are much in line with Miccailhuitontli, the Precolumbian celebration of deceased children. In the Postclassic period, offerings were made to the dead children during this feast to assuage the detrimental effects of hail on the crops in August and early September. In turn, Tlaxcalans of today acknowledge this dangerous agricultural time by customarily decorating the graves of infants and children with copious amounts of flowers in the month of August. Nutini clarified the modern practice.

The people believe that infants and children can intercede on their behalf before El Cuatlapanga and La Malintzi, the most prominent tutelary mountain owners in the Tlaxcalan region, regarded as masters of the natural elements (rain, thunder, and lightning, as well as hail). (Nutini 1988:59–60)

Certain themes emerge from these ritual practices. First, children who died serve as intermediaries with a special type of deities, rain deities. Whether Tlaloc of the Aztecs or El Cua-

tlapanga and La Malintzi of the Tlaxcalans, the gods the children entreat control the phenomena of storms. Second, mountains are the home of those rain deities, so they become an important symbol of child-related rituals. Indeed, in Postclassic times it need not be a child who spoke to the mountain deities. During the month of Tepeihuitl, the feast of the mountain, the Aztec fashioned mountain images for those who were buried but not cremated or who had died by drowning or being struck by lightning (Sahagún 1950–1982:II:131). This feast day, like the ritual for dead children, associated the deceased, especially those who died by the hand of the rain deities, with mountains. These strong continuities may suggest that Teotihuacan rituals directed toward the dead similarly concerned mountains and rain; that is, the prayers to the patio altars may have entreated the gods to send the life-giving waters.

This conceptual linking of ancestors with mountains may be found outside of central Mexico as well. Vogt (1965) described the Zinacanteco Maya belief in *chanul*, an animal spirit companion that comprises part of the soul. The animal companions live in a corral inside a volcano called "older brother" or "senior large mountain" (Vogt 1965:34). Holland (1964) reported that the Tzotzil recognize five types of gods, and one category includes the lineage and ancestor gods who reside in the sacred mountain. In the Tzotzil belief system these ancestral deities are conceptually linked with the animal companion, or *wayijel*, that accompanies each individual. When a person is born, there is a simultaneous birth of a *wayijel* in the sacred mountain. The mountains are segregated, as all of the animal companions of one patrilineage dwell inside the same mountain. The Tzotzil call the sacred mountain *ch'iebal*, which may stem from *che'*, or tree, in the sense of a family tree. Within the mountain there is a hierarchy of thirteen levels, and as people mature, they rise through those levels. Animal companions of the elders live at the highest point in the mountain, and they have the most power over the lives of the living. Among the duties of the elder animal companions are the protection of the lower status companions, curing of illness, and punishment of those who transgress traditions. In sum, Tzotzil beliefs strengthen the argument that ancient Mesoamericans associated ancestors with mountains.

The Tepantitla compound murals indicate that the ancient Teotihuacanos held many similar conceptions about mountains (Figures 2.7, 3.2). Previously, I discussed the personified mountain-tree with the representation of the natural mountain painted directly below; that is, the Tepantitla mural depicts supernatural and earthly expressions of the same concept. When viewed in light of the rituals and beliefs of the Aztecs, Tlaxcalans, Zinacantecos, and Tzotziles, the meaning of the murals emerges with greater clarity. Both the personified and natural mountains have streams of water flowing from their interiors, which corresponds to the central Mexican belief that mountain deities control the waters. In the lower register, water is not the only thing that emerges from the mountain: small human figures pop out of crevasses in the mountain or swim about in the waters of the cave. The mountain serves as a shelter and an origin for these figures. I would suggest that these figures are a version of the Tzotzil *wayijel* who live inside the mountains. As such, the figures are the ancestrally related soul companions shown in their sacred mountain. Even the Tzotzil word for the sacred mountain, *ch'iebal*, has its parallel in the Teotihuacan image. If the derivation from *che'*, or tree, is accurate, the word describes exactly the mountain-tree in the upper register, a mountain flowing with water and crowned by entwined floral branches. In all, the continuities would attest that Teotihuacan shared such Mesoamerican beliefs about mountains. The Teotihuacan mountain-tree was like the *ch'iebal*, the sacred tree-mountain in which the ancestors and soul companions of a lineage resided. The mountain-tree also controlled the life-giving waters. Standing in their principal patios, the Teotihuacanos spoke to the ancestral dead underneath the altars. The infants had a special bond with the personified mountain, and the revered ancestral adults had gained greater power with age. Living inside the *ch'iebal*, they served as mediators and carried the wishes for the release of the waters to the personified mountain. Hopefully, the supernatural being represented by the mountain-tree obliged, and the worship of the deceased in the principal patios ensured that

the Teotihuacan agricultural fields would have sufficient water.

Principal patios, then, emerge as an important location of ancestor veneration in the city of Teotihuacan. Burial data suggest that residents of an apartment compound were probably related by lineage and celebrated a revered ancestor from which they all claimed descent. They gathered in their patio for perhaps a variety of rituals, and the ancestral dead buried in those patios functioned as mediators between the living and the gods.

In rural Tlaxcala the majority of houses still reflect this type of familial organization (Nutini 1988:186). They most often consist of a rectangular structure with one entrance and rooms oriented to a central courtyard. Commonly, extended families live in these units. In a few cases the extended family does not have a compound, and a single construction house surrounded by a wall serves as the "ancestral household." The designated house becomes the locus for extended family living elsewhere, and the *ofrenda,* or table honoring the ancestral dead, is usually set up in this household. Still to this day the altar is an important feature of extended family compounds.

The household altar is the hub of the family's ritual and ceremonial life. Hardly a week goes by without the family congregating before it for some religious or social event. To put it differently, the household altar, and the room that contains it, is the locus of the private, individual religion, as contrasted with the public, collective religion centered on the church and the *mayordomía* system, a system of brotherhoods organized around the veneration of particular saints and categories of dead souls (Nutini 1988:186).

Such descriptions could easily apply to the Teotihuacan principal patios if the number of individuals involved is allowed to expand. Members of a lineage living in an apartment compound could gather there to celebrate their identity as a unit and include among their membership even the dead below their feet. The rituals in the patios, then, served to strengthen immediate familial ties, yet there is a danger in recognizing only the separate rituals of each apartment compound, for it is evident that rituals at a community level were critical in a city the size of Teotihuacan.

If the apartment compounds functioned as

FIGURE 3.2. Copy of the Portico 2 mural, Tepantitla, Teotihuacan, by Agustín Villagra in the Museo Nacional de Antropología, Mexico City. INAH photograph courtesy of CNCA-INAH-MEX.

so many independent lineages, one must wonder if there were community-level mechanisms that served to bond these disparate groups. Isolated inside their insular walls, the residents of apartment compounds were free to honor their particular ancestors, which could potentially

fracture the unification of the city as a whole. Furthermore, though each compound may have had its own founding ancestor, it is likely that founders of different compounds were related; that is, the residents of two or more compounds may have recognized an even greater, more distant, and shared ancestor. The lineage ties may have lessened the autonomy of each compound and grouped the compounds into alliances of a much larger nature. The key to understanding community-level lineage organization at Teotihuacan just may lie with a particular funerary custom practiced in Mesoamerica.

COMMUNITY ANCESTORS AND THE MESOAMERICAN MORTUARY BUNDLE

One of the most striking features of Teotihuacan burial data is that we have no clearly identifiable information about high-level elite burials (Cowgill 2003b:320). Adding to this frustrating circumstance is the possibility that we may never find these burials. The city's most elite ancestors may never emerge because the Teotihuacanos might not have buried them beneath their temples or under the floors of their apartment compounds. Instead, the highest ranking ancestors could have received a burial treatment that consisted of preserving their remains aboveground in wrapped assemblages called mortuary bundles. This burial custom would have allowed the dead to remain among the world of the living, even though it threatened their ability to survive in the archaeological record of the present. There is tantalizing evidence that such bundles may have played a prominent role at Teotihuacan, but documenting the practice requires the gathering of many fragments of data into a whole.

The archaeological recovery of intact mortuary bundles is exceedingly rare, for the organic remains of the human body are subject to the ravages of humidity and decay, and such bundles were also the target of Colonial priests trying to stamp out the idolatry they perceived (Pohl 1994:39). The Classic Maya site of Calakmul represents one extraordinary occasion where a mortuary bundle survived. Found in Structure VII and shedding light on bundle preparation, Tomb 1 contained the remains of an adult male, but some bones were missing, and there were cut marks on the bones. The individual was apparently defleshed before they wrapped his remains in cloth, encased this bundle in a mat, and exposed the whole to fire. The bundle may

have been dressed before its deposition: archaeologists found evidence of a jaguar skin cape, and a jadeite mosaic mask with obsidian pupils and pyrite eyebrows was on the floor near the bundle. A Postclassic period tomb from Coixtlahuaca in Oaxaca contained a bundle similarly wrapped in a woven reed mat painted with alternating bands of red and black. The condition of the tomb was such that archaeologists even found remains of the cords once used to bind the bundle.[7] Bernal (1948–1949:Photograph 5) further includes a photograph of a wooden mask encrusted with turquoise and jade mosaic that was probably once attached to the bundle. The overall appearance of the bundle probably resembled a reconstructed Mixtec bundle now in the Museo Nacional de Antropología (Figure 3.3).[8]

Some of the clearest evidence of mortuary bundle construction and function comes from artistic sources, primarily the codiacal paintings of the Mixtec manuscripts. There are numerous mortuary bundles and other types of sacred bundles in the visual histories left by the Mixtec, where the depiction of mortuary bundles is standardized to enhance the viewer's ability to recognize this element (Figure 3.4). Often the bundle sits on a low altar or throne and appears as a round oval about which a series of ropes binds the figure like a package. This wrapped bundle contains the body of the deceased ancestor, although sometimes the Mixtec artist included feet emerging from the bottom of the bundle. The only other body part appearing on Mixtec bundles is the head, which partially projects from the top of the bundle. Invariably, the eyes are closed as a standard visual element to indicate that the individual is dead. The artist seems to show enough details to identify the object as human, but carefully records that the individual is deceased and incapable of movement.

Mortuary bundles appearing in the artistic record elsewhere in Mesoamerica establish that other cultures shared many Mixtec conventions for bundle depiction. Stela 40 from the Classic Maya site of Piedras Negras includes a figure that is certainly a deceased ancestor but is probably a mortuary bundle (Figure 3.5). The stela depicts a Maya lord in the upper register who sprinkles a substance into a chamber below him. The distinctive shape of a corbel vault signals that the nals that this figure can no longer walk on earth. He is a deceased ancestor who may still be animated through ritual, but who is forever bound to the altar in his tomb. This mixing of life and death was a hallmark of Mesoamerican bundle depiction.

The Terminal Classic period offers two more instructive images of deceased, bundled ancestors. One similarly appears on a stela, but this monument was tellingly found within a tomb and dates to around A.D. 700 (Figure 3.6). Recovered from Tomb 5 at the Oaxacan site of Cerro de la Campana, the composition consists of two registers, each with paired figures facing one another. The lower register includes a man and

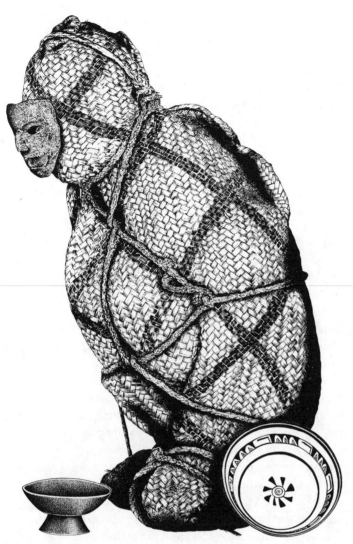

FIGURE 3.3. Reconstruction of a Mixtec mortuary bundle in the Museo Nacional de Antropología, Mexico City. Drawing by L. F. Luin after Baquedano 1993:35.

lower space is a stone tomb, which asserts that the figure waving a feather fan in the tomb is dead. The sculptors used the juxtaposition of the two figures to clearly relate the status of each. While the upper figure appears full-bodied with both legs visible as he kneels, the other lord has no lower body; only his head, hand, and richly beaded chest appear. In place of his body is a small altar on short legs which is too small to contain the rest of his body. As in the Mixtec codices, the artist attempted to depict an individual that was at once capable of life but clearly dead. In this example the figure is much more animated, with his eye open and hand holding a fan, but the odd termination of the body sig-

FIGURE 3.4. Lord 3 Skull's mortuary bundle, manuscript illustration, Codex Selden, Postclassic. Drawing by L. F. Luin after Codex Selden 1964:16.

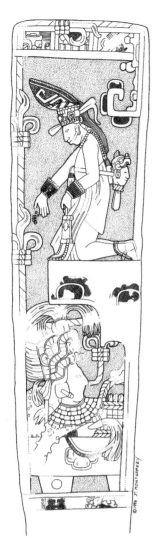

FIGURE 3.5. Stela 40, Piedras Negras, A.D. 746. Drawing by John Montgomery.

FIGURE 3.6. Stela from Tomb 5, Cerro de la Campana, Terminal Classic. Drawing by Jenni Bongard after Miller 1991:217.

woman, with the woman on the left wearing a *quechquemitl*. The male figure's skirt reaches only to his thigh and reveals the bottom of his foot. This detail serves as a visual cue that this is a full-figured person who is still among the living. Above this scene is another pairing, but this time one of the figures has attributes of a deceased mortuary bundle (Miller 1991). While the knee and foot are visible on the male to the left, the

figure on the right has the peculiar combination of animate and inanimate qualities that mark him as dead. Just as in the Maya stela, this individual seems to wave one hand about, and his head emerges from a similar low altar. Here, too, the artist eliminated the lower body to indicate that the figure is incapable of full movement. Above the scene, the hieroglyphs identify the mortuary bundle as Lord 13 O and offer his death date. The

FIGURE 3.7. Mural of a mortuary bundle, Las Higueras, Terminal Classic. Drawing by L. F. Luin after Sánchez Bonilla 1993:134.

name glyphs associated with this date include a head with a closed eye and slack jaw, effectively proclaiming his deceased state.

Another Terminal Classic mortuary bundle depiction comes from the mural art of Las Higueras, a site near El Tajín in Veracruz (Figure 3.7). As did the Maya and Oaxacan examples, this bundle sits on a low altar with short legs, indicating that such altars were a common furnishing for mortuary bundles in Mesoamerica. The wrapped body in the mural takes on a conical shape crowned by the head of the deceased. There is an ornament on the figure's forehead, and a swath of feathers falls from the back of the head. Following artistic conventions, at least one hand emerges from the bundle to hold a few strips of cloth or paper. Presumably, the hand and the face function to animate what would otherwise appear to be an inert object, and the face of the Las Higueras bundle is particularly telling because it is not fully integrated with the rest of the bundle and has simplified features that seem especially rigid. These qualities probably arise from the fact that the face is actually a mask similar to those found in the Calakmul and Coixtlahuaca tombs.

The presence of masks on mortuary bundles is confirmed in a document called the *Relación de Michoacán*. The *Relación* is part of a series of texts compiled for the Spanish court in the sixteenth century. Wanting to know the nature of the lands it had acquired, the court sent out a questionnaire requesting information about the various regions of Mexico. The document from Michoacán included a great deal of information about the indigenous Tarascan population, including a description of the funerary rites for a king. The text records that the king's body was placed on a great funeral pyre in front of the main pyramid. After the body had burned, they collected the ashes, as well as the bits of gold and silver from the king's costume, and wrapped them in a cloth bundle. Then, the *Relación* states, "On the bundle they put a turquoise mask, his gold earrings, his green feather headdress, his gold bracelets, his turquoise and seashell necklaces, and a round of gold on the back" (*Relación de Michoacán* 1989:237–238, translation by author). The importance of this account is that it confirms much of what is seen in the visual depictions of mortuary bundles. As in some images, the bound body has a mask affixed to it, and just as the Maya and Oaxacan bundles wear earrings and necklaces, the Tarascans decorated their bundles with opulent jewels.

The use of masks as funerary adornment has a long, rich history in Mesoamerica (Westheim 1965:96–97). Although the body was not bundled, the mask covering the face of K'inich Janaab' Pakal I, a Maya king of Palenque, is a prominent example of masks used to cover the face of the elite dead. Pakal's mask consists of jade mosaic pieces fitted into a portrait of the ruler.[9] Archaeologists found a similar wooden mask covered with turquoise and jade mosaics during excavations of Tomb 6 at Coixtlahuaca (Bernal 1948–1949:26). Writing in the early seventeenth century, Fray Juan de Torquemada (1977:229–300) explained that painted masks were put on the mortuary bundles of rulers before cremation.

The common use of masks in funerary context is of special interest to Teotihuacan because stone masks are an important part of the city's artistic record. The Teotihuacan masks are made of high quality polished stone such as greenstone or calcite (Figure 3.8). The heads often have an overall triangular shape with a wide forehead tapering to a pointed chin, and there is a planar quality to the flattened foreheads and smooth cheeks. They generally have parted lips that look as if the artist captured their image mid-speech, plus there is substantial evidence that the masks once had inlays giving them a more lively appearance. On a few rare examples there are tiny shell teeth in the mouth, or traces of iron pyrite fill the sockets of the eyes. Some masks, like the one illustrated here, have staining around the eyes which may be the remains of decayed iron pyrite. Frequently, the lobes of the ears have holes to suspend earrings.[10] In their original state—with open mouths, inlaid eyes, and elite status markers like earrings—the faces on the masks would have looked altogether lifelike.

A consistency of style instantly makes the masks recognizable as Teotihuacano, but the truth is that few of the masks come with a firm provenience. Almost all of the masks were looted from the site and worked their way to museums throughout Mexico, the United States, and Europe. Although hundreds of these masks exist, excavators have found only three in archaeological context (Berrin and Pasztory 1993:184; Pasztory 1992a:295). One example came from a palace along the Avenue of the Dead (Delgadillo 1991). It was found in a corridor that contained more than half of the palace's burials, which may indicate a funerary context for the masks, but its uniqueness is statistically unsettling. Without sound archaeological evidence, determining the function of the masks must come from other avenues.

There is much to support an argument that the masks once appeared on the mortuary bundles of Teotihuacan's dead. The widespread Mesoamerican tradition of tying masks onto mortuary bundles alone makes this a logical conclusion; in addition, the masks themselves offer evidence of mortuary bundle use. The masks are solid, and although the artists drilled deeply into the stone to create the eyes and mouths, they never fully pierced the stone. In a similar manner, the nose holes do not cut through to the back of the masks. Turning the masks over, some of them do have holes drilled on the back to secure them to some object; however, the masks are also

FIGURE 3.8. Serpentine mask with staining around the eyes, Teotihuacan style. Photograph courtesy of Dumbarton Oaks, Pre-Columbian Collection, Washington, D.C.

rather heavy, which would make them difficult to wear in a ritual context. In sum, the masks do not provide holes for breathing or seeing, and their weight makes them unlikely candidates for human costume.

A remarkable find near the Ciudadela indicates that the holes on the masks were probably used to attach them to mortuary bundles. Excavating in a ceramic workshop attached to the large compound, archaeologists found a ceramic bust with a small mask that fit over the otherwise featureless head (Figure 3.9). Like its stone counterparts, the mask has small holes that would facilitate attaching it to the bust. Noting that the bust is similar in form to depictions of mortuary bundles elsewhere in Mesoamerica, Carlos Múnera Bermúdez (1991) suggested that the bust and mask constituted an effigy mortuary bundle. To be sure, the compact body without any appendages, along with the complete truncation of the lower body, has much in common with the bundles in the Mixtec codices and the Las Higueras mural. The human features of the mask fit within Mesoamerican artistic conventions,

FIGURE 3.9. Ceramic effigy bundle with a removable mask from the Ciudadela ceramic workshop, Teotihuacan. Drawing by L. F. Luin after Múnera Bermúdez 1991:341.

the head was left hollow, and they then burned a part of the body and placed its ashes there, and plugged it up; afterwards they stripped off the dead body the skin of the back of the head and stuck it over this place and they buried the rest as they were wont to do.[11]

Several important bits of information can gleaned from Landa's observations. First, he established that effigy ceramics were receptacles for mortuary remains among the Postcontact Maya. Second, he documented that the Maya placed these remains in hollow areas of sculptures. Third, he recorded that the individuals receiving such treatment were elites, and fourth, his report indicates the form in which ancestral remains were preserved. Landa explained that the Maya deposited a portion of ashes from the burned body in the effigy, and in a parallel fashion, cremation was the preferred method of mortuary treatment for Teotihuacan elites (Rattray 1992:53). If the hole in the ceramic effigy bundle once held ashes from a deceased elite, the effigy would closely resemble medieval reliquaries where a portrait of the deceased, most commonly those approaching sainthood, housed a bone or other physical belonging of the individual. This is a compelling solution for the hole in the effigy, yet given more local traditions, it is just as likely that a mirror, shield, or bit of stone once filled the hole. As seen in some Teotihuacan ceramic figurines, a shield on the chest might include a hieroglyphic name identifying the individual.

As for the ceramic mask, its presence on the bust is critical for understanding the stone masks of Teotihuacan. Together, the mask and bust offer strong evidence that the stone masks also may have been tied to busts, but in their case, it is more likely that the busts consisted of cloth-wrapped human remains. The inlaid eyes and open mouths of the stone masks would have conferred an animate quality to the bundle whose wrapped contents were otherwise totally stationary.

Apart from the masks, the artistic record of Teotihuacan provides other possible examples of mortuary bundles. In their bundle depictions, Mesoamerican artists effectively conveyed the duality of life and death within the figure, but another characteristic was the low altar upon

for they provide the animated quality common to bundles just as the abbreviated body asserts its deceased state. The commingling qualities of life and death found in mortuary bundles typify this work.

The hole in the chest of the effigy bundle is intriguing in this context because its contents surely augmented its meaning. Information on Maya practices recorded by Landa suggests that it could have once housed a physical memento of the deceased individual represented by the effigy. His account of mortuary treatment is intriguing.

At this time it has been discovered when they [the dead] were of very high rank, they enclosed their ashes in statues of pottery made hollow. The rest of the people of position made for their fathers wooden statues of which the back of which bundles often sat. Among the Teotihuacan figurines is a category called "enthroned" figurines that may indicate that this element also existed at the city (Figure 3.10).[12] These small-scale works consist of a low throne with a small back similar to ones seen supporting bundles in the Mixtec codices. The human figures on the thrones wear elaborate costumes, and the particular headdress worn by the figure may, as it does in the Mixtec codices, record the name of the individual. Tellingly, there are no visible hands or feet, as the body is limited to a restricted, triangular form. Also among the ceramic remains are the half-conical figurines that clearly do not have legs (Figure 3.11).[13] There is no evidence of thrones for these figurines, but with their missing legs and overall shape, they fit many of the artistic conventions for mortuary bundles. In all, the half-conical and enthroned figurines share so many characteristics with the Mixtec images that they emerge as three-dimensional versions of the mortuary bundles in the codices.

Another possible depiction of mortuary bundles appears in a mural from the Temple of Agriculture that has troubled most people who have studied Teotihuacan (Figure 3.12). The mural was destroyed and only exists in a few fragments and through drawings made before

FIGURE 3.11. Half-conical figurine, ceramic, Teotihuacan. Drawing by Jenni Bongard after Séjourné 1966c: Figure 126.

it was damaged (Miller 1972a, 1973:173–174). It shows a perplexing scene with a number of small figures engaged in a variety of activities between two large forms with vaguely human characteristics. Some of the people seem to bargain over oval-shaped objects, while others sit holding offerings such as a bird or plate of food. Near several of the figures are ritual bundles of rubber that indicate the sacred nature of the scene.[14] Múnera Bermudez (1991:339) asserts that the larger forms depict mortuary bundles burning on altars as the smaller figures actively worship before them. Given the account of the Tarascan king's funeral, the flames may indicate the cremation phase of bundle preparation, and the Teotihuacan scene may be equally regal. The fanged noseplaques positioned in the midst of earflares and large necklaces may indicate that the deceased wore the costume of the personified mountain-tree, so it is possible that the Temple of Agriculture mural records royal burial. Thus, the details of the mural provide not only information about bundle fabrication at Teotihuacan but also emphasize the reverence with which the bundles were held.

The specter of burning fits in well with mortuary bundle traditions. In Mesoamerica, bundles were created either by wrapping the seated, flexed body or its cremated remains, and the Teotihuacan burials seemingly include both of

FIGURE 3.10. Enthroned figurine, ceramic, Teotihuacan. Drawing by L. F. Luin after Séjourné 1966c: Figure 87.

FIGURE 3.12. Temple of Agriculture mural, Teotihuacan. Drawing by L. F. Luin after Miller 1973:63.

these methods (Múnera Bermudez 1991:335). Most burials from the relatively recent 1980–1982 field seasons were flexed burials that commonly included fragments of cloth that may have once served as the wrapping of bundles (Cabrera 1987b:523; Serrano 1993:111). In earlier work, Laurette Séjourné (1966a:219) identified a number of burials with disarticulated skeletons in association with cloth and burning. By comparing this burial treatment with illustrations of bundles in the Aztec and Mixtec codices, she reasoned that mortuary bundles were part of Teotihuacan funerary rituals. On occasion, bundles in the codices have smoke rising up from them, indicating that they have been set on fire. It appears in certain cases that this is a malicious act meant to destroy the bundle, but the Tarascans who burned the body of their king before wrapping the remains demonstrate that burning could be a more reverential act.[15] The offerings being made to the large burning forms in the Temple of Agriculture mural are more in line with the Tarascan example; therefore, we may interpret the burning and cloth frequently exhib-

ited in Teotihuacan burials as residue of bundle burning for the honored dead.[16]

Multiple avenues suggest the likely presence of mortuary bundles at Teotihuacan. Burial data include several features that conform with bundle preparation practices, and although the possible bundles are not intact, they intriguingly share some properties of bundles. The artistic record also mirrors bundle depictions elsewhere in Mesoamerica, including ceramic figurines of legless human forms sitting on low altars. They exhibit that curious blend of animate and inanimate features that typify a deceased entity that still harbors a life force. Perhaps most fascinating of all, the stone masks from Teotihuacan have characteristics that suggest they were once tied onto bundles, but the masks have not been securely associated with human remains in documented archaeology. Because the masks were ripped from their archaeological context, a broader net must be cast to reconstruct their function. By looking outside of Teotihuacan, we may come to understand the function of mortuary bundles in Mesoamerica and see that the masks belonged to a special category of bundles that played an important role in Teotihuacan's social and political structure.

MORTUARY BUNDLE FUNCTION: LESSONS FROM THE MIXTEC

Even though no explicit evidence about mortuary bundle function survives from Teotihuacan, the bundles of the Postclassic Mixtec culture have received extensive attention and provide an interesting model for their Teotihuacan counterparts. John Pohl and Bruce Byland have conducted the most comprehensive research on Mixtec bundles, revealing a culture where the remains of elite ancestors were pivotal to the social structure (Byland and Pohl 1994; Pohl 1994). Instead of reverting into forgotten figures buried in the ground, some Mixtec ancestors stayed above the earth where their descendants could converse with them and strategically use their remains for political ends. The ancestors did not fade into the past, for they continued as a vital constituent of the living world.

The most important, and to the modern mind, the most exotic role of the Mixtec bundles was their function as oracles that offered advice on important human events. The oracular role of the bundles involved a certain figure who appears on several occasions in the Mixtec codices. Identified in the manuscripts as Lady 9 Grass, she presided over a cave near Chalcatongo where the wrapped remains of many elite ancestors were stored. Although there is no evidence that she ever ruled any particular area, she nevertheless held a deeply embedded role in political events. She seems to have been the priestess who served as an intermediary between the bundles and Mixtec rulers, conveying oracular messages to the living. We can get a sense of bundle visitation in the Nuttall Codex where two rulers, Lady 6 Monkey and Lord 8 Deer, sit before a mortuary bundle and Lady 9 Grass (Figure 3.13). The priestess presides in her skull-decorated temple and points at the bundle as she appears to talk with the visitors, perhaps speaking for the bundle itself. Such pilgrimages to Chalcatongo occur in the codices before events such as war or mar-

riage, so consultation of the bundles seems to be a requisite stop before undertaking important actions.

A belief in oracular ancestors was not limited to the Mixtec, for one of the most revered culture heroes of the Aztecs was probably a bundle who conversed with his followers. Often spoken of as a god, Huitzilopochtli more closely corresponds with the features of a Mesoamerican mortuary bundle.[17] In the Codex Boturini the only body part visible is his head framed by his trademark hummingbird headdress (Figure 3.14). A bound bundle conceals his exceedingly short lower body, and individuals called *teomamas,* or god-bearers, carry him on their backs. Invariably in this codex, small speech scrolls emanating from his mouth demarcate his oracular role. Because the Codex Boturini relates the tale of the Mexica migration, the constant speaking of Huitzilopochtli is particularly fitting. The instructions Huitzilopochtli gives to his followers largely drives the narrative of the story, as the Mexica move from one place to another, constantly prodded by Huitzilopochtli's mandates. The account of Huitzilopochtli in the migration follows a pattern similar to the Mixtec, for consultations with the oracular bundle precede military conflict or decisions to relocate. Bundles in Mesoamerica shaped the course of history as, through their interpretive priests, they expressed their opinion about events in the living world.

It is critical to note that not all Mixtec individuals became oracular bundles. This was an exclusive club restricted to the most elite ancestors of the ruling families and served as a means to limit access to power. One needed to have a close ancestor in one of the sacred caves to achieve elite status. The elite class was largely a closed hereditary system, and the bundles were physical evidence of one's membership (Byland and Pohl 1994:206–208). Occasionally, an enterprising individual like the famous Lord 8 Deer broke into the system by marrying well and conquering territories, but the ancestral bundles made this a relatively rare occurrence (Pohl 1994:83–93). The mortuary bundles emphasized lineage ties and helped the powerful maintain their status.

The Mixtec means of reckoning descent from a mortuary bundle followed a system of pre-

FIGURE 3.13. Lord 8 Deer and Lady 6 Monkey consult with Lady 9 Grass and the mortuary bundle of Lord 3 Lizard at Chalcatongo, Codex Nuttall, manuscript illustration, Postclassic. Drawing by Jenni Bongard after Nuttall 1975:44.

ferred primogeniture in which the eldest male generally became the lineage head (Byland and Pohl 1994:192–193; Pohl 1994:20–21). In turn, the distance between an individual and the direct line of descendants determined one's status. Even though everyone in a particular group claimed descent from the same ancestor, their status was not equal because some were more closely related to the senior line; that is, the direct line

of male descendants. Individuals descended indirectly fell into junior lines that continued to get even more distant with the passing of each generation. Those on the senior lines relied, in part, on the existence of the mortuary bundles to confirm their position, for the tangible nature of the bundles provided a verifiable means of doing so. This explains why the burning of mortuary bundles often followed periods of conquest. The

FIGURE 3.14. Huitzilopochtli carried on migration, manuscript illustration, Codex Boturini, Postclassic. Drawing by L. F. Luin after Heyden 1989:108.

newly ascendant rulers erased the ancestral legitimacy of their rivals by destroying the physical evidence in the form of ancestral bones. Among the Mixtec, direct male descent from an ancestral mortuary bundle was the surest route to a position of status in a system where the dead were constantly invoked to justify the social order.

The final lesson of the Mixtec is instructive because it explains how a system of ancestral reckoning can introduce instability into a society. Caves such as the one at Chalcatongo did not hold the bundles of just one elite family, but of several lineages. The result was that there were multiple founding ancestors each with their own

descendants vying for power with one another. Though still circumscribed by some restrictive forces, the multiplicity of ancestors fostered constant friction between the ruling elites. Couple this with intermarriage between the senior lines, and the outcome is a turbulent history of fluctuating power. Supremacy was always contestable because there was no clear method of determining the relative status between senior lines, and no one ruler ever dominated the whole of the Mixtec region. It was a fractious system built upon alliances and constant realignment among the various lineages (Byland and Pohl 1994:219).

SOCIAL STRUCTURE AND MORTUARY BUNDLES AT TEOTIHUACAN

How then might we apply the Mixtec model to the city of Teotihuacan? The archaeological and artistic records bear strong evidence that lineage ties were important to the city's residents, and the data indicate that Teotihuacan rituals may have included the fabrication of mortuary bundles. Beyond the mere existence of such bundles, the question remains whether the Teotihuacan bundle practices were akin to those of the Mixtec.

The visual arts suggest that mortuary customs of the city shared some characteristics with their Postclassic counterparts. One of the constant features exhibited in the Teotihuacan stone masks as well as the enthroned figurines is an open mouth that is poised to speak. In truth, an open mouth is a common attribute of figures in Teotihuacan art, and frequently a speech scroll emerges from the mouth. This characteristic led Pasztory (1992a) to argue that speech held a certain primacy over writing at the city and served as a symbol of local identity. Despite acknowledging the ubiquity of speech, I would venture that the open mouths of the masks held a special meaning. The mouths signified that the masks were capable of speech, which is of critical importance if the masks once belonged to mortuary bundles. With their inlaid eyes and earring-festooned earlobes, the masks provided the element of animation, a prerequisite of all Mesoamerican mortuary bundles. The open mouths fortified the animate nature and additionally signaled the bundles' oracular role. As was the case for mortuary bundles among the Mixtecs and Aztecs, the Teotihuacan bundles seem to have been capable of talking with their descendants and offering advice about momentous life events.

The example of Lady 9 Grass might also reveal how the Teotihuacanos stored their bundles. The fact that the Mixtec priestess presided over a cave that held the bundles recalls the sacred cave found underneath the Sun Pyramid, a long tunnel that culminates in a four-lobed chamber (Figure 1.9). The cave's original contents are largely a mystery. The archaeologists who found the cave reported that ancient looters had removed most of the remains. In the long shaft leading to the final chamber there were fragments of seventeen to nineteen blockages dating to the later part of the Tzacualli or Miccaotli phases. These had once compartmentalized the cave into smaller chambers, but the looters had penetrated these (R. Millon 1981:233).

The absence of significant artifactual remains shrouds an interpretation of these blockages, but Oaxacan funerary customs shed some light on the matter. The Codex Bodley includes an image elaborating upon the storage of Lord 8 Deer's bundle. Inside the cave at Chalcatongo, the bundle rests in a walled structure accompanied by offerings (Figure 3.15). Archaeologists have actually found stone structures like the one surrounding 8 Deer in caves that have strong funerary evidence. The masonry structures in the caves are invariably damaged but include as-

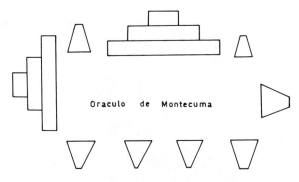

FIGURE 3.16. Map of Teotihuacan in the *Relación geográfica*. Drawing by L. F. Luin after Heyden 1975:142.

sociations of human bone and inlaid turquoise masks, the very components of mortuary bundles (Byland and Pohl 1994:201; Moser 1975, 1983). Thus, the Oaxacans stored their bundles in stone chambers built inside caves, and the blockages of the Sun Pyramid cave suggest this possibility for Teotihuacan as well.

There are additional reasons to see the Teotihuacan cave as a container for ancestral bundles. The Mixtec practice of placing their bundles in caves is also documented among the Huichol, which indicates that this was a widespread Mesoamerican practice (Burgoa 1989, I:372; Lumholtz 1902; Pohl 1994:75). The fantastical nature of caves resulted in numerous ritual associations for these mystical underground spaces; nevertheless, the association of caves with ancestors is one of the more frequent symbolisms in Aztec place-names for caves. The Aztecs gave caves such monikers as Colhuacan, "place of those who have grandfathers or ancestors," and Teocoluacan, "place of the divine ancestors" (Heyden 1981:15). An early colonial map of Teotihuacan prompted Doris Heyden (1975:142) to assign an oracular role to the Teotihuacan cave. The 1580 map from a *Relación geográfica* shows a crude rendition of the main structures of the city with the words "Oráculo de Montecuma" (oracle of Montecuma) directly beneath the Sun Pyramid (Figure 3.16). The storage of mortuary bundles in the cave would explain the oracular association offered by the map.

If the Sun Pyramid cave once served as the receptacle for Teotihuacan's most elite ancestors, the looting of the cave means that the location of the mortuary bundles may have drastically

FIGURE 3.15. The mortuary bundle of Lord 8 Deer, manuscript illustration, Codex Bodley, Postclassic. Drawing by Jenni Bongard after Codex Bodley 1960:14.

changed during Teotihuacan's history. Indeed, the oracle on the *Relación* map may not have been the Sun Pyramid cave but the avenue that sat in front of the pyramid. The evidence for this, I believe, rests in the center of Teotihuacan and concerns the name of the main street, the Avenue of the Dead.

The name of Teotihuacan's broad thoroughfare may be a misnomer because thus far tombs have not been found in the structures lining the street. To date, the name can only be traced securely back to a sixteenth-century map called the *Mapa de San Francisco Mazapán*. On the document, the street is identified in Nahuatl, the language of the Aztecs. The words *mica ottica* marking the location of the avenue translate as "Avenue of the Dead."[18] The late date of the appellation and its Aztec origins certainly challenge any assertion that the Teotihuacanos called this street something similar, yet we should also entertain the idea that the Nahuatl words for the avenue represent an oral history that survived the city's demise. That is, through oral speech the Aztecs may have preserved the local knowledge that the deceased ancestors of the Teotihuacanos were associated with the avenue. Given that the bodies of these ancestors have not emerged from the many structures along the thoroughfare, then perhaps it was the mortuary bundles who were the dead who resided on the street.[19]

The perishable nature of organic material explains why the human remains of the bundles no longer exist, so the stone masks that might have served as the faces of the deceased emerge as the only tangible evidence of the bundles themselves. It is lamentable that few masks have a secure provenience; consequently, hearsay and tradition provide the majority of information about the masks' origin. Any scholar would prefer to discuss sound archaeological recovery, but the masks are such a recognizable feature of the corpus of Teotihuacan art that Pasztory struggled to identify their provenience.

Because so many of them were found by looters at the end of the nineteenth and beginning of the twentieth centuries, I suggest that they came from the temple structures lining the Avenue and from other highly visible buildings. (Pasztory 1992a:295)

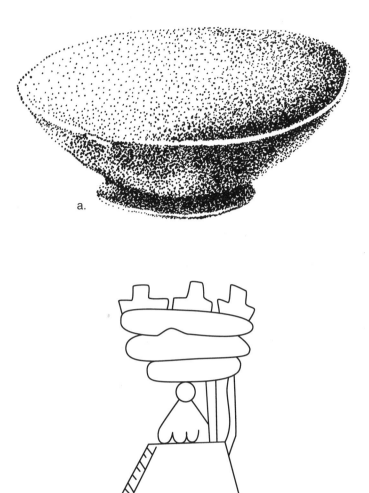

a.

b.

FIGURE 3.17. Metepec Polished Brown ring-base bowl with mortuary bundle decoration. Drawings by Jenni Bongard after Rattray 1992:26.

Pasztory reasoned that the looters naturally exploited the most conspicuous mounds at the site at a time when the site was less protected.

Fortunately, two vessels may record what the looters obliterated when they removed the masks from the site. Both vessels have incised graffiti that may record mortuary bundles housed within the architecture of Teotihuacan. The bottom of one Early Tlamimilolpa (A.D. 225–300) bowl from Tlajinga 33 shows what Evelyn Rattray (1992:27) has described as a "burial bundle associated with an altar." The second vessel is a Metepec (A.D. 550–650) bowl from Pueblo Perdido, a Teotihuacan-influenced site (Figure 3.17). This bowl includes an image of a possible mortuary bundle inside of a structure that looks much like the modest-sized temples that probably once stood along the Avenue of the Dead. The simple conical form of the bundled body surmounted by a round head sits in a temple crowned with *almenas,* the typical Teotihuacan roof decoration.

While heretofore I have stressed the storage of bundles in caves, the codices provide ample evidence that Mesoamericans also housed oracular bundles in temples. In the Codex Bodley, two mortuary bundles sit on the top of a Mixtec temple (Figure 3.18).[20] Likewise, the Aztecs placed Huitzilopochtli's bundle in a temple at Coatlicamac (Figure 3.19). In the latter image only the head and bird headdress appear just above the temple stairs, with the artist having completely eliminated the body in an effort to convey his bundled status. Given the Nahuatl name for the city's main avenue, the Teotihuacan images of bundles in temples, and the tradition of placing bundles in temples elsewhere in Mesoamerica, the Avenue of the Dead may have been a street lined by the ancestors—specifically, bundled ancestors enshrined in the many temples on the long road (Figure 3.20).

Even the name of the site itself, again a Nahuatl word, may allude to the creation of divine ancestors at the city. Numerous translations of the word *teotihuacan* include "the place where men became gods," "the place where one becomes deified," "place of those who have the road of the gods," "the place where divinity comes into being," and "at the place of the owners of the Elder Gods."[21] Each of these certainly associates the city with the concept of divine beings, but given the current discussion, it is interesting that these translations variously associate those divinities with the avenue itself or suggest that gods were created at the city or were actually owned. Consequently, the translation of *teotihuacan* could potentially incorporate references to the presence of deified ancestors in the form of mortuary bundles, the creation of these divine bundles, and the possession of ancestral bundles. The Avenue of the Dead, therefore, comes into focus as a long line of temples dedicated to the ancestral gods, a gauntlet of the gods who served an oracular role and represented the lineages in a highly visible fashion.

Who then, were these ancestral gods? The Mixtec example informs us that only the most elite individuals became oracular bundles; hence, we can assume that mortuary bundles in temples along the Avenue of the Dead would represent an equally restricted group. It is likely that Teotihuacan followed the Mixtec pattern, and that the bundles were the ancestors from whom the lineage heads claimed direct descent. These lineage heads would have been on the senior line, and at least theoretically, they would have proclaimed a direct line of male descent from the bundles, affording these lineage heads an elevated status in society.

The Mixtec model further emphasizes that the physical presence of the deceased ancestor was a powerful tool in justifying elite status, and this does much to explain the architecture on either side of the avenue. The small temples where I have hypothetically placed the mortuary bundles are directly on the Avenue of the Dead, but these temples are integrated into elite domestic spaces that I would call palaces.[22] These resemble apartment compounds, but they are not independent constructions because they are joined together to create the long expanse of the avenue. The construction of these palaces is of the highest quality, with fine stone walls and thick plaster often covered with murals. Impressive stone sculpture in these spaces includes carved panels to decorate walls and sculpted animal heads functioning as the decoration for balustrades. The elaborate nature of the palaces indicates that the most elite Teotihuacanos resided in these spaces, and the mortuary bundles in the temples would have served as a reminder of why they held such status. The lineage heads in the palaces seemingly kept the mortuary bundles close at hand to emphatically justify their position.

If the senior lines with their ancestral bundles resided in the palaces on the main avenue, the junior lines must have inhabited the many apartment compounds that spread out from the city's central core. Among the apartment compounds are mid-level residences characterized by finely constructed stone walls with ample plaster. The inhabitants commonly decorated the interior spaces with elaborately painted murals, but sculpture in these compounds is less frequent and of a more modest nature than that found in

FIGURE 3.18. The mortuary bundles of 12 Vulture and 12 Lizard on a temple with Lord 3 Flint sitting nearby, manuscript illustration, Codex Bodley, Postclassic. Drawing by L. F. Luin after Codex Bodley 1960:35.

FIGURE 3.19. Huitzilopochtli's mortuary bundle in a temple at Coatlicamac, manuscript illustration, Codex Boturini, Postclassic. Drawing by L. F. Luin after Heyden 1989:106.

FIGURE 3.20. View of the temples along the west side of the Avenue of the Dead.

the palaces. Although they have lavish qualities, they lack the grandeur and prime location of the palaces.

Through special burial treatment, these compounds apparently recognized a lesser ancestor that may have had a weaker claim of descent from a mortuary bundle on the avenue. The high-status burials incorporated into the foundation of some compounds and the elaborate burials associated with the central patio altars would be candidates for compound founders who represented offshoots from the senior line. A singular small mask fragment found at Xolalpan leaves open the possibility that some compounds displayed bundles, but the archaeological evidence predominately suggests that any bundle made for these compounds was buried (Linné 1934:Figure 275). In a discussion of burial patterns Rattray (1992:53) noted the special role of cremation at Teotihuacan. Within a compound, archaeologists have only recovered one or two cremated personages, and the contexts indicate that this is a treatment reserved for high-status individuals. Because cremation is a documented method of mortuary bundle production, some apartment compound founders seem to have shared in this aspect of elite burial treatment even if they were not bundled with stone masks.

As the number of founders, both elite and lesser, explodes in the archaeological record, a comparison to the segmentary lineage system of ancient China proves profitable. K. C. Chang (1983) argued that junior lines periodically broke off from the senior line and established new lineage founders. These new founders, however, were still of lower rank than the senior line lineage head who was more directly descended from the original ancestor. Chang also explained how the system affected the acquisition of territory by referring to a second-millennium Chinese text. Shih "Mien" (The Book of Odes) records that the process of establishing a new household required the founders of junior lines to conduct divination and measure the boundaries of their territories. In the case of the ancient Chinese, the new founder might receive vast land grants, a scenario which has no clear parallel at Teotihuacan. However, when a lineage-based apartment compound became overcrowded, a new subordinate founder of an offshoot lineage

may have similarly emerged, established a junior line, and acquired sufficient land to build a new compound. The integrated nature of Teotihuacan residential areas, however, indicates that these junior founders may not have moved very far away.

The downward mobility inherent in a system of preferred primogeniture offers an explanation for the status distribution of the apartment compounds. Recent excavations of contiguous apartment compounds have confirmed a particularly interesting residential pattern first identified by the Teotihuacan Mapping Project (R. Millon 1981:211). Instead of neighborhoods in which apartment compounds exhibit relatively homogenous status markers, there seems to be a mix whereby compounds of high and low status may be directly next to one another. The La Ventilla 1992–1993 project exposed several neighboring compounds with extraordinarily divergent status levels. In close proximity to more-elite apartment compounds with stone walls and lime plaster, archaeologists found compounds with less costly construction materials and, surprisingly, murals painted on mud plaster.[23] In these low-status structures, the residents sometimes reserved the precious lime plaster for their small central patio with its attendant altar (Cabrera, personal communication 1993). This same pattern holds for the fringes of Teotihuacan: excavations 10 km from the site revealed that some individuals lived in structures with plaster floors while their neighbors had to do without plastered surfaces (Charlton et al. 2003).

In a like manner, burial data indicate that the inhabitants of the low-status compounds were much weaker participants in the lineage system of Teotihuacan. The number of cremation burials significantly drops in these compounds to the point that some structures have none (Storey 1987:91–95). The elite associations of cremation burials and their implications for bundle production suggest that lower-status Teotihuacanos made few pretenses at having powerful ancestors. Certainly we must acknowledge that members of low-status compounds could have been servants attached to their wealthier neighbors, but they could equally have been poor cousins whose social standing was greatly reduced by the vast distance between them and their bundled founding ancestor.[24] Thus, the spatial differentiation of status at Teotihuacan resembles a patchwork quilt whose heterogeneity may reflect a lineage system in which junior lines periodically fractured off, resulting in their diminished social status. While they may have only moved next door, their new home reflected their increased distance from the revered ancestors. When commenting upon this model of ranked lineages, Cowgill (2003a:43) argued that they may have been ranked clans, a possibility that seems quite fitting. A city with the social complexity of Teotihuacan could surely foster the emergence of such large kin-based groups.

This model must acknowledge a critical trend in Mesoamerican scholarship. Of late, the field has come to question the suitability of lineage in the context of Precolumbian corporate groups in Mesoamerica. One of the most important contributions to the debate is that of Susan Gillespie (2000), who eloquently reviewed the literature on the topic of Maya social organization and proposed an intriguing new approach.[25] She noted that kin-based models such as lineage have certain drawbacks when applied to the Maya. Because lineage, as generally used in the literature, employs descent as the principal determinant in group affiliation, the model does not fully account for group members whose inclusion arises from different circumstances. Examples of this would be in-marrying wives or any individual whose membership was not technically determined by unilineal descent. This issue is particularly related to an inherent problem with many descent-based corporate models. Such approaches do not take into account the differences between descent groups and residential groups. For instance, Gillespie noted that unilineal groups are usually exogamous; therefore, some members of the lineage would marry outside and subsequently live elsewhere. When considering Teotihuacan apartment compounds, it seems highly likely that some of the members, particularly women who married into the compound, would claim descent from a lineage primarily based in another compound.[26] An additional critique of the lineage system arises from the consensus view that patrilineal descent is the rule. Gillespie identified many aberrations in the archaeological record that belie this assumption.

Burial treatment of Maya women often parallels the most elaborate tombs of men; public art frequently depicts women prominently engaged in consequential activities; and hieroglyphic inscriptions document the acknowledgement of matrilineal descent.

For a solution, Gillespie (2000) suggested the adoption of the term *house* as discussed by Lévi-Strauss (1982:174, 1987:152). She defined a house as

corporate, long-lived units that are organized for specific ends. House members strategically utilize relationships of consanguinity and affinity, real and fictive, in order to legitimate expressions of unity and perpetuity. (Gillespie 2000:468)

The benefits of house over lineage are many. For one, lineage approaches have a certain rigidity because they must conform to clearly defined kinship rules, while house models have an elasticity that accommodates the variety seen in the archaeology and ethnography. Moreover, consanguineal claims dominate in the lineage system, while houses may incorporate other forms of affinity as well as descent. Gillespie (2000:476) further recognized that the lineage system has certain incompatibilities when it is integrated with "large hierarchical polities," and houses better fit within these circumstances.

Certain archaeological evidence at Teotihuacan indicates that Gillespie's proposal has merit for this city. In particular, Monzón's (1987:164) report that a female burial was the richest found in one apartment compound correlates with Gillespie's recognition that models assuming exclusive patrilineal descent may be problematic. This burial demonstrates that female ancestors held significant prominence in Teotihuacan society. Furthermore, the close proximity of apartment compounds with differing status poses considerable challenges to the lineage model, as does the complexity of Teotihuacan's political structure. While I have argued that low-status compounds may represent cadet lineages, it is also possible that unrelated servants resided in these structures.[27] Yet even in the latter case, the servants may still have considered themselves members of the same corporate group that included a nearby high-status compound. Furthermore, Gillespie emphasized that nobles more frequently assert genealogical claims to status than commoners; hence social organizational models do not have to apply a singular and unified means for group identification. As she related,

ancestors are therefore a focus of group identity without necessitating recourse to a genealogy that encompasses the entire membership, although a pedigree for high-ranking members may be preserved. (Gillespie 2000:477)

Overall, the house model could help explain the integration of various social levels at Teotihuacan and acknowledge other forms of group determination that may have ensued from the pressures of the city's dense population and complex political structure. Instead of imposing conformity upon the entire population, it allows for the adaptation that emerges from the forces of human creativity.

LINEAGE AND ITS IMPACT ON THE POLITICAL SYSTEM

This foray into the possible lineage structure of Teotihuacan has identified the evidence for lineages or houses as a component of the city's social structure and suggested their impact on residential life; however, it is the impact of the lineages on the office of the ruler that is most pertinent to the broader argument of this book. Even if the house model better approximates the social structure of Teotihuacan as a whole, the evidence for mortuary bundles indicates that select elites determined their standing through descent, and for them the term *lineage* probably best characterizes the dynamics of their social identification. I would propose that the lineages, or those strata of society that reckoned proximity to the elite ancestors, held a pivotal role in the shaping of Teotihuacan history, forming one point of a triad of elements that forged the sociopolitical structure of the city. Furthermore, the elites actively engaged in lineage determination may have been a factor that influenced the ruler's actions more than any other.

The model for the Mixtec drawn up by Byland and Pohl (1994) is one of such intense factionalism that rulers were never secure enough to establish absolute power. They present a history where many individuals contended for dominance because there were multiple routes to power. Namely, the plurality of the ancestral bundles resulted in members of several lineages who each could formulate a rationale for their supremacy. The result was a tumultuous history with persistent shifts in power as the lineages and the historical actors within them constantly realigned their relative status.

In light of the factionalism witnessed in the Mixtec area, the stone masks serve as an essential clue to the dynamic social and political relationships of Teotihuacan. Within collections both public and private, there are hundreds of masks said to have come from the city, but calculating their number entails more than a simple count. Their uncomplicated and instantly recognizable style made them easy targets for modern reproduction, so numerous masks may be forgeries made to feed a voracious art market (Berrin 1993:77). Nevertheless, one could reduce the number manifold times and still comfortably assert that many masks and their associated bundles could have existed at any time during the height of Teotihuacan. Because the bundles would have presumably represented founders of lineages and other exalted ancestors, Teotihuacan seems to parallel the Mixtec in celebrating several lineages, and thus the specter of competition between the lineages emerges at the city. One wonders how, with so many recognized founders, the Teotihuacanos addressed the relative ranking between those lineages.

Couple this reasoning with the evidence of rulers who shunned personal narrative and portraiture, and you have a foundation for a city in which divisiveness between competing elements was a consistent trait. Rulers with secure hereditary claims to office might have followed a tradition similar to that of the Maya and asserted their power by recording a more personal history of their reigns and orchestrating the ascendance of their offspring. If, however, the existence of multiple founding ancestors engendered numerous pretenders to the throne, rulers might not invest significant capital in dynastic arguments. Instead, the celebration of the office and its accoutrements would dominate the royal presence, resulting in images like those seen at

Teotihuacan. The rulers emphasized their position by dressing in the garb of the mountain-tree and proclaiming their own names while neglecting claims of their heirs. Instead of a city where one lineage continuously held the sovereign role, the multiple mortuary bundles may reveal that royalty periodically shifted between the elites involved in reckoning lineage. Thus dynastic change may have frequently appeared at Teotihuacan and altered monarchical behaviors.[28]

Competing claims of the various lineages would have placed heavy constraints on the office of the ruler and likewise increased the potential for instability within the city as a whole as the lineages adjusted to realignments of relative status. In the Mixtec example, this meant that power never coalesced sufficiently for a centralized state to develop. Mixtec rulers only temporarily conquered large territories to assemble a petty state, but inevitably new aspirants emerged and the polity reverted to a fractured condition. Consequently, there seems to be some inconsistency in the applicability of the factional Mixtec model to the organized state of Teotihuacan; however, competing social components do not necessarily exclude the rise of states. The Zapotec, from whom the Mixtec may have inherited much of their system, probably developed a powerful state in the face of intense competition.

Sitting at the confluence of three valleys, Monte Albán emerged as the central power of the region even while bowing to the various factions that coalesced to create this state. In an intriguing parallel to Teotihuacan, the Zapotec capital harbors tantalizing evidence of powerful lineages within its burial data. The elite tombs that have surfaced at Monte Albán are not in the immediate ceremonial center but within high-status residential structures. Access to the tombs is generally through plaza floors, and they were meant to be periodically opened, as evidenced by their well built stairs and disturbed remains. The residential location of the tombs simultaneously allowed lineages to maintain control over their ancestral relics and reduced one lineage's ability to fuse its identity with the state (Flannery 1983:135). This distribution of power among the lineages probably reflected the origins of the state, for as Blanton (1978:106–108) contended, Monte Albán may have resulted from a confed-

eracy of different polities from the valleys. The various barrios that some archaeologists identify at the site may represent the vestiges of these regional groups (Blanton 1983:129; Kowalewski 1990:48–51). Blanton's confederacy model, therefore, explains how a dense urban center can indeed emerge from competing polities, and reveals that the social rivalries at Teotihuacan may be more the rule than the exception. This pattern is borne out when looking even further afield.

The dynasties of ancient China were far more successful in controlling large amounts of territory despite the presence of competing lineages. As Chang (1983:9–32) outlined, many hundreds of clans existed in early China. The members of each clan claimed descent from a common mythological ancestor whose birth was generally miraculous. In turn, the myth of the divine ancestor generated a name and emblem for the clan. During particular periods, the ancestor of one clan was recognized as superior to all the others, which justified this clan's hold on the royal title. The Three Dynasties of ancient Chinese history merely represent shifts in the preeminent clan. Within each clan were the various lineages, which, like those of the Mixtec, ranked themselves by comparative descent from the founding ancestor. Intermarriage between clans further complicated loyalty, authority, and descent. As Chang summarized the situation,

Available evidence from the Three Dynasties makes it clear that the political landscape of ancient China was dotted with hundreds of thousands of towns inhabited by members of discrete clans and lineages, and that these towns were linked in political hierarchies according to the kinship relations and interaction patterns of their inhabitants. (Chang 1983:32)

It would seem that if the dynasties of ancient China could coalesce sufficient power despite the competition, then the factions of Teotihuacan also could devise some sort of ranking system that gave one faction power, if only for a limited time.

Gillespie's (2000) house model also offers solutions for the fractiousness inherent when elites reckon their power through descent. Because her proposal includes routes to membership beyond the consanguineal ones, not all Teotihuacanos would have had to personally engage in the lineage debate. Some—in particular, the commoners—may have identified their primary means to membership through other affinities. Thus, the positioning of lineages, as proposed here, may be thought of as primarily involving the jockeying of elites, a select section of society whose political and social standing was sufficient to buffet the waters of Teotihuacan's history. While commoners may not have had the social capital to directly affect the political structure, their lack of participation in the lineage system might have had a positive effect towards unifying the city. These individuals extolled bonds outside of descent that contributed centripetal social forces. That is, the corporate identities of houses may have provided an element of stability even as certain members of these houses participated in a contentious system. Those polemical members ostensibly would have been the ones who tried most assiduously to link themselves to the mortuary bundles.

Particularly germane to this discussion is the question of the mortuary bundles' original location. If they were stored in the cave under the Sun Pyramid, potential existed for a more centralized imposition of control (Figure 1.9). A priestly class mirroring Lady 9 Grass could have easily restricted access to the bundles and enforced their exclusive role as oracular interpreters. Whether such priests were independent of the ruler or acted purely by royal directive, the state could have regulated access to the bundles, prevented lineages from communicating with their ancestors, and mandated that interpretations of the oracular messages be in the state's favor. Nevertheless, at some point the Teotihuacanos emptied the cave of its contents, leading to the second hypothetical location of the bundles.

The installation of the bundles along the Avenue of the Dead would have dramatically altered the relationship between the bundles, the state, and the lineages (Figure 3.20). Housed in the temples lining the street, the lineages could have asserted much more authority over their ancestors because the temples were integrated into the residential palaces. Possessing physical evidence of their lineage rights, the lineage heads could have had immediate access to the bundles and may have bypassed state efforts to monopo-lize oracular intercourse. If the Teotihuacanos did indeed move the bundles from the cave to the temples, the shift may have signaled an assertion of power by the lineages in which there was a realignment of power between the rulers and the lineages. Interestingly, this mirrors the work of several scholars who see strong evidence for an adjustment in the political structure of Teotihuacan. Pasztory argues that there was increased centralization of power as Teotihuacan developed. Likewise, Cowgill and René Millon suggested that powerful individual rulers governed early Teotihuacan, but the excesses of the ruler who sponsored the Feathered Serpent Pyramid led to subsequent checks on the royal office by the elite.[29] The presence of the mortuary bundles on the main avenue would be one more corroborative element in such a line of reasoning. The dispersal of the bundles among the lineages surely would distribute power to a greater number of social components.

Some degree of caution must temper this vision of independent lineages each controlling their own oracular bundles. One of the compelling features of the Avenue of the Dead is its unified quality wherein individual palaces architecturally join into one harmonious whole. Despite tensions between the various lineages and competition between the lineage heads and the state, a political apparatus was in place to coordinate a building campaign that celebrated at once the individual players and their participation in the greater social structure. The compelling manner in which the state projected a message of solidarity is one of the remarkable accomplishments of Teotihuacan, but it is critically important to recognize that this was a message formulated by the state to marshal these constituent parts.

In sum, the archaeological picture from Teotihuacan is far too murky to specifically identify the different lineages, let alone explore their relative hierarchy. For now, we must content ourselves with postulating their existence and assuming their competitive nature and the effect this had on the office of the ruler. It is possible that the characteristics of royal art are at least partially a response to the intense pressure that the lineages imposed on their rulers. As they curtailed the rulers' abilities to establish incontestable dynasties, they forced them into a position of articulating their roles more than their individual personalities. While there may have been periods where one lineage dominated the others over several generations, the generalities of the artistic record imply that shifts in power between the lineages were both possible and probable.

It would, however, be quite a mistake to assume that Teotihuacan rulers had no means of countering a hostile takeover by other lineages. The kings of the city did not rest passively and let history take its course without their intervention. The visual and archaeological record reveals that they countered aggressive attacks by sponsoring other social groups that attenuated the encroaching tendencies of the lineages. These royally sanctified bodies were institutionalized and broad based to incorporate as many Teotihuacanos as possible. Like so many others in history, the rulers of Teotihuacan looked to the military for support.

CHAPTER 4

ANIMALS, CANNIBALS, AND THE MILITARY

The final component in the Teotihuacan trinity, joining the ruler and the lineages, was the military. While the ruler may seem elusive, and the ancestral bundles of the lineages all but vanished, evidence of a military presence at the city is extensive. Militaristic individuals populate the visual arts in large numbers, marching on painted walls near the city center and out in the more secluded apartment compounds. Likewise, warriors circle around the painted and stuccoed vases or boldly appear on the carved surfaces of Thin Orange ceramics. Teotihuacan's censers consist of mold-made appliqués adhered to a conical core, and many of these appliqués have a military theme. Because the censers were probably used for more private household rituals, the decorations inform us that martial symbolism transcended the state to enter the individual conscience. Furthermore, material remains that resemble the painted military imagery have been recovered. Thus both art and archaeology indicate the expansive role played by the military in Teotihuacan society.

Although the imagery depicts a great deal of diversity in military costume, strong threads of continuity equally typify this genre. One of the most visible and diagnostic traits of a warrior was a bundle of darts and an accompanying atlatl with which the combatant propelled the darts with an incredible deadly force (Figures 4.1 and 4.2). The business end of the darts clearly shows a chipped stone point hafted onto the shaft. Quite often a circular element, which may be a puff of cotton, marks the transition from stone to wood, and similar round balls decorate the fletched end of the dart. Binding the darts together is a piece of cloth or fur grasped in the warrior's hand, allowing for a more easily carried package. The atlatl is invariably positioned in an active

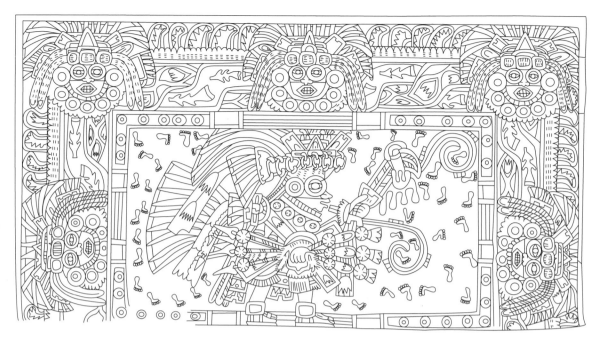

FIGURE 4.1. Mural of a warrior carrying atlatl darts and a heart on a sacrificial blade, lower *talud* wall, Portico 3, White Patio, Atetelco, Teotihuacan. Drawing by Jenni Bongard after Villagra 1971:Figure 20.

manner with the warrior's index and middle fingers slipped through parallel holes in the device (Figure 4.2). Above the fingers a knot seems to attach decorations to the atlatl; these may consist of the trapeze-and-ray year sign, strips of paper, a small bit of fur, and a bunch of feathers. The way in which warriors hold their atlatls aloft and prominently display their darts conveys the importance of these weapons to their identity.

Another crucial costume element of a Teotihuacan warrior is the mirror worn on his back. Although the preferred position was at the small of the back, artists sometimes shifted the device higher towards the shoulder so that the viewer could see costume elements that might be obscured by a more accurate placement. Called a *tezcacuitlapilli* by the later Aztecs, the mirror consisted of a small stone disk to which pieces of iron pyrite were attached in a mosaic.[1] Two beautiful archaeological examples from the site of Chichen Itza attest that some mirrors had an outer rim of decorative stone mosaic; however, visual depictions indicate that feathers commonly ringed the Teotihuacan mirrors. An additional decorative touch might include a knot securing a swath of feathers to the mirror.

Many of the other costume elements of the warriors are not restricted to the military. Bril-

liant sprays of feathers fall from their various headdresses and trail behind them. They wear sandals, shell or bead necklaces, large earflares, and short skirts with a loincloth, all clothing of a typical, if elite, Teotihuacan male. The main militaristic emblems tucked amongst this otherwise ordinary clothing are year signs, owl pectorals, and the ultimate warrior costume element, circular Tlaloc goggles. The goggles usually ring the human eye, but they were sometimes shoved up on the forehead in a style similar to modern goggle wearing.

A final characteristic of Teotihuacan military uniforms is, nevertheless, the most interesting because it opens a window not only onto attire but also onto the conceptual underpinnings of warfare itself and the social organizational properties of the military. Teotihuacan warriors did not enter battle solely with protective armaments of the material sort: they wore spiritual armaments as well. A curious feature of the city's military imagery is the incorporation of animal attributes in the costumes of most warriors. For instance, a plaque found in a ceramic workshop attached to the Ciudadela presents a spear-holding warrior who sports feathered serpent imagery on both his headdress and belt (Figure 4.3) (Sugiyama 1992, 2005:62). On this

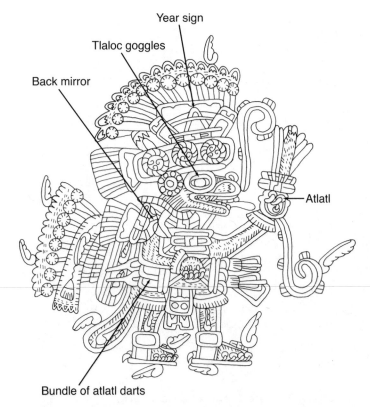

Year sign

Tlaloc goggles

Back mirror

Atlatl

Bundle of atlatl darts

FIGURE 4.2. Mural detail with canine warrior, Portico 1, White Patio, Atetelco, Teotihuacan. Drawing by Jenni Bongard after von Winning 1987:I:95, Figure 3c.

choose to dress as a ferocious feline or a screeching eagle. One explanation comes from military practices found throughout the world wherein costume serves to intimidate one's opponents. Plains Indians of North America applied facial paint, and successful warriors wore richly embellished clothing and feathered bonnets to advertise their expertise (Penney 1996:40; Penney and Longfish 1994:85). Proving that those going into harm's way sometimes push aside logic, fighter planes in the U.S. military often have fanged mouths painted onto the nose of the fuselage. Whether the paint job is meant to strike fear into a foe watching the planes on television or merely boost the drive of the pilot climbing into the cockpit, the effect is similar. The decoration's psychological impact engenders both fear and courage, motivates its user to engage in a dangerous act, and encourages the enemy to rethink his position. However, an examination of intrinsically Mesoamerican beliefs and practices may

individual, the animal features are obviously part of the uniform, but this distinction is not as clear in other examples. Although they wear back mirrors and carry shields to fend off blows, some warriors appear more animal than human (Figure 4.2). Such warriors have fur-covered bodies, the heads of canines, or the claws of a bird. Furry tails emerge from behind the back mirrors, and their mouths are full of sharp fangs. The heads of these beasts are anatomically correct for animals and have few human qualities other than the headdresses they wear. However, the clothing and the upright, two-legged stance imply that these probably represent human actors wearing animal costumes. Teotihuacan warriors, it seems, dressed as fierce animals when they went to war. On occasion this odd marriage is humorous, as when the dew claws of a canine project from the heel of a sandal or when the claws of a bird curl though the holes in an atlatl, but overall the artists successfully integrated the animal and human features to produce a believable composite creature.[2]

There are many reasons why a warrior would

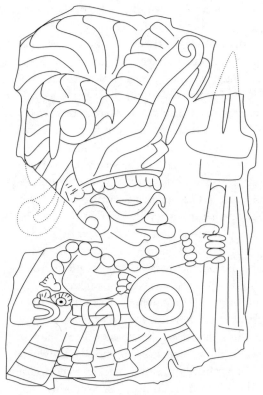

FIGURE 4.3. Ceramic plaque depicting a warrior with a feathered serpent headdress from the Ciudadela ceramic workshop, Teotihuacan. Drawing by Jenni Bongard after Sugiyama 1992:Figure 9.

FIGURE 4.4. Drawing of the Altar de Sacrificios vase, ceramic, Late Classic. Drawing by Linda Schele, © David Schele, courtesy of the Foundation for the Advancement of Mesoamerican Studies, Inc., www.famsi.org.

reveal another reason for the animal costuming of Teotihuacan warriors, and this explanation involves a broad cultural belief in nagualism, or the ability of humans to transform into animals.[3]

NAGUALISM AND THE MILITARY

Even the earliest Europeans to write on Mesoamerica reported the practice of nagualism. The sixteenth-century Franciscan Bernardino de Sahagún (1950–1982:IV:42–43) stated that people born on the day One Rain were sorcerers and had the ability to turn themselves into animals. Another Spanish friar, Diego Durán, described a case of nagualism during the reign of Motecuhzoma the Elder. This Aztec king sent sixty sorcerers to seek the mythical island of their origins, Aztlan. When the sorcerers reached the hill called Coatepec at Tula, they conducted a ritual. As Durán wrote,

The Devil, conjured by these spells and pleas, turned them into birds or wild beasts such as ocelots, jaguars, jackals, wildcats, and took them, together with their gifts, to the land of their forebearers. (Durán 1964:135)

Thus, the act of transformation allowed these humans to travel in magical ways to the world of their ancestors. Even though Durán does capture a uniquely indigenous belief, it is worth noting that his referral to the devil as the causal agent reveals his own cultural proclivities. Louise Burkhart (1989:40) investigated the linguistics of such biased statements in her treatment of the intersection of Nahua and Christian beliefs. She pointed out that friars appropriated the Nahuatl word *tlacatecolotl,* which refers to shamans who changed into birds. Instead of respecting the specificity of the term, the friars used it indiscriminately as the word for "devil," thereby acknowledging the practice even as they condemned it.[4]

Using the words of ancient indigenous writers, epigraphers have documented the presence of *naguals,* or *wayob,* in ancient Maya belief. A hieroglyph that has been read as *way,* means "to dream, to sleep, and to transform into one's animal companion."[5] The glyph appears repeatedly on the famous Altar de Sacrificios vase, which depicts dancing jaguar and serpent men (Figure 4.4). Positioned next to the composite animal-human figures, the *way* glyph probably records that these elites have transformed into supernatural creatures.

The ability to metamorphose into otherworldly animals was also a documentable aspect of Mesoamerican warfare. In a masterful analysis of early colonial texts, Victoria Bricker (1981:38–42) compared the Spanish and K'ichee' accounts of the conquest of Guatemala and revealed that this was a war fought between peoples with radi-

FIGURE 4.5. Aztec counterattack at Tenochtitlan, manuscript illustration in Durán's *The History of the Indies of New Spain,* sixteenth century. Drawing by Jenni Bongard after Gruzinski 1992:46–47.

cally different views of war and reality.[6] In typical fashion, the Spanish records betray a Western emphasis on strategies and ultimate outcome, whereas the K'ichee' focused on the supernatural aspect of war. In the indigenous version the appearance of their leader, Tecum Umam, received much attention.

Captain Tecum, before leaving his town and in front of the Chiefs, demonstrated his fortitude and his courage and immediately put on wings with which he flew and his two arms and legs were covered with feathers and he wore a crown, and on his chest he wore a very large emerald [jade?] which looked like a mirror, and he wore another on his forehead. And another on his back. He looked very gallant. This captain flew like an eagle, he was a great nobleman and a great sorcerer. (Translation of Recinos 1957:86–91 by Bricker 1981:39)

Bricker recognized the significance of this passage and its suggestion that K'ichee' warfare had a magical element. She entertained the idea that the early colonial Maya may have viewed Tecum Umam's transformation as reality, not hyperbole.[7]

A careful look at the precise wording, however, reveals just how difficult it is to know the K'ichee' position on the issue. When the author

labeled Tecum Umam a "sorcerer," he implied a magical aspect to the transformation, but he also allowed for the physical world by admitting that the captain "put on the wings" and "flew like an eagle." The latter two statements concede that Tecum Umam probably donned a costume and that while his flight was "like" an eagle, it was not exactly the same as an eagle's. The point of this discussion is to establish that while Mesoamericans may have believed that they could tap into supernatural forces and change themselves into an animal companion, they were not above using costume to heighten the effect. Furthermore, it would be nearsighted to assume that there was a monolithic Mesoamerican position on the comparative reality or theatricality of animal transformation. The safest supposition is that some Mesoamericans probably believed that humans could physically change into animals, while others might have interpreted these events in a more metaphorical light or even dismissed them as fakery.

This discussion permits us to approach images of Mesoamerican warriors from a more emic perspective. For example, an Aztec artist working at the behest of Durán drew a scene of the Mexica attacking the Spanish, who were

FIGURE 4.6. Olmec figure of a kneeling shaman in partial transformation, serpentine. Photograph courtesy of Dumbarton Oaks, Pre-Columbian Collection, Washington, D.C.

FIGURE 4.7. Olmec figure of fully transformed shaman, serpentine. Photograph courtesy of Dumbarton Oaks, Pre-Columbian Collection, Washington, D.C.

then positioned within the city of Tenochtitlan (Figure 4.5). Reflecting the polarity of K'iche' and Spanish views of war, the Spaniards emphasized technology, surrounding themselves with metal armor, stone fortifications, and crossbows. The artist certainly included the Aztec weapons, carefully painting the spears and decorated shields, but he also expended a good deal of time on the warriors' costumes. In contrast to the European emphasis on physical defense, the Aztec warriors wear bird, jaguar, and other animal costumes, and they have backracks that are perhaps more cumbersome than protective.[8] One explanation for these features is that they offered protection of a different sort: spiritual protection.

An examination of the Olmec indicates that the Mesoamerican belief in nagualism has great time depth. Peter Furst (1968) has been a strong proponent for the existence of shamanism and its attendant belief in human transformation. Expanding upon Furst's ideas, Kent Reilly (1989) demonstrated that numerous figurines depict Ol-

mec kings in various states of ritual transformation. Even though the figurines lack provenience, he argued that they carry the same conceptual intent regardless of their authorship or original location. That is, while each figurine shows a different moment from the process of ritual transformation, when viewed collectively, they convey the whole process sequentially. For instance, one figurine has mostly human features and sits on his lower legs with his hands on his knees.[9] The suggestion of his shamanic role arises from tiny lines inscribed on his head, which Reilly identified as the *Bufo marinus* toad, and the metamorphosis of the *Bufo* from tadpole to toad provides a worthy metaphor for nagualism.

A second figure sits in a similar pose but has different facial features (Figure 4.6). His nose, eyes, and ears now resemble a jaguar. Moving further along, a third figure walks like a human and has human hands and feet, but the face exhibits jaguar features.[10] In the last figure of Reilly's group, the transformation is complete (Figure 4.7). The head is fully jaguarian and the

FIGURE 4.8. Mural depicting a jaguar warrior with a shield and back mirror, Zacuala, Teotihuacan. Drawing by Jenni Bongard after von Winning 1987:I:80, Figure 3a.

sequent transformation that is strikingly similar to that depicted by the Olmec figurines.

The narrative begins on the side walls, where warriors stride within a net of diamond spaces (Figure 4.9).[11] These human warriors are identified by their Tlaloc goggles, back mirrors, year-sign headdresses, and bundles of atlatl darts, but instead of an atlatl in their other hand, they curiously hold some sort of club with which they strike birds in the head. Drops of blood spurting from the heads indicate the birds' ultimate death. The wounded birds on these walls could represent one of two things. First, they could be actual birds sacrificed in a ritual. Substantial ethnographic evidence records that this occurred in both ancient and modern times. Sahagún, for example, discussed the ritual events the Mexica practiced on the day One Dog.

figure sprouts a tail. Only the upright, dancing position indicates the human qualities of the transformed shaman.

Given this tradition of nagualism in the various temporal and cultural groups—that is, from Olmec to Aztec—Teotihuacan's animal imagery seems not so much an anomaly but a participant in a tradition. Like the fully transformed Olmec figurine, a Teotihuacan jaguar from Tetitla also walks or dances in a human fashion (Figure 1.12). Similarly, on a wall in Zacuala Palace the accoutrements of warfare, including a defensive shield and back mirror, emphasize the true human nature of this otherwise jaguarian individual (Figure 4.8). In light of the overwhelming evidence that nagualism was practiced throughout Mesoamerica, the best interpretation is that Teotihuacanos held similar beliefs.

The Olmec figurines are particularly convincing because they show the stages of the transformation. In a sense, it happens before our very eyes as the art reconstructs the process. Interestingly, the same stages of transformation appear at Teotihuacan in the murals of the White Patio in the Atetelco apartment compound (Figure 2.4), which also includes possible portrayals of a ruler in the middle portico. In the flanking porticos, however, the artists painted images of warriors in animal costume. In particular, the walls of the north portico tell a story of ritual action and sub-

And they decapitated quail. It seemed that before the hearth, they kept fluttering and beating their wings. Their

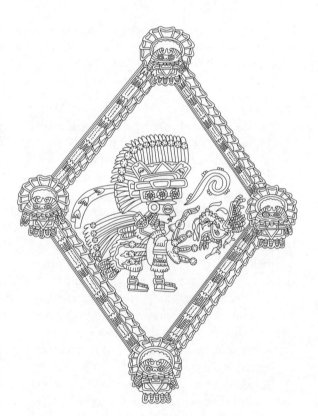

FIGURE 4.9. Detail of mural with a warrior striking a bird, upper *tablero* side wall, Portico 3, White Patio, Atetelco, Teotihuacan. Drawing by Jenni Bongard after Pasztory 1974:Figure 15.

blood was scattered by their fluttering, so that the earth before the hearth was struck in various places. They spattered and poured forth their blood. (Sahagún 1950–1982:IV:87)

Sahagún's description is extraordinary in its resemblance to the images in Portico 3. The emphasis on the fluttering wings and flying blood are consistent themes in the Teotihuacan visual account and the Aztec written version of bird sacrifice, a practice that still continues today. During the Great Seeing ceremony, the Maya of Zinacantan sacrifice two chickens which they call *k'exoliletik,* or substitutes, because the chickens are a replacement for the patient being cured by the shaman (Vogt 1976:91–94). The Zinacantecos view the chicken's body as a substitute for the human's soul.

K. C. Chang's (1983:45–73) work on Shang China offers other interesting parallels for the function of animals in shamanic rites. In ancient China the king and a retinue of assistants were shamans who accessed the supernatural realm to consult with ancestors before undertaking important actions such as a war, hunt, journey, or ritual. They believed that animals were able to help them establish contact with the ancestors and had images of these shamanic enablers cast on their ritual bronzes. Chang (1983:65) argued that sacrificial animal offerings were a means of achieving communication between heaven and earth. In that the traits of shamanism evidenced throughout Mesoamerica reflect those found in China to some degree, the animals killed in Portico 3 may have similarly served as agents of communication. Perhaps the birds were enablers of these warriors on a shamanic quest.

In an alternative interpretation, the bird may represent a human bird warrior, captured in war and sacrificed in a ritual at Teotihuacan. Because evidence suggests that Mesoamericans fought their wars in the guise of their animal companions, the foes of the Teotihuacanos may also have had naguals. Mexica images of battles show that animal costumes were not exclusive to one army.[12] Eagles and jaguars fought on both sides because all participants shared a belief in the supernatural nature of warriors. Furthermore, Mexica conceptions of their war captives might elucidate why sacrificial victims may appear in

the Teotihuacan murals as birds. The Mexica referred to their captives as "eagle men" whose reward was a heaven better than that where most people went (Sahagún 1950–1982:II:48). As Sahagún explained,

The eagle man is taken upwards, because indeed he who died in war went, went looking, sat resting in the presence of the sun. That is, he did not go to the place of the dead. (Sahagún 1950–1982:II:49)

Perhaps the Teotihuacanos held a similar belief, and the birds executed in the White Patio were warriors who went to reside with the sun. The artist may have shown Teotihuacan's foes in their fully transformed state, which could simultaneously convey the role of nagualism in warfare-related sacrifice and dehumanize one's enemy.

The scenes shown on the lower walls of Portico 3 strongly support a human identity for the dying birds in the walls above (Figure 4.1). Just below the warriors who strike the birds are warriors dancing in a space reminiscent of Teotihuacan architecture. Documented by a haphazard series of footprints, the dance occurs within a rectangular enclosure that has stairs on each of its four sides. The configuration of the space could easily be the sunken courtyard of the White Patio itself, or it may describe a raised dance platform within the city center. In either case, the architecture most likely places the event at Teotihuacan. The dancers still wear their war costumes, but now with the addition of sacrificial embellishments. The headdress has a vertebral column, possibly human, on its brim, and three obsidian knives emerge from the top. The warriors carry another obsidian knife, this time hafted, in their hands.[13] The hearts impaled on these knives are arguably human, and the close proximity of these images to those above suggests that the hearts came from bird warriors. That is, the dance appears to be a sequential scene that follows the bludgeoning above. In the cycle of events, a Teotihuacan warrior may have sacrificed a captured bird warrior and then danced about with his captive's heart stuck on a large obsidian blade.

Whether the sacrificed individuals were animals or humans, the ultimate result of this deed appears on the back wall of the White Patio's

FIGURE 4.10. Fully transformed bird warrior, upper *tablero* rear wall, Portico 3, White Patio, Atetelco, Teotihuacan. Drawing by Jenni Bongard after von Winning 1987:I:95, Figure 3b.

Portico 3. It is important to note that the portico's rear wall has different figures filling the net spaces than the side walls (Figure 4.10): they are composite creatures with human and animal characteristics. The warriors have bird's tails, beaks, and feet, and feathers cover much of their bodies. In one hand they hold aloft their atlatls, and bird claws curl through the finger holes. Nevertheless, they walk in an upright, human fashion and carry atlatl darts in human hands. These figures very clearly represent Teotihuacan warriors fully transformed into their naguals.

The imagery of the side and back walls mirrors the Olmec figurines by showing two stages in the transformation process. The side walls depict the ritual leading up to and permitting the transformation (Figure 4.9). In turn, the back wall displays the result of the sacrifice: the complete transformation of the human into a supernatural creature (Figure 4.10). Like the Zinacantecos, the Teotihuacanos may have viewed the sacrificial victim as a substitute; the offering of a bird or bird warrior might have substituted for the soul of the Teotihuacan warrior, who was now able to access the supernatural realm (Vogt 1976:91–94). The modern Zinacanteco gains renewed health through this access, but the Teotihuacan

warrior achieved an altered state. Just as with the Olmec figurines, the artists of the White Patio wanted to convey the process of ritual shamanistic transformation.

An even more complete view of transformation appears in the central building in the White Patio (Figure 4.11). The lower walls of Portico 2 depict canines and net jaguars (identified by its interlaced design). The animal nature of these figures is even more pronounced, for they walk on all fours. The only hint of their true human nature comes from their headdresses. The net jaguar underscores that not all naguals are creatures from the natural world. The interlaced design marking the pelt of this creature also appears on the wall space above, but it has no counterpart in any feline. The net jaguar is a creation of human fancy, and parallels for this appear amongst the Maya *wayob*. At Palenque a dancing skeleton was an important *way*, and Grube and Nahm (1994) have pointed out that deities and composite creatures such as tapir jaguars serve as *wayob* (Freidel et al. 1993:191–192). Of course, there is no reason that we should be surprised by the suspension of reality when we are dealing with a phenomenon so grounded in belief.

Other murals at Atetelco offer more evidence of the role of sacrifice in animal transformation. Excavations at Atetelco conducted by Séjourné and Manuel Romero Nogueró (1982) uncovered murals just north of the White Patio. The stratigraphic elevation of the North Patio indicates that these murals date later than those of the White Patio, yet their imagery seems to deal with similar concepts. One mural, featuring a feathered canine in a U-shaped depression, offers a concise view of the process of nagualism at Teotihuacan (Figure 4.12). The canine sits back on its tail and waves its front paws in the air as a speech scroll curls from his mouth. The lower border consists of a repetitive series of curved obsidian knives and biznaga cacti.

In a discussion of murals at Tetitla, Taube (1992a:171) identified the object that holds the canine as a bowl in cross section. Such bowls also held mirrors and were used in divination. At Tetitla the divinatory rituals possibly materialize the image of a deceased ruler (Figure 2.11), while at Atetelco divination produced a canine nagual. Both the Tetitla and Atetelco images

a.

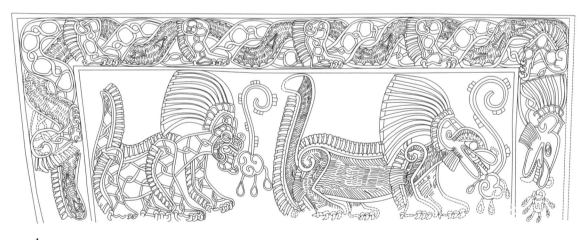

b.

FIGURE 4.11. Photograph and drawing of the lower *talud* mural of Portico 2 depicting canines and a net jaguar eating hearts shown in tri-scroll and profile views, White Patio, Atetelco, Teotihuacan. Drawing by Jenni Bongard after Villagra 1971:Figure 19.

FIGURE 4.12. Mural with canine sitting in a bowl, North Patio, Atetelco, Teotihuacan. Drawing by Jenni Bongard after Cabrera 1992:Figure 15.

FIGURE 4.13. Biznaga mural, Atetelco, Teotihuacan. Drawing by Jenni Bongard after Villagra 1965:Figure 3.

FIGURE 4.14. Zone 2 mural with feline-dressed figures above felines, Teotihuacan. Drawing by Jenni Bongard after Miller 1973:Figure 22.

have a war shield tassel hanging from the edge of the bowl, suggesting a conflation of war with divination and nagual transformation. Taube's (1992a:192) work on mirrors demonstrated the close association of war shields and mirrors.

The remaining imagery reveals just what type of divinatory rituals led to the appearance of the canine. The lower walls of Portico 3 (Figure 4.1) explain the curved knives below the bowl because there the knives function as a tool of heart sacrifice. Likewise, the biznaga cactus shown in the North Patio has long thorns, which were also effective bloodletters, though probably for auto-sacrifice. A nearby mural shows the biznaga with obsidian knives dripping with blood, and rows of pointed bloodletters arch above these biznaga (Figure 4.13). On the North Patio mural there are obsidian blades and pointed bloodletters inside the bowl itself. These implements are probably floating in the blood that was spilt into the bowl. Reiterating themes seen in the White Patio, this later mural shows the connection between sacrifice and nagualism.

Further corroborating this process is a fragmentary mural from Zone 2 just south of the Palace of Quetzalpapalotl that relates the same sequence of events (Figure 4.14). The lower register includes the large hooks of the obsidian sacrificial blades. Amongst the blades the artist has inserted war shields with their falling tassels. Doubling as divinatory mirrors or bowls, the war

shields have headdress-wearing pumas emanating from their surface. To emphasize the quality of emergence, the bellies of the pumas blend with the upper surface of the shields. Above this the top register records the final outcome. Only the lower portion of these figures survives, but the remaining costumes, especially the animal tails and paws, announce the presence of warriors dressed in the guise of their puma nagual.[14]

Portico 3 of the White Patio thus depicts how the death of birds or sacrificed warriors could result in fully transformed bird warriors. The biznaga in the murals north of the White Patio indicates that auto-sacrifice, as well as human sacrifice, enabled the manifestation of canine naguals. The consistency of the theme on richly painted walls indicates that the rituals of animal transformation were crucial to the practice of Teotihuacan religion, and if sacrificial victims were a necessary requirement for that transformation, then the machinery of war seems to have assured an ample supply.

ANIMALS AS CANNIBALS

The close examination of a particular looted mural can help explain the complex relationship of animals and humans in Teotihuacan art and perhaps further justify viewing the bleeding birds in the Atetelco murals as human victims. The canine-deer scene is a mural fragment now in the Fine Arts Museums of San Francisco (Figure 4.15). In the well-known exhibition catalogue, *Feathered Serpents and Flowering Trees,* René Millon (1988b) successfully argued that this, and a selection of other looted murals, came from an apartment compound in the northeast section of Teotihuacan referred to by archaeologists as the Barrio of the Looted Murals. The looting destroyed the finer details of the mural's original context, yet the narrative nature of the scene still allows it to participate in a reconstruction of Teotihuacan.

Compositionally, the mural is rather simple. Two profile canines mirror one another as they face inwards. The canines bracket the composition, and they lean forward, forming a triangle that draws the eye up the diagonals. At the apex of this triangle are the prominent heads of these two animals. Their intense, forward stares focus the viewer's attention on the third animal—a small deer positioned at the center of the composition. Unlike the diagonals of the canines, the deer is primarily vertical, providing a central axis about which the whole composition pivots.

The symmetrical balance and stability of this composition is jarringly at odds with the explicit violence of the subject matter. The two canines tear at their impotent victim as they proceed to subdue their prey in a graphic scene where the artist provided us with details that emphasize the brutal nature of this attack. The deer's head is thrust backwards, and its tongue lolls out of its parted mouth. With its arms outstretched and feet lifted off the ground, it is powerless against its larger attackers. The canines' brilliant white teeth are carefully delineated in their open mouths, which allow us to see the sharp canine

FIGURE 4.15. Mural from Teotihuacan of canines attacking a deer, the Fine Arts Museums of San Francisco. Drawing by Jenni Bongard after C. Millon 1988c:Figure V.11.

teeth behind the shorter front teeth. Likewise, the white of the canine claws starkly contrasts with the blood red background. The claws extend, and these curved hooks menacingly thrash at the small body of the deer. One paw grabs at the deer's chest and succeeds in extracting the heart. We see the hole leading to the inner chamber of the heart and three large drops of blood oozing off this essential organ. The heart appears at the very center of the composition, giving it the most prominent place in the whole scene.

Yet, it is this very prominence of, or emphasis on, the heart which seems the most curious element in this image. Canines, it would seem, would have no preference as to which organ they would first consume. Indeed, this prominence most assuredly says more about the interests of the humans who painted this image than the animals depicted here.

The canine-deer mural has been the topic of much discussion because scenes of explicit violence are rare in Teotihuacan art, and the mural is thus far unique in providing a vivid narrative of a violent act. In truth, evidence of violence does abound, for even in the White Patio warriors dance with human hearts impaled on large obsidian knives. Nevertheless, a distinction can be made between images showing the aftermath of bloodshed and the actual act of taking a living being's life. By depicting just the heart, the artist depersonalizes the event and diffuses sympathy for the victim. In contrast, the Maya and Aztec were not squeamish about depicting narrative imagery of sacrifice, and artists went to great lengths to show the victims' pain. The Maya institutionalized the presence of the sacrificial victim, either living or dead, in the stela format.[15]

The general consensus on the canine-deer mural seems to be that it represents a "metaphorical human heart-sacrifice scene" (C. Millon 1988a:219). The argument goes that unlike their Maya contemporaries, Teotihuacanos abstained from showing human beings involved in actual sacrifice scenes. As Clara Millon stated, "Even in this rare painting, where violence is explicit, the artist employs avoidance of a sort. He does not paint men engaged in violence" (C. Millon 1988a:220). In a similar manner, Pasztory argued that "any overview of Teotihuacan art as a whole must conclude that the images for the most part emphasize natural bounty, order, and harmony rather than violence, and when violence is shown it is rarely represented charged with emotional force; its force is neutral and distanced" (Pasztory 1993:48–49). Pasztory concluded that violent animal imagery justifies, in a sense, the practice of heart sacrifice by the elites. These scenes declare that the gods established the natural order, and it is the duty of the elites to duplicate the patterns seen in nature. In other words, carnivores kill the weak, and humans sacrifice those defeated in battle. While I agree with these scholars that the canine-deer scene refers to human sacrifice, I part with their insistence that the scene is metaphorical. I disagree that there is any form of avoidance or distance in this imagery.

The canines and net jaguars of the White Patio's Portico 2 are of particular importance to this assertion because a tri-scroll element dripping with liquid sits in front of each animal's mouth (Figure 4.11). Neys and von Winning (1946:82) described the sign and argued for its association with water, presumably because of the droplets falling from it. However, it was Séjourné (1956:119) who first realized that the drops consisted of blood and correctly identified the motif as a cross-sectional view of a heart. Images where the tri-scroll sign appears with knives support Séjourné's interpretation (Figure 4.16), as do the many hearts seen from the more recognizable profile view. In the lower wall of Portico 2, a canine serpent frames the space and nibbles at a side-view heart that also drips with blood (Figure 4.11). These hearts, like

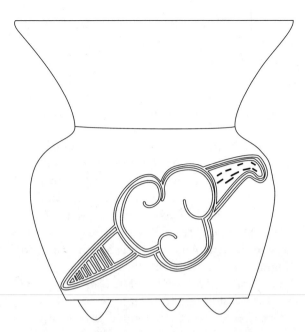

FIGURE 4.16. Thin Orange vessel with tri-scroll heart pierced by a knife, Teotihuacan. Drawing by Jenni Bongard after von Winning 1987:II:13, Figure 5e.

the hearts carried by the dancing warriors in Portico 3, are most likely human hearts, which raises a question that challenges ethical boundaries. I have argued above that many, if not all, of the animals in Teotihuacan art are actually humans shown in the guise of their naguals. With their headdress-covered heads, the canines and net jaguars are two such human actors; therefore, the event taking place on the lower walls is arguably an act of ritual cannibalism.

Cannibalism is difficult to prove archaeologically, but there is sufficient evidence to demonstrate that it was part of the ritual practices of Mesoamerica. Coe and Diehl (1980:91, 386, 390) contended that cannibalism accounts for the human skeletal remains found broken and burned in culinary middens at the Olmec site of San Lorenzo. Storey (1987:103) found bones with cut marks that were not associated with burials at Tlajinga 33, and she interpreted these as the remains of human sacrifices at Teotihuacan. Working in Oaxaca, Ronald Spores (1983b:157) reported adult and human bone with evidence of burning and cut marks in the refuse deposits of Yucuñudahui. He also found cannibalized human bone mixed with refuse containing animal and plant remains in Ramos Phase (200 B.C.–A.D. 300)

Yucuita (Spores 1983a:120). Nearly contemporary is the Period II (100 B.C.–A.D. 200) high-status residence at San Martín Huamelulpan where excavations revealed human bone in the hearth. Because these remains occurred near public buildings and in association with large vessels, Flannery and Marcus interpreted this as evidence of public feasting involving "the cooking and eating of humans around the altars, and perhaps the distribution of substantial cannibalistic meals at the nearby residences of community leaders" (Flannery and Marcus 1983d:124).

Sahagún (1950–1982:I:3) reported that cannibalism continued in Postclassic central Mexico. During the feast of Xipe Totec, captives had their hearts extracted and bodies rolled down the pyramid. These bodies were then taken to be dismembered and divided for communal eating. At Teotihuacan remnants of dismembered bodies were found in the habitational palace structures north of the Feathered Serpent Pyramid, and these fragments of torso, vertebra, and feet had cut marks and showed signs of burning (Serrano 1993:114). The public nature of this nevertheless residential area is reminiscent of San Martín Huamelulpan, suggesting that cannibalism was a civic event at Teotihuacan as well.

I want to emphasize the ritual nature of cannibalism. This is not consumption of human flesh for protein or other dietary needs. Presumably, the act would have taken place only within a carefully prescribed ritual context. In fact, it is possible that the Teotihuacanos themselves did not even recognize this act as cannibalism, and the experiences of Hans Staden can clarify this seemingly duplicitous statement. Staden was a sixteenth-century German captured by the Tupinamba Indians of Brazil. At one point Staden watched the Tupinamba king gnaw at the leg bone of a human war captive. He asked the king how he could do such a ghastly thing, how he could eat the flesh of another human. The king responded that he was a jaguar and, he added with humor, it tasted good (Staden 1928:110). This story illustrates the two different concepts of reality that were operational during this dialogue: the reality of the German and the reality of the Tupinamba king. The Tupinamba king did not see himself as human when he conducted

this ritual act, and therefore it was not cannibalism.[16] The story also suggests that nagualism was not limited to Mesoamerica, but may be a core element in many cultures in the Americas.

The sentiments of the Tupinamba king may also help explain the iconography of the White Patio. In Portico 3 the sacrificial victim might appear as a bird rather than a human warrior because the event transpires in the supernatural realm (Figure 4.9). I would propose that in the belief system of the original audience the victim was indeed a bird. The canines and net jaguars may depict Teotihuacan warriors, even specific individuals who lived at Atetelco and engaged in cannibalism, yet there was no need to chastise one's relative for these acts because it was not your acquaintance who ate the flesh of another human but a supernatural partner (Figure 4.11). That is, this otherwise repulsive act is palatable because the actors temporarily cede their human existence. Like the Tupinamba king, a Teotihuacano eating a human heart might have offered in explanation that he was a canine or a jaguar at that moment. The rules of the sacred world apply to these murals, and to look for logical explanations or counterparts in the natural world is to miss the point. Though animal imagery was initially inspired by aspects of nature, the Teotihuacan artists continually molded these characteristics to explore human concerns.

This position challenges the traditional belief that images of animals served as surrogates for the violent acts of Teotihuacan elites. Previously, it seemed that the city had a distaste for overt violence in its art, so its artists substituted scenes from nature as analogies for human behavior. In the Teotihuacan artistic tradition the animals did the dirty work. The art never showed humans conducting sacrifice. Instead, the viewer was supposed to infer the human act from the animal scene, and, in turn, the conduct of the animals justified human activities because the violence was seen as the normal pattern of nature.

The canine-deer scene fueled much of this debate. Pitting a defenseless deer against predatory canines, the mural clearly shows the death of a victim and the responsible parties. Interpreting this as metaphor—a natural scene painted by artists reluctant to present humans as violent actors—develops a picture of an artistic tradition that softens violence through avoidance by never showing humans in the act of sacrifice. With the recognition that Teotihuacan, like the rest of Mesoamerica, believed in nagual transformation, animals in Teotihuacan art lose their bestial aspect. The animals in many cases are not animals at all but humans in their nagual guise. The violence conducted by these figures cannot be explained away as the innocent acts of nature because cognizant human beings perform these deeds. The evidence suggests that the canine-deer mural portrays not animals involved in eating their prey, but humans, transformed into their naguals, consuming the heart of their warfare captive, an act of cannibalism. The same is true of the net jaguars and canines in Atetelco's White Patio. These fully transformed Teotihuacanos eat the human hearts before their mouths.

The original Teotihuacan viewer would not see the animal behavior as metaphor nor as violent acts, softened and distanced with analogy. There is no avoidance of the human presence because these scenes are explicit. Teotihuacanos would see the animals instead as pictures of real events, events witnessed by them, and done by warriors they knew. The animals do not substitute for their human counterparts; they are the humans. The images are graphic, and their message is threatening. All who viewed the violent acts of the naguals recognized the awesome power of the Teotihuacan warriors. The artists presented human sacrifice not through analogy but in reality.

The White Patio goes further to illuminate the relationship between nagualism and sacrifice. Portico 3 illustrates one of the ways the Teotihuacanos induced a shamanic state and underwent transformation into a nagual. The sacrifice of the birds, which could easily be naguals themselves, enabled the Teotihuacan ritualists to attain their nagual state. The canine mural north of the White Patio reiterates this theme (Figure 4.12). It shows the bloodletters in the bottom of a divinatory bowl and the supernatural canine generated from the sacrificial blood. Emergence of naguals is dependent on sacrifice, and this necessitated a steady supply of sacrificial victims.

This ritual demand for sacrificial victims offers one reason for the prevalence of martial themes in Teotihuacan art, for artists devoted much time to portraying the detailed military costumes. Further, it was the success of these warriors on the battlefield that ensured human victims for ritual events. Mesoamericans did not typically annihilate their enemy on the battlefield because their objective was to return home with captives (Durán 1994:141). Durán explained this well when he related the Aztec philosophy of war.

In this way the object of the battle or encounter was more to capture than to kill. This was their goal: to seize yet not slay; to do no harm to man or woman, to a home or cornfield, but to feed the idol! (Durán 1971:93–94)

The lower walls of Portico 3 emphasize this practice (Figure 4.1). A Tlaloc-goggled warrior holds up a human heart impaled on a knife as he dances within a structure built in the Teotihuacan style. He killed his hapless victim, a captive taken in war, during great festivities held in the city of Teotihuacan.

MASCOTS AND MILITARY ORDERS

When exploring the nature of nagualism and the military at Teotihuacan, a cautionary note concerning individual versus collective belief needs mention. The Atetelco murals depicting sacrifice and transformation as well as the images of naguals engaged in cannibalism imply that the animal costumes of Teotihuacan went beyond clothing and engendered a mental conception of oneself as a transformed being. Yet, it would be foolhardy to propose that every individual embraced the supernatural implications. Many may have performed the act of dressing in costume without believing that their corporeal presence had altered, but the Teotihuacan system allowed for such non-believers because it institutionalized the animal imagery of warfare. Although a shamanic rationale may have underlain the existence of animal warriors at Teotihuacan, the real strength of the costumes was their ability to foster collective identities. The animal costumes of Teotihuacan do not seem to represent an individual as much as they designate groups of warriors who wore the same costume and shared an animal companion.

Clara Millon (1988c) has developed a very convincing argument that Teotihuacan had a series of military orders similar to the eagle and jaguar knights of the Aztecs.[17] Military orders are essentially elite groups of warriors who share titles, costumes, and heraldic symbols. A vessel from the site of Las Colinas near Teotihuacan expresses this concept in the clearest terms. On the bowl each warrior in the procession walks behind the symbol of his military order (Figure 1.19). Here, the heraldry includes such things as a bird, canine, feathered serpent, and a tassel headdress, the latter indicating that animals were not the only emblem of the military groups.[18] According to the argument, the animals and headdress function as heraldic images and signal the military order of each human. The military badges float above the humans just as name glyphs do in other Mesoamerican cultures, but in the Teotihuacan tradition there is a generic sense to the labels.

For instance, the bird and canine are not exclusive to the specific individuals on the bowl because elsewhere at Teotihuacan a particular animal costume appears on numerous individuals assembled together. In the murals of the White Patio, multiple copies of the bird and canine warriors cover the walls of the porticos (Figure 4.17). Because they all walk in the same direction, the arrangement seems to record a procession in which lines of bird and canine warriors move through space in some sort of ritual. In the apartment compound of Tepantitla, individuals wearing canine headdresses also process in a straight line, just as bird-costumed figures walk in single file on murals found along the Avenue of the Dead (Figures 1.11a and 4.18).[19] These last two examples pose a certain challenge because they do not carry implements that unequivocally identify them as warriors; however, even though they carry incense bags instead of atlatls or atlatl darts, they still have attributes that associate them with warfare. In both cases, the processing figures have obsidian blades incorporated into their costumes. The canine-clad individuals wear their blades in their headdresses, perched just below a spray of feathers. In a more obvious manner, the bird-costumed figures hold their blades aloft, each with a bleeding heart impaled upon the tip. Because the Teotihuacanos used these sacri-

FIGURE 4.17. View of mural with bird warriors, Portico 3, White Patio, Atetelco, Teotihuacan.

ficial blades on captives, the murals may show the aftermath of war. All in all, the similarity of their costumes to bird and canine warriors seen elsewhere suggests that these warriors have put down their atlatls and taken up the knives with which they sacrifice their captives.

Archaeological evidence corroborates the visual record through the preservation of the warriors' costumes themselves and the residue of rituals performed by these warrior orders. Included in the many sacrificial burials under the Pyramid of the Feathered Serpent are a number of warriors buried in mass graves.[20] Although debate continues as to how many of these warriors were Teotihuacanos or war captives from foreign sites, the remains indicate that the victims

FIGURE 4.18. Mural with procession of bird-costumed figures holding knives with impaled hearts, Portico 19, Zone 5-A, Teotihuacan. Drawing by Jenni Bongard after Séjourné 1966b:Figure 173.

wore Teotihuacan-style warrior costumes when they died.[21] Near the small of the back, archaeologists found small slate disks, and clusters of obsidian points were recovered next to the skeletons. Once covered with reflective mosaics, the disks are the remains of the warriors' distinctive back mirrors, and the points are all that survives of the atlatl darts placed with the victims. A number of rather brutal necklaces found on the bodies project an attitude of vicious bravado. Some consisted of actual human maxillae and a few mandibles strung together, while others were manufactured of shell fashioned to imitate teeth. Another subset included necklaces of canid maxillae, presumably affiliating the wearers with the canine warrior military order.[22]

Even more pertinent are the spectacular finds recovered from underneath the Pyramid of the Moon. Positioned under the structure's *adosada,* Burial 2 is an extraordinarily rich offering that sacrilized the fourth incarnation of the Moon Pyramid. The first three temples were rather modest in size, but Structure 4 was enormous compared with the earlier constructions. The offering dates to around A.D. 150 and included some of the most impressive artifacts ever found in archaeological context at the site (Schuster 1998; Cabrera and Sugiyama 1999; Sugiyama and Cabrera 2000; Sugiyama 2005:205). To one side of the chamber sat a sacrificed male with his hands tied behind his back. Copious offerings of greenstone, shell, and obsidian filled the rest of

the roughly square space. Near the center a large greenstone figure stood on a pyrite mirror ringed by obsidian bifaces placed in a radial pattern. Similarly, two exceptionally large figurines, one of greenstone and the other of obsidian, rested on another concentration of bifaces.

Anticipating the later burials at the Feathered Serpent Pyramid, the sacrificial male wore a shell necklace of imitation human maxillae, and numerous projectile points appeared in the chamber's offerings. The costuming and weapons of war provide strong evidence of military symbolism. Most interesting of all was the other skeletal material because it positions the military orders at this early point in Teotihuacan history. Placed in various locations within the space were the skeletal remains of several animals, including two pumas, a wolf, three rattlesnakes, one falcon, one owl, and nine eagles (Sugiyama and Cabrera 2000; Sugiyama 2005:205)

Tunneling even deeper, archaeologists found a second large offering, Burial 3, which was part of the next enlargement of the Moon Pyramid. Structure 5 was the first in this location to consist of a pyramidal base with an *adosada,* adopting the architectural format of the Moon Pyramid that is now visible. In a depression cut into the *tepetate,* the Teotihuacanos placed four sacrificial victims with their hands tied behind their backs. Following the pattern of the earlier deposit, these individuals were surrounded by obsidian projectile points, greenstone figurines, and shell pendants. One individual continued in the tradition of Burial 2 by wearing a necklace of imitation human maxillae made of shell. However, in this offering the ritual deposition of animals differed, for here only the heads of four pumas, fourteen wolves, and an incomplete owl skull were included. Presumably, these animals were sacrificed by decapitation, and their bodies were placed elsewhere (Sugiyama and Cabrera 2000; Sugiyama 2005:205).

Precisely matching the animal imagery that warriors wear in the art of Teotihuacan, the animals in the Moon Pyramid offerings seem to represent the various military orders. As stand-ins for the different groups, the animals function as substitutes for the warriors themselves, and the act of placing their mascots in this central pyramid highlights the prominent position the orders held in Teotihuacan society. Furthermore, the context of these offerings may indicate the critical role played by the military in Teotihuacan's growth. As Sugiyama and Cabrera (2000) noted, the first of these impressive burials coincided with the massive enlargement of the Moon Pyramid, which led them to conjecture that the increased prominence of military symbolism may have occurred at a time of dramatic expansion for the Teotihuacan state. In other words, these deposits may acknowledge that military conquest was a vital part of Teotihuacan's success.

The presence of the military pervades the site of Teotihuacan, constituting one of the most prominent iconographic themes in the city's vast artistic record. Reproduced in multiples, the costumed warriors are in constant motion, marching in parades long since over, but through the art, we can almost still hear their footsteps. The Teotihuacanos saw this imagery not only on their painted walls, but they held it in their hands when they picked up a vase decorated with a warrior's image. The impressive discoveries found within the Moon and Feathered Serpent Pyramids may include some of these very soldiers, although they could equally hold substitutes—animals and humans captured and sacrificed to represent this powerful social constituent. These rich caches positioned in the most public of architecture surely bespeak of the importance the military orders had to the state. By choosing the military orders as a central symbolic element of their civic architecture, the Teotihuacanos explicitly declared that the military was an integral component of state identity. The next question to be asked concerns the military's complex integration with the state, and the evidence points to the military as the unifying force that held together a fractious mixture of competing interests.

CHAPTER 5

A MARRIAGE OF CONVENIENCE

THE KING AND THE MILITARY

Like the mortar that holds a house together, the military orders provided the unifying force that bound the city into a concordant whole. While the military may have risen as a necessary part of establishing a new city, its later manifestation when Teotihuacan was at its apogee reflects an urgent need to counteract the oppositional forces of the other elements of the triad. Inherent tensions between the ruler and the powerful lineage heads would have been rife with detrimental effects. Such fractious relationships, not only between the ruler and the lineages but among the lineages themselves, could have threatened the stability of the city had the Teotihuacanos not devised social institutions that defused the pressure. The military seems to have done just that by engaging otherwise antagonistic parties into a common service that engendered a Mesoamerican form of civic responsibility.

Although evidence suggests that the lineages were well entrenched in every facet of the military, it was the ruler who stood to gain the most from a healthy military that stimulated widespread participation by the population. Reassessment of relative power and the subsequent realignment between lineages was evidently a chronic condition at Teotihuacan, and unchecked, it doubtlessly would have led to self-promotion and independent actions with little consideration of the social whole. Furthermore, as individuals tried to maneuver their lineages into the royal position, their loyalties to the ruler would have been extremely limited. The military, however, seems to have provided a social vent by establishing corporate bodies composed of otherwise antagonistic elements. Furthermore, it rallied these groups behind goals that were beyond individual motives. By fostering bonds of cooperation and fidelity, the military probably reduced oppositional pressures on the ruler and may even have created an environment in which his competitors might become his advocates.

Apart from the overwhelming quantity of visual imagery and archaeological remains, the subtleties concerning the nature of these military groups are largely missing. Fortunately, the Spaniards wrote down their observations on the military organization of the Aztecs, and this material may provide a model upon which to develop a hypothetical reconstruction of the Teotihuacan military orders. Durán (1971:197) devoted a whole chapter to an elite military class he labeled the Knights of the Sun. In his explanation, he described the various temples in Tenochtitlan, one of which was the Cuauhcalli, or House of the Eagles. Both his text and archaeological excavations indicate that this structure stood within the sacred precinct of Tenochtitlan, just to the north of the main pyramid.[1] In function, the Cuauhcalli served the purposes of warriors whom Durán called the eagle and jaguar knights. As he dutifully conveyed the elite status of these warriors, Durán explicitly stated that these men were celebrated in Aztec society.

They were the men whom the sovereigns most loved and esteemed, the men who obtained most privileges and prerogatives. To them the kings granted most generous favors, adorning them with brilliant, splendid weapons and insignia. No decision in war could be reached without them; not even the monarch could contradict their ordinances and command, and soon confirmed them. (Durán 1971:197)

Three important details may be gleaned from this passage. First, the eagle and jaguar knights enjoyed an elevated social status that allowed for certain privileges. Second, the sumptuary rights bestowed upon them by the king were one of these privileges. Third, they held a consultative position with the king in matters of war. Durán went on to state that there were other military orders, and a soldier rose through the ranks by distinguishing himself in battle. With each elevation in status, warriors were permitted to wear clothing that symbolized the new position. The highest and most coveted position was inclusion in the eagle and jaguar knights (Durán 1971:197–199).

The early colonial Codex Mendoza pre-

serves within its pages some of the many costumes worn by various military ranks (Figure 5.1).[2] Composed as a record of tribute owed to the Mexica, the manuscript documents the towns conquered by Tenochtitlan and the payment expected from each locale. From some defeated towns the expected tribute included warriors' military costumes, and the codex has detailed images of these highly perishable costumes that were otherwise lost to archaeology. The variety of animal and even skeletal costumes in this tribute list are well in accord with the military uniforms depicted at Teotihuacan and with the *wayob* that surface in the Maya area. The animal headdresses and furry one-piece suits manufactured for the Aztecs are so markedly similar to the costumes seen in the Teotihuacan murals that there must have been some continuity between these two central Mexican cultures. Furthermore, the Aztec system of ranking the different military costumes allows for a comparable stratification of the different Teotihuacan military orders.

Durán (1971:194–202) documented another important characteristic of Aztec social structure when he explained that there were both commoners and elites or, as he called them, aristocrats. Noting that the eagle and jaguar knights were certainly elites, he elaborated upon the rituals performed by the king when installing a new member of the order. After proving himself particularly courageous on the battlefield, the warrior received a new title, hairstyle, shield, and jewelry from the king. When not in his military costume, the warrior could also wear sandals and the cotton clothing so preferred over the scratchier maguey cloth. In addition, the ruler also exempted the knight from taxes, and many of his new rights were transferable to his descendants.

Ross Hassig (1988, 1992) mined rich ethnohistoric materials such as Durán to produce the most thorough studies of Aztec warfare to date. He focused on the ramifications of the military on the class system by emphasizing that the House of the Eagle and Jaguar Knights provided a sort of pressure valve for tensions between the classes. Of particular note is a category of warrior identified by Durán (1971:199) as the Gray Knights who literally fought their way out of

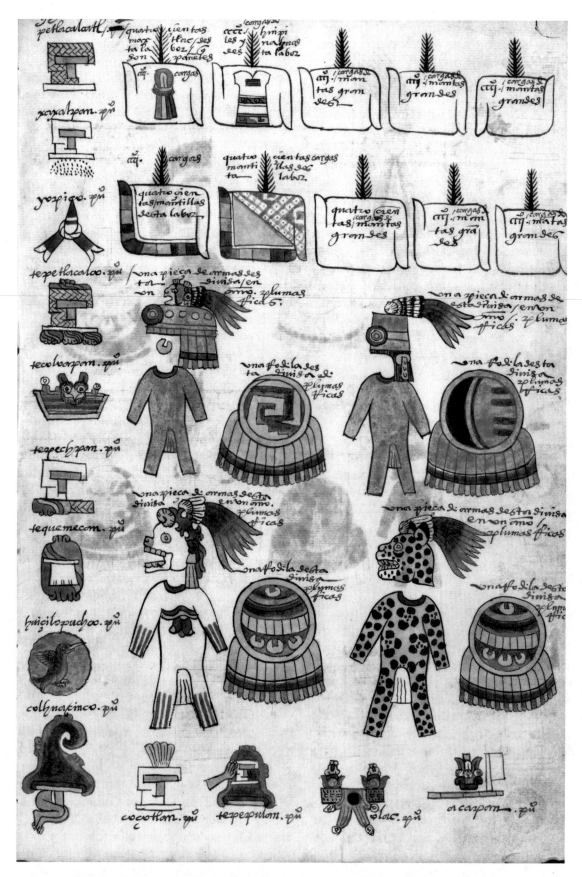

FIGURE 5.1. Page from the Aztec Codex Mendoza illustrating warrior costumes given in tribute, manuscript illustration, MS. Arch. Selden, A.1, fol. 2or. Photograph courtesy of the Bodleian Library, University of Oxford.

the commoner class to enter the ranks of the elites. Born into the lower classes, these men proved their bravery through military prowess and earned entrance into the eagle and jaguar knights. Because the arrangement allowed for social mobility, military service became especially attractive to commoners who had few other means of escaping their unfortunate birth.

Before we assume that the system was uniformly fair to all Aztecs, we must acknowledge that the elites received preferential treatment that almost guaranteed their military success. Noble sons went through special training in exclusive schools that virtually assured their initiation into the ranks of the eagle and jaguar knights, and a seasoned warrior accompanied the elite novice into battle to assist him in taking his first captive.[3] Even though anyone could rise in status through success in battle, the system was rigged in favor of the elites. Nevertheless, the promise of advancement was sufficiently attractive to motivate men to go into war and accept the social arrangement.

The abundant evidence of lineages at Teotihuacan implies that social mobility may have had an equally restrictive set of rules at this city. If descent was reckoned by preferred primogeniture, then it would not take many generations before an individual was sufficiently removed from the founding ancestor to warrant his demotion from the elite class. A safety valve similar to the one developed for the Aztecs would have been a particularly effective strategy for the Teotihuacan state. Those joining the military would have satisfied personal ambitions even as they acted in concert with the goals of the state, and if they were lucky enough to rise through the military hierarchy, they would be much less likely to contest the codified nature of hereditary rule.[4] Providing a more temperate view, Cowgill countered such materialistic arguments by suggesting that other irrational and less tangible motivational factors existed. He speculated that the virtue inherent in being a good soldier may also have driven the Teotihuacan citizenry (Cowgill 1993a:568, 1997:145–146, 2000b:59). Taken as a whole, a variety of motivational forces seems to characterize the Teotihuacan military. Hereditary ranking may have offered one form of stability to the state, but the military absorbed those pressures that fell outside the system by tolerating personal ambition and taking advantage of individual talent. In addition, something as familiar as patriotism may have fostered widespread participation in the military, but the result was the same: loyalty to the state functioned as a unifying force and bound the disparate voices into a whole.

Modeling the Teotihuacan military after the Aztec example offers a rationale for the popularity of martial themes in the city's art, but it is imperative that we address the idiosyncratic aspects of Teotihuacan's iconography to tease apart its differences from this later culture. First and foremost is the fact that Teotihuacan seems to have celebrated groups of people dressed in the same military costume, and several such groups existed. The groups that most frequently appear are the warriors wearing bird, canine, snake, and feline imagery. Often when depicted, these military units cluster in exclusive assemblies and do not mingle with members of other orders. That is, a mural commonly depicts only bird warriors moving in a procession, while another mural includes only canines (Figures 1.11a, 4.18). Notable exceptions to this appear on the Las Colinas vessel, where all of the orders assemble together, and at the Moon Pyramid, which contains the animal mascots of each order (Figure 1.19). These may represent rare occasions where the orders came together to show the unity of the state, but more often the different military branches appear to have been rivals. The visual isolation of the orders from one another as well as their oppositional arrangement in murals and archaeological contexts support this assertion.

By mapping animal imagery against archaeological stratigraphy, Rubén Cabrera (1987a) found evidence of hierarchies among the different military orders, and furthermore, he argued that these hierarchies fluctuated throughout Teotihuacan history. He suggested that the serpent order dominated the city in one period, while at another time, people associated with felines held power. With the preponderance of snake imagery on the Feathered Serpent Pyramid, he logically connected it with the snake order (Figure 5.2). This association is all the more interesting when we consider the dramatic remodeling that the temple underwent in the fourth century. At that

FIGURE 5.2. Feathered serpents and war serpent headdresses on the Feathered Serpent Pyramid, Teotihuacan.

FIGURE 5.3. View of the *adosada* (*left*), which covered the front façade of the Feathered Serpent Pyramid (*right*), Teotihuacan.

FIGURE 5.4. Serpent balustrades (*lower*) later replaced by jaguar balustrades (*upper*), West Plaza Complex, Teotihuacan.

time looters ransacked burials in the pyramid, and a new mural-decorated *adosada* replaced the sculpted facade (Figure 5.3). Apparently, the Teotihuacanos were not satisfied by simply covering the temple's front facade because there is overwhelming evidence of violence directed at the specific imagery of the Feathered Serpent Pyramid. Saburo Sugiyama noted that many of the sculptured heads were defaced by smashing, and some decorative stones were removed and used at other places in the city.[5] Although René Millon (1992:397, 1993:42) reported that the faded mural remains of the *adosada* once had imagery of a goddess, the murals are so deteriorated that this is difficult to confirm. Nevertheless, the imagery on the *adosada* could have represented a change in the Feathered Serpent Pyramid's imagery. Because the Ciudadela may have served as the residence of Teotihuacan's rulers, an iconographic

substitution could signal a change in the ruler's political alliance (Armillas 1964:307; R. Millon 1973:55).[6]

Two sets of stairs in a palace along the Avenue of the Dead preserve a shift in allegiance of a different sort. During excavations in the West Plaza Complex, archaeologists found two superimposed levels in the main patio (Morelos 1982:311, 1993:102–116). The lower level included a balustrade decorated with serpent heads, but at a later date, the patio was remodeled, and the new balustrade featured feline heads (Figure 5.4). Assuming that the animal imagery represented different military orders, there are two possible scenarios for this situation: the occupants could have changed their military affiliation at some point, or new individuals with different allegiances moved into the space. Taken together, these incidences of destruction and replacement

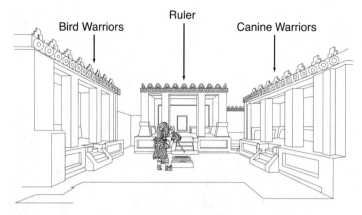

Bird Warriors   Ruler   Canine Warriors

FIGURE 5.5. Reconstruction of the White Patio, Atetelco, Teotihuacan. The patio is open to the west. Drawing by Jenni Bongard after Villagra 1952:Figure 1.

of animal imagery support theories incorporating the rise and fall of various military orders.[7] In the case of the Feathered Serpent Pyramid, the iconography engendered such feelings of anger that some people literally destroyed the imagery, while in the West Plaza Complex they obliterated it by burial. Thus, it appears that the prestige of heraldic animal imagery was a fluid thing throughout Teotihuacan history.

By affording careful attention to the relative arrangement of military imagery, we can also speculate upon the relationship of the military orders with the office of the ruler. To this end, the White Patio in the Atetelco apartment compound poses an interesting question because its murals ignore other military orders to exclusively pair the bird and canine orders with the ruler. One thematic element dominates each of the structures in the White Patio (Figure 5.5). The central and largest building has murals devoted to the ruler, with repeated images of the king filling the upper walls (Figure 2.8). To the north of this structure, the portico space celebrates bird warriors, while canine warriors command the final, southern building (Figures 4.2, 4.10). Physically the north and south porticos face one another, creating an opposition or pairing of the two military institutions. In turn, these paired orders seemingly support the king as they flank the royal iconography of the center. This thematic pairing may have been a long-lived topic at Atetelco; although the evidence is scant, canine- and bird-decorated plaques reportedly were found in association with the later Painted Patio.[8] Details

of the terra-cotta plaques were never published, but their mention suggests that the coupling of birds and canines continued at Atetelco after the abandonment of the White Patio.

Bird-canine pairing also appears outside Atetelco in murals from the nearby Tetitla apartment compound. In contrast to the White Patio, which may have been the main ceremonial area of Atetelco, Tetitla's Patio 25 is a minor patio with only two structures facing onto its central area (Figure 5.6). Nevertheless, the iconographic pattern is consistent with the White Patio. Canines with fanciful spots walk along the lower walls of the west portico, and canine heads cover the upper walls. Opposing this on the other side of the patio are bird heads and birds with outstretched wings. A wall seals one of the two remaining sides, and the other side of the patio opens onto a corridor. Both the flat wall and the corridor repeat the bird imagery, giving it a slight edge in importance due to its greater frequency.

The White Patio avoids privileging either the bird or canine because its middle space features the office of the king. The bird and canine orders are in equilibrium with the king at the fulcrum. If we view this triad of structures as a unified program where the arrangement of the iconography itself conveys a message, then there is one interesting conclusion. The physical positioning of the three decorative themes may express the actual political relationship between these social institutions. More clearly stated, there may have been a supportive arrangement between the ruler and these two orders, with the king recognizing the prominence of the bird and canine warriors, and the orders responding by supporting the office of the ruler.

Yet again, the Postclassic Aztecs provide intriguing parallels that help contextualize the arrangements seen at Atetelco and Tetitla. Indicating the social importance of military orders, the rationale for the eagle and jaguar knights was embedded in creation mythology. Aztec accounts of creation relate that the sun and moon first emerged at Teotihuacan where the gods Nanahuatzin and Tecuciztecatl modeled self-sacrifice by throwing themselves into a fire (Sahagún 1950–1982:III:1, VII:4). Metaphorically this act is described through animal imagery as the myth describes Nanahuatzin as an eagle whose blackened feathers resulted from scorching in the hot fire. Likewise, Tecuciztecatl takes the form of a jaguar whose spots are attributed to the burning he experienced when entering the fire (Sahagún 1950–1982:VII:6). These two gods then became the sun and the moon, and the animal imagery surrounding their brave act inspired the naming of the eagle and jaguar knights. Aztec mythology, therefore, connects the eagle and jaguar knights with creation, the two most important celestial bodies, self-sacrifice, and the admirable quality of bravery. The interesting placement of the event at Teotihuacan suggests that the Aztecs may have associated the origins of the military orders with the city. That is, the myth may record that the Postclassic Aztecs inherited the tradition of military orders from this earlier culture (Taube 1992c:78–79).

Just as the myth inextricably links the fate of the eagle and jaguar, so too Sahagún repeatedly coupled the Aztec eagle and jaguar knights, to the extent that he rarely mentioned one without referring to the other. The pairing is evident in his account of an aquatic battle.

And once again two boats came, so that there were four. Then there rose up two eagle warriors [and] two ocelot (i.e., jaguar) warriors. The first eagle warrior was Topantemoctzin; the second, Tlacotzin. And the first ocelot warrior was Temilotzin; the second, Coyoueuetzin. Thereupon arose an ocelot warrior [and] an eagle warrior. They poled them in with all their force; it was as if the boats flew. They went cautiously to Teteuhtitlan to head [the foe] off, to cut them off. And when they had gone, once again they dispatched two, another eagle warrior and another ocelot warrior. (Sahagún 1950–1982:XII:115)

Sahagún painted a picture where eagle and jaguar knights alternated in the tactics of war. The same is true after the war, for in the ritual of gladiator sacrifice, first a jaguar warrior brought out his captive and then an eagle warrior presented his captive (Sahagún 1950–1982:II:50–51). In life as in death, the eagle and jaguar warriors were companions, a belief epitomized in a prayer describing the warrior's heaven.

May there be peace, repose, for whomsoever is brought unto the lap, the bosom. . . . And may they in peace, in repose,

arrive among the valiant warriors, those who died in war, . . . the several eagle warriors, the ocelot warriors who are in the heavens where they gladden the sun, the turquoise prince, the valiant warrior, the one who died in war—they cry out to him there. (Sahagún 1950–1982:VI:11–15)

Throughout Sahagún's Florentine Codex, the repetitive coupling of the prose eternally binds the eagle and jaguar knights to one another, creating a bond that transcended even their earthly existence.

Mention of the eagle and jaguar knights also repeatedly tied them to a third political institution: the office of the king. A salient example is Durán's (1971:197) statement that the eagle and jaguar knights shared decisions concerning military matters with the king. In a rather poetic manner, Sahagún (1950–1982:VI:23–26) recorded that the status of the ruler directly affected the

FIGURE 5.6. Artist's reconstruction of the Portico 25 murals with birds and canines, Tetitla, Teotihuacan. Drawing by Christopher Wray after Séjourné 1966b:Figure 183.

members of the eagle and jaguar orders. When the ruler abused his position, the eagle and jaguar knights were troubled and wept. Likewise, so intimately was their well-being tied to the ruler, that when the ruler died, the knights professed their desire to die. Although such statements may reflect the exaggeration of public displays, a symbiotic relationship of power seems to have existed between the king and the military orders.

Such beliefs might extend to the sometimes fanciful way in which the Aztecs viewed the natural world. In a description of a creature called a *chimalcoatl*, or shield-serpent, Sahagún related that a person who saw the snake ". . . gains merit: he merits the eagle mat, the ocelot mat; it is said that he merits the estate of ruling general, of general" (Sahagún 1950–1982:XI:81). Especially pertinent is the mention of the mat, a well-established symbol of rulership throughout Mesoamerica. Durán (1994:297) said that the Aztecs called their king's throne the Cuauhipalli, which translates as "eagle seat," but he also called it a "jaguar seat." In turn, both eagle feathers and jaguar skins decorated the throne. The accounts of these Spanish friars coincide with the throneroom of another Aztec site, Malinalco, where eagle and jaguar thrones are sculpted into the living rock of a room once used for the installation of provincial rulers (Townsend 1992b:37). The Borgia Codex follows this tradition by pairing the eagle and jaguar thrones on the House of Corn page (Taube 1986:69). The thrones indicate the powerful role played by the military orders in the authority of the king, and the overall picture is one where the office of the king is intimately linked to the two military bodies.

David Webster's (1975) analysis of the evolution of the state provides a model for just this type of connection between the ruler and military orders. He began with the basic premise that others covet the status of the chief. While kinship can sanction a hierarchical organization, others of nearly equivalent rank and genealogy can easily challenge the current system. Warfare, initially, is unrelated to this inherent friction as it results from the emergent state's need to acquire limited resources. Eventually, however, military systems come to address challenges to the ruling office with the development of profes-

sional soldiers. Webster argued that two aspects of the military serve as a release valve for the pressures resulting from competition for rulership. First, membership in the military is not based on kinship; thus it provides a means for social mobility outside of lineage. Next, the institution itself provides offices and recognition for any emerging powerful individuals or groups of individuals. Webster highlighted the benefits of his model as follows:

Constant warfare not only provided an important and highly adaptive managerial function for emergent elite segments of society, but it also stimulated the acquisition of small amounts of "wealth" (i.e., basic resources) which were external to the traditional system and could be manipulated in various self-serving ways by these same groups to dampen internal dissension and attract supporters. Out of this milieu developed political and economic special interest groups which ultimately provided the basis for social stratification. (Webster 1975:469)

The integration of warfare into the structure of the state therefore offers new routes to power and wealth through non–kin-based alliances that have no genealogical claim to the office of the ruler.

Redmond (1983) adopted Webster's model in her study of early Zapotec developments in the Cuicatlan Cañada. She too believed that militarism contributes to the rise of the state, but she went on to stress that the military organization eventually acquires decision-making functions of its own. Her study of colonial writers in Oaxaca concluded that the Postclassic military institutions in this region were similar to those reported for the Aztecs. The military offered the potential to rise in society and had a political function that ranked below the ruling lineage (Redmond 1983:29). Archaeologically, the greatest evidence for Zapotec military orders appears in Period II (100 B.C.–A.D. 200). During this period, certain tombs and burials include jade nose plugs, a military insignia awarded to brave warriors. Furthermore, Redmond interpreted anthropomorphic urns depicting men in jaguar or bird costumes as the imagery of military orders (Redmond 1983:171–175). Citing the prominence of jaguar-suited men on Period IIIa

(A.D. 200–500) public monuments, she argued that military leaders assumed political positions.

Evidence from the Aztecs and Zapotecs reveals a Mesoamerican tradition of intimate connections between the military and the position of the ruler. In particular, the Aztecs developed a system of two military orders that ranked directly below the king, shared their insignia with the king, and contributed to the decision-making process of the state. Far from being absolute monarchs, the Aztec kings ruled with at least the partial consent of the eagle and jaguar knights.

The structural relationship between the murals of the White Patio suggests that a similar co-dependency may have characterized the political structure of Teotihuacan, a structure that probably inspired the later Aztecs. In that each portico has one thematic element, the physical arrangement of the murals seems to suggest the relationship of the actual political bodies (Figures 2.4 and 5.5). The imagery of the king appears in the central structure. This structure is larger, has a floor that is elevated above the other two, and probably had a higher roof. All of these elements indicate that this was the most significant building in the group. Certainly it is fitting that imagery of the highest political office appears in the most important structure.

Accordingly, the flanking buildings have a subordinate status. Ritual activities in these two structures probably supplemented the primary rituals in the central structure. It therefore follows that the imagery in these two buildings represents political institutions of secondary importance to the office of the king. The king may have needed the orders of the bird and canine warriors for support and legitimization, but the king nevertheless held the supreme position of power. What I am suggesting is that the physical arrangement of the murals reflects the actual political structure of Teotihuacan. The politics of Teotihuacan may have been envisioned as a triadic structure in which the primary governing bodies may have been the king and the military orders of the bird and canine warriors.

If Aztec parallels hold true for Teotihuacan, then the bird and canine orders may have supported the office of the ruler, and their symbols

may have been absorbed into the verbal and visual iconography of royal power. Teotihuacan expressions of kingship may have incorporated imagery of the military orders as a nod not only to their support for the office of the ruler but also as an acknowledgement of the very real power held by these military institutions. In the case of the Aztecs, the warrior orders seem to have held decision-making powers in the arena of warfare, and the orders of Teotihuacan may have held similar rights. The arrangement may have benefited and restrained each of the participating parties at the same time.

A system of mutual dependence between the ruler and the orders would also explain the location of the White Patio murals. Set outside the immediate public performance space of the Avenue of the Dead, the Atetelco apartment compound easily could have served as the residence of elites, but it could hardly house the ruler himself. What then would be the purpose of such royal imagery within this domestic structure? The most logical assumption would be that the inhabitants of Atetelco used the White Patio murals to assert their social position within the city. That is, they had something to gain from the messages stated in the artistic program. If residents of the compound held membership in either the bird or canine orders, then the murals would proclaim their political proximity to the highest office of the city. As a public space within an otherwise domestic sphere, the patio not only reminded the compound's inhabitants of their prominent social standing, but also informed visitors that the compound's participation in the military orders closely associated them with the ruler. The system of mutual benefit was complete because the Atetelco residents gained social status by proclaiming their intimate relationship with the ruler even as they relinquished potential hereditary rights by acknowledging the ruler's legitimacy.

The pairing of the bird and canine warriors in a select number of Teotihuacan mural programs may signal another critical aspect of the military orders. Webster (1975) emphatically argued that military institutions are not based on kinship; therefore, they directly address the friction inherent in a kin-based system. The murals of the

White Patio and Tetitla are in accord with this model (Figures 5.5 and 5.6). If the military orders were kin-based, then we would expect mural programs in lineage-based domestic settings to feature only one military order. However, these murals include imagery of the bird and canine orders, implying that members of both orders may have resided in the compounds. The murals therefore document group loyalties outside of kinship, alliances that were held in such esteem that the residents chose to feature them in their domestic spaces.[9]

Further parallels for the socially integrative characteristics of military orders come from the katsina societies among the Pueblos of the United States Southwest. While modern katsina societies are primarily involved in rainmaking rituals, Adams (1991:90) suggested that they were originally warrior societies. These societies may have developed in response to the pressures of migratory incursions and the subsequent re-structuring of populations. The period when the katsina societies first emerged coincided with a concentration of the population in a reduced number of locales and an escalation of conflict between villages (Adams 1991:145–151; McGuire 1986). Most importantly, the katsina societies functioned as sodalities that may have been open to all male members of the village. As Adams stated,

This katsina society, therefore, crosscut the social system in place in the late 1200s and 1300s. It served to integrate both the immigrant and the indigenous segments within the society, involving them in a common ritual purpose rather than individual or kin-only goals. (Adams 1991:155)

Thus, the katsina societies offered an alternative to kin rituals and a cohesive element to the Pueblo culture. They helped unite concentrated populations composed of different clans.

Ethnographic analogies with the Aztec also suggest that Teotihuacan's military orders probably crosscut the boundaries of kinship. The eagle and jaguar knights of the Aztecs included members of many different lineages. Like the katsina societies, the eagle and jaguar knights conjoined the various units that comprised Aztec society. The Aztecs recognized social divisions based on heredity and residential districts. As for the latter, the *calpolli,* or wards, were the most important. As Hassig proposed, the military had ties to a variety of these social institutions and was not, therefore, allied to any one element.

The members of the Aztec army had many different and cross-cutting loyalties—to the city, the *calpolli* (ward), the king, the calpolli headman, and so forth—and their rank did not depend merely on their position in a monolithic, centralized military hierarchy. (Hassig 1988:27)

The very complexity of competing loyalties seems to have created a web of common interests that interfused the various factions.

Although the katsina societies and Aztec military orders may have incorporated members of different lineages, it would be a simplification to suggest that such institutions were completely independent of kinship ties. For instance, ancestor veneration is an important feature of katsina societies, leading Plog and Solometo to question Adams' model and suggest that katsina societies may have had a lineage component (Adams 1991:9; Bunzel 1932:901; Plog and Solometo n.d., 1997; Titiev 1944). They emphasize that a single clan owns each modern katsina society and its rituals, even though general membership pulls from various clans (Plog and Solometo 1997:176–177). As for the Aztecs, certain conventions regulated membership in the eagle and jaguar knights. Although any warrior who took four captives gained entrance into the prestigious association, the nobility had advantages in this quest (Hassig 1988:45). Sons of noble families were sent to military academies, the *telpochcalli* and *calmecac,* which gave them substantial training. Besides having enhanced military skills, they had veteran warriors to assist them in their first battle. Such advantages eased the acceptance of nobles into the military orders. Furthermore, a young boy's lineage largely determined which *telpochcalli* or *calmecac* he would enter. The eagle and jaguar knights may have had a diverse membership, but it was surely skewed toward the powerful noble lineages.

At Teotihuacan, there is some evidence that lineage affected membership in warrior sodalities. Because the canine also appears on the lower walls of the White Patio's central portico, the members of this compound may have signaled their greater allegiance to the canine order by placing the canines in this otherwise royal space (Figure 4.11).[10] In contrast, the Tetitla artist of Patio 25 placed birds as a central motif, making this order more prominent (Figure 5.6). During the remodeling of the Feathered Serpent Pyramid and the West Plaza Complex, serpent imagery was likewise replaced with new iconographic programs, which may indicate new affiliations for these lineages. Such examples indicate that the Teotihuacan warrior sodalities may have mirrored the Aztec and Pueblo cultures with a complex system of membership that had elements both dependent on and independent of lineage.

Remarkably, the laws governing the military academies of the United States reflect this same delicate balance of diversity and heredity. In an effort to maintain a broad territorial distribution, entrance into the United States army, air force, and naval academies is effected by nomination. Every United States congressman and senator is allowed five postings at each academy at any one time. These laws ensure that no one state or region of the country can dominate the officer corps of a particular military branch. The system likewise acknowledges the executive office by allowing the vice-president to nominate candidates. The breadth which is legally mandated for these institutions is nevertheless tempered by what might be loosely termed lineage in the United States. There are special slots for individuals with a parent currently in the military or one that served a sufficient period, and the superintendent of each institution is able to appoint cadets who are the children of that particular branch of service. That is, at the air force academy a special category of nominations is reserved for the offspring of individuals enlisted in the air force. This special allowance as well as family traditions of serving in a particular branch of the military adds a kin-based character to the military, even in a nation founded in direct opposition to the hereditary traditions of Europe. The application of this process onto Teotihuacan reveals that military membership can depend on different modes of entrance that

need not be mutually exclusive. Mechanisms that both emphasized and undercut lineage could operate in tandem, resulting in sodalities with complex membership and competing alliances.

Discussing the American Southwest, Plog and Solometo (n.d., 1997) suggested that katsina societies may not have crosscut lineage; however, they did agree with Adams (1991) that the warrior societies had an integrative function. They argued that each katsina society may have had specific ritual functions or duties, with the full expression of community ritual dependent on the joint participation of all the katsina societies. The integrative qualities in their model stem from cooperative ritual instead of membership.

Warrior imagery at Teotihuacan is particularly illustrative when viewed in this light. Despite the frequent appearance of warriors in the city's art, narrative scenes of warfare are conspicuously absent. Instead, artists concentrated on images of ritual events after and perhaps before the war. Warriors dance in public spaces with sacrificial hearts or process in large assemblies fully arrayed in their military costumes. The depicted events seem to record the pageantry of ritual rather than the historical specifics of the battle and thus appear to have transpired within the city itself. The residue of these integrative public military displays is preserved inside the Moon Pyramid. By including the mascots of different military sodalities, the offerings reveal that civic rituals were designed to incorporate the various military groups. These characteristics indicate that warrior societies played an important role in the ritual life of Teotihuacan. Ritual performance by the warrior societies thus offered community-wide activities that strengthened bonds between the city's residents, and such performances unified the city in ways that went beyond simple membership in the military orders.

The social and political arrangement of the ruler and the military orders seemingly succeeds through its ability to address the tensions that arise from hereditary systems of rulership. In a discussion of state formation, Norman Yoffee explained that "[t]he ruling elite must also be able to reproduce itself, in part by providing access to its own inner structure" (Yoffee 1991:287). The open nature of warrior sodalities performs this function because status within the military satisfies ambitious individuals through non-hereditary routes. For the Aztecs, we have evidence that the association of the eagle and jaguar knights with the ruler was justified by creation mythology because the bravery of the eagle and the jaguar resulted in the emergence of the sun and moon. There is no clear evidence that the bird and canine warriors held these same celestial associations, but the murals in the White Patio similarly integrate these orders with another creation belief. As we shall see, at Teotihuacan, the political structure was viewed as the very expression of cosmic organization.

CHAPTER 6

THE GODS DID IT

THE DIVINE SANCTION
OF POWER

The murals of Atetelco's White Patio provide a unique opportunity to reconstruct at least one version of Teotihuacan's political structure because the three separate murals were so clearly designed as a unified program. While each discrete portico celebrates a particular social body, as a cohesive unit the structures describe the inter-relatedness of these social institutions. The north portico expresses the correlation between sacrifice and transformation, just as the centrality of the east portico records the ruler's supremacy over the groups upon which he is paradoxically dependent. The physical placement of the imagery in the White Patio is of critical importance, for the artists arranged the thematic elements with the intent of expressing the nature of Teotihuacan's social structure. This aspect of the White Patio underscores the significance of the architecture itself, and the exploration of the architecture, in turn, reveals the integration of Teotihuacan's political structure with the city's creation mythology.

The White Patio fundamentally consists of three structures arranged in a triad around an open patio. Each portico faces the patio, so anyone standing within the patio can easily view the murals. In the middle of the patio is the upper surface of a small altar that has never been fully exposed. A wall, probably a later construction, blocks the fourth side of the patio.[1] As a whole, the patio faces to the west, and stairs on the largest and most central structure indicate that the preferred movement through the space was from west to east; that is, moving though the patio and up the steps on the eastern portico.

The architectural space of the White Patio is notable not because it is special in any way, but because it is so typical of the sacred spaces constructed in the city. Numerous other spaces

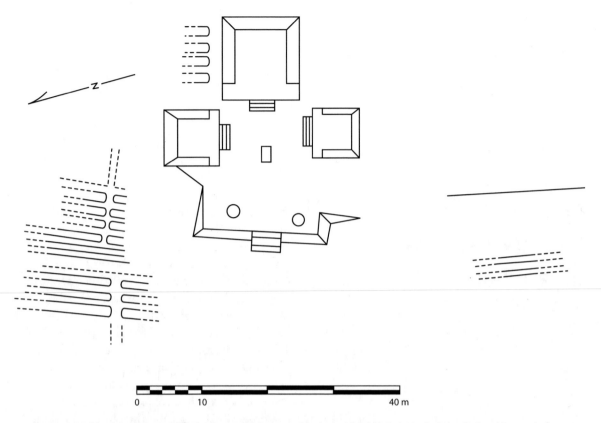

FIGURE 6.1. Residential structures of Operation 11 with furrows of agricultural fields, Tetimpa. Drawing by Jenni Bongard after Plunket and Uruñuela 1998:Figure 6.

throughout Teotihuacan have the same essential format, suggesting that Atetelco merely conforms to the city's dictates for religious space. Referred to as three-temple complexes, they consist of a triad of temples in which the central temple is usually larger (Wallrath 1966; Angulo 1987b). As a rule, these complexes are freestanding and not incorporated into apartment compounds; however, the similarities of the compound principal patios are sufficient to include them within this category. Resembling the White Patio, the three-temple complexes surround a quadrangular patio that has an altar or platform at its center. Further excavation is required for precise dating of the three-temple complexes, but Cowgill (1974:388) and Rattray (1992:4–6) assign them to the Tzacualli phase (A.D. 50–150).[2]

More recent work at the site of Tetimpa in the state of Puebla suggests that the triadic arrangement is a very old idea in central Mexico (Plunket and Uruñuela 1998). The importance of this site cannot be overstated because Tetimpa emerges as a "missing link" for those on a quest

to understand early Teotihuacan domestic architecture. The site's Late Tetimpa phase (50 B.C.– A.D. 100) immediately precedes the period when Teotihuacan built its apartment compounds and closely overlaps Teotihuacan's Tzacualli phase (A.D. 50–150), about which we have little information concerning residential architecture. As Plunket and Uruñuela revealed, these coexistent time periods share many ceramic features, which explains why Tetimpa architecture closely resembles aspects of Teotihuacan's subsequent constructions.

During its later phase, the fundamental housing unit at Tetimpa consisted of three structures opening onto a patio with a ritual altar at its center (Figure 6.1). The residential spaces could be described as Teotihuacan principal patios without the surrounding maze of rooms and delimiting outer wall. Instead of the dense urban concentrations of apartment compounds seen at Tlamimilolpa and Xolalpan period (A.D. 225–550) Teotihuacan, the domestic groupings are dispersed, and the furrows of agricultural fields are tucked right next to the houses of the more rural Tetimpa. Further paralleling Teotihuacan, the Tetimpa structures use *talud-tablero* construction, and modeled-daub decorations sometimes fill the recessed spaces of the *tablero*. On one structure the balustrades on either side of the stairs had long, undulating red forms of modeled-daub that Plunket and Uruñuela (1998:300–301) suspect are serpents. Such ornamentation would set a precedent for the serpent balustrades of Teotihuacan's Patio of the Jaguars and the Feathered Serpent Pyramid.

Even though they had a residential function, the Tetimpa triadic structures are not incorporated into apartment compounds, so they may represent central Mexican domestic architecture just before the full conception of the compound (Cowgill 2003a:48). Because the Teotihuacanos scraped the *tepetate* clean before building the apartment compounds, little information survives concerning early housing at the city. The archaeology of Tetimpa would suggest that the first domestic architecture was analogous to the Tetimpa tradition, with clusters of three structures (Manzanilla 2000). Later, as housing developed, the network of rooms comprising the apartment compound absorbed the triad, and this ancient form of domestic housing evolved into the principal patio with its three surrounding structures built in the *talud-tablero* style.

The Tetimpa model is important for several reasons. To begin, Tetimpa offers significant time depth to the triadic arrangement of structures around a patio and demonstrates that it predates the apartment compounds themselves. In addition, the retention of this triadic grouping within the apartment compound suggests that it carried important meaning for the Teotihuacanos. The conservative preservation of this architectural assemblage was apparently revered to the point that it was considered an essential component of domestic architecture. Finally, the original domestic function of the triadic space may indicate that the "ritual" patios may have held a residential function at Teotihuacan as well (Cowgill 1997:143). That is, the lineage head of the apartment compound may have lived in the central structure in addition to using the space to preside over ritual events in the patio outside.

While I feel strongly that the structures around the principal patios had a domestic function, we should not ignore the evidence for ritual events in these locations. In efforts to conduct a thorough analysis of activity areas within the Oztoyahualco apartment compound, Linda Manzanilla assembled a team of archaeologists and physical scientists that conducted chemical analysis of the floors, providing a picture of the floors not visible to the human eye (Barba 1986; Barba and Manzanilla 1987; Manzanilla 1990, 1991, 1993a, 1993b; Valadez and Manzanilla 1988). Minute traces of carbon and other chemicals identified areas where cooking occurred, and with flotation they obtained detailed data on plant remains that are often lost. The project also carefully recorded the location of larger faunal remains. Using the latest archaeological strategies, the daily life of the compound came to light, and an especially important pattern emerged from the faunal data. The remains of animals from distant regions—including bear, armadillo, marine mollusks, and jaguar—were concentrated in the principal patio, whereas the bones of animals consumed for food were concentrated in habitational areas. The difficulty in obtaining the foreign animals would have made them prestige items; consequently, their appearance in the patio identifies this as the locus of ritual activities or elite consumption of exotic foods (Valadez and Manzanilla 1988; Manzanilla 1990:82, 1991:8).

A look at the city as a whole reveals that three-temple complexes appear in several different scales and are ubiquitous, suggesting they permeated the religious thought of the Teotihuacanos. The triadic structures of the apartment compounds represent the smallest scale of this architectural feature. Proving its universal appeal, the grouping appears in the lavish palaces along the Avenue of the Dead as well as in the comparatively modest housing of Atetelco (Figure 6.2). Significantly larger versions of the three-temple complex are the freestanding examples identified by the Teotihuacan Mapping Project (Figure 6.3). During this survey, archaeologists found more than twenty of these complexes (Cowgill 1974:388). Most of these intermediate-sized triads are along the Avenue of the Dead. A limited few are away from the ceremonial center, within the residential areas but not physically attached to the apartment com-

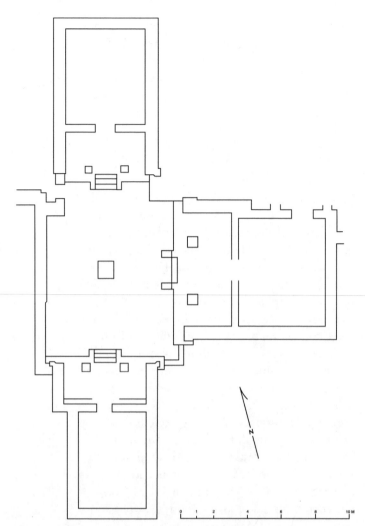

FIGURE 6.2. Plan of the White Patio three-temple complex, Atetelco, Teotihuacan. Drawing by Jenni Bongard after Miller 1973:Plate XIV-A.

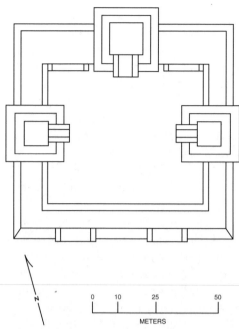

FIGURE 6.3. Plaza One, a three-temple complex in the northwest quadrant of Teotihuacan. Drawing by Jenni Bongard after R. Millon 1973:8, 17.

pounds. René Millon (1973:40; 1981:212–213) suggested that the temple complexes away from the avenue were barrio temples used for administrative purposes. However, Cowgill (1993b:123) cogently identified serious problems with viewing these temples as part of barrio-level administration. He noted that some pyramids seemed too large, while others were isolated from their proposed barrio. Furthermore, the midsized three-temple complexes are not evenly distributed throughout the city; although modestly concentrated in some areas, they are only sparsely represented in others. Most troubling is the fact that there are simply too few three-temple complexes embedded in the various Teotihuacan neighborhoods to justify their interpretation as administrative centers. Despite their apparent

ineffectiveness for broad administrative purposes, the midsized three-temple complexes could easily have served the needs of some select neighborhood rituals. As such they may have echoed the ceremonies of the more private apartment compound patios, but with a larger, more diverse group, thereby fostering neighborhood bonds. In a city as vast as Teotihuacan, participation in neighborhood-level civic and religious obligations could have furthered political control through the unification of ritual activity. However, the absence of the three-temple complexes in large portions of the city reveals the limited nature of this strategy.

The grandest three-temple complexes incorporate the two largest structures at the site, the Pyramids of the Sun and Moon (Figure 6.4). Each of these pyramids has a decidedly smaller pair of temples in front that frame a plaza with a platform at its center (R. Millon 1973:52, 1992:309; Pasztory 1992a:296). Although the scale of these pyramids is staggering, the ritual space is essentially the same as that found in the residential areas. If the rituals performed in these spaces were also similar, then the city would have promoted a unification of thought and belief through the replication of ritual at different levels. Thus, the magnificent public events performed before the Sun Pyramid may have been duplicated at a smaller scale within the increasingly private spaces of the barrio and apartment compound principal patios. Such replication would have fostered the development of civic identity and shared experience between the many people of Teotihuacan.

The enormous size of the Sun and Moon Pyramids argues for their role as models for Teotihuacan's other religious spaces. Many of the midsized three-temple complexes face to the south, suggesting they may have replicated activities that occurred in the Plaza of the Moon, but these appear to be exceptions. Most of the apartment-level three-temple complexes position the central, most important structure on the eastern side of the patio, with the principal building facing west, just as the Sun Pyramid does.[3] The organization of these architectural spaces indicates that the Sun Pyramid was an archetype for a large number of three-temple complexes in the city. Reiterating the importance of the westerly facade, the small altars or platforms in the apartment compound patios usually have a set of stairs on their western side. Whether symbolically climbing the tiny stairs of the miniature temples or entering the main structures in the patios, the flow of motion is from west to east. The same is true of the Sun Pyramid. To enter its space requires climbing the stairs on the east side of the Avenue of the Dead. Inside, the central altar has its stairs on the west side, as does the Sun Pyramid itself. In all these examples, movement is from west to east.[4]

The paradigmatic westerly orientation of the Sun Pyramid may have derived from an astronomical phenomenon visible from the cave underneath it. During the Tzacualli period (A.D. 50–150) observers at the entrance of the cave could watch the sun set on the same spot on the western horizon two times a year.[5] The critical sightline between the cave and the western horizon is 15°30' north of west, which is perpendicular to the 15°30' east of north seen in the Avenue of the Dead (Cowgill 2000a:360–361; R. Millon 1973:36, 52–53, 1993:35). This indicates that the astronomical observation from the cave was the baseline from which the Teotihuacanos determined the arrangement of their main

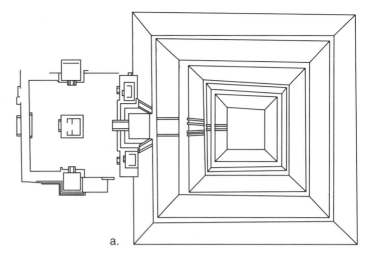

a.

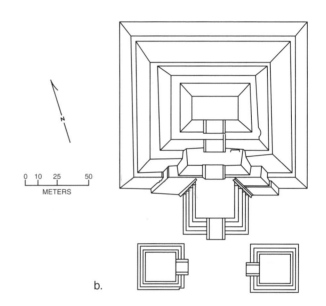

b.

FIGURE 6.4. The Sun Pyramid (*a*) and Moon Pyramid (*b*) as three-temple complexes, Teotihuacan. Drawing by Jenni Bongard after R. Millon 1973:18, 19, 31, 45.

street. One of the most distinctive characteristics of Teotihuacan is how many of its structures rigidly adhere to one of two axes within the city (Cowgill 2000a:360–361, 2003a:43). The most prominent is the orientation of the main avenue, while the other is an east-west axis of 16°30' south of east. Based on readings taken of the Sun Pyramid, R. Millon (1973:53) suggested that the east-west axis evolved later; therefore, during the Tzacualli phase the astronomical event associated with the Sun Pyramid cave may have dictated the early site plan. In turn, if this astronomical event could influence the map of the entire city, it is

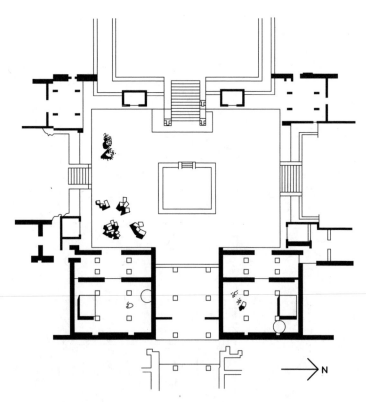

FIGURE 6.5. The West Plaza Complex with stairs on the west side of the central altar, Teotihuacan. Drawing by Jenni Bongard after Morelos 1991b:Figure 1.

easily believable that the pyramid constructed over the cave could have been a model for other religious structures in the community.

Doris Heyden has argued that the cave under the Sun Pyramid was probably the earliest focus of ritual at Teotihuacan, possibly even a pilgrimage destination before the building of the city as we know it.[6] Later, an architectural construction of three temples replaced this cave, and perhaps the architectural grouping itself subsumed the meaning of the cave as the Teotihuacanos built three-temple complexes all over the city. A few of these broke with the traditional orientation, but by far the majority preserved the directional reference by maintaining a west-facing arrangement.

Slight alterations to three-temple complexes on the west side of the Avenue of the Dead reveal just how much the Teotihuacanos valued the symbolism of a western orientation. Living on the west side of the street posed an interesting dilemma. Unlike compounds on the east side, entrance to these compounds is from the east, necessitating an east to west movement. Such an

approach precludes a west-facing structure without forcing the visitor into a circuitous route. In addition, the strong linear directionality of the Avenue of the Dead reveals the Teotihuacan preference for direct routes and clearly defined approaches with straight access. Apparently, this latter need overrode the lesser requirement of patterning a three-temple complex after the Sun Pyramid.

A perfect Teotihuacan solution to this problem appears in the West Plaza Complex positioned along the west side of the avenue (Figure 6.5). The main building (Structure 40A) of this compound faces east, which is the opposite orientation of the Sun Pyramid but allows the structure to face a visitor entering the compound. To compensate for the unorthodox orientation, the small altar in the patio has its stairs on the traditional west side. Usually the principal structure and the altar share the same directionality, but the modification here allowed the patio to maintain a symbolic connection with the Sun Pyramid.[7] This same adjustment in the altar stairs appears just to the south in the Superimposed Buildings Compound (Figure 6.6a), but even farther south, architects came up with another solution. The principal structure in the Northwest Compound has stairs on both the east and west sides of the building (Figure 6.6b). This may represent an attempt to provide a western access to the structure, paralleling the Sun Pyramid, even though it breaks with the more common singular access seen in most Teotihuacan temples.

Any discussion of three-temple complexes should note that some apartment compounds have four structures arranged around the principal patio. This is best seen at Tetitla and Zacuala, where structures enclose the principal patios on all four sides; nevertheless, these patios do retain the traditional directionality by placing the largest building in the east (Figure 6.7). However, careful attention must be given to the plans of such patios, for some triadic arrangements could easily be misconstrued as groupings of four. Upon initial investigation the Painted Patio at Atetelco and the main patio of Yayahuala appear to be quadratic arrangements (Figure 6.8).[8] Closer examination reveals that the fourth structure on the west side has a doorway piercing the rear wall. Thus, the additional building func-

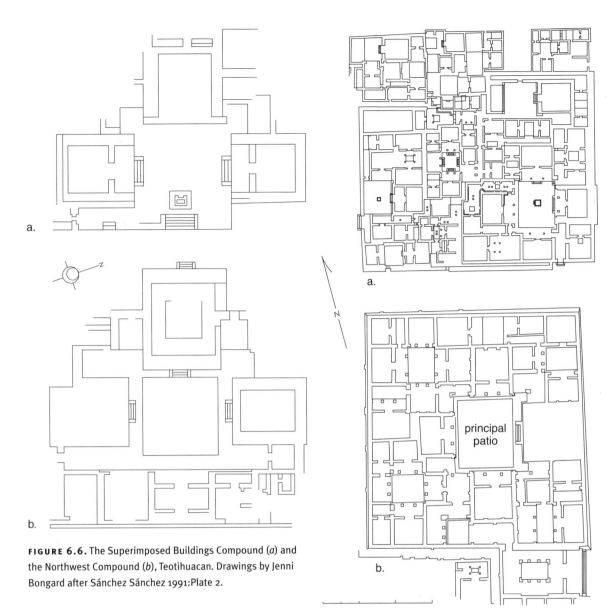

FIGURE 6.6. The Superimposed Buildings Compound (*a*) and the Northwest Compound (*b*), Teotihuacan. Drawings by Jenni Bongard after Sánchez Sánchez 1991:Plate 2.

FIGURE 6.7. Plans of the Tetitla (*a*) and Zacuala Palace (*b*) apartment compounds with their four-temple complexes. Drawing by Jenni Bongard after Miller 1973:Plates XIII, XI.

tions not so much for housing people or events, but as an elaborate doorway to a triadic patio. In the case of Yayahuala the western doorway allows access from the exterior of the apartment compound itself. This would have created an impressive entrance for visitors as they entered Yayahuala, for their first view would be the grand space of the principal patio. Entrance into this compound would have also mimicked the experience of entering ritual spaces in the city center. To reach both the Sun Pyramid and the principal patios of the compounds directly on the Avenue of the Dead, a visitor would have climbed up a set of stairs, crossed a platform, and then descended into the patio space. The main entrance to the Yayahuala apartment com-

pound reproduces this sequence and thereby forges special connections between the center and periphery.

At Atetelco, where there is some relative stratigraphy, the White Patio dates earlier than the Painted Patio, indicating that the elaborate structural doorway may have been a later adaptation of the triadic patio. Currently, there is insufficient evidence to state just how early the true quadratic arrangements date. The desire to recover murals has driven most excavations of Teotihuacan apartment compounds, so only a

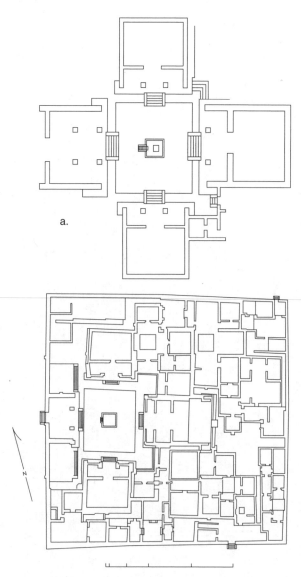

a.

FIGURE 6.8. Four-temple complexes with a door in the west temple: *a)* Painted Patio, Atetelco, Teotihuacan; *b)* Yayahuala, Teotihuacan. Drawings by Jenni Bongard after Miller 1973:Plans XIV and X.

pan (A.D. 300–450) residents also moved their ritual space farther south than the initial Early Tlamimilolpa (A.D. 225–300) temple (Widmer 1987:330–338). Atetelco and Tlajinga 33 suggest that only full excavation of Tetitla and Zacuala would reveal if quadratic patios always characterized these compounds. Likewise, excavation of the Xalla Compound to the southeast of the Moon Pyramid may explicate the nature of its patio surrounded by four structures. Clarification of this issue will require further testing to determine if the quadratic patio always existed at Teotihuacan or represents an important remodeling of ritual space. In either case the existence of quadratic patios indicates that Teotihuacan had an alternative to the three-temple complex or experienced modification of its ritual activities.

With the quadratic patios serving as one qualifier, the quantity of three-temple complexes constructed at Teotihuacan clearly demonstrates the importance of this architectural space. The Sun Pyramid stands as the greatest expression of the three-temple complex, and smaller versions reproduced this most sacred location. Copies of the Sun Pyramid space maintained the west-facing orientation or tried in some way to acknowledge this precedent. The astronomical events associated with the Sun Pyramid may explain the orientation of the structures but do little to elucidate the rationale behind their triadic nature. To understand this, it is necessary to look broadly to Mesoamerica's mythological traditions.[9]

THE THREE STONES OF CREATION IN MESOAMERICAN COSMOLOGY

The triadic arrangement of ritual structures frequently appears in Mesoamerica and is not unique to Teotihuacan. Among the most memorable are the three temples on Stage 1 of Structure A-V at Uaxactun. Tatiana Proskouriakoff memorialized this structure in a stunning set of drawings that showed how the triadic arrangement eventually evolved into a complex palace (Proskouriakoff 1963:111–129). Furthermore, the addition of Temples I and II in Tikal's Great Plaza may have been done to restore an earlier triadic arrangement that had been con-

sparse number have been excavated uniformly to bedrock. More importantly, few have been excavated with careful attention to the contents of different stratigraphic layers, resulting in uneven information on construction sequences. Some excavations have demonstrated that the location of a principal patio may shift within an apartment compound. For instance, the Painted Patio, which replaced the White Patio at Atetelco, is farther south than its predecessor. At Tlajinga 33 the Late Tlamimilolpa–Early Xolal-

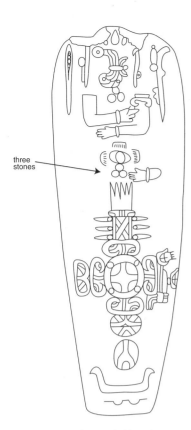

three
stones

FIGURE 6.9. The Humboldt Celt, greenstone, Olmec.
Drawing by Jenni Bongard after Joralemon 1971:25.

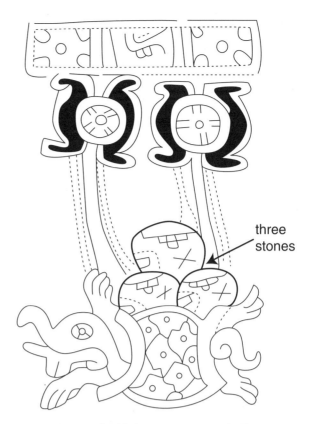

three
stones

FIGURE 6.10. Turtle with three stones, manuscript illustration,
the Codex Madrid, Postclassic. Drawing by Jenni Bongard after
Freidel et al. 1993:Figure 2.16.

cealed on the North Acropolis. This penchant
for building ritual structures in threes is effectively explained through the creation story that
survives in fragments scattered throughout the
various Mesoamerican cultures.

One of the clearest accounts of creation appears on Stela C from the Maya site of Quirigua.[10] The text on the monument states,

On the date 4 Ahaw 8 Kumk'u
The three stones were set.
The Jaguar Paddler and the Stingray Paddler seated
    a stone.
It happened at the First-Five-Sky-Place, the
    Jaguar-throne-stone.
The Black-House-Red-God seated a stone.
It happened at the Earth Partition Place, the
    Snake-throne-stone.
Itzamna seated the Waterlily-throne-stone.
It happened at the Lying-down-sky place, the
    First-three-stone place.
(Freidel et al. 1993:66–67; Schele and Looper 1996:92)

This passage describes one of the first acts of creation, which involved placing three stones at the
heart of the world. Corroborating this Classic
period text are numerous other textual and visual
accounts of this same event. The Humboldt Celt
(Figure 6.9) from the Formative Olmec shows
the event as it happened (Reilly 1994). Above a
cluster of symbols probably representing the four
cardinal directions, a disembodied hand places
three circular elements. In this case cloud symbols and an eye signal that the stones are stars in
the sky. A much later Maya document, the Postclassic Madrid Codex (Figure 6.10), also indicates
that the three stones are a constellation. In this
image, the stones are clearly identified by their
cauac, or stone markings. Just as the Olmec celt
positioned the stones in the sky, the codex stones
rest upon the back of a turtle constellation that
hangs from a skyband.

Further textual evidence of the widespread
nature of this myth comes from the Postclassic

Aztecs. The Codex Chimalpopoca includes instructions that were given to the ancestors of the Aztecs. After shooting arrows in the four cardinal directions, they were told,

And when you have shot your arrows
place them in the hands of Xiuhtecutli,
the God of Fire, the Old God
the three who are to guard him—
Mixcoatl, Tozpan, and Ihuitl
these are the names of the three hearth stones.
(Knab and Sullivan 1994:63)

In this version, even the names of the hearthstones survive, and the god of fire definitively sits in the midst of the stones.[11]

Another Postclassic example comes from the Mixtec culture in a codex image that collapses different moments of the creation story. At the beginning of the Selden Codex, three stones appear just below a tree from which the Mixtec ancestors emerge (Figure 6.11). The image closely matches Classic period Maya texts in which the placement of the three stones is subsequently followed by the separation of the sky from the earth

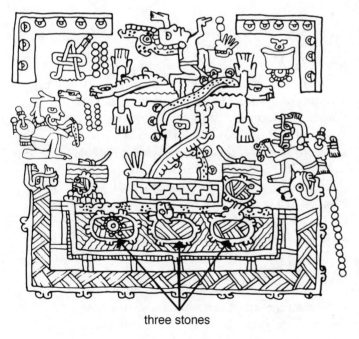

three stones

FIGURE 6.11. Three stones under the world tree, manuscript illustration, Codex Selden, Postclassic. Drawing by Linda Schele, © David Schele, courtesy of the Foundation for the Advancement of Mesoamerican Studies, Inc., www.famsi.org.

and the erection of the world tree at the center of the universe.[12] Thus, the tree in the Selden Codex represents the creation of vertical space and the centering of the world, and the emerging Mixtec figure above signifies the first peopling of the world.

Given that the placement of the three stones is the initial act of creation, it can be viewed as the incipient action that set all other events on their inevitable course. By situating the stones, the gods established the center and created a location from which the rest of the world could emanate; therefore, the stones came to represent not only the heart of the world but its very creation. While Olmec and Maya images unequivocally identify the stones as a constellation in the sky, the stones also existed on the human plane of the earth.[13] Every traditional Maya household has its own version of the three stones in the form of its hearth, which consists of a griddle balanced on three stones, an arrangement physically mirroring the Aztec triad of stones surrounding the Old Fire God. In a beautifully prosaic manner the three stones existed on the earth as well as in the sky, and all Maya lived at the center by virtue of placing a reproduction of this symbol in their houses. On a grander scale, the Maya of Santiago Atitlan believe that the three volcanoes that surround their town are the sacred stones of creation, although in their version, the mountains were the first land to emerge from the primordial waters. This notion fits well within the Atitecos' contention that evidence of supernatural presence in the world is visible in objects such as lakes, mountains, or a small piece of jade. One of the lessons to be taken from Santiago Atitlan is that natural mountains as well as manmade ones can be physical expressions of the mythical first stones.[14]

If individual households actively claimed to inhabit the center, efforts to assert this distinction for communal spaces was even more pronounced. The construction of soaring triadic temples in Maya cities was an overt declaration of the centrality of ritual space and the city as a whole.[15] In turn, the widespread nature of this myth indicates that the Teotihuacanos shared a creation story that included the placement of the three stones. Because there is evidence of this myth throughout the temporal and geographic areas of Mesoamerica, it would be logical to assume that the Teotihuacan three-temple complexes mirrored triadic arrangements elsewhere and symbolized the three stones of creation. Indeed the obtrusive embeddedness of the three-temple complexes at every level of Teotihuacan life forcefully argues for their high degree of symbolism. With these complexes appearing in apartment compound, neighborhood, and community versions, Teotihuacanos were never very far from architecture that reminded them of the creation story and their own centrality to the universe. All Mesoamericans, it seems, believed that they uniquely lived at the center, but the Teotihuacanos ratcheted up the proposition by looking to the natural features surrounding their city and asserting that the earthly stones of creation were tangibly present in the Teotihuacan Valley.

THE THREE MOUNTAINS OF TEOTIHUACAN

A review of Teotihuacan iconography reveals several motifs used repetitively in the art of the city. One of these is referred to as the three-mountain motif. The design consists of three inverted U-shapes clustered in a triangular arrangement (Figure 6.12). In some cases small circles punctuate the faces of the mountains, while in others a diagonal line across the top is strikingly similar to a mountain snowcap. Curious antennae-like lines occasionally emerge from the superior mountain, but an example where flowers grow from the same spot indicates that these lines represent vegetation. Long recognized as a standard symbol in Teotihuacan's visual vocabulary, scholars have associated the motif with fertility, water, and vegetation—qualities commonly applied to imagery with a more opaque meaning (von Winning 1987:11–12). In light of the ubiquitous nature of the three stones of creation in Mesoamerican myth, I would argue that an affiliation with the creation story is a more likely identification.[16] Teotihuacanos, like the Maya of Santiago Atitlan, apparently interpreted the three stones as three mountains, and it is the natural environment that justifies this assertion.

Teotihuacan is located in a broad basin encircled by mountain ranges, among which three

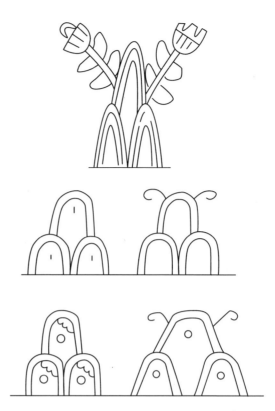

FIGURE 6.12. Three-mountain motif, Teotihuacan. Drawing by Jenni Bongard after Séjourné 1966a:Figure 94 and von Winning 1987:II:13, Figure 14a.

peaks emerge as the most prominent: Cerro Gordo in the north, Cerro Patlachique to the south, and Cerro Malinalco on the western horizon. In his extensive study of Teotihuacan Valley geography, Manuel Gamio (1979:8–14) emphasized the visual distinction of these mountains, publishing a photograph and extensive description of each one. Although there is no indication that he made any connection to the three-mountain motif, he seems to have recognized the visual particularity of Cerros Gordo, Patlachique, and Malinalco. Gamio's isolation of the three mountains could be coincidental, but there is much to suggest that the Teotihuacanos similarly acknowledged the special nature of these three prominent peaks.

The position of Cerro Gordo within the city planning of Teotihuacan is so obvious that it takes little to assert its importance (Figure 1.1). The Avenue of the Dead runs directly on access with the wide, sprawling mountain, so much so that the street seems designed to take the visitor to the mountain's base. In a very profound manner, Cerro Gordo serves as the focal point for the entire city. The mountain's relationship with the city reveals another strategy used by the Teotihuacanos to assert its symbolic presence: the integration of architecture with the natural environment. The city's design places the Moon Pyramid directly in the middle of the mountain, synthesizing the two masses into a unified whole. The pyramid's sloping diagonals mimic the mountain's profile so that Cerro Gordo symmetrically frames the structure. Nevertheless, the most dramatic contrivance incorporated into the architecture surfaces as one walks north up the avenue. As one nears the temple, the Moon Pyramid appears to get ever larger, just as Cerro Gordo seemingly submerges behind the structure. In effect, the Moon Pyramid replaces the mountain, indicating that the temple is the manmade replication of Cerro Gordo (Cowgill 2000a:361; Linné 1934:32–33; Tobriner 1972:104). Through this optical illusion, the Moon Pyramid is visually and symbolically Cerro Gordo.

The name *Cerro Gordo,* or "fat mountain," is unfortunate given the distinct importance the mountain held in ancient times. The original appellation may have been much closer to the name used by the Nahuatl speakers living in the area when the Spanish arrived. The Nahua called the mountain Tenan, "mother of stone," which more clearly matches the mountain's particular characteristics (Berlo 1992:147; Nuttall 1926:11:47; Tobriner 1972). The cleft at the peak of Cerro Gordo communicates its original symbolism to the inhabitants of Teotihuacan. Marking the mountain as an extinct volcano, the cleft is a highly diagnostic feature of the mythological Sustenance Mountain.[17] Found repeatedly in different Mesoamerican cultures, Sustenance Mountain typically has maize vegetation sprouting from the cleft, designating it as the source of this staple food. Aztec accounts of this myth have Quetzalcoatl transforming into an ant, whereby he burrows into the mountain and emerges with maize kernels in each color of the four cardinal directions. The Maya, on the other hand, frequently envisioned the mountain as a turtle carapace from which the Maize God emerged after his sons cracked open the shell (Freidel et al. 1993:281; Taube 1985, 1986).

Apart from maize imagery, the iconography of Sustenance Mountain frequently has streams of water and fish at its base, thereby conflating this mountain with the Aztec concept of *altepetl,* or "hill and water" (Heyden 2000:176; Matos Moctezuma 2000:188). The water symbolizes the mountain's role as a microcosm of the world, which was fundamentally a mountain floating in a primordial sea. Even today, large pools of water often collect in the Plaza of the Moon after a rainstorm. The sight of the Moon Pyramid rising up from the glassy, water-filled plaza may have periodically heightened the effect of the pyramid as Sustenance Mountain.[18] Furthermore, oral tradition in the Teotihuacan Valley preserves an intimate connection between Cerro Gordo and water.[19] Teotihuacan's agriculture benefited from irrigation made possible by a number of natural springs, but local tradition maintains that Cerro Gordo is the source of all the valley's water. The mountain was likened to an inverted *olla,* or ceramic vessel, filled with water. Adding some realistic basis for this belief are reports of locations on the mountain where one can even hear the water sloshing about in the vessel. Though difficult to scientifically verify, these sounds are thought to result from the auditory effect of lava tubes threading through the mountain (Cowgill 2000a:361; Nuttall 1926:76; Tobriner 1972:110–111; Taube 1986:52). Thus, in concert, the Moon Pyramid and Cerro Gordo represented the two most vital staples of life: maize and water. Through their massive size and looming presence, the mountain and pyramid surely suggested the city's role in providing its residents with sustenance, a beneficent message that was difficult to escape.

Teotihuacan's design initially draws the visitor into the Plaza of the Moon, but one only needs to pivot 180 degrees to understand how purposefully the second mountain was incorporated into the city's symbolism. The optimal location is from atop the Moon Pyramid, where the view south exposes the close association of the Sun Pyramid with Cerro Patlachique (Figure 6.13). With remarkable accuracy, the pyramid precisely echoes the profile of the mountain behind it as both descend in a series of matched, uneven steps. Even though the cave beneath the Sun Pyramid may have prompted the building of the structure, the final design appropriated the

FIGURE 6.13. View of the Sun Pyramid with Cerro Patlachique in the background as viewed from the Moon Pyramid, Teotihuacan.

surrounding landscape and married the two into one fused vision. Just as the Moon Pyramid is an artificial reproduction of Cerro Gordo, the Sun Pyramid is a manifestation of Cerro Patlachique.

The mirrored effect of pyramid and mountain is all the more astounding when considering the unorthodox excavation practices of Leopoldo Batres near the turn of the nineteenth century.[20] Batres believed that he would find an earlier, better preserved version of the temple in the interior, so using dynamite, he removed a layer measuring approximately 5 meters. When no such building emerged, he began to consolidate the fragile exposed areas without clearly distinguishing between the consolidated and removed layers. The resulting appearance of the structure has certain anomalies, including the odd split staircase and the thin fourth body of the temple that is singularly smaller than the other four bodies comprising the pyramid. Both of these features are most likely artifacts of excavation practices, and it is likely that neither reflects the structure's original appearance. Bastien (1967:64–65) believed that the original pyramid only had four bodies and that the small body "discovered" by Batres was really a misinterpreted drainage canal. He held that the fourth body is actually part of the third body. A remarkably detailed

panoramic drawing of Teotihuacan published by W. H. Holmes in 1897 supports Bastien's assertions (Holmes 1897:Plate XLIX). Made before any excavations had commenced, the drawing shows the Sun Pyramid with only four bodies, and no small body disrupts any of these. Troubling as the circumstances surrounding its excavation are, the Sun Pyramid's correlation with the mountain beyond maintains that all was not lost in these early years of archaeological exploration. The overall general silhouette of the pyramid imitates the outline of the mountain behind. Battered and bruised, the pyramid still forges its symbolic attachment to Cerro Patlachique, thereby associating the structure with a foundation stone of creation.

To reveal the final mountain, the apex of a pyramid once again provides the optimal view. This time the climb must be up the Sun Pyramid, from which the view to the west has fewer large geological features than the other directions. To the north and south, Cerro Gordo and Patlachique definitively dominate the visual experience. Behind the Sun Pyramid is a long, relatively consistent range of mountains from which no peak emerges with any distinction. But to the west, there are areas bereft of projecting mountains, and the mountain range that does

FIGURE 6.14. View from the Sun Pyramid including Cerro Colorado (*left*) and Cerro Malinalco (*right*), Teotihuacan.

emerge is significantly more modest in scale. Viewed from the Sun Pyramid, the western horizon has a low set of mountains that gradually rise to the most prominent peak, Cerro Malinalco (Figure 6.14). The relative smallness of Malinalco might challenge its identification as the third stone of creation, but this would ignore the substantial effect resulting from its isolation. Because the western horizon is so unencumbered with visual elements, the punctuation of Cerro Malinalco is all the more effective. Even today Mexico recognizes the mountain's visual prominence with an enormous Mexican flag planted at its summit.

Another disconcerting aspect of the mountain is the fact that Cerro Malinalco sits just off center, slightly to the north of the main axis of the Sun Pyramid. More directly across from the pyramid is the much lower Cerro Colorado. The

Teotihuacan tendency to integrate architecture with the natural environment raises questions. If Malinalco was the third hearth stone, why did the Teotihuacanos not pivot the Sun Pyramid to face it? Furthermore, is it possible that Cerro Colorado is the more likely candidate, despite its unremarkable appearance? The answer to these questions involves the astronomical observations of the western horizon that were so important to the Teotihuacanos.

While exploring the astronomy of Teotihuacan, Anthony Aveni investigated the phenomenon of pecked crosses, which generally consist of two concentric circles of dots bisected by a cross (Figure 6.15).[21] They appear on Teotihuacan's plaster floors, on stone outcroppings in the mountains surrounding the city, and in several other locations in Mesoamerica.[22] The one that most intrigued Aveni was a pecked cross on the

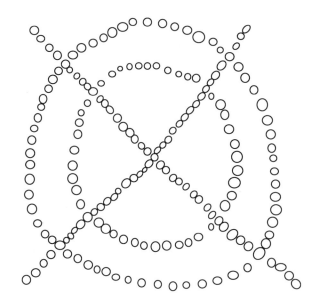

FIGURE 6.15. Pecked cross from Cerro Gordo, Teotihuacan. Drawing by Jenni Bongard after Aveni 1980:223.

slopes of Cerro Colorado that marked the setting of the Pleiades star cluster on the day of solar zenith passage. Occurring around May 18, the sun would have cast no shadows at noon on this day, and it would have coincided with the arrival of spring rains that made planting possible.[23] In combination with the sightline from the Sun Pyramid cave, this pecked cross documents the astronomical significance of the western horizon and Cerro Colorado. These mountainous ridges were arguably associated with stories of creation that influenced the city's distinctive orientation.

The astronomical associations of Cerro Colorado may have led to its identification as the third creation stone, even though the isolated prominence of Cerro Malinalco would have made it the obvious choice. While I favor the visual impact of the latter, there is a real danger in underestimating the importance of astronomical events to the ancient Mesoamericans. Another factor to consider is that the Teotihuacanos may not have categorized mountains in the same fashion that we do, and they may have conceptually affiliated Cerro Colorado with Cerro Malinalco. When viewed from Teotihuacan, the mountains appear connected by a low ridge, which may have justified their identification as one mountain. Certainly it would have been

more spectacular had the astronomical event occurred over Cerro Malinalco, but by clustering the mountains, the Teotihuacanos may have massaged their environment to fit their mythological ideals.

The painstaking care with which the Teotihuacanos harmonized their architecture with the landscape and the stars suggests a reverence for particular characteristics of the natural environment. By constructing their architecture to reflect and recognize Cerro Gordo, Cerro Patlachique, and Cerro Malinalco, they advertised their particular interpretation of the creation story. Standing in the ceremonial heart of the city, Teotihuacanos could merely look around them to see that their city was extraordinarily blessed because, they may have reasoned, the three mountains in their valley were the actual stones placed by the gods at the beginning of time. With this belief they saw themselves at the sacred heart of the universe, and, as René Millon once wrote, "the place where time began."[24] Because all Mesoamerican cultures tended to argue for their own centrality, this strategy was probably not unique to the city; however, at Teotihuacan we see a rather aggressive campaign to promote their location as the place of creation. The repetitive use of the three-mountain motif codified this message by constantly fostering an association between the city and its sacred landscape. The massive scale of the built environment would have reinforced the city's assertions, as would the manmade replications of the three stones in the form of architecture.

Once the three mountains of the Teotihuacan Valley emerge as the three hearth stones of the creation story, the meaning of the three-temple complex appears with greater clarity. The temples can easily be viewed as symbolic mountains because there is a long tradition connecting Mesoamerican ritual structures with mountains. Locally at Teotihuacan, the visual coupling of the Sun and Moon Pyramids with their respective mountains is clear testament that temples were metaphorical mountains. Maya hieroglyphic inscriptions use the word *witz,* or mountain, to refer to pyramids, and the Aztecs of Tenochtitlan called their main temple Coatepec, or Snake Mountain. Given this precedent and evidence of

Teotihuacan's celebration of the three creation stones, the numerous triadic architectural groups in the city appear as nothing less than symbolic versions of the first act taken by the gods. In essence, the three-temple complexes were ritual surrogates for the three mountains, architectural attempts to promote this ideal and provide spaces within which to celebrate Teotihuacan's exalted position in mythological history. From the triadic temple cluster of the Sun Pyramid to the neighborhood and compound versions, the three-temple complexes reinforced the mythical centrality of Teotihuacan at all ritual levels.

Because Mesoamerican traditions consistently associate the three stones with a hearth, we would expect to see evidence of fire rituals within Teotihuacan's three-temple complexes. Signs of such activities are most clearly visible at the apartment compound level. Séjourné (1964) found burners in front of the altar in the central patio of Tetitla, and Old Fire God braziers frequently appear in or near the principal patios of Teotihuacan's apartment compounds, some directly associated with the patio's central altar (Figure 6.16).[25] These braziers depict the same hunched over and aged man that the Aztecs called Huehueteotl, and the Codex Chimalpo-

poca recorded that the three stones were to guard this god. Moreover, the miniature temples at the center of the principal patios may themselves fall into the cult of the Old Fire God. Robert Zingg described a Huichol shrine to this deity.

The Shrine of Grandfather Fire is one of the most highly sacred spots in the entire Huichol country. It is a miniature temple no larger than a god-house, near Santa Catarina. It is made in miniature, since everything of the gods is small, like toys. (Zingg 1938:352)

Such a description closely fits the diminutive pyramids found in Teotihuacan apartment compound patios (Figure 3.1). The archaeological recovery of braziers within the associated spaces implies similar rituals among the Teotihuacanos and the Huicholes. Overall, the strong evidence of fire rituals inside the three-temple complexes strengthens the proposition that this architectural space symbolizes the three stones at Teotihuacan. Just as the triad of temples provided a landscape appropriate for creation reenactments, the patio inside served as a location to ignite the primordial fire in the hearth.

ATETELCO'S WHITE PATIO: RECONCILING MYTH AND POLITICAL STRUCTURE

The standardization of art and architecture at Teotihuacan is a notable characteristic of this great city. Remarkable for a preindustrial metropolis, a great deal of art was made by using molds, which allowed imagery to be mass produced and widely distributed. The city's streets adhere to a rigid grid, aligning to one of two directions, and the apartment compounds represent another attempt to systematize life (R. Millon 1973). By including ritual spaces reflective of the ceremonial center, the apartment compounds fostered common experience and unification of belief. If an apartment compound had its own three stones in the form of its principal patio, then we might expect the replication of state political agendas within these domestic spaces.

One of the most intriguing examples of this replication of political agendas appears in the White Patio of Atetelco, where the art and architecture work together to contrive a logical

FIGURE 6.16. Old Fire God brazier, Teotihuacan. Drawing by Jenni Bongard after von Winning 1987:I:114, Figure 1.

justification for human political constructs. Already, I have offered much explanation of this principal patio with its three porticos. Imitating the Sun Pyramid's orientation, the central structure opens to the west, with flanking temples to the north and south (Figure 5.5). The image here identified as the king decorates the upper walls of the central portico, just as members of the bird military order dominate the northern portico, and canine warriors commandeer the southern portico. This much has been explicated, but the final symbolic coup de grâce emerges when the mythological significance of the space is taken into consideration.

At their most fundamental level, the structures of the White Patio represented the three stones of creation about which Teotihuacan seems to have formed its identity. However, the application of imagery onto the walls of those structures amended the message and provided a distinct interpretation of the creation story. Rather like the notational gloss of a medieval manuscript, an apartment compound's choice of decoration offers insight into the beliefs of that particular familial group. What makes the White Patio so interesting is that its residents employed the space to promote a supernatural rationale for the nature of Teotihuacan's political structure. The patio represents an incidence of state propaganda within the context of domestic ritual space.

When the artists used their red and white paint to affix images on the White Patio's walls, they not only fused pigment but ideology with the architecture. By placing the image of the ruler in the central and largest structure, they conveyed the king's position in the social structure. His centrality in the patio reflected his apical status in society. Likewise, the deposition of the military orders on the flanking portico walls symbolized their political affinity with the ruler and possibly a mutually supportive arrangement with him. Just as the eagle and jaguar knights sustained the Aztec *tlatoani,* the Teotihuacan military orders may have bolstered the royal office through political and martial assistance. However, the White Patio took this one step further when it overlaid this political message onto the mythological narrative, for in essence the White Patio likens the three social institutions to the three stones of creation.

The programmatic nature of the murals and the mythically infused symbolism of the space indicate that the White Patio makes an analogy between the three political bodies and the first act of the gods. Thus, the residents of the White Patio may have associated the king with one stone, the bird warriors with another stone, and the canine warriors with the final stone. In other words, as the gods placed the stones, they not only marked the center, but also created the various social groups that would govern the city. The genius of this strategy is that it allows for a politically charged interpretation of the creation story. If each stone is ideologically merged with a specific political institution, then, it could be argued, the gods actually ordained the city's political structure. The creation story would emerge not only as the establishment of the physical world, but also as the conception of a political structure.

Because the gods devised this political arrangement at the beginning of time, challenges to the system could always be rebuffed with divine justification. The marriage of the political structure with the creation story would vindicate many avenues designed to defend the status quo. For instance, political rhetoric might assert that the gods would unleash their wrath on anyone who might try to alter their celestial plan, and the ruling parties could easily label alternative suggestions as unnatural or heretical. The strategy allowed for the fundamentalist claim of an absolute divine mandate that was rigidly permanent. Seemingly flawless with its heavenly backing, the argument for this particular political arrangement would have seemed unassailable.

But Atetelco's White Patio is simply one of many such ritual spaces, and it is possible that others viewed the creation story differently and attached alternative meanings to their triadic arrangements. Statistically, the number of apartment compounds excavated at Teotihuacan is simply too small to fairly judge if the White Patio's recognition of the bird and canine warriors as the ruler's favored groups was a widely held belief. To complicate matters more, the upper walls of these structures rarely survive, so our knowledge of their iconography is further jeopardized. These voids in our understanding of the great city necessitate the customary ac-

FIGURE 6.17. Door jamb murals with eagle and jaguar warriors, Cacaxtla, Terminal Classic. Drawing by Jenni Bongard after Stuart 1992:124, 129.

knowledgement that the interpretation of an archaeological culture is always conditional.

Data that temper the White Patio's elevation of the bird and canine warriors include the archaeological and iconographic evidence that other warrior orders existed at various times in Teotihuacan's history. One of the grand offerings

under the Moon Pyramid included raptorial birds and canines that could arguably represent the warrior orders seen on the White Patio's walls. However, the offering additionally contained the skeletal remains of a feline and a serpent, which may suggest the presence of these warrior orders in the ritual deposition of these materials. The subsequent Moon Pyramid offering omitted the birds and only celebrated felines and canines, so by the time this cache was placed, maybe bird warriors had fallen in stature. Echoing the materials buried within the Moon Pyramid are the militarily dressed felines among the Zacuala murals and the heraldic appearance of the snake on the Las Colinas vessel. Such imagery would imply that a number of orders used animal imagery, which further confuses any determination of their relative hierarchy.

We should recognize that the political situation in Teotihuacan certainly changed over its roughly 600 years of existence, and the prominence of particular orders may have been temporary. The suppression of serpent imagery at the West Plaza Complex coupled with the wholesale destruction of this creature on the facade of the Feathered Serpent Pyramid are important indicators of political realignments (Cabrera 1987a; Cowgill 1997; Sugiyama 1998). Whether new inhabitants commandeered these spaces, or the existing residents simply repositioned themselves to fit with evolving political fashions, the alteration of costly status markers such as sculpture certainly projected a public statement about the inhabitants' political or social affiliations. The danger for the modern researcher may be the quest for a single, static explanation of Teotihuacan's political structure; nevertheless, Atetelco's White Patio may not be the isolated vision of one familial group.

Patio 25 at the apartment compound of Tetitla also pairs bird and canine imagery, suggesting that Atetelco's residents were not alone in distinguishing this political couplet (Figure 5.6). In this more minor patio, birds with broadly spread wings face off with spotted canines in an arrangement that harkens back to the White Patio. However, Tetitla is rather close to Atetelco, and the proximity of these two compounds may indicate that this was a barrio-level argument. These two examples, in any case, are far from providing a statistically comforting number. It is when one looks beyond the immediate scope of Teotihuacan to the cultures that rose in its aftermath that the pairing of warrior orders seems more solid and less like the isolated assertion of a few people.

Fresh on the heels of Teotihuacan the murals from the Terminal Classic (A.D. 650–900) site of Cacaxtla incorporate a message of militaristic dualism that may have grown from traditions established at Teotihuacan. The battle mural overlooking an open patio features bird and, in this case, jaguar warriors pitted in violent opposition. The scene exhibits an interesting mix of narrative and staged elements as the obvious victors of the battle, the jaguar-clad warriors, proceed to subdue the bird warriors in a most gruesome manner.[26] Just off the patio is a set of door jambs that echo the coupling of these two animals (Figure 6.17). Each door jamb has one warrior painted on its surface; one wears a jaguar costume replete with jaguar boots and mittens, while the other is clad in eagle feathers. Unlike those in the larger mural, the jamb figures are removed from the fray of battle even though the jaguar figure's enormous bundle of atlatl darts references war. Each warrior stands on a serpent whose skin consists of either feathers or a jaguar pelt to match the individual above. In essence, the jaguar or bird imagery consistently infuses the imagery of each jamb so that these two figures emerge as iconic representations of the bird and jaguar militants seen in the more narrative battle mural. The pairing of these figures on the door jambs is clearly purposeful, so their iconic nature not only revolves around each of these representative warriors, but the very coupling of the warriors becomes an icon in and of itself.

A final example of the bird-jaguar motif at Cacaxtla definitively asserts that this militaristic couplet was a dominant ideological theme at the site. This set of murals appears on the walls flanking a stairway (Figure 6.18). The walls are seemingly free from any overt martial imagery save the clear pairing of the bird and jaguar. These walls depict a rather lush natural setting in which feathered serpents ascend the stairs with accompanying bands of water filled with copious life forms. The walls are almost identical, but much like a reflection of opposites, the pres-

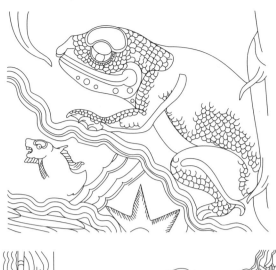

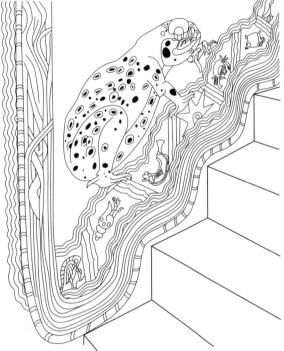

FIGURE 6.18. Opposing murals with a blue frog and a jaguar frog, Cacaxtla, Terminal Classic. Drawing by Jenni Bongard after Stuart 1992:135, 136.

ence of a different animal dominates each side. In an almost comical manner a toad covered in jaguar skin opposes a more common looking blue toad that blends in with the blue feathers of the serpent. The repetitive use of the pairing throughout the Cacaxtla complex speaks to the symbolic importance of the animal dualism at the site even as it resonates similar couplings at Teotihuacan.

Much has been said here about the Aztec military orders of the eagle and jaguar knights, but further mention is warranted in the context of this discussion. In a manner resembling Teotihuacan imagery, the Postclassic Codex Mendoza illustrates a wide variety of military costumes that go well beyond eagles and jaguars (Figure 5.1). The costumes include skeletal, deer, and spotted creatures. Just as we see in the art of Teotihuacan, the manuscript reveals a diversity of military costuming.

In his extensive treatment of Aztec warfare, Ross Hassig (1988:27–46) explained that a host of accoutrements were used to designate a complex number of distinctions. Military accomplishments dictated everything from hairstyle to the fabric of one's clothes. A flower-decorated mantle was the reward for the taking of the first captive, and by taking a second captive, the warrior earned a red-trimmed mantle. Noble members of the military orders wore feathered costumes into war, but commoners who had gained entrance into this prestigious group fashioned their suits from animal skin. Apart from the various insignia awarded to men who took captives in war, the *tlatoani* conferred other insignia on his warriors as a form of encouragement before important battles. Some members of the military, including the ruler, had personal insignia, such as the human skin on the standard of King Axayacatl or the *tlauhquechol* bird used by Motecuhzoma. The picture of Aztec military costume is decidedly complex and infinitely adaptable over time. This fluid example, which allowed for the whims of rulers and accommodated individual accomplishments, provides a worthy comparison for the variety seen in Teotihuacan military dress. As Aztec costume recognized a number of factors—rank, class, achievement, historical events—so too may the apparel seen on Teotihuacan's warriors reflect numerous social categories.

Despite the many costumes recorded in the Codex Mendoza, the rhetoric of the Mexica consistently featured the eagle and jaguar orders at the expense of other groups. The text of Sahagún's Florentine Codex repeatedly includes metaphorical references to the eagle and the jaguar and clearly implicates their role in supporting the office of the king. In the poetic format that typifies the manuscript, the orders are symbolic of exemplary warriors and function as

societal role models. The codex suggests that the state nurtured a vision of the military orders as the ideal citizens of Tenochtitlan. Durán also devoted significant space to an explanation of the eagle and jaguar knights, recalling their connection with royal symbols and their participation in decision making.[27]

Furthermore, the rationale behind the names of the orders was grounded in the creation story. The Aztecs maintained that the gods gathered together at Teotihuacan to determine which of them would become the sun and moon. Tecuciztecatl, a rather self-confident god clad in exotic feathers and fine jewels, offered himself for the mission, but the more humbly dressed Nanahuatzin gladly agreed only after being nominated by the gods.[28] The gods then fashioned the Pyramids of the Sun and Moon as locations for the chosen gods to perform penance, and after four nights, they were dressed to sacrifice themselves on a great fire that had been laid. Despite four attempts to rally his courage and throw himself on the fire, Tecuciztecatl was unable to perform the task. The gods then called upon Nanahuatzin, who bravely entered the fire without hesitation. Realizing that his opportunity for greatness was passing him by, Tecuciztecatl finally cast himself on the fire. From the fire Nanahuatzin rose as an eagle representing the sun, and Tecuciztecatl emerged as a jaguar symbolizing the moon. The myth rationalizes the gods' appearance, explaining that the darkened wings of the eagle resulted from the searing heat of the scorching fire, but the skin of the jaguar was only burned in spots because the fire had cooled due to his hesitation. Thus, the gods had succeeded in creating the sun and moon, but to their dismay, the two celestial bodies did not move. To accomplish this, all of the remaining gods sacrificed themselves, after which Ehecatl, the wind god, set the skies in motion.

Even though Tecuciztecatl exhibited some vacillation in his resolution, the act of these gods was directly analogous to the bravery expected of the Aztec warriors. These two main protagonists had sacrificed themselves so that the world could come into existence, and as a reward, they became the most prominent features of the heavens. By naming the most elite corps of warriors after the eagle and the jaguar, the state made analogies to the creation story and encouraged emulation. The Aztecs similarly asked their warriors to sacrifice themselves for the good of the larger whole. Their acts of bravery essentially mimicked the very acts of the gods which made life possible.

These cultural and temporal comparisons reveal a picture of central Mexico in which there is a consistent pairing of animals in military imagery. The Classic period coupling of Teotihuacan's Atetelco apartment compound continues in the murals of Terminal Classic Cacaxtla, and in the subsequent Postclassic the Aztecs evidently appropriated this strategic rationale. In all of these examples two iconic animals function as mascots, and they are displayed in oppositional arrangements that definitively link them into a complete whole. At Cacaxtla, the martial association is overt because the artists positioned the two orders in the midst of a battle, while at Teotihuacan the inclusion of weapons may be comparatively more subtle, but the theme of militarism is ever present. The Aztec adoption of this military system was probably a major factor leading Tenochtitlan to conquer vast territories and effectively establish an empire. The union of paired animal imagery with military institutions was successful because it created a vehicle by which the state inspired individuals to do its bidding.

The constancy of this mythical and iconographic theme indicates that the pairings seen at Teotihuacan are not the isolated visions of individual families living in particular apartment compounds. Even though the surviving evidence for a bird and canine coupling is relatively slim in Teotihuacan's archaeological record, the reemergence of this theme throughout central Mexico argues for its existence as a state institution. In other words, it is highly possible that the canine-bird murals of Atetelco and Tetitla expressed state concepts of political organization even though they appear within the context of domestic space.

It is additionally clear that the Aztecs incorporated their mythological tradition within their political structure, and if the positions argued here are accurate, then Teotihuacan may have been the city where this strategy was first expressed. Indeed, the Aztecs even went so far as to say that creation occurred at Teotihuacan, which potentially indicates that the Aztecs inherited their mythological traditions from this earlier central Mexican city. Even though the Aztecs may have substituted jaguars for the Teotihuacan canines, the similar mythical and iconographic threads imply that Teotihuacan may have had a cognate myth about solar and lunar creation. Both cultures, it seems, manipulated the creation story to explain the close relationship of the ruler with the military orders. In an idiosyncratic twist, Teotihuacan looked to the natural environment and found there the expression of another aspect of the creation story. The city's residents interpreted their mountains as the sacred residue of the gods, as the very stones first placed at the beginning of time. Then, as the murals of Atetelco suggest, they rationalized their system of governance by linking the three stones of creation with the office of the king and the military orders that supported him. By equating human political constructs with religious doctrine, the state's preferred institutions gained logical and moral foundations even as they promoted certain kinds of behavior that were favorable to the state. It is this tendency of the state to shape the actions of its citizens that forms the next chapter in Teotihuacan's story.

CHAPTER 7

TEOTIHUACAN JIHAD

The pageantry of warriors parading across the walls of Teotihuacan and the fantastic deposition of the warrior orders' motifs within the Pyramid of the Moon bespeak the active and vital role played by the military in the great city. Their social prominence was sufficient to warrant the celebration of their imagery at the city's largest temples and in its most intimate domestic settings. By sharing the ideologically charged ritual spaces of the center with these orders, those who ruled Teotihuacan could acknowledge their indebtedness for the political support the orders offered even as they socially elevated the orders' members. Participation in these elite corps must have bestowed on these men a good deal of prestige, which they could then use as social currency.

Even though we must not discount the value of this social capital, there appears to have been another incentive program at Teotihuacan that further fueled the military machine. This motivational weapon was more personal in nature and appealed to the warrior's belief in an afterlife. It addressed concerns for self-preservation and preyed upon the ego as it promised heroic immortality. This catalyst to action was stunningly effective because it was perhaps the most prominent propagandistic tool used by the Teotihuacan state. Visual reminders of this coercive strategy were omnipresent in the city, thereby promoting a daily renewal of the vows between the state and its warriors. This brand of propaganda was inescapable because it lined the streets that Teotihuacan's citizens traversed every day.

The medium for this propaganda was architecture, and more specifically, it was the particular style of Teotihuacan's architecture, called *talud-tablero* (Figure 1.4 and Figure 3.20). This distinctive style is easily recognized by its two component parts. The upper portion consists of a rectangular box, or *tablero*. At Teotihuacan the *tablero* generally has a depressed middle with a projecting frame around its perimeter. Below this is a sloping element referred to as the *talud*. The architectural style is ubiquitous in the city, gracing many temples found in the ceremonial center and forming the facades of structures around the principal patios of the apartment compounds. *Talud-tablero* construction epitomizes the Avenue of the Dead, which is dominated by a continuous band of this architectural style.

The ensuing argument suggests that *talud-tablero* functioned as an identity marker for Teotihuacan's citizens, creating a sense of civic pride and fostering a collective ideology, especially for individuals involved with the city's military engagements. Although I maintain that the architecture communicated a specific ideology of warfare that shaped the actions of individuals and motivated the population to support state-sponsored activities, I in no way mean to suggest that *talud-tablero* architecture outside the city of Teotihuacan carried the same coded messages. The clear chronological evidence from Tetimpa decisively establishes that *talud-tablero* construction predates Teotihuacan in central Mexico, and there is no surviving evidence that the inhabitants of Tetimpa ascribed any military associations to the architectural style.[1] Furthermore, apart from areas like the Esquintla region of Guatemala, where there are suggestions of the most direct forms of Teotihuacan influence, there is little to indicate that *talud-tablero* constructions or imagery in Oaxaca or the Maya region necessarily had martial content. Instead, this argument intrinsically applies to Teotihuacan itself, and the audience for the militant symbolism of the architecture was primarily the city's own citizenry.

The repetitious use of *talud-tablero* at Teotihuacan has led many scholars to fuse this style with the city's identity just as Classic period peoples living elsewhere in Mesoamerica must have intimately associated the architecture with Teotihuacan. The connection is so complete that the appearance of *talud-tablero* structures abroad often leads scholars to suspect the foreign presence of Teotihuacanos or emulation of Teotihuacan. Thus, *talud-tablero* structures at Tikal have been

used as one indication of Teotihuacan visits to this site, and use of the distinctive style on the Great Pyramid of Cholula is interpreted as an ideological or political affiliation with the central Mexican power. Such conclusions have lately been challenged by arguments that the appearance of *talud-tablero* construction abroad may have stemmed from multiple catalysts.[2] Nevertheless, the omnipresence of *talud-tablero* construction at Teotihuacan warrants the suggestion that Teotihuacanos used this form of architecture as an identity marker, and even though scholars universally recognize the importance of *talud-tablero* to Teotihuacan's identity, few have attempted an explanation of its meaning. Most recently, Matos Moctezuma (2000:188) associated the form with the natural environment, likening the *taludes* to the slopes of mountains.

Although the relationship of architecture with landscape is well documented in Mesoamerica, I would submit that the *talud-tablero* of Teotihuacan was more narrowly defined with a cultural specificity that was unique to the city. Namely, the architectural style so distinctively associated with Teotihuacan had meanings entrenched in the institution of warfare, and which, interestingly enough, revolved around a delicate insect. To the Teotihuacanos, I hope to demonstrate, *talud-tablero* symbolized an ideology of warfare that was visually conveyed through the butterfly.[3]

THE BUTTERFLY IN TEOTIHUACAN ART

Support for this seemingly implausible hypothesis requires a full exploration of the butterfly in the art of Teotihuacan. This creature makes frequent appearances in the corpus of Teotihuacan imagery, and it sometimes appears at Teotihuacan–influenced sites abroad. Not restricted to one medium, butterflies flit along the surface of murals, ceramic vessels, and censers. The iconographic treatment of butterfly imagery even suggests that the butterfly was a popular theme for personal adornment: a certain segment of Teotihuacan society, a military group, wore butterfly-shaped noseplaques.[4] The most impressive store of butterfly iconography abroad appears on the Teotihuacan–influenced censers found in the Esquintla region of Guatemala,

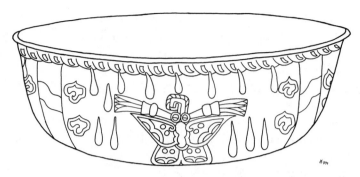

FIGURE 7.1. Frescoed bowl with butterfly, Teotihuacan. Drawing by Mareike Sattler after Séjourné 1966a:Figure 121.

where the Teotihuacanos may have attempted to export the philosophy associated with the image. In a masterful analysis of Esquintla's butterfly imagery, Berlo (1983b:81–82) asserted that the site's iconography more closely adhered to Teotihuacan art than the Maya-Teotihuacan hybrid traditions seen at Tikal and Kaminaljuyu. This led her to conclude that Teotihuacan contact might have been more direct at Esquintla, perhaps resembling the Aztec *pochteca* model, with Teotihuacan warrior-traders using the location as a staging area from which to penetrate deeper into the Maya highlands and the Peten. So familiar is the butterfly to Teotihuacan iconography that von Winning (1987) devoted an entire section to this insect in his influential compendium of the city's imagery.[5] The very popularity of the butterfly in Teotihuacan art indicates its strong presence within the psyche of the city's inhabitants.

A set of codified visual components results in easy identification of the butterfly within the artistic corpus. On one particular fresco-decorated bowl a butterfly spreads its wings in the midst of raindrops (Figure 7.1). Typical of Teotihuacan representations of the insect, this example has a tubular body with forewings branching to the sides and lower wings positioned like a tail. The artist portrayed the eyes with two circular rings, a motif quite distinctive to the city. Above the eyes the curled form of the proboscis emerges, and to either side are the antennae. This depiction, for the most part, is anatomically correct, which indicates not only the artist's familiarity with the subject, but also that time was taken to render the insect's features accurately. The colors used on the vessel

may be somewhat fanciful, but they nevertheless manage to convey the brilliance so characteristic of a butterfly. A bold green appears on the round eyes and the tips of the antennae, and it outlines the wings and proboscis. Yellow and red brighten the body, antennae, and proboscis. All of the colors repeat on the wings, which have fanciful patterns of dots and curved lines. The vivid colors and the lively quality of the butterfly amidst the multicolored raindrops project a scene of lighthearted fertility, but the positioning of these various elements within Teotihuacan's iconographic tradition exposes a more ominous meaning.

To the original viewer, the strong round forms of the butterfly's eyes would have instantly recalled one of the most diagnostic features of a warrior's dress. Images at Teotihuacan of men dressed in military costume repeatedly include round goggles through which their normal, human eyes peer. The goggled warrior from the White Patio murals serves as a typical example (Figure 4.1). On this individual, red face paint from the nose to the ear accentuates the round goggle. Above this the rather gruesome vertebral column serves as the brim of his headdress, which is further embellished with a year sign, strips of rubber-splattered paper, and curved obsidian knives.[6] The year sign has strong connections with military imagery, and because rubber was a symbolic substitute for blood, the paper, blood, and vertebral column give this individual sacrificial connotations.[7] Even more direct than these already less than subtle sacrificial elements is the handled knife with the curved blade held in the warrior's left hand. Jammed onto the blade is the bleeding heart of a probable human sacrificial victim. The three atlatl darts clutched in the warrior's right hand firmly announce that the victim was a casualty of war.

The goggled eyes of warriors and butterflies undoubtedly associate these figures with the god Tlaloc. In a Tetitla mural fragment we see his general features, including the circular goggles adopted by the warriors and a down-turned mouth with sharp, menacing fangs (Figure 7.2). Often water or other liquid flows from the mouth, and not uncommonly he grips a water lily in his teeth. The items in his hands continue this watery theme. He holds a jar from which

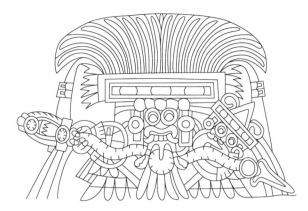

FIGURE 7.2. Mural fragment depicting Tlaloc with a lightning atlatl dart, Corridor 21, Tetitla, Teotihuacan. Drawing by Jenni Bongard after Séjourné 1966b:Figure 160.

he pours water, and he has two fingers through the holes of an atlatl loaded with a distinct, wavy atlatl dart.[8] The Aztec version of this deity provides sufficient evidence for this odd weapon, for the Aztecs associated Tlaloc with water, rain, and lightning (Sahagún 1950–1982:I:7). Thus, the Tetitla Tlaloc's curvy atlatl dart is a visual pun for lightning as it snakes down from the sky.

Tlaloc's watery symbolism illuminates the appearance of raindrops surrounding the butterfly on the frescoed bowl from Teotihuacan (Figure 7.1). Both the rain and the goggles connect the butterfly with the life-giving properties of water. Another fragmentary mural recovered near the Avenue of the Dead exhibits further integration of Tlaloc and butterfly iconography (Figure 7.3). The form of the butterfly is clearly delineated, with the proboscis sitting on top of the goggles and the wings to either side. In place of the body, however, the artist has substituted the U-shaped mouth of Tlaloc dripping with liquid.[9] In this incidence the fusion of Tlaloc and the butterfly is complete, although it is important to acknowledge that this may be for a different purpose. Directly under the mouth is a hand, which transforms this image into an assemblage that resembles a glyphic compound. Perhaps the mural records the name of an individual who carried a butterfly-Tlaloc insignia.

Although Tlaloc's identity as a water god has long been established, his equal connection to war has been slower to emerge. The historical reason for this is rooted in the standard interpretation of the central pyramid of Tenochtitlan.

When the Spaniards arrived, the Mexica informed them that each of the two temples atop the pyramid had a patron deity. The north temple was dedicated to Tlaloc, and the south temple celebrated Huitzilopochtli.[10] Given the ethnohistoric documents that definitively associate Tlaloc with water, and numerous caches on the northern side that included water-related iconography, scholars have justifiably connected the Tlaloc side with a cult of water. Huitzilopochtli, in turn, was interpreted as the war god because militant activities typify the account of his birth and subsequent exploits (Matos Moctezuma 1987:57). Such an interpretation of the Aztec Templo Mayor is well founded, but it neglects one critical aspect: Huitzilopochtli was not the only military presence on the pyramid, for there is a long tradition connecting Tlaloc to war.

Schele and Freidel (1990) have been vocal advocates of this position, particularly as it applies to Teotihuacan contact with Tikal.[11] On the famous Stela 31 from Tikal, a Teotihuacan-clad warrior stands on the sides of the monument (Figure 7.4). This individual is Yax Nuun Ayiin I, who, as David Stuart (2000) argues, may be a Teotihuacano who disrupted the Maya royal line when he acceded to the Tikal throne. He wears two versions of a war headdress and carries an

FIGURE 7.3. Tlaloc mouth on a butterfly in a mural fragment, Room 12, Zone 5-A, Teotihuacan. Drawing by Jenni Bongard after von Winning 1987:I:122, Figure 3.

FIGURE 7.4. Drawing of Stela 31 sides, Tikal, A.D. 445. Drawing by Linda Schele, © David Schele, courtesy of the Foundation for the Advancement of Mesoamerican Studies, Inc., www.famsi.org.

atlatl in his right hand. The left hand clutches a square shield with a detailed image of Tlaloc. Schele and Freidel (1990) see this and other such imagery as evidence of Tlaloc's military symbolism, and they argue that the appearance of Tlaloc coincided with a type of Venus-regulated warfare that they christen "Tlaloc-Venus" war. Their work indicates that the militant associations of this deity were so powerful that the Teotihuacanos effectively exported a system of warfare symbolized by Tlaloc.

The consistent appearance of the atlatl within the iconography of this warfare may have some bearing on the goggles that so prominently figure in Tlaloc's visage. Essentially, an atlatl consists of a shaft of wood that curves at one end to make a hook. In Mesoamerican versions a pair of circular rings are attached to the main shaft. To use the atlatl, the warrior would place an atlatl dart on the atlatl, securing it in the curved hook at the end. He would then slip two fingers through the rings and use them for purchase while pulling the atlatl over his shoulder and propelling the dart with a forceful throw. In an interesting manner, the rings on the atlatl resemble the goggles of Tlaloc, but even more compelling is the playful visual correspondence between the butterfly and the atlatl. Returning to the frescoed bowl, the goggled eyes mimic the fingergrips on the atlatl, while the proboscis imitates the atlatl hook (Figure 7.5). On both the atlatl and the butterfly, the paired circles and the curved, hooked shape are in close proximity, which serves to reinforce this visual pun. Seen in this light, one wonders if the butterfly is an inventive representation of an atlatl, and whether, with his goggled appearance, Tlaloc also may reference this weapon. In other words, Tlaloc and the butterfly may be animated images of the Teotihuacan warriors' weapon of choice; that is, they are personified or deified atlatls.

In addition to the goggles, another anatomical feature of the butterfly has visual overtones of a military nature. A comparison of butterfly antennae with Teotihuacan atlatl darts reveals a distinct similarity (Figure 7.6a, b). The long shafts of both antennae and atlatl darts terminate in a round ball with a feathery tip. The artists seem to have drawn the antennae so that they closely approximated the fletched end of atlatl

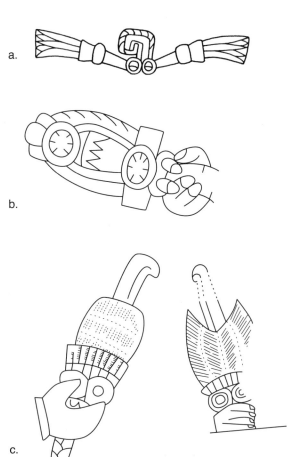

FIGURE 7.5. Comparison of butterfly eyes and antennae with an atlatl: *a*) detail of butterfly from ceramic bowl, Teotihuacan; *b*) atlatl from mural in Corridor 21, Tetitla, Teotihuacan; *c*) atlatls from Stela 31, Tikal, A.D. 445. Drawings: *a*) by Mareike Sattler after Séjourné 1966a:Figure 121; *b*) by Jenni Bongard after Séjourné 1966b:Figure 160; *c*) by Jenni Bongard after von Winning 1987:I:80, Figure 1h.

darts. This visual similarity might be dismissed were it not for a fragmentary mural found in Zone 5-A, a complex of rooms near the northwest corner of the Sun Pyramid (Figure 7.6c). Even though the middle section of the mural is missing, the proboscis at the top clearly identifies the main figure as a butterfly. Portions of the round goggles sit just below the proboscis, and the aft wings spread on either side at the bottom. Curled forms to the left and right of the proboscis may be antennae that flop to either side. Next to these curled forms are what looks like a second pair of antennae with the round balls and feathered tips that typify both butterfly antennae and atlatl darts. That this pun is meant both literally and figuratively is clear from the atlatl

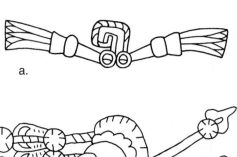

a.

b.

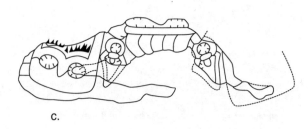

c.

FIGURE 7.7. Butterfly warrior with shield on frescoed vase from Teotihuacan, Museo Diego Rivera, Mexico City. Drawing by Jenni Bongard after Séjourné 1966a:Figure 94.

FIGURE 7.8. Butterfly-bird warrior on frescoed vase, Teotihuacan. Drawing by Mareike Sattler after Séjourné 1966c:Figure 130b.

FIGURE 7.6. Comparison of butterfly antennae and atlatl darts: *a)* detail of butterfly from ceramic bowl, Teotihuacan; *b)* detail of mural with atlatls carried by a warrior, Portico 3, White Patio, Atetelco, Teotihuacan; *c)* mural with butterfly and atlatl darts, Zone 5-A, Teotihuacan. Drawings: *a)* by Mareike Sattler after Séjourné 1966a:Figure 121; *b)* by Jenni Bongard after Villagra 1971:Figure 20; *c)* by Jenni Bongard after Miller 1973:Figure 134.

points positioned just inside the aft wings at the bottom. Looking at the whole assemblage, it appears to depict a butterfly with a pair of crossed atlatl darts behind it. Most interesting of all is that the artist plays upon the visual similarity of antennae and darts by placing the fletched ends of the darts in the same location as the antennae. The visual comparison associates the two motifs and offers another militaristic layer to the Teotihuacan butterfly.[12]

The military symbolism of the butterfly goes well beyond the goggled eye and atlatl-like antennae, appearing consistently in warriors' costumes. On one frescoed vase we see only the head of the warrior because his shoulders are hidden behind his round war shield (Figure 7.7). Spreading to either side of the shield are the fore and aft wings of a butterfly, and the proboscis curls at the front of the warrior's headdress. Behind the proboscis is another frequent characteristic of butterfly iconography, an ovoid eye with a feathered edged, commonly called a feathered eye. Finally, an antenna extends down the length of the headdress behind the feathered eye.

Another frescoed tripod vase may help explain the substitution of the feathered eye for the goggles (Figure 7.8). The warrior costume on this vase displays a mixture of butterfly and

FIGURE 7.9. Rollout of relief-decorated vase with frontal figure containing bird and butterfly elements, Teotihuacan. Drawing by Jenni Bongard after Séjourné 1966c:Figure 130.

bird iconography. Similar to the previous vase, his shield partially obscures the warrior's body, but the predominant costume element seems to be avian. His face emerges from the jaws of a bird beak, and a bird's tail sweeps behind him. The feathered eye sits just above the upper beak, while the proboscis on the crown of his head provides the main butterfly element. The dominant avian appearance of this warrior seems to suggest that he belongs to a bird warrior order but has added butterfly attributes to his costume. Apparently, butterfly costuming could include imagery of other animals.

The conflation of bird and butterfly imagery is particularly common in Teotihuacan art (Mayhall 1991; Parsons 1988). Another tripod vessel includes two complementary images that each reference both creatures (Figure 7.9). The frontal human figure stretches out both arms to shake rattles whose music is indicated by the speech scrolls emanating from them. Broad, outstretched wings spread below his arms, and on his chest is the head of an owl. The strong avian iconography is once again balanced by the headdress, which has a proboscis at its center. On the opposite side of the vase is a composite creature with the same costume elements seen on the human figure. The beak and tail feathers of a bird are clearly present, but the round goggles, proboscis, antennae, and forewings of the butterfly merge to make a creature of fantasy.

The most complete integration of the bird and butterfly appears on a relief-decorated vessel (Figure 7.10). Here the artist displayed the butterfly's body in its full frontal splendor. The fore and aft wings make a cruciform shape around a four-petaled flower, but a tiny bit of the insect's tubular body emerges below the flower. The head

FIGURE 7.10. Avian butterfly from relief-decorated vessel, Teotihuacan. Drawing by Jenni Bongard after von Winning 1987:I:122, Figure 7a.

of this composite creature is somewhat amusing in its attempt to successfully integrate these two animals into a unified image. The strong forms of the bird beak and feathered eye appear in profile just above the flower. The feathered eye is so thoroughly integrated into the head of the bird that I suspect that this eye is a decidedly avian element. In fact, the feathered eye may have been so strongly associated with birds that its singular presence on a butterfly may have been enough to suggest an avian conflation. This bird head, however, has a proboscis jammed into its forehead, and an antenna arches over the eye. This assemblage of these animal forms is somewhat monstrous but fluid at the same time and conveys further evidence of the butterfly's martial symbolism.

FIGURE 7.11. Theater-type ceramic censer with butterfly motifs, Teotihuacan. Museo Nacional de Antropología, Mexico City.

The birds that appear in this avian butterfly conflation have a distinctive short, hooked beak, which von Winning (1948:131–132, 1987:I:85–90, 121) has identified as the beak of an owl. This identification is especially pertinent to this discussion because he made a strong argument that the owl was an important military symbol at Teotihuacan. When coupled, as it often is, with a shield and atlatl darts, the owl is part of an assemblage that von Winning dubbed the *lechuza y armas,* or owl and weapons, sign. He argued that it is an emblem for war and also a heraldic symbol for a warrior class.[13] In an investigation of Teotihuacan-Tikal interaction, David Stuart (2000) proposed a different understanding of the owl and weapons, reading them as the glyphic writing of a name, perhaps the name of a powerful Teotihuacan ruler. The profound implications of this inspired interpretation have forced Teotihuacan scholars to reconsider the relationship between iconography and writing at Teotihuacan. As Karl Taube (2000b, 2003) has wisely argued, much of the imagery previously treated as iconography may be better understood as glyphic assemblages. Thus, the bird-butterfly conflation could represent the name of a specific group or individual, or it could function as a more overarching martial symbol. In either case, the butterfly itself has strong warfare associations that transcend this issue.[14]

A return to one of the previously discussed vases reveals another critical element of butterfly costume. This profile depiction of a butterfly-bird warrior places heavy emphasis on a particular noseplaque that appears on the vessel twice (Figure 7.8). It dangles in its proper place below the nose of the central figure, but to allow for a clearer understanding of the noseplaque's shape, the artist has employed multiple viewpoints and has shifted the noseplaque to a frontal position. In addition to its function as jewelry, a noseplaque decorates the warrior's shield. It is simple in form, consisting of a triangle surmounted by a rectangular bar with a depression at its center to accommodate the nose.

While not uncommon on painted images of warriors with butterfly attributes, the noseplaque most frequently appears on censers found both at Teotihuacan and Teotihuacan-influenced Esquintla (Berlo 1984; von Winning 1987:I:118–124).

FIGURE 7.12. Ceramic relief-decorated vase with a noseplaque surrounded by butterfly wings, Teotihuacan. Drawing by Jenni Bongard after von Winning 1987:II:60, Figure 3b.

One example clearly exhibits the conflation of butterfly and bird iconography (Figure 7.11). At the two upper corners are the owls with their carefully delineated eyes. Between and below the birds are mirrors with mica centers, and superimposed over the mirrors are three realistically rendered butterflies. In the center of the ceramic frame is a clay mask that strongly resembles the more costly stone masks. The mask wears a pair of large earflares and the same noseplaque seen on the butterfly warrior.

The association of this noseplaque with the butterfly was first made by Séjourné (1962), and Caso (1966:260) agreed, further labeling the noseplaque with its Nahuatl name, *yacapapalotl.* In a similar vein, von Winning (1987:II:59) argued that it was an accoutrement of his "Butterfly God," and although I disagree with his deity identification, the noseplaque's connection with the butterfly is made explicit in Teotihuacan iconography. One plano-relief vessel leaves little doubt that the noseplaque represents a stylized butterfly body (Figure 7.12). The perimeter of the noseplaque depicted on the vase is surrounded by butterfly wings, and a bit of the insect's body projects beneath it. In a very literal sense the artist connects the forewings with the upper rectangular bar, and the aft wings with the triangular portion of the noseplaque. This visual integration indicates that the butterfly and the noseplaque are two versions of the same concept.

A delightfully animated version of this same message is seen on a frescoed vessel found at Tetitla (Figure 7.13). On this vase the artist substituted the noseplaque for the entirety of the butterfly's body. A pair of feathered and goggled eyes, along with the antennae and proboscis, finish off the image. The complete replacement of

FIGURE 7.13. Frescoed vase with butterfly head above a noseplaque, Tetitla, Teotihuacan. Drawing by Jenni Bongard after Séjourné 1966b:Figure 100.

the insect's body by the noseplaque unequivocally states their interchangeable nature. The noseplaque is nothing less than a stylized version of a butterfly's body.

ARCHITECTURAL BUTTERFLIES

While Teotihuacan artists articulated the noseplaque's butterfly symbolism with an explicit directness, a second association for this object is equally clear to anyone versed in the city's art and architecture. The noseplaque with its rectangular bar and triangular base hauntingly mimics the shape of Teotihuacan's dominant architectural form, *talud-tablero*. Specifically, the upper portion of the noseplaque corresponds to the *tablero* of Teotihuacan architecture, just as the lower, triangular section mirrors the sloping *taludes* seen on the city's buildings. Thus, in addition to the noseplaque's butterfly symbolism, the noseplaque also conveyed the architectural style so identified with the city.

It was von Winning (1947b, 1979:321, 1987: II:60) who first noted that Teotihuacan artistic representations of *talud-tablero* architecture have the same fundamental shape as stylized butterflies.[15] An architectural scene on a tripod vessel offers a typical representation of a *talud-tablero* temple in Teotihuacan art (Figure 7.14a). On the

bottom a set of stairs bisects the *talud* base and rectangular *tablero*. Above this are the walls and thatched roof of the temple, crowned by the *almenas* that are so characteristic of the city's architecture. In this depiction the stairs provide the most powerful indication that the image is a temple and not a noseplaque. Another artistic rendering of Teotihuacan architecture appears in the headdress of a small figurine (Figure 7.14b). Here, there are three temples, each with a *talud-tablero* base, upper room, and *almena*-decorated roof. Although considerations of scale and clarity

a.

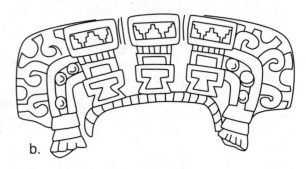

b.

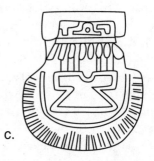

c.

FIGURE 7.14. Temple depictions: *a)* a Teotihuacan temple on a plano-relief tripod vessel; *b)* three temples in a figurine headdress, Teotihuacan; *c)* molded ceramic plaque with butterfly noseplaque serving as temple substructure. Drawings by Jenni Bongard: *a)* after von Winning 1947b:Figure 1; *b)* after Séjourné 1966c:Figure 44; *c)* after von Winning 1987:II:60, Figure 6a.

may have caused the artist to eliminate the stairs, the *almenas* on the roofs conclusively identify them as architecture.

To date, the proverbial "smoking gun" that demonstrates that the Teotihuacanos recognized the visual similarities of the noseplaque with *talud-tablero* architecture appears in the modest form of a mold-made clay appliqué once attached to the base of a vessel (Figure 7.14c).[16] The plaque clearly depicts a temple because it includes the upper walls and thatched roof surmounted by *almenas*. Much like the temples on the figurine headdress, the *talud-tablero* foundation does not have stairs, but there is an interesting departure from most depictions of temples. In this case the artist has included a small depression at the top of the *tablero* in a manner similar to the cutout seen on noseplaques to accommodate the nose. Instead of having his audience make the theoretical leap from architecture to jewelry, this artist is more literal. The plaque tells us that there is a visual coupling between the two, which leaves open the possibility of a conceptual superimposition as well. In some manner the butterfly noseplaque is analogous to the *talud-tablero* base of a temple.

Even though artists typically included visual markers to distinguish architecture from noseplaques within the corpus of Teotihuacan art, similarities between the shapes of temples and the bodily adornment are difficult to dismiss. *Talud-tablero* structures were omnipresent within the city; therefore, it would have been difficult for a Teotihuacan citizen to spend a day without seeing such a structure. If the ceramics are to be a guide, the butterfly noseplaque was an important part of military costume, so most inhabitants would have seen them frequently, even if this jewelry was only worn during ritual celebrations. Because both were quite prominent in the visual experience of Teotihuacanos, it seems unlikely that residents of the city did not recognize the visual parallels. Much like a pun, the warriors who wore the noseplaque carried both the butterfly and the architectural style of their state below their nose. The noseplaque gave the wearer two identities. The first was an association with a social entity within the culture, his identity as a warrior. The second was his larger cultural association, his identity as a Teotihuacano. In a reciprocal manner, the architecture too could have engendered multiple readings of its symbolic content. Apart from its ability to project a unified style that promoted a sense of state inclusion, *talud-tablero* may have conjured the specter of butterflies within the minds of those indoctrinated into the city's cultural beliefs. Yet the suggestion of a dual meaning for *talud-tablero* architecture begs a simple question. Just why would a powerful city want to associate its public architecture with a butterfly?

BUTTERFLIES AND THE AFTERLIFE

The frequent appearance of butterfly body parts and stylized butterfly noseplaques on Teotihuacan warriors suggests an intimate connection between the insect and warfare. Far from being the docile creature of springtime romance, Teotihuacan's butterflies were quite belligerent in nature. Butterfly-emblazoned figures boldly position their war shields towards the viewer in a pugnacious manner. When the Teotihuacanos saw the butterfly in art, it must have raised the specter of war and its bloody aftermath in the form of ritual human sacrifice. In turn, the visual mimesis of the noseplaque for the architecture imparted this militant symbolism onto the temples of the city. Striding down the *talud-tablero*–lined Avenue of the Dead, an individual probably associated the temples with the butterfly and its warlike character (Figure 3.20). The architecture may have projected an image of Teotihuacan as a bellicose state, a city with an identity grounded in conquest and domination.

The aggressive message of Teotihuacan architecture was surely one of its most important aspects because it set the ideological tone. For both visitor and inhabitant it created a set of expectations about the very nature of the city. The architecture communicated a message of power, a particular brand of power based on hostility and taking by force those things which the city claimed. Yet to end here would be to neglect a deeper, more proselytizing feature of this ideological association. Even as Teotihuacan's *talud-tablero* architecture conveyed a message of war, it also imprinted a social duty upon its own residents. Entrenched within the militant symbolism of the butterfly was a religiously based enticement for engaging in warfare.

The absence of ethnohistoric documents for Teotihuacan itself warrants the application of other cultural models to understand the patterns seen at this site. One persuasive model of the ideological function of the butterfly is offered by the Aztecs and mirrors the iconography seen in Teotihuacan's visual record. Despite the hundreds of years that separate the Aztecs from the Teotihuacanos, the symbolic use of the butterfly by both cultures is striking in its congruency. This implies, in turn, that the Aztecs inherited some of their beliefs from the earlier Teotihuacanos.

In his rather encyclopedic manner, Seler wrote several papers that included discussion of the butterfly in various Mesoamerican cultures. However, it was his analysis of Aztec concepts, filtered through the lens of Sahagún's ethnohistoric work, that proves most poignant. During an investigation of Aztec creation mythology, Seler (1990–1998:V:39) began by examining Sahagún's account of Aztec beliefs about the afterlife. In the Aztec system the souls of the dead inhabited various places dependent on the cause of death. This system reserved a particularly exalted celestial afterlife for warriors who gave the ultimate sacrifice. As Sahagún wrote,

The third place to which they went was there to the home of the sun, in heaven. Those went there who died in war, who perhaps right there indeed died in battle, in the warring place, where they despoiled them, where their breathing ceased, where they laid down their cares, or only were taken in, those who were to die later. Perchance one was slain in gladiatorial sacrifice, or cast into the fire, or pierced by darts, or offered up on the barrel cactus, or shot by arrows, or encrusted [and burned] with pieces of resinous wood: all went to the home of the sun. (Sahagún 1950–1982:III:49)

From this it is clear that warriors who never returned from battle were a special category of the dead. Sahagún was explicit that this classification included those who died in battle or those who were marched back to enemy cities and sacrificed in the aftermath of war. He also definitively stated that their heaven was in the company of the sun.

In Book Six, Sahagún's portrait of Aztec rhetoric and moral philosophy, the warrior's existence with the sun is more fully explained.

The brave warriors, the eagle-ocelot warriors, those who died in war, went there to the house of the sun. And they lived there in the east, where the sun arose. And when the sun was about to emerge, when it was still dark, they arrayed themselves, they armed themselves as for war, met the sun as it emerged, brought it forth, came giving cries for it, came gladdening it, came skirmishing. Before it they came rejoicing; they came to leave it there at the zenith, called the midday sun. (Sahagún 1950–1982:VI:162)

Sahagún painted a picture of the sun's dawning that has a decidedly martial flavor. Mimicking their most heroic moments in life, the deceased warriors dressed themselves in their military costumes each day to lead the sun into the sky. The cries they made to call the sun out resembled the yelling that warriors did before bursting onto the battlefield, and words such as "skirmishing" are clearly the language of war. This glorious accompaniment of the sun was the initial reward for the fallen warriors, but with time, their eternal lives transformed into a more idyllic existence.

Sahagún explained what ultimately happens to the warriors who joined the sun in the sky:

And when they had passed four years there, then they changed into precious birds—hummingbirds, orioles, yellow birds, yellow birds blackened about the eyes, chalky butterflies, feather down butterflies, gourd bowl butterflies; they sucked honey [from the flowers] there where they dwelt. And here upon earth they came to suck [honey] from all the various flowers. (Sahagún 1950–1982:III:49)

This passage completes the story for the warriors by transmuting them into birds and butterflies with carefree lives of sucking the sweet nectar of flowers.[17] The picture it paints is a pleasurable one, with the beauty of their plumage being a metaphor for their charmed existence. Interestingly enough, Sahagún contended that this life took place in the human realm as well as the supernatural. Thus, the noble warriors actually maintained contact with the living when they visited this world in their avian and butterfly forms. Returning to the topic at hand, the mention of butterflies as a manifestation of deceased warriors resonates with the themes seen in the Teotihuacan iconography of war.

Seler (1990–1998:III:102, IV:9, V:39) latched on to this final passage from Sahagún to assert that butterflies represented the souls of dead warriors. In Seler's time there was insufficient archaeology to carefully parse out the time depth between Teotihuacan and the Aztecs, but nevertheless, many subsequent scholars have accepted Seler's basic argument and applied it, in varying degrees, to Teotihuacan.[18] In his study of the insect, Beyer (1965b:465–468) proposed that butterflies represented the souls of dead warriors, but he also argued that they represented fertility and flames. Concerning the connection between Teotihuacan and the Aztecs, he held that the latter culture absorbed and adapted concepts deeply rooted in the Classic period. Von Winning (1987:I:116–117) acknowledged the lengthy history of Teotihuacan itself and constructed a model in which butterfly symbolism changed over time. He posited that the fertility aspects of the butterfly were quite ancient, and through time the Teotihuacanos added the associations of warfare and the souls of the dead. As one of Mesoamerica's staunchest critics of continuity, Kubler (1972:81) characteristically avoided direct comparisons with the Aztec, yet his methodology of iconographic clusters still led him to see a funerary meaning for butterflies. He reasoned that the butterfly's frequent appearance on censers indicated that it could represent a soul.

The association of the butterfly with censers is especially pertinent because many scholars argue that censers seem to have functioned in funerary rites.[19] The typical Teotihuacan theater-type censer consists of a base in a rough hourglass shape (Figure 7.11). Above this is a conical lid with a mask-like human face at its pinnacle. Surrounding the mask is a rectangular frame on which mold-made clay plaques, or *adornos*, have been affixed. The upper conical form with its decorated mask can be removed to place incense inside. When lit and reassembled, a cloud of perfumed smoke would emanate from a chimney behind the elaborate decoration.

It is the burning incense and smoke that so demonstrably connects the censers with funerary elements. Throughout Mesoamerica, incense was one of the primary means of contacting

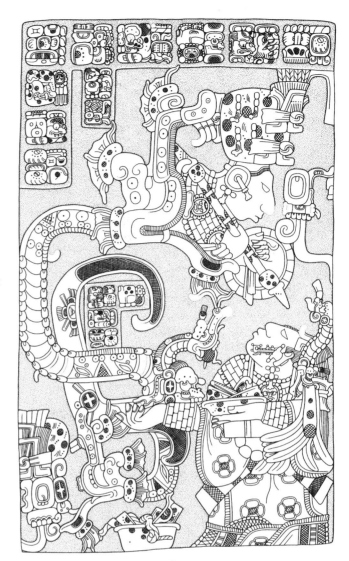

FIGURE 7.15. Lintel 25, Yaxchilan, A.D. 723. After *Corpus of Maya Hieroglyphic Inscriptions,* volume 3, part I, *Yaxchilan,* reproduced courtesy of the President and Fellows of Harvard College.

deceased ancestors. The rising smoke created a conduit between the human plane and the celestial, linking them in a profound if ephemeral way. As demonstrated on Yaxchilan Lintel 25, the Maya apparently believed that the face of an ancestor emerged from the smoke (Figure 7.15). On this well-known and oft used example, Lady Xoc burns her own blood and gazes up at an armed warrior, who emerges from a cloud of smoke envisioned as a serpent (Schele and Miller 1986:187–188; Schele and Freidel 1990:267). If we imagine the smoke flowing around the masks of the Teotihuacan censers, the image we get is quite similar. The smoke would both reveal and mysteriously obscure the small face, which would seem to inhabit the cloudy realm of the ancestors.

Von Winning's (1987:I:122) suggestion that the mask at the center of the censer is a portrait of a deceased individual thus appears to have much merit. In overall form the clay masks of the censers are stylistically similar to the more costly stone masks (Figure 3.8). Both have a generalized and generic representation of the face with a broad forehead that tapers to the chin. Remembering that the stone masks were likely attached to mortuary bundles, this stylistic format probably carried a distinct message, denoting the face as a deceased individual. The masks may even suggest socioeconomic implications, with the clay masks used to commemorate a midlevel-status person, and the stone masks reserved for the highest elites. Noting that the conical shape of the censers closely approximates the contours of a mortuary bundle, Taube (2000a) has argued that the censers are effigy mortuary bundles.[20] The high frequency of censer fragments in apartment compound principal patios further augments this model. If the mortuary bundles with stone masks were objects of devotion along the Avenue of the Dead, then the ceramic censers may have served a similar function for apartment compound ancestor worship. The fact that a number of archaeologically recovered censers came from burials lends further support to their funerary context.[21]

While Kubler (1972) and von Winning (1987) associated butterflies with the general category of the dead, Berlo (1983b, 1984) built upon the work of Seler (1990–1998) and Beyer (1965b), who restricted the butterfly to dead warriors. These scholars found the ethnohistoric analogies compelling, and a particular censer mask does much to support their position. The mask was found with several other masks by Linné (1934) during excavations in Tlamimilolpa (Figure 7.16). The remains of face paint still exist and help individualize the mask. Below the nose is the commonly seen butterfly noseplaque, but with two notable additions. Three skulls grace the upper portion, and a V-shape converts the noseplaque into the trapeze-and-ray year sign.[22] The repetition of the skulls forthrightly projects a message of death and may corroborate arguments

FIGURE 7.16. Ceramic censer mask with butterfly noseplaque and skulls, Tlamimilolpa, Teotihuacan. Drawing by Jenni Bongard after Berrin and Pasztory 1993:cat. 74.

FIGURE 7.17. Feet from ceramic tripod vases decorated with the year sign, Teotihuacan. Drawing by Jenni Bongard after Séjourné 1966a:Figures 72, 83.

for the funerary function of censers. As for the year sign, the tripod feet of cylindrical vessels reveal that the coupling of the butterfly or *talud-tablero* shape with the year sign was a frequent trope for Teotihuacan ceramists (Figure 7.17). Many of these tripod feet take the form of *talud-tablero* architecture, and a V-shape often decorates the triangular base, thereby transforming it into a year sign. The mask and the tripod feet presumably have martial connotations because the year sign consistently appears in war-related contexts. The headdresses of Teotihuacan warriors typically incorporate the year sign, and it is one of the dominant military symbols adopted by Mesoamerican cultures with Teotihuacan contact (Berlo 1984:111–112; Coggins 1979a; Proskouriakoff 1993; Schele and Freidel 1990; Stuart 2000). When viewed in tandem, the skulls and the year sign on the Tlamimilolpa mask could easily serve to identify the individual as a deceased warrior.

BUTTERFLIES AND STATE PROPAGANDA

The proposal, then, is that the Teotihuacanos, like the Aztecs, believed that fallen warriors received a reward that was both honorable and pleasurable, and which surpassed the afterlife existence of the average individual. By gloriously accompanying the sun, they achieved a form of immortality and power through their close proximity to the preeminent celestial entity. Upon their transformation into butterflies, the recompense warriors earned for giving their lives was a delightful existence, free from the worries of life. Of special note, however, is the exclusivity of this afterlife: Sahagún (1950–1982:III:49) clearly indicated that it was warriors who died on the battlefield or were sacrificed as war captives who received such honors. The ethnohistoric record suggests a system of inducement whereby the social, political, and religious systems promised a special afterlife for those who went into war and risked their lives for the state.

The Aztec beliefs about fallen warriors provide a compelling explanation for the martial butterfly imagery at Teotihuacan, and they suggest a military incentive program that pushed people into battle. However, to fully comprehend the way states use afterlife beliefs to motivate large segments of their populations, it may prove useful to look much further afield. Specifically, there are interesting correspondences between Mesoamerican, and perhaps Teotihuacano, propagandistic tools of warfare with some factions of the Muslim world. Although this is certainly a vast cultural and temporal leap, it is justified by human factors; namely, the unfortunate but often unavoidable need to encourage individuals to jeopardize their lives for their state.

Certain expressions of Islamic fundamentalism have had, and continue to incorporate, incentive systems that are similarly founded on beliefs of a more advantageous afterlife for culturally designated heroic figures.[23] The following is a decidedly broad overview that neglects to explore the numerous variations that have emerged throughout the vast geographical and temporal history of Islam. However, it does aim to distill this phenomenon to its essential fundamentals and expose the basic mechanics of state manipulation of individual belief. Although the word

Islam, like any name for a religion, has many meanings, in its simplest translation the word means "submission," specifically the submission to Allah, or God (Johnson 1997:161). The Muslim submits to the will of Allah, but because there is a long tradition of political and religious integration in Islam, this submission is also expected by other factions. The goals of religious and political elements are deeply entwined, and a Muslim is expected to submit to the will of the state that represents his god. Interwoven into the system is a set of devotional duties, or obligations, ranked from mandatory, to recommended, to forbidden. One of the mandatory duties that the state may require is *jihad* (Peters 1979:3–12, 1996:3).

The term *jihad* has recently acquired a new level of charged emotionalism as Islam collides with states that are predominantly Christian and Jewish; however, it is important here to pare down the term to its essential meaning and most canonical use. While the Western media often translates *jihad* as "holy war," a more precise translation might be "to struggle" or "to strive." Books on Islamic law and the Koran offer the best route to comprehending the concept, and they indicate that the term means "to struggle against unbelievers." In practice, whenever a Muslim leader, or caliph, announces a *jihad,* it is a Muslim's duty to fight unbelievers (Martin 1991:92; Peters 1979:9, 1996:1–3). Despite the fact that this is a mandatory duty, not all members of the community must directly fight in the war. *Jihad* belongs to a category of universal duties in which a set of individuals may satisfy the obligation for the community as a whole. All community members are considered to have fulfilled the duty as long as the participating members, who in the case of war would be able-bodied men, can accomplish the goals of the *jihad* (Peters 1977:9–10, 1979:12).

An interesting paradox arises from this system in which *jihad* is mandatory but executed by a subset of the population because it necessitates some motivational tool to urge individuals into taking on the burden of the collective whole. Likewise, because the activity is war, the stimulus must address the individual desire for self-preservation. Islamic *jihad* tackles this issue with a two-pronged approach firmly grounded in beliefs that are inculcated into the society. The first is a fundamental principle of Islam which holds that it is a Muslim's duty to bring all of humanity into the submission of Allah. Underpinning this goal is the belief that an individual's actions can eliminate the forces of deception and unbelief, which will, in turn, lead to the restoration of proper order in the world (Martin 1991). The second motivational tool is more personal in nature, appealing not so much to conceptions of world order, but to individual needs and perhaps even a sense of heroic immortality. To directly confront the natural fears of risking one's life, the individuals who die in battle are declared martyrs. Although this designation as a sacrificial offering of the state may offer some personal aggrandizement for posterity, more clearly the title of martyr conveys a very specific reward. Verses of the Koran suggest that entrance into Paradise without any preconditions is guaranteed to such martyrs (Peters 1977:4, 1996:5). The compensation is a delayed one that is only captured after the ultimate sacrifice, but it is an enticing one nonetheless. Moving back to Mesoamerica, this latter incentive, the promise of an easier afterlife, provides an appealing model.

The correspondence between the Islamic and Aztec systems of state warfare is striking. Both traditions implemented the afterlife as the "carrot" with which to lead individuals into actions for the state. The Muslim believer expects expedited admittance into Paradise if he dies while engaged in the activities of *jihad*. Similarly, the Aztec martyr became a companion of the sun, the most powerful supernatural entity. After four glorious years of assisting the sun's ascent, the warrior returned to earth as a bird or butterfly drinking the nectar of flowers, imagery that resembles the Islamic paradise. The most poignant similarity between the two cultural traditions is their efficacy in persuading segments of their populations to offer their lives for the goals of the state. Essentially, a warrior's actions are somewhat counterintuitive to the logical mind; therefore, a state must counteract the individual's fears with some greater goal that transcends the drive for self-preservation. The deadly beauty of both systems is that they manage to devise individual incentives that are in harmony with the collective objectives of the state. It may be that the reward in both systems had to be an intan-

gible one based on belief because the stakes were so incredibly high.

As for Teotihuacan, the martial aura of the butterflies in its art implies that this city had a military incentive package that was remarkably similar to that of the Aztecs. Consequently, the parallels seen between the Aztec and Muslim states may be overlaid onto Teotihuacan, suggesting that it too had a form of holy war. If Teotihuacan warriors believed that there was a special afterlife reserved for those among them who died in the pursuit of war, then they would similarly have had a greater reason to do the bidding of the state. Such a motivational strategy would help explain the success of the Teotihuacan state, especially in the arena of warfare.

The Tepantitla image of the mountain-tree may represent the fullest expression of the Teotihuacan ideology of holy war (Figure 1.14). Often referred to as the Tlalocan mural, the central figure has the harsh frontality frequently seen in deity depictions. To either side, figures scatter offerings on the ground, and the personified mountain returns the favor tenfold. Water drops fall from its hands, and a torrent of water flows from a vaginal opening at the base. The summit of the mountain is radiant with fertility, with two branches of a flowering tree sprouting from the headdress, and birds flying about and singing, as indicated by their speech scrolls. The register below the mountain-tree contains a myriad of small human figures engaged in numerous activities.

In early analyses of the Tlalocan mural most scholars accepted Caso's (1942a) suggestion that the central figure represented the deity Tlaloc.[24] The first important challenge to this assertion came when Furst (1974) argued that the figure was a goddess, and Pasztory (1976) published her seminal research on the Tepantitla murals. In that study Pasztory was more open-ended in her identification of the figure, but as she refined the distinctions between Tlaloc and the "Great Goddess," she eventually came to firmly identify the Tepantitla deity as the goddess (Pasztory 1974, 1988, 1997). Berlo (1992) further articulated the iconography of the "Great Goddess," and this identification was widely accepted. Recent critiques of the goddess iconography by Cowgill (1997) and Paulinyi (2006) have demonstrated that identifications of a goddess are too indiscriminating, which is why I refer to the Tepantitla image by using the descriptive term *mountain-tree*. Another important contribution towards understanding this figure emerged when Taube (1983) explored the spiders that appear on a branch of the tree. Pulling upon Mesoamerican and North American cultural traditions, he positioned the image within the Spider Woman myths. Taube's work is critical because it revealed the multifaceted nature of the image's meaning, but I would like to balance his suggestions by incorporating the other branch of the tree.

Although the tree emerging from the mountain's peak diverges into a multitude of branches, its base reveals that it consists of two trunks winding up into the sky. Just as Taube (1983) emphasized, one branch has spiders decorating it, but the other has butterflies.[25] From a simple formal viewpoint, the two branches have a juxtaposed equality that suggests a paired duality. Neither the spider nor the butterfly dominates the image; instead, they are balanced in the composition. The pairing in this image is critical, I would argue, because the Tepantitla mountain-tree expresses the fundamental concept of gender roles. In essence, the two branches of the tree represent an archetypal opposition of male and female.

Given the interpretation of butterflies as the souls of dead warriors—who in Mesoamerica, with some interesting exceptions, are male—the butterfly half of the tree may be considered male. The choice of the butterfly to represent the male has interesting implications. The artist of the Tepantitla mural did not choose a symbol that emphasized male food acquisition or craft production; instead, the image projects warfare as the quintessential male activity. More than that, the butterfly accentuates the sacrificial and subservient aspects of war through which an individual sets aside his personal safety and devotes himself to the service of the state. The butterfly would remind male viewers of their duty to become warriors for the state, for which they would be rewarded in the afterlife if there was an unfortunate outcome.

Pasztory's (1976:160–161) analysis of the spiders on the Tepantitla tree (Figure 1.14) provides a basis for identifying the other tree branch

with females. She connected the spiders with the female activities of spinning, weaving, and childbirth. One of the clearest expressions of this association comes from the Maya, whose Goddess O is the deity of spinning and weaving, and the spider is seen as a symbol of this goddess because its activities of spinning and weaving a web were seen as analogous to the process of cloth production (Taube 1992b:99–105; Thompson 1970:247). For a host of Mesoamerican cultures, including the Maya, Aztec, and Mixtec, the goddess of spinning and weaving was additionally coupled with childbirth (McCafferty and McCafferty 1994b). The consistency of the associations throughout Mesoamerica makes a strong case that the spider branch of the tree represented females and their paradigmatic tasks of weaving and childbirth.

In the case of the butterfly symbol for male gender, the Tepantitla tree goes beyond instructions for proper male occupations to celebrate the individual's important role in the machinery of the state. The state valued such actions further because it would have enhanced the power of Teotihuacan. If the Teotihuacanos had a system of tribute tied to war like the Aztecs and the Maya, then successful military actions also would have benefited the city economically. On the other side, the activity of weaving symbolized by the spider may have had similar designs because the weaving of women could have made an important economic contribution to the state. Surviving Aztec manuscripts such as the Codex Mendoza document that cloth was a frequent component of tribute payments. Likewise, this system continued after the conquest because sixteenth-century tax records from northern Yucatan record that the Spaniards received *mantas* woven by Maya women as tribute (Pohl and Feldman 1982:306). The production of cloth by women in Teotihuacan society could have similarly furnished vast economic resources that the state could use for trade or tribute.[26]

Another resource that women could provide to the state was children, and the city may have been in desperate need of this commodity. In her study of the Tlajinga 33 skeletal material, Storey (1992:246–249) noted a high rate of infant mortality and reasoned that women would have worried over their surviving children and closely spaced their pregnancies to compensate for the frequent loss of their children.[27] Furthermore, she modeled a population that was in decline and in need of replenishment: "Teotihuacan was probably not able to maintain its numbers and was dependent on at least some migration. Again, as in the other preindustrial cities, infant and child mortality was a large reason for the demographic difficulties" (Storey 1992:249). Recognizing the significant population decline, the state may have taken measures to promote childbearing, and ethnohistoric information about the Aztecs may explicate the nature of this propaganda.

Sahagún records that childbirth by women was analogous to the battlefield exploits of men. In Aztec conceptual thought, a woman experiencing labor pains was likened to a warrior. The relationship is explicitly stated in Sahagún's (1950–1982:VI:167) description of birth: "When the baby arrived on earth, then the midwife shouted; she gave war cries, which meant that the little woman had fought a good battle, had become a brave warrior, had taken a captive, had captured a baby." Sahagún's text clearly articulates the metaphorical relationship between childbirth and warfare, with the child as the captive and the struggle of delivery as the battle (Berlo 1983b:92–93; Headrick 2002:97, 2003a:165; Klein 1988). In the unhappy event that the mother died during childbirth, the military symbolism continued. These women were called mociuaquetzque and became goddesses who assisted the sun. Just like their male counterparts, these female "warriors" went to the exalted celestial afterlife where, as Sahagún (1950–1982:VI:163) explained, "the women arrayed themselves, armed themselves as for war, took the shields, the devices." Hence, in Aztec thought, each day the deceased male warriors would lead the sun from dawn to its noontime zenith, and then they would hand the sun to the female mociuaquetzque. Dressed as warriors, these women would help the sun through the remainder of its journey to the place where the sun set. At this point the sun would go to the land of the more average dead, called Mictlan. A prayer said by midwives over the body of a woman who died in childbirth indicates that these women were heroic and deserving of a reward. Included in the prayer are the words

"seeing that thou hast now suffered affliction, for thou hast done penance, thou hast deserved, thou hast merited good, the pleasing, the precious death" (Sahagún 1950–1982:VI:164). Clearly, their death was considered valiant and righteous. In sum, women who died in childbirth were conceptual counterparts to male warriors: both gained prestige through their courageous acts and earned a more advantageous afterlife.

The Aztec conceptual linkage of childbirth and warfare credibly illuminates the tree of the Tepantitla mural. Essentially, this image conveys the ideal Teotihuacan gender roles and promotes adherence to these roles through incentives based on faith. The butterfly branch symbolized the exemplary vocation for men. They were to be warriors who fought the battles of the state. The spider side of the tree encapsulated the consummate roles for women, weaving and motherhood, especially the reproductive aspect that contributed to the population of the state. Each of these gendered ideals incorporated a great degree of risk, but the potential rewards motivated the population nonetheless. If the individual survived the experience, the compensation was very real and tangible. A man would probably gain social prestige and mobility through state recognition of his military prowess. The female prize was her child, with whom the emotional bond was a valued reimbursement. Yet the tree, viewed through the Aztec ethnohistoric material, makes another promise to those who died in the pursuits of the state. These intrepid martyrs received a superior afterlife in the celestial paradise of the sun.

The paired genders seen on the Tepantitla tree and in Sahagún's text were probably not restricted to Teotihuacan and the Aztecs. More likely, this particular conception of ideal gender roles was widespread in Mesoamerica. Another image of a tree from the Mixtec culture demonstrates that the same dual vision existed in Oaxaca. Found in the Codex Vindobonensis, the image depicts the tree of Apoala, from which the ancestors of the noble Mixtec lineages emerged (Figure 7.18).[28] At the base of the tree two figures named 7 Rain and 7 Eagle jab cutting implements into the trunk to release the ancestors inside. Similar to the Tepantitla image, the Apoala tree is predominantly female, and the ancestors issue

FIGURE 7.18. The birth tree of Apoala, manuscript illustration, Codex Vindobonensis, Postclassic. Drawing by Jenni Bongard after Codex Vindobonensis 1963:37.

from the vaginal opening in the branches of the tree.[29] Addressing the topic at hand, the Apoala tree is bifurcated with distinct symbols marking each half of the tree. One side has atlatl darts; the other, circles. The atlatl dart easily translates as the male symbol of warfare. In turn, circles are an almost universal symbol of females, but their interpretation as spindle whorls is a more culturally specific identification. The left side of the tree thus represents the female pursuits of spinning, weaving, and presumably childbirth. With such clear congruencies between these Classic and Postclassic period trees, the possibility exists that the Mixtec also shaped the actions of their populations by modeling proper gender roles.

A remarkably intact shaft tomb from the west Mexican state of Jalisco included tangible evidence of similar gendering of deceased individuals.[30] Dating between 300 B.C. and A.D. 400, the Huitzilapa tomb belongs to the Teuchtitlan culture and consisted of two chambers, each

with three occupants. Archaeologists found atlatl hooks with three of the four interred males, and rings for atlatl finger holes were even found close to one of these hooks. Positioned near the right hands of these men, the atlatls were ready for use in the afterlife, even as they symbolically proclaimed the ideal male role of warrior. Two females similarly took gendered objects to the otherworld. One woman lay on two metates, and the other had spindle whorls at her right hand and left foot. The objects gripped in the hands of these individuals signal just one more occasion where a Mesoamerican culture used atlatls and spindle whorls to designate an individual's sex and social value, thereby giving great breadth to this gender tradition.

The comparison of Teotihuacan to other Mesoamerican cultures has a twofold benefit. On one hand it assists efforts to explicate a culture for which there is no direct ethnohistoric material. Because Teotihuacan collapsed almost a millennium before the Spaniards arrived in the New World, scholars are left only with the archaeological remains. The integration of cross-cultural comparison with the archaeological material increases the prospect of understanding the site, and the fact that imagery such as the Tepantitla mountain-tree resonates with cultural, archaeological, and artistic data from several cultures makes interpretations more tenable. While reliance on one culture has inherent dangers, a broad cultural base of support is profitable. On the other hand, comparison of Teotihuacan with the Mixtec, Maya, Aztec, and Teuchtitlan cultures can also reveal Mesoamerican cultural paradigms. It may show that certain concepts, including state promotion of gender roles, were widespread and fundamental ideas among the greater Mesoamerican world.

ART, PROPAGANDA, AND WAR

If butterfly imagery indicates that incentive warfare played a critical role in the foundations of power for the Teotihuacan state, it would have been important for the state to effectively indoctrinate its population with the belief system behind this form of war. To advance a universal compliance with this state ideology of war, the elite of Teotihuacan had to develop mechanisms by which to instruct its population. For this reason, the art and architecture of the city became invaluable tools through which to communicate state propaganda.

To this end, butterfly imagery appears in a variety of artistic media from the city. The painted murals that once covered the city commonly include butterflies. They flit in the background among large central figures or smaller humans in a manner that reflects the harmonious life that Sahagún described for dead warriors. Warriors clad in butterfly costumes also process around Teotihuacan vessels decorated with relief or fresco techniques. These images may represent the living warriors who wear the state's promise on their bodies in an effort to bolster their courage, or these vessels depict and commemorate fallen warriors. In the latter case the vessel would record the last image of the warrior in his battle clothes and a suggestion of the afterlife to which he went. Another category of ceramic objects, censers, may have served similar memorializing purposes.

The censers provide particularly fascinating examples of butterfly imagery in Teotihuacan's artistic record because they are so convincingly associated with funerary rituals (Figure 7.11). If, as has been proposed, the central mask represents a portrait of a deceased individual, then the censers with butterfly motifs could arguably represent heroic, dead warriors (Berlo 1983b, 1984). Perhaps more than any other medium, the censers mirror what was unique about the art of Teotihuacan. The basic censer container and framework were made without any decorative embellishments and followed a standardized format. All of the decorative elements were manufactured separately and attached later. Furthermore, the vast majority of censer fragments seem to be mold-made, which allowed for mass production of the component parts. Even though the intent of the masks may have been to represent an individual, they too were mold-made, and the facial features are generalized. The aspect of portraiture entered when the parts were assembled into a composite whole. By picking and choosing from among the many decorative elements and arranging them in a number of ways, the Teotihuacanos could construct an infinite

variety of censers. Rather like our own Christmas trees, one could use mass manufactured decorations to create a customized religious image. The facial paint applied to some masks may have transformed the generic mask into an individual representation; likewise, the very choice of adornos may have served as a reflection of the intended person (Berrin and Pasztory 1993:219–220). One almost imagines that upon the death of a loved one, the family could visit a censer vendor, pick out the little ceramic plaques that fit with the occupation and interests of the deceased, and then request that they be assembled into a portrait. What is paradoxical about this scenario, however, is that the portrait was created completely with mass-produced materials.

A further irony of the censers is related to who may have manufactured and distributed some of them. In excavations near the northwest exterior corner of the Ciudadela, archaeologists found a workshop with approximately 20,000 ceramic fragments (Berrin and Pasztory 1993:21; Múnera Bermudez 1985; Múnera Bermudez and Sugiyama n.d.). In particular, the workshop contained extensive quantities of censer fragments, including censer bases, adornos, and the molds used to manufacture censer parts. By means of stairs on the Ciudadela's north platform, the workshop fully communicated with the large compound. Furthermore, significant quantities of censers similar to those in the workshop appear among materials found in the North Palace of the Ciudadela. Taube (2000a) interpreted this as evidence that censer activities were an important part of ritual events at the Ciudadela; however, it is also possible that some censers were manufactured at the Ciudadela and used elsewhere in the city.

If the palaces to either side of the Feathered Serpent Pyramid are indeed royal residences, it is somewhat surprising that the rulers of this great city were so actively engaged in sponsoring censer manufacture. One must question the motivation behind royal promotion of a populist form of ancestor worship. Because so many censer fragments are found within the apartment compound patios, one possibility is that some of these censers had their origin at the Ciudadela ceramic workshop. Under this scenario, it would seem that the central power of Teotihuacan had a vested interest in encouraging the veneration of ancestors within the apartment compounds. Through the distribution of censers, the rulers of Teotihuacan may have subsidized the art associated with household-level ancestor veneration. Such actions could have developed continuity between the center and the surrounding populace because veneration of lineage elites on the Avenue of the Dead would be replicated within the domestic sphere. However, Teotihuacan's rulers may have had an even greater need to encourage ancestor veneration within the apartment compounds.

Among the many censer parts found in the Ciudadela workshop, some included butterfly imagery, and royal sponsorship of militarily related censers fits within the model proposed here. In his delicate dance of balancing power, the ruler used the military to undercut the elites of the dominant lineages because the military provided a base of support that was outside of familial interests and pulled from many segments of Teotihuacan society. It is difficult to believe that the ruler used the Ciudadela workshop as a straightforward economic enterprise; thus any distribution of the censers from the royal compound must have been in exchange for a social category of capital. In the case of butterfly-decorated censers, it seems plausible that the recipients were family members of a fallen warrior. If the censer represented a portrait of the dead warrior, the royal gift would have served to commemorate the memory of the warrior even as it celebrated his sacrifice for the state. A censer such as this could even be displayed within the apartment compound to project the family's loyalty to the state and their prominent role in maintaining the state. The frequency of censer parts found within the principal patios makes these areas a fitting location for such display.

The most obvious parallel to this hypothesis can be seen in the actions taken by the United States government upon the death of a soldier. If the death occurred in action, his family receives a folded flag, which is frequently displayed in the living room, the most public room in the house. The flag doubly serves to sustain the memory of the deceased even as it projects the family's support of the cause for which he died. The cause, of course, is the military activities of the state. In all, the Ciudadela workshop may have pro-

vided one route through which the ruler could promote the ideology of warfare and loyalty to the state, and the medium of the censer may have allowed him to infiltrate the domestic spaces of citizens and engender a form of patriotism.

Compared to the city's architecture, the censers seem a rather modest vehicle through which to convey the ideology of war. Given the unmistakable visual similarities of *talud-tablero* architecture to the butterfly noseplaque, Teotihuacanos must have associated their civic architecture with the city's cult of war. Like a mnemonic device, the architecture would have reminded residents of the intimate relationship between the individual and the state, and would have embodied culturally normative gender roles as well as the reward for compliance with state ideals. *Talud-tablero* was nothing less than a propagandistic tool through which the sociopolitical forces of Teotihuacan shaped behavior by cultivating a set of expectations within its population. The architecture reminded residents that their duty was to pursue the goals of the state; that is, to fight in the wars that the city declared. In return, Teotihuacan promised its citizens that the rewards of an extraordinary afterlife would shower down upon the martyrs created in these wars.

An insidious quality of this propaganda is that it was inescapable. *Talud-tablero* structures lined the Avenue of the Dead on both sides. Walking up the avenue, *talud-tablero* walls frame and delimit one's space and largely dominate the visual experience. Rather like the blinkers put on racehorses, the walls force a particular vision upon the individual, and the vision here carried a symbolic component that was deadly serious. There was no respite for Teotihuacan's citizens because they could not evade the state propaganda by retreating to their domestic spaces. In the form of the structures clustered around the principal patios, *talud-tablero* invaded the apartment compounds and further imprinted the doctrines of butterfly war upon the inhabitants. By fostering similar ideology in public and domestic spaces, the architectural style was one more vehicle used to unify the city. *Talud-tablero* was all-pervasive, and this omnipresence perpetually hammered the ideology of war into the minds of every Teotihuacano.

CHAPTER 8

FIESTA TEOTIHUACAN STYLE

Thus far the emphasis has been on architectural and visual mechanisms used by the state to structure a unified ideology for its citizens. The subjects covered have included architectural arrangements and the stylistic components of the architecture. The murals that frequently grace these architectural environments have also served as evidence, as have the painted and carved decorations on ceramics. Sculptural resources in the form of the stone masks have likewise emerged as remnants of perishable cult objects that affected social hierarchies. Enhanced with ethnohistoric data and cross-cultural comparison, the artistic record has revealed much about Teotihuacan's possible sociopolitical organization and the interactions between the disparate constituents. However, the art can illuminate one more facet of Teotihuacan state activity that profoundly contributed to the successful functioning of the state.

Ritual performance is, by nature, ephemeral; therefore, it is difficult to reconstruct from the archaeological record. Although there are inherent difficulties in revealing the transitory events of an archaeological culture, cultures endeavor to document these activities for posterity in numerous ways, and the artistic and architectural record of Teotihuacan does reflect such attempts to archive ritual occurrences. The lines of striding figures in the Teotihuacan murals indicate that procession was an important aspect of the city's ritual life and one of the primary means for displaying prestigious costume elements such as the butterfly noseplaque. Similarly, the elaborate caches under the Moon Pyramid, which included both human and animal remains, likely represent the residue of magnificent public spectacles. As a last foray into Teotihuacan's past, I want to turn to one specific ritual and attempt a reconstruction of this event. Doubtless, a city like Teotihuacan had many public rituals with considerable sociological and ideological impact, but this particular one is critical because it may have been the single most important annual event in the Teotihuacan ritual cycle.

Evidence for this ritual comes from the so-called Tlalocan murals in the apartment compound of Tepantitla. Already discussed in previous chapters, the murals deserve much more attention because they are conceptually grand; furthermore, the inclusion of large numbers of human figures suggests that the artists attempted a comprehensive image of a Teotihuacan event. The rich density of various activities within the murals has consistently drawn scholars to them, and they may be the most discussed murals from the ancient city.

The Tepantitla murals appear on all four sides of the compound's Portico 2. Like many murals at Teotihuacan, artists let the architectural format dictate to some degree the arrangement of the composition. The upper walls, which correspond to the *tablero,* serve as one compositional space, while the lower walls, paralleling the *talud,* provide another (Figure 3.2). As a result, the walls include two separate but complementary scenes. Framing is also an essential component of Teotihuacan compositions, and at Tepantitla, frames reinforce the distinction between the *talud* and *tablero* spaces. Even though there are differences in the preservation of the various walls, it appears that a frontal image of the mountain-tree dominated the superior section of each one (Figure 1.14). Villagra's reconstruction of the murals indicates that pairs of priests, perhaps even the rulers themselves, approached the mountain-tree and sprinkled offerings before it.[1] The rather formal and austere nature of the upper walls contrasts markedly with the free-spirited environment of the lower walls (Figure 2.3). Here, much smaller figures frolic about, engaged in a myriad of individual and group activities. Instead of the repetition seen above, the *talud* spaces vary from wall to wall. In an effort to standardize references to the different walls, Pasztory gave them names such as the Water Talud, the Medicine Talud, and the Ballgame Talud based on thematic elements included in each wall.

The contrasting styles of the upper and lower walls prompt the viewer to continually compare the two areas. Scale forcefully projects that the large upper figures carry more importance than the tiny figures that populate the nether region. In addition, the costume and features of the priests and the personified mountain are intricately detailed. The artists carefully delineated the skirts and capes of the priests, and the portions that survive exhibit elaborate feathered headdresses on these figures. The *talud* figures, in contrast, are scantily clad in simple loincloths, many are bald, and only a few of those with hair have rudimentary headgear. While the upper figures rigidly adhere to their profile or frontal positions, the people in the lower section twist, turn, squat, stand, and tumble. These individuals are a lively bunch in contrast to the stoic pomp and circumstance seen above.

The dense population of figures and the narrative characteristic of the *taludes* have naturally intrigued many scholars. It was Caso's (1942a) important early study that identified the central figure of the upper compositions as Tlaloc. Instead of discussing all of the lower walls, Caso focused on the Water Talud, which includes figures playing games and waving lush branches in the midst of butterflies. He maintained that the seemingly happy people represented the souls of Tlalocan, the paradise of those who died from water-related causes.

Many who followed accepted Caso's Tlalocan hypothesis until Pasztory (1974, 1988, 1997) and Furst (1974) eventually countered by pointing out that the large deity was not Tlaloc, but a female who would later carry the name "Great Goddess." Their insight was pivotal because the U-shaped opening near the bottom of the personified mountain and the waters that torrentially flow from it decidedly convey a vaginal opening emitting life-generative birth waters. Pasztory also emphasized the tree growing from this goddess, and she brilliantly developed an interpretation of a goddess as the cosmic mountain at the center of the universe with the world tree emerging from the top. Furthermore, she not only saw the goddess as Teotihuacan's version of the *axis mundi,* but she importantly removed the image from the supernatural world of Tlalocan. The priests, she reasoned, indicated an image from this world; that is, a scene that took place at Teotihuacan. In turn, the goddess, she posited, was actually a decorated idol used by the priests in their ritual. Expanding beyond the restrictive scope of Caso, Pasztory incorporated all of the murals into her model and argued that the lower walls depicted a variety of ritual events that regularly took place at Teotihuacan. Her arguments masterfully brought the Tepantitla murals down to earth and absorbed them into the ritual life of the city.

Pasztory's assertion that the murals record human activities that took place within Teotihuacan leads to productive conclusions if we use this lens to explore the central figure on the upper walls. Even though I refrain from calling the image a goddess, I heartily concur with Pasztory that the mural does not depict a vision of a deity existing in the supernatural plane but instead offers an image of an idol, one that the Teotihuacanos created. The implications of this interpretation are significant. Following Caso's view that this scene exists in the supernatural world, the artists would have attempted to capture the intangible world. The presence of the priests sprinkling offerings would primarily convey the devout homage of the people for the mountain-tree. If, instead, the upper murals depict an actual ritual, the need to define the abstract world and praise a supernatural entity may still exist; however, it is tempered by a motive to document an historic event and the role of the human actors in that event. It elevates the position of humans and makes their actions the central theme. I would build on this distinction and suggest just what the specific ritual event was on the upper walls of the Tepantitla murals. Furthermore, the identification of the particular ritual implies the likely location of the ceremony. By incorporating the Tepantitla murals into the archaeological and ethnohistoric record, the dynamic function of Teotihuacan civic festivities can gradually emerge.

THE MESOAMERICAN TRADITION OF TREE RAISING

The frontality and dominant size of the mountain-tree in the murals clearly indicate that

FIGURE 8.1. Olmec ruler raising a staff, stone, Monument 1, San Martín Pajapan, Formative. Drawing by Linda Schele, © David Schele, courtesy of the Foundation for the Advancement of Mesoamerican Studies, Inc., www.famsi.org.

it is the focal point of the entire mural program (Figure 1.14). The priests who walk toward it additionally direct the eye to the personified mountain, especially with their hands extended toward it. The mountain-tree is a composite entity with the cave-like vaginal opening correlating with the underworld and the wavy branches of the tree extending into the realm of the heavens: it thus represents the three cosmological levels of under, middle, and upper worlds connected into a fluid whole, an *axis mundi*. It is the tree on top of the mountain, however, that may suggest the particular activity documented in the Tepantitla murals because the erection of trees was a common and profoundly essential ritual throughout Mesoamerica.

An early example of a tree-raising ritual was found near the crater of the volcanic mountain of San Martín Pajapan (Figure 8.1). This Formative period sculpture depicts an Olmec ruler who leans forward and grasps a bar in his hands. His headgear consists of a cleft-headed were-jaguar headdress sprouting with foliage that marks the crown of kings (Fields 1989, 1991; Schele and Freidel 1990:115). He has one leg tucked underneath him and the other leg planted on the ground, indicating that he is about to push his weight onto his vertical leg and stand. Meanwhile, he holds his hands with one palm to the ground and the other towards the sky. If he were to stand, his hands look as though he would turn the staff so that it would assume a vertical position. The quadripartite decoration on the top of

FIGURE 8.2. World tree on the Tablet of the Cross, Temple of the Cross, Palenque, A.D. 690. Drawing by Linda Schele, © David Schele, courtesy of the Foundation for the Advancement of Mesoamerican Studies, Inc., www.famsi.org.

the staff as well as the activities of the ruler led Kent Reilly to interpret the staff as a world tree that the ruler is about to raise.[2] As he moved to a standing position, the ruler would rotate the tree from horizontal to vertical and symbolically erect the tree, and the act of raising a tree seems to have been a royal prerogative with sufficient importance to warrant carving the event in the permanence of stone.

The ancient Maya interest in tree raising surfaces through the integration of hieroglyphic texts and visual imagery. To date, Freidel, Schele, and Parker (1993:59–122) have presented the most thorough reconstruction of Maya concepts on this issue. Their model highlighted texts

from Quirigua and Palenque that told the ancient Maya version of creation.[3] On the day that this world began, the texts speak of "raising up the sky" and the *Wakah-Chan.* The authors identify the *Wakah-Chan* as the world tree, or *axis mundi,* most beautifully depicted at Palenque on the Tablet of the Cross and K'inich Janaab' Pakal I's sarcophagus (Figures 2.6 and 8.2). They then compare the texts to events seen in the night sky and argue that the Maya viewed the Milky Way in its north-south orientation as the *Wakah-Chan.* By observing the movement of the Milky Way on nights associated with creation, the Maya could watch as the Milky Way rotated into an upright position and created the "raised up sky" that separated the heavens from the earth and established vertical space. Their account intimately links tree raising with the creation of the physical world and, furthermore, the beginning of time because the heavenly clock begins its rhythm subsequent to the erection of the tree.

Taking a bold leap to the present, a version of the tree-raising ritual still continues today in the form of the *palo volador,* or flying pole dance, of Veracruz and the highlands of Puebla (Toor 1947:317–323). Many tourists have witnessed the *palo volador* in reenactments at the archaeological sites of Teotihuacan and El Tajin. At the appointed time, five costumed men enter a space containing a large, permanently erected pole. To the awe of the onlookers they climb to the top of the pole and position themselves precariously around a small platform. While one individual stands on the tiny platform playing a drum and flute, the other four attach themselves to ropes and plunge off headfirst to begin spinning around the pole as the ropes unwind. Without any cultural understanding of the event, most tourists are left to admire the bravery of the *voladores* and to consider it a quaint version of something that might once have been "authentic."

Because of the staged nature of these versions, it would be easy to dismiss the modern *palo volador* as a faded remnant of the past, yet even though these reenactments have been sanitized and isolated from their surrounding events and populations, they still carry the imprint of their ritual nature. Each of the four men revolves around the pole thirteen times, resulting in a total of fifty-two circumambulations, the number of years in the sacred calendar round (Durán 1994:143, n. 1). During Aztec times one of the most symbolically charged celebrations occurred at the conclusion of the fifty-two year count. Called the *toxiuhmolpilli,* or the "binding of the years," it commemorated the creation of the world and the rising of the first sun (Durán 1994:445–446). Temples and households throughout the Mexica empire extinguished their fires for four days and destroyed common household utensils and devotional objects. The people tossed out images of deities, hearthstones, and manos as a form of cleansing their communities

in preparation for the new era. Then, on a mountain called Huixachtecatl, the Mexica drilled a new fire on the breast of an elite captive, and from this virgin fire all of the empire's hearths were reignited (Durán 1994:107, n. 2; Sahagún 1950–1982:VII:25–32). The rekindling of the fires reenacted the ignition of the fifth sun and marked the dawn of a new calendrical cycle. As for the *palo volador,* the fifty-two circumambulations indicate a strong calendrical association for the ritual and implicate the tree in creation symbolism. Although the tourist-driven performances of the *palo volador* place no emphasis on the erection of the pole, there is substantial evidence that this activity is of great consequence in more traditional versions.

When the *palo volador* is part of community rituals, the acquisition of the tree proceeds in an intensely sacramental fashion. Once a proper tree is located, the men beg the tree's forgiveness for cutting it. To lessen the tree's pain as its branches are cut, they pour a fermented beverage called *tepache* on it, and they sing and dance around it as they fell the tree. The men take great care when they carry the tree, so much so that they pour additional alcohol on the ground when they need to set it down to rest. The celebration that ensues when the men enter town implies that the tree is a sacred object. The celebrants shoot fireworks and ring church bells to welcome the tree into their community. Mirroring the caches often found beneath Precolumbian stelae, the hole dug for the tree's erection is a receptacle for sacred offerings. Customarily, food, liquor, and a live chicken are placed in the hole to sacrilize the event (Durán 1971:163, n. 2; Toor 1947:319–321). The care and deference offered to the tree before its erection highlight the symbolic underpinnings of the eventual climb and descent of the *voladores.* Because the calendrical number of fifty-two characterizes the main spectacle, the ritual aspects of the tree's erection indicate close ties to the Maya creation story. In both cases tree raising designates the beginning of a calendrical cycle that ultimately represents the inception of time.

Two important tree-raising rituals performed by the Aztecs offer more insight into this Mesoamerican tradition. The Mexica referred to one of these trees as Tota, or Our Father, during the Feast of the Waters.[4] The ritual may have mirrored others and had calendrical significance because the Aztecs cut the tree on the mountain of Huixachtecatl, the same place where priests drilled the new fire every fifty-two years. The selection of the tree and its treatment are also akin to the *palo volador*. The chosen tree had to be the largest and most perfect specimen with especially lush foliage. This tree was never to touch the ground, so they used ropes to elevate it even as they cut it down, and the ropes then helped the men carry the tree back to Tenochtitlan. This tree ceremony was somewhat different than that of the *voladores* in that the Mexica did not climb the tree. Instead, the tree was part of a temporary artificial landscape created in the main plaza of Tenochtitlan on Tlaloc's feast day. The Tota tree stood in the center of the imitation landscape, and four smaller trees marked each of the corners. Positioned in the archetypal Mesoamerican quincunx shape, the corner trees represented the four cardinal directions, while the Tota tree was the *axis mundi* of the center. As seen in the illustration accompanying Durán's text (Figure 8.3), a series of ropes tied between the trees emphasized the interconnectedness of the four directions and the center. In essence, the Tota ritual created a verdant cosmic model of the world.

During the festival the artificial forest was the location of song, dance, and games; moreover, the terminus of the celebration was equally loaded with ritual content. In a logical nod to the significance of the tree, its disposal was carried out with considerable respect. As the Mexica took down the tree, they bound its branches and placed it on a raft in Lake Texcoco. The procession to the lake also included priests and lords who carried a sacrificial girl in a litter. At the water's edge, they boarded canoes and took the girl and the tree to a location in the lake called Pantitlan. The Aztecs thought of it as the drain of the lake because a large whirlpool often formed there, and it was here that they unbound the tree's branches and plunged it into the lake. In the final act, the priests slit the young girl's throat and watched as her blood flowed into the water. They then threw her into the lake along with offerings of jewelry and stone. To the Aztec mind, this "drain" must have facilitated their offering to the supernatural world.

The second Aztec tree ceremony described

FIGURE 8.3. Aztec Tota festival from Durán's *Book of the Gods and Rites,* sixteenth century. Drawing by Mareike Sattler after Durán 1971:Plate 14.

by Durán more closely resembles the *voladores* ritual because it involved climbing a tree called the *xocotl,* or "precious pine." The tree climbing took place during the Small Feast of the Dead and the Great Feast of the Dead, a time for remembering deceased children and adults (Durán 1971:203–209; Sahagún 1997:60, n. 26). In this case the Aztecs cut all the branches from the tree and carefully smoothed the trunk. Once erected, they put a bird made of amaranth dough on top of the pole, which may have conveyed the celestial connotations of the upper portion. Great feasting ensued, and young girls and boys danced below the tree. The culminating event occurred on the last day just prior to sunset when the boys stopped dancing, took off their feathered dance clothes, and vied to be the first to climb up and capture the amaranth dough bird. The skill and bravery required to ascend to the top of the *xocotl* markedly resembles the heroics of the *voladores,* with both events providing an opportunity for the display of athletic abilities. In contrast to the ritual deposition of the Tota tree, the Aztecs cut down and dismembered the *xocotl* as Tenochtitlan's residents each tried to grab a piece as a memento of the event. The covetous nature of

a.

b.

FIGURE 8.4. Aztec Xocotl rituals from the *Primeros memoriales*, manuscript illustrations, sixteenth century: *a*) bringing in and erecting the tree; *b*) dancing around and climbing the tree. Drawings by Mareike Sattler after Sahagún 1993:Folio 251r–251v.

their actions would imply that the very substance of the tree was sacred.

The *xocotl* ritual also intrigued Sahagún (1950–1982:II:111–117), who offered his textual version of the events in the Florentine Codex. In this manuscript, Sahagún neglected to include an illustration; however, his earlier work, the *Primeros memoriales,* did contain two images and a brief text outlining the ceremony (Sahagún 1993:Fol. 251r–251v, 1997:60–62). In the first illustration (Figure 8.4a) four men enter from the left carrying the tree by means of ropes wrapped around its trunk. As with the traditional *palo volador,* the entrance of the tree into town warranted celebration, for a man in the upper left blows a trumpet, and a female stands before the tree with a shield and torch. Sahagún's text reveals that the female is probably an impersonator of the terrestrial deity Teteoinnan, who greeted the tree upon its arrival. Finally, in the back right corner, the men use the cords to erect the tree. With a nod towards continuity, the ropes attached to the tree parallel the cords used to carry the *voladores* tree, and they are reminiscent of the ropes wrapped between the Tota trees.

The subsequent image contains many of the details in the textual accounts and thus verifies Durán's description of the *xocotl* events (Figure 8.4b). Just below the tree a group of men hold hands, making a chain as they dance behind a figure bearing the deity Painal, who looks much like a wrapped mortuary bundle.[5] Behind the dancers are three men scaling the *xocotl,* and the uppermost has already succeeded in grasping the effigy figure on top. Sahagún's illustration and later text, however, add a more martial flavor to the event. The men who erected the tree were called warriors, and the individual who first reached the amaranth dough figure was considered its captor (Sahagún 1950–1982:II:111–117). Furthermore, Sahagún specified that the principal actors in the event were captors who carried shields and wore butterfly backracks. The *Primeros memoriales* image corroborates this because the lead dancer and the dough effigy wear paper butterfly ornaments in their hair, and several figures carry shields. The clear references to the butterfly reveal the dancers' desire to achieve the glorious afterlife of martyred warriors.

Sahagún's (1950–1982:II:113–117) description of events prior to the tree climbing attest to the centrality of warfare symbolism in the *xocotl* ritual. The dance showcased the military garb of the captors, which further included the eagle and jaguar imagery of the warrior orders. To publicly celebrate the warriors' prowess, the captors danced with their captives, who wore humble paper loincloths, and each captor received a hank of his captive's hair. Wrapped in a reed container, the hair became a visible trophy prominently displayed from the rafters of the captor's home. Eventually, the captor grabbed his victim by his remaining hair and pulled him to the foot of a temple, whereupon another group of men bound his hands and feet and carried him to the summit of the pyramid. Each captive warrior was temporarily roasted in a large fire before being extracted and having his heart removed. In a condensed fashion, the *Primeros memoriales* shows two men carrying a near naked man above their heads, and a bird's eye view of a victim burning in a rectangular fire pit (Figure 8.4b). Only after these sacrificial events transpired did the young warriors stampede the *xocotl* and race to the top, with the victor seizing the amaranth dough figure and breaking it apart as he sprinkled it upon the crowd below. On the whole, the *xocotl* festival provided a grand stage for successful warriors to receive public recognition of their triumphant deeds.

The militant flavor of Sahagún's account makes the presence of butterfly imagery in the visual record all the more pertinent. The headdresses worn by the lead dancer and the dough figure on top of the tree consist of a band around the head with two paper extensions terminating in notched forms. The same headdress also appears in another image of the *xocotl* from the Codex Magliabecchiano, implying the critical symbolism of this headgear (Figure 8.5).[6] The notched forms represent stylized butterflies, which, in turn, refer to the souls of dead warriors—the same warriors who transform into birds and butterflies.[7] Through text and imagery, Sahagún explained that the *xocotl* feast day honors both successful warriors and their heroic captives. On two occasions he referred to the sacrificial victims as brave and therefore worthy

FIGURE 8.5. Pole-climbing ceremony, manuscript illustration, Codex Magliabecchiano. Drawing by Mareike Sattler after Nuttall 1903:38.

of admiration. Even though the text does not directly state the ultimate fate of these sacrificed warriors, the paper headdresses allude to their eventual metamorphosis into butterflies. In turn, the reference to the afterlife of martyred warriors provides a link to Durán's version of the *xocotl* ritual (Durán 1971:203–209). He stated that the tree was a component in the Feast of the Dead. When married into one uniform account of the festival, it appears that a prominent category of ancestors celebrated during the *xocotl* events was the souls of dead warriors.

The mere fact that at least three separate tree-raising rituals existed in central Mexico during the Postclassic and modern times attests to the consequential role such events played in the region's religious cycle. When coupled with the evidence for tree erection among the Olmec and Maya, the ritual emerges as central to Mesoamerican religions.[8] In truth, there is some variety between the different versions of tree raising, but, nevertheless, a number of consistent themes surface that suggest the ceremony's conceptual underpinnings. First and foremost, tree-raising events have definitive ties to the calendar that recall the erection of a tree in the creation story. At a fundamental level, all tree raisings must have symbolized the erection of the *axis mundi,* which offered the world a spatial dimension and allowed for celestial motion; that is, the establishment of time. The second aspect of tree rituals followed two dominant paths. While some trees allowed for heroic climbing displays, others were part of artificial landscapes that conveyed notions of cosmological order. Thus, in its centrality, the Tota tree became the clear embodiment of the *axis mundi.*

Two other prominent themes are the celebration of warriors and ancestors. Because some versions include butterfly imagery, one especially important category of ancestors was the sacrificed warriors. Finally, sacrifice often accompanied tree raisings. In the *xocotl* ritual, sacrifice was intimately interwoven into the glorification of warriors, with the deposition of the girl and tree into the lake during the Tota celebration indicating associations with water and fertility. Each of these rituals was multivocal in its symbolism, permitting the actual celebration to fulfill many social needs. However, when applying these accounts back upon Teotihuacan, there is no reason to believe that one of these specific rituals was practiced at this Classic site. Rather, the Postclassic ceremonies may have evolved out of earlier rituals, and, therefore, the material remains of Teotihuacan may harbor aspects of tree raisings practiced by other Mesoamerican cultures.

THE TEPANTITLA TREE RAISING

Given the widespread nature of tree festivities throughout the temporal and cultural boundaries of Mesoamerica, the tree painted on the upper walls of Tepantitla's Portico 2 seems much more convincingly an image of a human ceremony than a picture of a distant supernatural realm (Figure 1.14). The Tepantitla tree has verdant foliage spreading out above the personified mountain. The branches terminate in flowers surrounded with birds in full-throated song. Both the hands and vaginal opening of the mountain flow with water, irrigating a fertile landscape that sustains four more trees. The lush setting and the centrality of the mountain-tree in the midst of the smaller trees are reminiscent of the Tota festival. Although the ropes connecting the trees

are missing, the Teotihuacan image could similarly depict an artificial forest with five trees denoting the quincunx-arranged cosmological directions. Viewing the Tepantitla murals as an antecedent to the Tota ritual further explains the fullness of the branches on the Teotihuacan tree. In all other tree raisings, the celebrants removed the branches and smoothed the trunk to enhance the difficulty of climbing the tree. The curving branches of the Teotihuacan tree seem wholly unsuited for climbing, but they do correspond with Aztec requirements for a Tota tree. Such trees were supposed to be perfect specimens with dense foliage, and the floral and avian embellishments of the Tepantitla image comprise a tree bursting with life.

Yet, these same birds—in addition to the butterflies emblazoned on one tree branch—indicate that the Tota ritual is not the sole useful source for understanding the Teotihuacan tree. The great likelihood that the butterflies, and possibly the birds, represent the souls of deceased warriors is in accordance with other Aztec tree raisings such as the *xocotl* celebration. Occurring during the Small and Great Feasts of the Dead, the *xocotl* ritual was in part a time to remember the ancestors; however, Sahagún's account (1950–1982:II:111–117), with its overt military elements, asserts that deceased warriors received special recognition. More precisely, the butterfly headdress of the amaranth dough figure atop the *xocotl* tree as well as mention of butterfly backracks on the dancers specifically target sacrificial warriors as the most exemplary ancestors. Just as butterfly imagery was notably present in the Aztec ritual, so too do the upper and lower murals of Tepantitla incorporate this insect. Mirroring the tree with half of its branches dedicated to the celebration of dead warriors, the butterfly frequently appears in the lower portion of the murals (Figures 2.3, 8.6). Butterflies fly about the heads of many ritual participants in the Water Talud, and one figure even brandishes a staff decorated with a butterfly. Because this mural also includes a fecund mountain that sends water to agricultural fields sprouting with life, the butterflies could be construed as a general indication of the city's fertile well-being, yet this would ignore Aztec conceptions of the butterfly. In the lower mural, the butterflies are in close proximity to the many

human figures; if they are the souls of dead warriors, then the scene projects a ritual that brings
the honored dead into contact with their descendants. Such an interpretation accords well with
Sahagún's assertion that the *xocotl* tree raising
celebrated the dead.

Another figure in the Water Talud provides
further parallels between the Postclassic rituals and the Tepantitla murals. At the bottom
of the *talud*, rivers pouring from the mountain
lead to agricultural fields with sprouting plants
(Figure 2.7b). On the surviving portion, the river
comes to the edge of the composition and ter-
minates in a flower-shaped lake teaming with
aquatic life (Figure 8.7). At the top of the lake a
man stands on the shore and waves a leafy branch
as a particularly long set of speech scrolls emerges
from his mouth.[9] Interestingly, the glyph associated with the speech scroll nearest his mouth
is the three-mountain motif, which may be the
name of Teotihuacan or a reference to the Teotihuacan Valley.[10] Thus, the words of this individual may reveal the location of the Water Talud
activities; that is, he speaks the name of the town
where he was sacrificed. His status as a sacrificial
victim is clear, for lines of red and blue liquid
stream from his chest to merge with the waters
of the lake. A probable victim of heart sacrifice,
the tears flowing from his eyes demonstrate his
pain and, possibly, the rain expected from his
death. As such, the tears would be in concert
with Aztec child sacrifice, in which weeping
children slain on mountaintops encouraged the
Tlaloc gods to send plentiful water (Sahagún
1950–1982:II:1–2). Furthermore, the individual's
sacrifice in the proximity of a lake is strikingly
reminiscent of the final events in the Tota festival, even though the Aztec version concluded
with the slitting of a girl's throat before plunging
her into the lake. Nevertheless, the lush tree in
the Tepantitla mural and the sacrifice of a man
near a lake intriguingly correspond with two
critical components of the Postclassic festival.

A final point of comparison between the
Aztec tree rituals and the Tepantitla murals is
their overall festive nature. In the Water Talud
people frolic about in a seemingly infinite number of activities. One group holds hands, making
a chain as they perform a centipede dance, while
another individual holds a garland of flowers

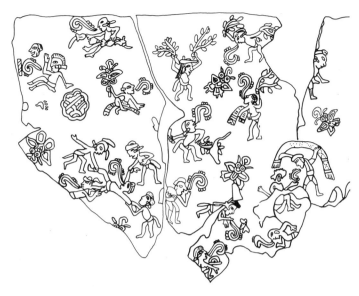

FIGURE 8.6. Butterflies with human celebrants, detail of the Water Talud
mural, Tepantitla, Teotihuacan. Drawing by Jenni Bongard after Pasztory
1976:Figure 36.

FIGURE 8.7. Sacrificial victim above a lake, detail of the Water
Talud mural, Tepantitla, Teotihuacan. Drawing by Jenni Bongard
after Pasztory 1976:Figure 36.

(Figures 8.6 and 8.8).[11] People play various games
in the upper left corner of the Water Talud, and
the central motif of the Ballgame Talud is a stick-
ball game complete with traces of a ballcourt and
markers (Figure 8.9).[12] As a composite whole,
the many lively figures seem to be at a fiesta that
involves the dancing, singing, and gaming that
Durán and Sahagún mentioned in their descriptions of the Tota tree and *xocotl* celebrations.

FIGURE 8.8. Centipede dance, detail of the Water Talud mural, Tepantitla, Teotihuacan. Drawing by Jenni Bongard after Pasztory 1976:Figure 36.

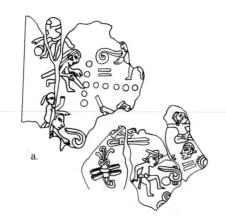

a.

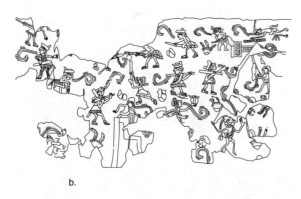

b.

FIGURE 8.9. Various games in the Water Talud mural (a) and the Ballgame Talud mural (b), Tepantitla, Teotihuacan. Drawings by Jenni Bongard after Pasztory 1976:Figures 36, 39.

Though more staid in nature, the priests in the upper mural also perform rituals in keeping with later traditions (Figure 1.14). The priests pay homage to the tree by sprinkling it with offerings in a manner much like the reverence given the *xocotl* and *palo volador* trees. One glaring difference, however, is the fact that the Teotihuacan tree is already fully erected when the priests anoint it. Unlike Sahagún, the Teotihuacan artists did not record practical information about transporting and erecting the tree. Instead they

provided a view of the finished product, a cult image decked in finery, with priests engaged in using the constructed image during ritual. While Sahagún may have taken an etic perspective and recorded the various steps taken by a decidedly foreign culture, the Teotihuacan artists, who were more concerned with documenting the event and conveying its religious meaning, naturally created an emic view.

Although the cult object was imbued with mysticism and spirituality, the painted image neglects to offer certain clues about the material construction of the Teotihuacan tree. Better communicating the animation that the ritual conveyed upon the object, the mountain itself is seemingly alive. The artists captured the mountain's hands in action as the arms spread to the sides and distribute the precious liquid. The curving vine-like branches of the tree almost seem to sway from the vigorous movements of the birds that dive in amongst the flowers. Yet a rather restrictive symmetry tempers the vibrancy of life otherwise exhibited in the image. The arch of the tree is perfectly balanced, and apart from the arms, the geometricized shapes that personify the mountain create a rigid and inhuman presence. Even the curling volutes that emerge from the mouth have a hard-edged quality, making the mountain appear rather blocky and stiff. The tension between the soft forms of the tree and the boxy configuration of the personified mountain may have some basis in reality because the Teotihuacanos may have erected their tree on a stone sculpture.

The Tepantitla image differs from other tree-raising rituals in that the Teotihuacanos did not set the tree directly into the earth. Sahagún (1950–1982:II:113) noted that a hole filled with small stones and soil secured the *xocotl,* and the Aztecs placed the Tota tree in a deep hole (Durán 1971:162). In contrast, the Tepantitla tree rises from a personified mountain, springing forth from a swath of feathers crowning its headdress. The inspiration for this may be metaphorical because there is a long tradition of trees growing from the body of an earth goddess.[13] In the Codex Borgia a reclining goddess with clawed hands has a tree rising from her abdomen (Figure 8.10). Similarly, the back of the *Teocalli,* a stone throne found at Tenochtitlan, has a supine

FIGURE 8.10. Tree emerging from a supernatural being, manuscript illustration, Codex Borgia, Postclassic. Drawing by Linda Schele, © David Schele, courtesy of the Foundation for the Advancement of Mesoamerican Studies, Inc., www.famsi.org.

FIGURE 8.11. Tree emerging from a goddess on the back of the *Teocalli,* Tenochtitlan, Aztec, Postclassic. Drawing by Linda Schele, © David Schele, courtesy of the Foundation for the Advancement of Mesoamerican Studies, Inc., www.famsi.org.

goddess in a pool of water (Figure 8.11). From the jaws of her open mouth emerge the fabled cactus and eagle of the Tenochtitlan foundation story. Both of these trees include a bird in their branches, which, along with the earthly symbolism of the water on the *Teocalli,* marks these trees as images of the *axis mundi.* Without a doubt, the Tepantitla tree carries the same symbolism, which may justify Pasztory's contention that the Teotihuacan mountain was conceptualized as a goddess.[14] However, the priests on either side and the activities in the murals below indicate that this tree is a human representation of a mythical concept rather than the supernatural itself. If we accept that the Tepantitla image documents an actual ritual performed by the Teotihuacanos, then we must also accede that they may have erected their tree on an image of the personified mountain. Colonial period chronicles frequently report that Mesoamericans decorated sculptures during rituals. Durán (1971) included descriptions of idols that were dressed with clothing, festooned with paper, and painted with sacrificial blood. By placing a tree on a sculpture, the Teotihuacanos would have

shared in a long tradition of enhancing inanimate objects.

Unfortunately, no surviving sculpture precisely mirrors the iconography seen on the Tepantitla mountain-tree. In the past I have argued that the battered sculpture in the Moon Plaza (Figure 2.17) was a promising candidate; however, the traces of iconography on this sculpture are decidedly inconclusive.[15] If this sculpture once wore a *quechquemitl,* it might represent a goddess, but the sculpture's ovoid eyes differ from the diamond-shaped eyes of the mural. The same applies to the Museo Nacional sculpture, and as argued earlier, these sculptures could just as easily portray rulers. Thus, while the identification of the physical object upon which the Teotihuacanos performed their version of the tree raising remains unresolved, the symbolism of tree raising in Mesoamerica suggests a plausible location in the city for this event.

CREATION CELEBRATIONS AT TEOTIHUACAN

Maya hieroglyphic texts reveal that tree raising was ultimately symbolic of the world's creation because the erection of the tree allowed for one of the most important events in the creation story, the movement of the sun in the sky. Unable to move in a world where the earth and the sky were sandwiched into one compact whole, the sun was given space to move when the tree separated these two features. The resulting motion of the sun instituted that other cosmic element: time (Freidel et al. 1993:59–122). In this light, the Aztec belief that solar creation occurred specifically at Teotihuacan is of particular interest.[16]

In Sahagún's Florentine Codex we learn that the gods convened at Teotihuacan to force the sun to move.

It is told that when yet [all] was in darkness, when no sun had shone and no dawn had broken—it is said—the gods gathered themselves together and took council among themselves there at Teotihuacan. They spoke; they said among themselves: "Come hither, O Gods! Who will carry the burden? Who will take it upon himself to be the sun, to bring the dawn?" (Sahagún 1950–1982:VII:4)

The author of the *Leyenda de los soles* concurred with this account, saying that the current fifth sun began at Teotihuacan (Codex Chimalpopoca 1975:121). Viewing this as evidence for Classic period concepts, René Millon has suggested that the Teotihuacanos shared this Aztec version of events and believed that their city existed at the very nucleus of creation.[17] Adding specificity to his argument, he contended that the cave under the Pyramid of the Sun was the actual location of solar creation.[18]

The integration of the cave into the architectural plan of the Sun Pyramid is remarkable in and of itself. Terminating in a four-lobed chamber that is quite close to the center of the pyramid's summit, the cave, in concert with the crest of the pyramid, links celestial and underworld into a cohesive statement of interconnectedness (Figure 1.9). However, this alone does not confirm the cave's identity as the birthplace of the sun. The strongest evidence for this comes from the role the cavern played in the orientation of the entire city.

As discussed earlier, the mouth of the Sun Pyramid cave seems to have served as the location from which to view the most important astronomical event recognized by the Teotihuacanos. The sun set on the same spot on the horizon twice a year during the Tzacualli period (A.D. 50–150): April 29 and August 12. August 12 is the most intriguing because it is one day before August 13, the Maya day of creation.[19] Thus, Aztec legend holds that creation occurred at Teotihuacan, and the Maya day of creation coincides with the sightline of sunset from the cave. These two factors substantiate Teotihuacan's participation within the greater Mesoamerican creation cycle; furthermore, the dates indicate that Teotihuacan shared in the calendrical tradition of Mesoamerica. The number of days separating April 29 and August 12 are 260 and 105, and 260 is the number of days in the calendrical count commonly referred to as the *tzolkin*.[20] When the 260-day *tzolkin* was paired with the 365-day calendar, the result was the 52-year sacred Calendar Round.

The calendrical significance of the cave was so charged with religious importance that it ultimately shaped the entire city of Teotihuacan. We cannot fail to remember that the sightline from the cave is perpendicular with the Avenue of the Dead, which leads to the conclusion that the celestial event determined the orientation of the city. The motion of the sun in the heavens above apparently inspired the designers of Teotihuacan, resulting in a city in which the very buildings recalled the creation myth. The power behind this strategy was that it reinforced the belief that Teotihuacan was the location where the pivotal moments in cosmic history occurred.

The prominence of this sightline would explain why the Sun Pyramid is not only the largest structure at the site, but also one of the most massive constructions ever built in Mesoamerica. Nevertheless, the size of the pyramid is somewhat paradoxical in relationship to its placement. As discussed in chapter 6, the Sun Pyramid's western orientation affected the directionality of many sacred spaces. From palaces along the avenue to the more private apartment compounds, ritual structures generally faced to the west; there-

FIGURE 8.12. Southerly view of the Plaza of the Moon including the Building of the Altars (*foreground*) and the central plaza altar (*background*), Teotihuacan.

fore, much of Teotihuacan ritual behavior may have moved along an east-west axis to mimic the arrangement of the largest pyramid. Yet interestingly, this east-west axis did not dominate the site as a whole because the north-south axis of the Avenue of the Dead was the unmistakable artery that shaped everyday life and arguably framed ritual activities as well.[21] Even today with so much of the architecture missing, one cannot help but imagine the pageantry that must have taken place in the vast expanse of this broad street.

Although the Sun Pyramid may astound us with its overwhelming bulk, the real focal draw of the city is the Moon Pyramid, which beckons at the end of the avenue. The planners designed Teotihuacan so that its visitors were drawn ever closer to Cerro Gordo and the Moon Pyramid; consequently, entrance into the Plaza of the Moon must have brought with it a feeling of

fulfillment in having attained the quest. Though the Moon Pyramid was slightly smaller, its commanding presence on the avenue would have made the enormous plaza before it a sensational location for grand public spectacles. Indeed, there is much about the Plaza of the Moon to suggest that it played a pivotal role in public rituals. More specifically, the Teotihuacanos must have staged magnificent ceremonies to commemorate its identity as the birthplace of the sun and "the place where time began."[22]

RITUAL AND THE PLAZA OF THE MOON

Although the pyramid's soaring presence initially pulls the visitor into the Plaza of the Moon, once in the plaza the enormity of the enclosed space profoundly shapes one's experience (Figure 8.12). The Moon Pyramid serves as the north barrier, and a number of smaller but still monumental temples form the eastern and western sides of the plaza space. Structures in the southern corners constrict movement in this direction to channel people into the Avenue of the Dead. The broad avenue and passageways between the encircling temples provide practical routes for entrance and departure, yet the sensation of containment still dominates in the framed space.

Two structures along the central axis break up the expanse of the plaza. The first of these is an altar with a nearby mutilated sculpture. This square altar has a set of stairs on each of its four sides, and it would be the first structure one would encounter upon entering the plaza. Significantly, it sits in the approximate middle of the enclosure, which could imply its centrality to ritual events. If the damaged sculpture once sat on the platform, its location would assert that this sculpture served as an important cult image for the entire community, sitting, as it does, at the apex of Teotihuacan civic space.

Beyond this altar, tucked right in front of the stairs to the Moon Pyramid, is another square building that has a unique configuration in Mesoamerican architecture (Figures 8.12 and 8.13). Although this building sits at the terminus of the north-south axis, the door on its west-

ern side makes an obvious nod to the east-west ritual orientation of the Sun Pyramid. Called the Building of the Altars, its interior consists of a number of oddly angled walls that may have once formed the bases of altars. The arrangement of these possible altars follows a symmetrical pattern around a rectangular altar in the middle of the building. Additional altars sit in each of the four cardinal directions. Even though two altars technically exist on the western wall, they should be conceptually conceived of as one altar because the need for an entrance on axis seems to have prompted its division.[23] Walls on either side of the eastern altar indicate that it was originally inside an interior room, and coupled with its larger size, this altar was probably the most important.[24] Near each of the four corners, curious diagonal altars project into the remaining space. Because the upper walls are damaged and there are no traces of decoration, interpreting the configuration and purpose of the internal space is impossible. Nevertheless, as Otto Schondube (1975) brilliantly asserted, the spatial arrangement is markedly similar to a famous image in the Codex Féjérvary-Mayer.[25]

The image in this Postclassic codex has received much attention because it seems to provide a visual conceptualization of cosmic space by diagramming the integration of time and geography (Figure 8.14).[26] The temporal component emerges from a series of dots and glyphs found around the perimeter of the image. The number of dots comes to 260; that is, the number of days in the *tzolkin*. Day names and the arrangement of the dots divide them into groups of 13 with 20 named days, which precisely mirrors the Maya 260-day calendar. In the four corners are cartouches with each of the four year bearers, thus the image further expresses the 52-year calendar comprised of four 13-year periods.

The spatial dimension rests on the four trapezoidal motifs that form a cross. The artist painted each arm of the cross a different color for each of the four directions. East is red, west is blue, north is yellow, and south is green. Just as within the Building of the Altars, the direction of east is paramount, appearing at the top of the map with a solar disk resting on a temple platform. In contrast, a death head labels the western region because this is where the sun dies each night;

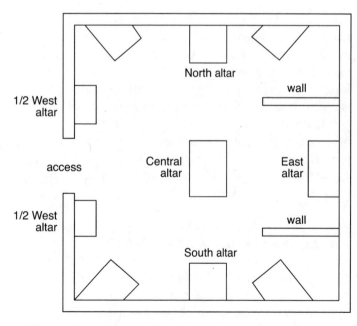

FIGURE 8.13. Plan of the Building of the Altars, Teotihuacan. Drawing by Jenni Bongard after Schondube 1975:Figure 1.

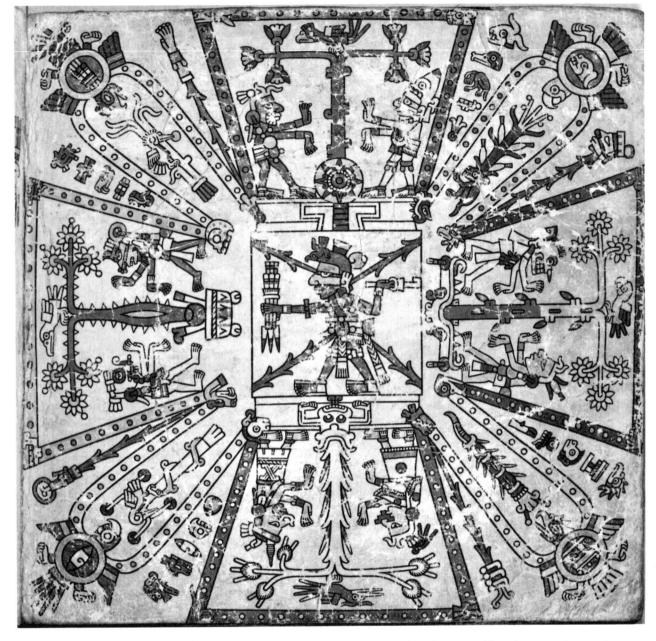

FIGURE 8.14. Calendrical page of the Codex Féjérvary-Mayer, manuscript illustration, Puebla-Mixteca area, fifteenth century. Photograph courtesy of World Museum Liverpool, © National Museums of Liverpool.

hence the vertical axis records the path of the sun. Not only does the Féjérvary-Mayer calendar designate the cardinal directions, but the looped forms in the corners represent the intercardinal points. As Brotherston (1976) and Aveni (1980) have noted, these intercardinals additionally symbolize the extreme solar positions of the winter and summer solstices.[27] Moving in a clockwise pattern from the upper left corner, the diagonals mark the summer solstice sunrise, winter sol-

stice sunrise, winter solstice sunset, and finally the summer solstice sunset. Viewed as an attempt to give tangible form to complex philosophical understandings of the world's natural order, the calendar in the Codex Féjérvary-Mayer is a staggering *tour de force*. Time and space are married into a cohesive visual model that conveys the essence of the world remarkably on a two-dimensional surface.

When Schondube (1975) compared the codex

image to the Building of the Altars, he justly proposed that the structure was a Classic period, three-dimensional version of the ideas recorded in the manuscript. He emphasized that the altars in the structure demarcate the center and the four cardinal directions, and I would persist in adding that the diagonal altars signify the inter-cardinals. The importance of the eight cardinal and intercardinal altars in the space arises not only from the spatial arrangement recorded in the Postclassic codex, but also from a Classic period text at the Maya city of Palenque.

The Tablet of the Cross includes a creation passage that describes a place called "the north house." The text reads,

hoy wakah chanal waxakna-tzuk u ch'ul k'aba yotot xaman
[it] was made proper, the Raised-up-Sky-Place, the Eight-House partitions, [is] its holy name, the house of the north. (Freidel et al. 1993:71)

In the passage, the "Raised-up-Sky" refers to the fact that at this point in the creation story the sky has now been separated from the earth.[28] Moreover, the Mayan words for the "Raised-up-Sky," *Wakah-Chan,* are also the name of the world tree. Therefore, the inscription reveals that the erection of the world tree, which produced vertical space, was intimately connected with the founding of the north house. By using the word *tzuk,* or partition, the Maya scribes character-ized the nature of this house, explicitly stating that it had eight partitions. In short, the culmi-nating events of creation are the raising of the tree and the establishment of the north house with its eight partitions. The continuity is re-markable when this information is overlaid upon the Building of the Altars. As a building, the structure easily qualifies under the generic des-ignation of "house" that many Mesoamericans applied to their constructions, and the altars in-side give this house its eight partitions. Located in the northern extreme of the site, this eight-partitioned house appears to be the same "north house" described in the Maya texts.

Just as the Féjérvary-Mayer calendar conveys notions of geographic space, so too does the in-ternal arrangement of the Building of the Altars recognize the spatial organization of the world.

One also wonders if the structure directly ac-knowledged the temporal element in its original appearance. If the diagonal altars commemorated the solstice points, then the structure would have incorporated a sense of temporality through solar motion. Furthermore, the decorative program of the building may have once documented the integration of time and space. Only patches of plaster survive on the fragmentary walls, but it is tempting to wonder whether the four colors of the cardinal directions or the 260 dots seen in the codex were manifest in the temple's decoration. The fact that the sightline from the Sun Pyra-mid cave marked two days separated by 105 and 260 days makes it possible that the Teotihuacanos recognized the 260-day calendar; therefore, the configuration of this building makes it a deeply viable candidate for celebration of the calendar and, more specifically, the day upon which that calendar began.

In sum, the Building of the Altars seems to reflect Classic and Postclassic conceptions of tem-poral and spatial reality, most notably as they are expressed through the creation sequence. Its northern location qualifies it as the mythi-cal north house, and the eight altars conform to Maya descriptions of this supernatural locale. The building's incorporation of the 260-day calendar is only speculative, but it is quite tenable that this structure was where the Teotihuacanos annually commemorated the division of the world into the eight directions. By performing a ritual cir-cuit inside the building, the priests would have recalled the creation of horizontal space, which conveniently reinforced the centrality of Teoti-huacan itself. After all, the arrangement of the altars inside the structure implies that the cardi-nal and intercardinal directions emanate directly from the Plaza of the Moon.

Although the Building of the Altars pos-sibly concentrates on time, it surely records the important element of horizontal space in the creation story. However, it would be unwise to neglect the critical role of vertical space in the creation events. The Palenque text couples the *Wakah-Chan* with the north house, and the Codex Féjérvary-Mayer alludes to tree raising, with the four trees tended by pairs of attendants in each of the cardinal directions (Figure 8.14).

Although trees could have been erected on the platforms inside the Building of the Altars, it seems more likely that the tree raising took place in the surrounding plaza, just as the Aztecs erected their Tota tree in their main plaza. The central altar of the Moon Plaza would have been a prominent and spectacular location for the tree raising, and it is possible the altar and the now-damaged sculpture played a role in this ritual. The plaza also would have offered the splendid backdrop of the Moon Pyramid and Cerro Gordo, which is all the more pertinent because the Tepantitla murals intimately connect the tree with a mountain. A decorated tree within the plaza would have had the mountain behind it and would have physically reproduced the visual connection between mountain and tree seen in the mural. Mesoamerican parallels forcefully assert that the Teotihuacanos erected their tree, their *axis mundi,* in close proximity to the north house in the Plaza of the Moon near the cosmic mountain filled with life-sustaining water.

Overwhelmingly, tree raising was the metaphor used by Mesoamericans to illustrate the establishment of vertical space, and one might expect the Moon Plaza to incorporate this crucial component of the story. The Tepantitla murals undoubtedly depict the veneration of a tree rising from a mountain. Because the entirety of the mural program shows humans interacting with that tree, the painting more likely documents a ritual that took place at Teotihuacan than a distant image of the supernatural. The prominence of tree-raising rituals throughout Mesoamerica justifies assuming the presence of a similar event at Teotihuacan, yet Tepantitla indicates that this version involved a tree placed on an idol or representation of a mountain. The interior of the Building of the Altars affirms that creation rituals occurred within its walls, and following the creation sequence, one would expect tree raising to transpire nearby. The plaza is the most public of spaces, and large enough to hold a swelling crowd. The surrounding buildings would have provided more viewing platforms and served as stages upon which performers could move about. Paired as they are within the plaza enclosure, the Building of the Altars and the altar with the sculpture constitute a space within which to pub-

licly reenact the creation cycle. Conjoined, they provide locations where elites could symbolically produce the vertical and horizontal ingredients of cosmic organization.

This model of ritual behavior leaves open two questions: when in the ritual calendar did this occur, and why was the culmination of the event in the Plaza of the Moon instead of the plaza in front of the Sun Pyramid? The first of these questions I have previously addressed somewhat. The most probable day for the celebration of creation would be August 12, when observers in the mouth of the cave beneath the Sun Pyramid could view the sun setting on the significant point on the horizon. This day may have generated the 260-day calendar, and the sightline arguably mandated the orientation of the entire city. In addition, this date closely coincides with Maya inscriptions that promote August 13 as the day of creation. As this was perhaps the most important annual festival at Teotihuacan, we could surely entertain the possibility that the ritual transpired over a number of days. The observation from the Sun Pyramid could have been the signal that initiated the commencement of the entire festival cycle.

If the creation ritual began at the Sun Pyramid, then why move up the avenue to conclude the sequence in the Plaza of the Moon? The solution to this question again emerges from the analysis of Maya creation texts and imagery. As Freidel, Schele, and Parker (1993:75–112) have asserted, the Milky Way was the physical manifestation of the *Wakah-Chan,* or world tree. More specifically, the world tree was visible in the heavens above when it was in its north-south orientation. Whenever it was in an east-west direction, the Milky Way was conceptually and artistically rendered as a canoe, and throughout the night the canoe rotated to eventually transform into the *axis mundi.*[29] This celestial rotation apparently evolved into the Mesoamerican tradition of raising the tree as seen in the spinning of the tree in the hands of an Olmec ruler or the motion from horizontal to vertical as ritualists erected a Tota tree. By raising their tree in the Moon Plaza, the Teotihuacanos would have conducted the ritual at the terminus of the north-south Avenue of the Dead. Such a scenario would be in accord with Mesoamerican doctrines of creation in which the world tree was definitively a north-south entity. In turn, when the festivities were over, the Avenue of the Dead remained as a bold reminder of ritual directionality and a permanent representative of the *axis mundi* (Cowgill 2000a:359).

The ritual, then, may have ensued as follows. The priests would have positioned themselves at the Sun Pyramid to watch for the setting sun on August 12.[30] Perhaps like the Aztecs who rekindled a central fire every 52 years, Teotihuacan officials lit a sacred fire at the Sun Pyramid that represented the newly created sun. Then, the celebrants may have moved north up the avenue, stopping in the plaza, perhaps on the central altar, to erect a tree symbolizing vertical space. The plaza may subsequently have been filled with the song, dance, and games seen in the Tepantitla lower murals. Finally, a select few elites could have entered the confined space of the Building of the Altars to memorialize the north house, the establishment of vertical space, and the division of the world into its eight partitions. In its entirety the creation festival would have explained the physical design of the world and honored the launch of the solar clock.

If this scenario is at all accurate, then Teotihuacan shared many of the traditions seen elsewhere in Mesoamerica. It possessed a creation story with similar components, and it designed its civic spaces to reenact these sacred truths. This hypothetical reconstruction of the ritual contends that the Teotihuacanos acknowledged the two most prominent celestial axes, with the view from the Sun Pyramid featuring the solar ecliptic and the Avenue of the Dead a crystallization of the Milky Way. With its sacred cave and its enormous success, Teotihuacan's claim to be the location of creation may have carried a certain legitimacy even outside of its direct cultural sphere. However, all Mesoamerican cities and the elites who governed them claimed to be at the center of the universe. The continuity of these ideas suggests that Teotihuacan inherited much of its creation beliefs from earlier cultural sources, yet the city nevertheless overlaid its own unique political agendas onto the more universal notions of creation.

As the best documentation of Teotihuacan's tree raising, the Tepantitla murals preserve the major thematic interpretations of the creation events. Surely, water and fertility were overt consequences of creation because the mountain generously sprinkles water from its hands, and streams literally overflow the bountiful fields below. The vegetation in the murals also provides an opportunity to codify gender roles, and the ritual itself probably incorporated motifs that further enhanced this message. In particular, the butterfly expressed the militant role expected of men, but it also conjured the realm of the ancestors. The butterflies record that the ancestors most revered were those who died in the proper service of the state.

When viewed under the lens of Tepantitla, the architectural elements of the Moon Plaza set a stage in which the creation story could periodically unfold. Other rituals certainly occurred within the plaza, for the space is simply too large and central to have one unique purpose. However, the permanent structures and the labor invested in them indicate that the celebration of creation was the most significant event of the ritual space and, arguably, the preeminent event in the ritual life of the city as a whole. It was here, in this space, that the city declared itself the *axis mundi* and proclaimed that all points on the compass ultimately led to Teotihuacan.

CHAPTER 9

CONTINUITIES
AND POWER

When I began to write my concluding thoughts
on Teotihuacan, the funeral procession for former
President Ronald Reagan was assembling on our
own broad national thoroughfare. Dense crowds
packed either side of Constitution Avenue while
various members of the military branches positioned themselves on the processional route. A
man in a large bearskin hat led the Army band,
followed by rows of sailors in pristine white
uniforms. Stern members of the Marines and
impeccably dressed soldiers walked in perfect
formation only to stop and await the arrival of
the dead president's body. As the body was trans-
ferred onto the caisson, the president's former
official residence, the White House, was visible in
the distance. Glorious black horses had smartly
dressed members of the Old Guard sitting ram-
rod straight upon their backs. When they began
to pull, the funeral cortege to the United States
Capitol began, and Americans witnessed the pageantry of leadership whose vestiges still survive
in our own society.

Another poignant tradition included in the
funeral was the riderless horse with reversed
boots in the stirrups. All of these horses were a
nod to the cavalry of the past through which the
United States secured its independence and rose
to world prominence. The Air Force contributed
its own funeral tradition by flying overhead in
the missing man formation. Certainly the line of
elite black limousines was impressive, but overall
it was the seemingly endless linear formations
of the marching military personnel, the solemn
drumbeat, and the dirges played by the band that
created the dominant effect of the procession.

The cortege ultimately concluded its stately
movement when it reached the Capitol, and the
body was placed on Lincoln's catafalque in the

rotunda, arguably the most symbolic location of the United States government. A prime minister, members of congress, and everyday Americans walked the circuit around the casket by the tens of thousands. Through it all, hour after hour, six men stood watch over the flag-draped coffin. Although the honor guard changed every thirty minutes, there remained at least one representative from each branch of the military—the Marines, Air Force, Army, Navy, and Coast Guard—all of whom shaped the tenor of the ritual with their unflinching watch. After years of exploring how Teotihuacan's rulers had sheltered themselves with the military orders of their day, I found it was these five individuals who most captivated me. Even in this country, where the powers of the executive office over matters of war are tempered by Congress, in his final moments the president was surrounded by his military.

While it might be easy to dismiss these events as insignificant traditions that have lost their meaning, the thousands of people who journeyed to the funeral or simply watched it on television would serve as testament that such symbolic rituals continue to have tremendous value in the modern world. Furthermore, as much as the United States proclaims itself a peaceable nation, we persist in using our militance to assert our values throughout the world as we accompany our rhetoric with the rattle of sabers. The heavy presence of the military in a presidential funeral should therefore come as no surprise because our own leaders at least partially support their tenure with the promise of strong military leadership. Presidents of the United States may serve as citizens, but those citizens still carry the title of Commander-in-Chief.

Step back 1,500 years, and we see the Teotihuacan ruler also encircling himself with members of his culture's various military entities. The caches under the Pyramid of the Moon, wherein the contributions of the military seem to have even eclipsed the ruler, offer the prime example. Although we will never know the precise circumstances surrounding the deposition of the animal mascots of the military orders, it is tempting to imagine the splendid ceremonies that must have accompanied the filling of these chambers. One wonders if the whole of Teotihuacan,

and even representatives from foreign political powers, gathered in the Moon Plaza to watch as members of the military orders assembled. How exciting it would have been if feline warriors carried the puma in its cage and placed it in the cavity, and if canine warriors followed with a caged wolf. Such speculation is unprovable, even though logic holds that the military orders must have had a role in furnishing the caches because their heraldry was so prominently figured in their contents.

In spaces like the White Patio, the ruler's presence is more forcefully projected. The bird and canine warriors flank their superior, and their placement on the walls implies that all process in a ritual event. The murals create a picture of a king who surrounds himself with his military and shares the public stage with them. As supported by parallels with later Mesoamerican cultures, the Teotihuacan rulers likely hitched themselves to the military because they provided a basis of power that was somewhat independent of the familiarly based groups who possibly contended for political authority. The evidence that the military orders functioned as sodalities that crosscut lineage ties explains the attraction of the military to the ruling parties. The orders provided avenues for loyalty to the ruler while simultaneously helping to bind the city into a unified whole. The support offered by the orders further clarifies the rulers' self-effacement in the Moon Pyramid caches because their elevation of the orders in large public spectacles translated into their own enhanced power. Perhaps the rulers shrewdly recognized that the appearance of conferring the limelight on others ultimately increased their own grip over the city.

On the other hand, the White Patio murals appear within a domestic setting, so the overarching agenda in this location must have been that of the residents themselves. The iconographic arrangement demonstrates that the inhabitants of Atetelco chose to feature the ruler, but this was probably more a strategy of closely associating themselves with him than selflessly celebrating his reign. The members of the Atetelco compound had something to gain through their close social proximity to the ruler, and they advertised this arrangement by memorializing it on their walls.

The profit in such strategies was likely the prospect of social advancement through exemplary service in the military. If Aztec models hold, there were routes to social elevation within the military that were independent of genealogical factors. The system would have allowed talented and charismatic individuals to garner public acclamation and receive material recompense. A resulting benefit was the suppression of disgruntled elements that might challenge the sociopolitical structure were there not avenues for personal enhancement.

All in all, the relationship of the ruler with the military was a mutually beneficial one where both parties flourished through their agreement. The military provided a solid base for the ruler, and he, in turn, saw to it that the military enjoyed social prominence in the city. The archeological record includes hints that the system allowed emotional incentives such as patriotism to flourish, so individual ambitions may have been augmented by nobler motivators. Counteracting explosive and disruptive pressures, the compact of the ruler and the military not only unified the city but also increased its power through successful military campaigns. Wars of conquest may have brought in tribute and human victims for sacrificial rites, and the expansive fingers of military elements may have brought in resources from foreign territories. The dazzling size of the city would indicate that the ruler and the military arrived at an advantageous balance in which a substantial segment of the population prospered.

The stone masks, however, are proof that military service was not the only trajectory for social prestige. From a pan-Mesoamerican perspective the masks probably had a mortuary function, and their semiprecious materials bespeak of their elite context. Their likely use on mortuary bundles, particularly the bundles of elite lineage heads, reveals a critical aspect of Teotihuacan social structure: lineage. Reckoning descent was an important preoccupation within the city and a critical determinant of social standing. As a consequence, the prominent use of genealogical reckoning exposes rifts in the harmonious social structure and identifies factions that may have contentiously vied for power with the highest authorities. The elites who participated in this

upper stratum of hereditary justification, more than any other component of Teotihuacan society, were the stimulus behind the rise of the military. Challenged on all sides by nobles with justifiable claims to power, Teotihuacan's rulers turned to the military for a solution.

Thus it is that the ruler, the lineages, and the military formed the trinity that most forcibly shaped the dynamics of power at Teotihuacan. Though at times oppositional, the genius of the arrangement was that the three elements were integrated to foster competing loyalties. The ruler could not function as an absolute monarch because the lineages could match his claims with legitimate assertions of their own. Despite their own familial interests, the lineages were loathe to dispose of the ruler because their own members benefited through participation in the military. The military orders found that the ruler was their greatest backer, who doled out public recognition in return for their steadfast support. And through it all, the ruler persevered with the assistance of the military orders. Each social constituent needed the others, and the complex web the system developed created an environment stable enough that a great city emerged.

This stability should be viewed on a macro level because there certainly were moments of instability, and individual principal players may have fallen and been replaced. Monarchies seldom exhibit perfect transitions over many generations, and thus the dominant lineage at the city may have varied over time. Evidence for strong competing lineages would virtually assure that the ruling family was periodically usurped, and the destruction of tombs, including the Feathered Serpent Pyramid, bolsters this idea. The absence of genealogical declarations in the form of hieroglyphic texts would also fit within a system wherein disruptions in the royal lineage occurred. In a parallel fashion, while the military may have been united in its support of the ruler, we should acknowledge the possible infighting between the different orders. Destruction and replacement of the iconographic motifs that served as mascots for the orders clearly demonstrate that ideals changed, and fortunes waxed and waned. Teotihuacan data are such that we often have trouble discerning the particularities of historical moments, and only with further investigation will we have the information with which to attempt this.

Although stability does not imply inertia, the one constant in Teotihuacan's history does seem to be the military. By A.D. 150, when the first massive cache was placed in the Moon Pyramid, the Teotihuacan military must have already had considerable stature. At this point their symbols were prominent enough to serve in the temple's consecration, and these animal symbols probably represented the supernatural animation of the structure. The prestige of the military continued with the next version of the Moon Pyramid and the construction of the Feathered Serpent Pyramid, where martial symbols typify the offerings. At this point the Teotihuacanos ceased building large pyramids, but the military orders evidently maintained their positions because the mural and ceramic art of the later periods contains a heavy load of militant iconography. The consistency of this theme throughout Teotihuacan's history raises the specter that the military may have been the crucial ingredient in the city's success.

Where, however, would the city have been were it not for the religious component that fastened together the minds of the city's inhabitants? Monopolizing creation myths that predated Teotihuacan, the city promoted an ideology of place. It relocated these myths to the Teotihuacan Valley and looked to the horizon for the acts of the gods. The three prominent mountains became the first stones placed by the gods, and Teotihuacan nestled within this symbolic hearth. Their identity as the hearth may have prompted their contention that the sun was created in their cave, and led the Teotihuacanos to declare that time commenced in their valley. Yet in Mesoamerica, time and space are related, so the Teotihuacanos oriented their city on a north-south axis to commemorate the establishment of vertical space. That done, the city, like the world, could expand to the four cardinal directions, and evidence for vast foreign connections reveals that expansion was just what the city's leaders had in mind.

These ideological doctrines needed reinforcement, so elaborate pageants reenacted the creation mythology. The Moon Plaza appears to be a place where the identity of the Avenue of the Dead was fused with the *axis mundi*. Odd constructions like the Building of the Altars emerge as ritual performative spaces that mark the division of the world into its eight partitions. The platform at the center of the plaza may have been where the Teotihuacanos raised a world tree each year, if we can interpret the Tepantitla murals through a Mesoamerican lens. Through these two acts the Teotihuacanos proclaimed their centrality to the rest of Mesoamerica, but they also seized upon the opportunity to instruct their own population.

Tepantitla, which harbors the surviving images of this ephemeral event, specifies the activities expected of men and women. Teotihuacan is not unique in its incorporation of gender roles into creation stories, but the militant flavor of these directives is compelling.[1] Women were given their marching orders during the tree-raising festival, and their roles were symbolized by the spider, who dictated the female endeavors of cloth manufacture and childbirth. Both of these may have had a military aspect because cloth could have been used as a tribute item, and Aztec parallels show that childbirth was a metaphor for war. Childbirth apparently was a woman's battle, and an untimely death during labor sent a woman to a coveted afterlife.

Opposing the spider was the butterfly, which Aztec sources also explicate. This insect was a motivational tool to prompt males into valiant heroics on the battlefield, and as for women, the promised reward was an exalted afterlife and the acclaim of Teotihuacan society. The men, it seems, were hit harder by the Teotihuacan state because their role model was more difficult to escape. Members of the military wore butterfly noseplaques and costumes to remind themselves of the proper attitude of a warrior. Butterfly-festooned censers probably commemorated exemplary warriors who had given their lives for the state. Greater yet, the symbolism of the butterfly was conceptually overlaid upon the *talud-tablero* architecture of the city. Buildings, therefore, became more than a place for shelter; instead they almost nagged the populace into conformity. As in all states that marshal propaganda for rather nefarious purposes, the resulting environment must have been somewhat oppressive.

What is singularly interesting about this circumstance is that Teotihuacan managed to couch this propaganda within the religious realm of creation mythology. That is, the expectations of the state were effectively married to intrinsic conceptions of the universe. Militant gender roles were portrayed as inextricable aspects of the world's very fabric. Similarly, the White Patio may offer a case where the political arrangement of the ruler and the military orders was coupled with the myth of the three creation stones. In each case the dominant Teotihuacan ideology held that institutions created by living people were part of the divine blueprint and had thereby existed since the dawn of time. Like most fundamentalist approaches to the world, this strategy must have made these assertions difficult to challenge.

The arguments put forward in this book make no pretense at producing a complete image of Teotihuacan. The city dominated central Mexico for roughly 500 years, and over that time Teotihuacan must have transformed itself many times. With an archaeological culture it is often much easier to see the large patterns of behavior than the peculiarities of individual historical events. The names of the actors who built the buildings, sacrificed warriors in showy displays, painted the murals, and presided over rituals in the plazas are still opaque to the modern world. Likewise, there are other parties who have been omitted in this study who contributed greatly to the

Teotihuacan world. Merchants who imported the Thin Orange ceramics and priests who assisted Teotihuacan's rulers must have shaped the city in significant ways. With further archaeological explorations and more scholarly attempts, some of these players will emerge, and we can enhance our understanding of this impressive city.

The route to this greater comprehension, I would propose, is a scholarly approach that values both intrinsic and external evidence. There are many things about Teotihuacan that are unique, and we should recognize the specific innovations that led to a Mesoamerican city of unparalleled success. Yet viewing the city in isolation stunts our ability to reap the harvests offered by other Mesoamerican cultures. When Teotihuacan is invited into the Mesoamerican fold, we can see much about the city that is similar to these other peoples. We now have documentation of communication between Teotihuacan and various parts of Mesoamerica, and the parallels tell us that they shared material and intellectual resources. The continuities discovered in this process replace some of the information that was lost over time. We must be mindful that these continuities need not be constant and monolithic because patterns can change and variations will emerge, but the basic melody may still yield critical data. Teotihuacan certainly had its own special song, and the music was so deafening that Mesoamerica invariably listened.

NOTES

1. The account of the compound's discovery appears in R. Millon 1973:18–20. Although some excavations took place in the compound, determining the function of this space is problematic because much of the archaeological evidence has been destroyed by modern construction, including the old museum at the site.

2. The names *Sun Pyramid* and *Moon Pyramid* derive from sixteenth-century Aztec appellations, and it is unclear whether they reflect Teotihuacan conceptions of these structures (Cowgill 2000a:358).

3. In her analysis of cave symbolism, Doris Heyden (1981:3–4) suggests that the Sun Pyramid cave was the religious focus for early Teotihuacan.

4. This version of Teotihuacan's history comes from R. Millon (1966a, 1966b). The precise dates for the various periods at Teotihuacan are problematic, but I will use recent chronologies proposed by Braswell (2003b) and Cowgill (1997, 2003b).

5. See, for example, the elevated bench on the exterior of Yayahuala (Séjourné 1966b:74).

6. René Millon (1970:1080) offered the original estimates for apartment compound habitation, but recent work by Linda Manzanilla (1990:83) incorporating burial data suggests that some calculations may be inflated by 25 percent. Considering that only three to four compounds have been excavated to an extensive degree with modern techniques, any population estimates of the apartment compounds or the city as a whole are notoriously difficult (Cowgill 1974, 1993b:118; R. Millon 1992:344).

7. The 1992–1993 excavations by Rubén Cabrera at the La Ventilla apartment compounds have offered a better picture of the variety of wealth among neighboring structures. Of two apartment compounds on either side of a street, one contained finely plastered walls with elaborate murals, while the other had only mud-plastered walls with small remnants of murals (Cabrera, personal communication 1993).

8. The strongest evidence for a permanent foreign population at Teotihuacan comes from the Oaxaca Barrio, also known as Tlailotlacan. A Oaxacan-style tomb as well as Zapotec-style urns indicate that the residents of the compound managed to preserve their Zapotec customs and beliefs over several centuries of occupation (Altschul 1987:214; R. Millon 1973, 1974; Rattray 1987b; Rattray and Ruiz 1980; Spence 1989, 1992). In addition, Gulf Coast and

Early Classic Lowland Maya ceramics found at the "Merchants" Barrio may signal a foreign presence (R. Millon 1981; Rattray 1987b). Rattray argued that the circular structures found in this area could indicate Veracruz ties for the residents of this compound (Rattray 1989).

9. These estimates of Teotihuacan's size are based on the work of Cowgill (1996, 2000a, and 2003a) and René Millon (1973:8, 1988a:113, 1992:354).

10. For one such different interpretation, see Braswell 2003b:23–27. An extensive variety of voices on the subject of Maya and Teotihuacan interactions may be found in the various articles contained in Braswell 2003a. Approaching the material from a Teotihuacan perspective, Cowgill (2003b) developed a better understanding of when in Teotihuacan's history such interactions took place.

11. Cowgill (1996:256) highlighted the numerous deficiencies within Teotihuacan archaeology. As he noted, excavations cover little more than 2 percent of the site; many have not been published adequately; collections have been discarded; and reports from early excavations before modern practices are problematic. Furthermore, he pointed out that many excavations proceeded with the goal of restoration, not identification of construction sequences.

12. Sugiyama (2005:119, 183–184) also discussed the staff and its association with rulership, although he is unsure whether this was a royal tomb.

13. Sugiyama (1992:224–225, 2005:235) also introduced the suggestion that a pit in front of the temple staircase is another possible location of a Teotihuacan ruler's tomb. This pit was looted during the construction of the *adosada,* a large porch-like platform that later covered the front of the original temple.

14. This lack of evidence is not entirely due to ancient looting, because there was a substantial loss of archaeological information both during and after the excavations. For the best account of the cave's excavations, see René Millon 1981:231–234.

15. For information about recent excavations in the Moon Pyramid, see Cabrera and Sugiyama 1999; Sugiyama and Cabrera 2000; and Sugiyama 2005.

16. This sequence of architectural campaigns is largely based on R. Millon 1992; however, until full-scale excavations with ceramic analysis are undertaken on the structures lining the Avenue of the Dead, this sequence is subject to modification.

17. The hieroglyphs discovered in the La Ventilla 1992–1993 project may be an exception to this (Rubén Cabrera, personal communication 1993). To date they represent the greatest concentration of Teotihuacan hieroglyphs ever found, and although most appear in isolation, there are some interesting groupings. However, even these hieroglyphs appear to lack syntax. Furthermore, this find in combination with the glyphs from Techinantitla suggest that hieroglyphic writing was more common in the decoration of apartment compounds than previously thought (C. Millon 1988c).

18. See Lintel 16, Yaxchilan, for an example of foreshortening (Schele and Miller 1986:38).

19. For more examples, see Miller 1973:Figures 58–62.

20. See Pasztory 1990:182, 1993:58. Cowgill (1996:271–

272) made a similar argument, stating that while costume elements do reveal hierarchies at Teotihuacan, humans do not appear in situations where they are subordinate to others. Furthermore, he also emphasized the "multiplicity and replication" that typify Teotihuacan art, suggesting that these traits indicate "that no one person is irreplaceable."

21. The central motif of the Tepantitla mural has most commonly been referred to as the "Great Goddess," a possible deity of the city (Berlo 1992; Pasztory 1976, 1997). However, others (Cowgill 1997; Paulinyi 2006) have called into question the identification of this deity and even the very existence of the goddess. In light of this work, I will use the more neutral and descriptive reference, the mountain-tree, to refer to the Tepantitla image. More discussion of this appears in Chapter 2.

22. Karl Taube (2000b) delivered a brilliant analysis of the presence of glyphs at Teotihuacan.

23. As of late it has become more common to refer to Tlaloc as the Storm God (Pasztory 1997; Sugiyama 1992, 2005) so as not to confuse the Teotihuacan manifestation of the god with the later Aztec version. While I find much merit in this strategy, I have retained the name *Tlaloc* because I see so many continuities between the central Mexican cultures. However, this decision must acknowledge that there are differences, and it is critical to be sensitive to the Classic period manifestation of this deity.

CHAPTER 2

1. See Coe 1975:102. For a critique of Coe's hypothesis, see Gillespie 2002.

2. Millon et al. (1965) reasoned that elites conceived of the construction of the large-scale Tzacualli (A.D. 50–150) structures and oversaw their construction. Later, Millon (1992:384–385) more directly argued that powerful rulers probably built the large pyramids and that tombs are feasibly at their core.

3. The Noguera tunnel cuts through the pyramid on its east-west axis. The full account of the reanalysis of this tunnel is in Millon et al. 1965. For a discussion of archaeological missteps at the Sun Pyramid, read R. Millon 1981:231–234 and Pasztory 1997:20.

4. See Sugiyama and Cabrera 2000. Sugiyama (2005:235) offered a tentative identification of a royal burial at the top of the Moon Pyramid's Building 5, although he noted that the fragmentary nature of the bones and offerings makes interpretation difficult.

5. Dating this mural and its associated patio is exceedingly difficult because the archaeological materials associated with it, including the ceramics, were not analyzed. For more discussion about the date, see R. Cabrera 1995:203 and Headrick 1996b.

6. A comprehensive study of blood symbols at Teotihuacan may be found in Parsons 1988.

7. In her essay, Schele (1995) accepted the moniker of "Great Goddess" for this image. Even though I avoid that term, the importance of the pivotal work of Pasztory (1974, 1976, 1997) and Berlo (1992) in identifying the critical

features of this entity cannot be overstated. Much of the description used here, including the female-gendered nature of the mountain, is firmly rooted in observations made by these earlier scholars. Critiques of the term *Great Goddess* appear in Cowgill 1997 and Paulinyi 2006.

8. Cowgill (2000a:361) similarly suggested that the upper image in the Tepantitla mural is a personification of Cerro Gordo.

9. This idea comes from a personal communication recorded in Schele 1995:113. Another case of conch shells in association with elites is in the west Mexican shaft tomb of Huitzilapa. Archaeologists excavating the tomb surmised that it held the remains of the political authority of the site, and two of the male skeletons had conch shells over their pelvic areas (López Mestas Camberos and Ramos de la Vega 1998).

10. A comprehensive discussion of this staff and others like it appears in Headrick 2003b.

11. As George Cowgill (personal communication 1996) pointed out, the identification of the upper portion as an eccentric point must remain tentative at present, for no point with a similar shape has yet appeared in the archaeological record of Teotihuacan.

12. The three spears held by warriors on Kerr vase 2352 are a typical example of this (Kerr 1990:240).

13. Cowgill (1997:149–151) questioned whether the fanged noseplaque and bird headdress of the Tepantitla image are diagnostic attributes of a female "Great Goddess." Nevertheless, he also argued that the sculpture from the West Plaza Complex was a ruler, although he was unsure whether it depicts a particular ruler or the general idea of a ruler. Furthermore, he noted that the fanged noseplaque in the Tepantitla mural has three decorative circles that mirror a noseplaque found at the Feathered Serpent Pyramid. I am not fully convinced by this association because the Feathered Serpent Pyramid noseplaque is bifurcated and lacks the multiple fangs seen in the murals.

14. Most consistently, this image has been identified as the "Great Goddess." For the most pertinent discussion of it in this context, see Cowgill 1997; Berlo 1992; Pasztory 1974, 1976, 1997; and Paulinyi 2006.

15. Pasztory (1976:119–120, 1997:86) offered a clear discussion of the *quechquemitl* or *huipil* and skirt as female clothing, and she also explained why the presumably male priests to either side of the Tepantitla mountain-tree wear similar clothing. Essentially, there is a long tradition of male elites donning female attire as part of their strategy of legitimacy.

16. Studies accepting the existence of a "Great Goddess" include Berlo 1992; C. Millon 1988c; Pasztory 1972, 1992a, 1997; Taube 1983; and von Winning 1987. For critiques of the identification, see Cowgill 1997 and Paulinyi 2006.

17. The Tetitla image (Figure 2.11) has also been interpreted as the "Great Goddess" and similarly sprinkles water from its hands. However, as suggested in this study, the Tetitla image may portray a deceased ruler, and the generosity from the hands may be an indication of the ancestor's association with the water-filled mountain.

18. The confusion about the Museo Nacional sculpture's original location is understandable, and the existing information is imprecise and difficult to interpret. In an earlier article I too assumed an intimate connection between the sculpture, the Plaza of the Moon, and the other colossal sculpture found in the Moon Plaza (Headrick 2002).

19. Holmes 1897:296. In an earlier publication Holmes (1885:364) also provided an image of the partially buried sculpture, and the surrounding debris offers evidence that it was in a smaller courtyard.

20. See Taube's (1992a) seminal paper on mirrors for a full account of the appearance and function of mirrors at Teotihuacan.

21. The stain around a serpentine mask in the Dumbarton Oaks collection (Figure 3.8) probably resulted from the decay of iron pyrite (Berrin and Pasztory 1993:186).

22. The Viking Group is on the east side of the Avenue of the Dead approximately 300 meters south of the Sun Pyramid. Here, Armillas (1944) found one of the most dazzling offerings in the city: large sheets of mica beneath the floor of an interior patio. The cache consisted of two 6-centimeter layers of mica separated by earth that covered 10.4 by 2.8 meters, and the mica was carefully cut to fit the contours of walls and corners.

23. In his book of 1700, Gemelli Carreri (1995) wrote about two sculptures that Juan de Zumárraga, the first bishop of Mexico, had destroyed. However, it is not clear whether this refers to the sculpture in the Moon Plaza.

CHAPTER 3

1. Despite this suggestion, Cowgill (2003a:41–42) does not rule out the possibility that kin ties might have been looser and even included patron-client relationships.

2. For additional excavation information, see also Widmer 1987.

3. Sahagún recorded a Precolumbian parallel for the category of accidental death. In the thirteenth month, *Tepeihuitl,* the Mexica had a feast celebrating those who had drowned or been struck by lightning. In addition, they honored those who were buried but not cremated on this day (Sahagún 1950–1982:II:131). Such parallels indicate strong continuities in veneration of the dead between the Precolumbian and present periods.

4. The difficulty in discerning Precolumbian ties to the past stems from the syncretism of merging Precolumbian traditions with the European Christian All Saints' Day and All Souls' Day, which also involve rituals for the deceased. For more discussion of the Precolumbian roots of Day of the Dead rituals, see Cook and Leonard 1949; Scheffler 1976; Nutini 1988; and Carmichael and Sayer 1991.

5. In a discussion of these ideas with Randolph Widmer, he noted that the entire compound of Tlajinga 33 has not yet been fully exposed. He wondered if there was a second patio functioning during the Late Tlamimilolpa/Early Xolalpan period (A.D. 300–450) that would have had adult burials so that there would have been separate patios for each of the age divisions (Widmer, personal communication 1995).

6. Susan Gillespie (2002:72) similarly addressed the question of whether Maya child burials could be considered ancestors and resoundingly asserted that they could. Noting that children are the replacements or reincarnations of their ancestors, she reasoned that everyone is an ancestor.

7. Accounts of these archaeologically recovered bundles are in Bernal 1948–1949:23–26; Folan et al. 1995:319–320; and El Universal 1995.

8. I am indebted to Susan Toby Evans (personal communication 2005), who pointed out that the stone mask in the museum reconstruction is not the same as the wood and mosaic mask reported by Bernal.

9. The beautifully expressive mosaic facial masks found in Structure VII, Tomb 1, and Structure III, Tomb 1, at Calakmul are two other prominent examples (Folan et al. 1995).

10. See, for example, Berrin and Pasztory 1993:cat. nos. 25, 26, and 28.

11. Landa 1966:130–131. McAnany's (1995:36) pivotal work on Maya ancestors must be credited with bringing this information to my attention. Landa's mention of hollow ceramic sculptures may provide insight into the large-scale effigy figures seen in Postclassic Yucatec ceramics. Although many of these seem to depict gods, it must be remembered that the bundled remains of Aztec rulers were clothed in the garments of deities, thus complicating the distinction between elites and gods (Klein 1987:343).

12. Harold McBride (1969) was the first to suggest that the enthroned figurines may depict mortuary bundles.

13. Rebecca Storey and Randolph Widmer (personal communication 1995) brought these to my attention as possible candidates for mortuary bundle depiction.

14. Andrea Stone (2002) compiled a wonderfully thorough discussion of rubber depictions and ritual use.

15. A possible malicious case of bundle burning may appear on page 20 of the Codex Zouche-Nuttall. As part of the devastation surrounding the War from Heaven, the mortuary bundles of Lords 4 House and 3 Monkey are placed on a burning pyre. Because 4 House is seen captured by one of the Stone Men, it appears that the destruction of these bundles was the ultimate goal (Byland and Pohl 1994:110–112).

16. See Headrick 1999 and Taube 2000a for similar discussions. Of further interest is the flexed burial found in Burial 3 of the Moon Pyramid. Archaeologists reported traces of fiber near this and the other three burials, which may indicate the presence of bundle burials (Sugiyama and Cabrera 2000:168)

17. For a more complete discussion of Huitzilopochtli as a mortuary bundle, see Headrick 1999.

18. References generally attribute the name *Avenue of the Dead* to sixteenth-century Nahuatl speakers; however, René Millon (personal communication 1995) traced the first appearance of the name to the *Mapa de San Francisco Mazapán* and recognized José María Arreola (in Gamio 1979:I:556) as the first to translate the Nahuatl text.

19. Placing the ancestors on this north-south road may have held particular symbolic significance. As I will dis-

cuss in Chapter 8, the avenue may have been associated with the Milky Way. In Mesoamerica, the Milky Way was conceptualized as a road taken by the ancestors upon their death. This is most clearly expressed in the text of K'inich Janaab' Pakal I's sarcophagus at Palenque, which includes the phrase *och bih,* "he entered the road," to describe Pakal's fall down the Milky Way, which appears on the sarcophagus lid (Freidel et al. 1993:76). If the mortuary bundles were installed along the Avenue of the Dead, then they too would metaphorically be on the Milky Way upon their death.

20. Byron Hammon (personal communication 1997) brought this example to my attention.

21. These various translations appear in Carrasco 1990:40; Millon 1992:359; and Robertson 2007. Of these, Robertson is one of the most explicit, stating that his translation, "the place where divinity comes into being," derives from,

teoti⟨denominal verb "to become divine," "to become a god"⟩; –**hua**⟨impersonal suffix⟩; and –**can**⟨locative noun "place where"⟩ (see Launey 1992:135 ff., 225). Andrews (2003:498) has recently translated the word as "at the place of the owners of the Elder Gods." This intriguing translation might make better sense of the observed locative –**can** (the locative –**yan** might be expected after the impersonal verbstem *teotihua-* that I posit), but this reading also requires restoring a glottal stop in the position immediately preceding—*teotihuahcan* instead of *teotihuacan.*

22. George Cowgill (2000a:358, 2003a:40) joined me in recognizing these structures as elite residences.

23. Margáin (1951:77–79) noted the vast amounts of wood burned to make lime during work at Palenque and proposed that the lime plaster used in the roofs, walls, and floors of Teotihuacan structures must have led to deforestation. The added expense of obtaining the necessary wood or lime from distant regions must have made lime-plastered walls an important marker of wealth.

24. Cowgill (2003a:41) questioned whether the proximity of less prosperous compounds next to well-built compounds might indicate craft specialization, with craftsmen living near their patrons.

25. Gillespie's (2000) contribution provides a fabulous review of the pertinent literature, and this article is especially commendable for its clearly defined critical terms and analysis of the benefits and pitfalls of each model.

26. The evidence for this comes from Spence 1974.

27. For a debate on similar issues at Copán, read Hendon 1991:912 and Sanders 1989:102–103.

28. When commenting upon my model, Cowgill (2003a:43) stated that these lineages or clans may "have formed an elite oligarchy from which heads of state were recruited."

29. The most salient writings on this are Pasztory 1992a, 1993; Cowgill 1983, 1993a, 1997; and R. Millon 1988a, 1992, 1993.

1. For an excellent and comprehensive discussion of mirrors, see the seminal article by Karl Taube (1992a).

2. Although the literature tends to refer to these animals as coyotes, I am using the term *canine* because of recent archaeological finds in the Moon Pyramid. Burial 2 contained a number of animals, and the canine included in this offering has been identified as a wolf (Cabrera and Sugiyama 1999:30; Sugiyama and Cabrera 2000:167; Sugiyama 2005:205). While it may be more accurate to refer to these animals as wolves, the extent to which the Teotihuacanos distinguished between wolves and coyotes is unclear. Thus I will use the more generic term until we have a better grasp of Teotihuacan classifications.

3. Although I am using the Nahuatl term for this phenomenon, this in no way assumes that this was the language of Teotihuacan or the word the Teotihuacanos would have used to refer to this practice. There are many indigenous words for the transformation of a human into an animal counterpart. I use the Nahuatl because of its geographic proximity and because of the rich amount of ethnohistoric information, but we should be mindful that any Teotihuacan conception of nagualism would have had its own unique flavor.

4. George Foster (1944) wrote some of the earliest modern work on nagualism. In scanning the ethnohistoric documents, he found numerous incidences of nagualism among many Mesoamerican cultures, including the Nahua, Zapotec, and Maya. William Holland (1964) documented this belief in his ethnographic work with the Tzotzil, and Peter Furst (1968) compared the Olmec were-jaguar to South American shamans.

5. Credit for the decipherment of this glyph goes to several epigraphers, including Houston and Stuart (1989) and Grube and Nahm (1994). For a specific account of the events leading to this decipherment, see Freidel et al. 1993:442–443. The application of this glyph to the art appears in Freidel et al. 1993:52, 188–193. For a cautionary note about the applicability of shamanism to Mesoamerica, see Klein et al. 2002.

6. The K'iche' version comes from the *Títulos de la casa Ixquín-Nehaib,* which probably reflects the voice of the Nehaib K'iche' (Bricker 1981:38; Carmack 1973:32–33).

7. Although Bricker deserves credit for fully exploring the implications of the K'iche' account, Foster (1944:88) was the first to recognize that Tecum Umam went into war as his nagual. Indeed, Foster's work provides the basis for much contemporary work on nagualism (Freidel et al. 1993; Grube and Nahm 1994; Houston and Stuart 1989).

8. On the other hand, these backracks may have served a vital functional role. As Hassig (1992:50) has noted, control of a large army demands communication strategies that extend beyond the oral. Military leaders wearing large backracks may have allowed Aztec troops to see where their commander was and to know whether to advance or retreat.

9. See Reilly 1989:Figure 1.

10. See Reilly 1989:Figure 16b.

11. Earlier and much reduced versions of this discussion appear in Headrick 1994 and 2001.

12. See, for example, the battle between Mexico-Tenochtitlan and Tlatelolco in Durán 1964:154.

13. Preforms of these knives have been found at Teotihuacan. One came from Palace 3 in the Plaza of the Moon, and another was found near the road that circles the archaeological zone. These blades measured 37 centimeters and 51 centimeters, which accords with their size in the murals (Berrin and Pasztory 1993:268). In addition, the Type B bifacial knives exhibiting an S-curve found in the Feathered Serpent Pyramid deposits resemble the knives in the murals (Sugiyama 2005:131–135). The appearance of the actual knives further secures the identification of the knives as obsidian.

14. Another way of viewing this mural is to interpret the lower portion, consisting of the shield and puma, as a hieroglyphic name for the puma warriors above.

15. Cowgill (1996:255) commented on the absence of vanquished foes in Teotihuacan art. For an example of a Maya image with a captive, see Piedras Negras Stela 11, where the king sits above a victim whose belly appears slit open (Schele and Miller 1986:Figure II.4).

16. In his studies of shamanism and hallucinatory imagery, Reichel-Dolmatoff (1971, 1975, 1978) provided ample evidence that shamanism and, in particular, an association of shamans with jaguars existed in South America.

17. Cowgill (1997:146) also accepts the presence of military orders at Teotihuacan.

18. As Clara Millon (1988c) noted, the tassel headdress seems to have preferential treatment because it also appears on the Tlaloc face at the bottom of the bowl. This, coupled with the use of the tassel headdress both within and without Teotihuacan, may indicate that this headdress signals a different, elevated rank of militaristic trader similar to the Aztec *pochteca.*

19. Scholars have often neglected to precisely identify the animal used for the headdresses of the processing Tepantitla figures (Figure 1.11a) and other figures with similar headdresses. Generally, the motif has been referred to as a generic animal or serpent headdress (Miller 1973:101; C. Millon 1988b; Sugiyama 1992:206, 2005:57–58). While acknowledging that it is rather difficult to distinguish canine and serpent headdresses, I refer to the Tepantitla headdresses as canines because they have molars for rear teeth, and their feathered eye resembles the eye of more clearly represented canines (C. Millon 1988a:Figures VI.27, Plate 37).

20. The prime example of this is Burial 190.

21. Discussion of this issue appears in Cabrera 1993:106; Spence et al. 2004; Sugiyama 1989a, 2005; and White et al. 2002. It should come as no surprise that the warriors could have been dressed by their captors because the Aztec ethnohistories document the arraying of captives in special costumes. For one of many such accounts, see Sahagún 1950–1982:II:113. Regardless of the origin of the Pyramid of the Feathered Serpent warriors, the fact that their hands were tied behind their backs reveals that these men were not willing victims.

22. Thorough accounts of these burials may be found in Cabrera 1993 and Sugiyama 1989a, 1992, 2005, and information about the origin of the human war trophies appears in Spence et al. 2004.

CHAPTER 5

1. For discussion of archaeological excavations of this structure, see Fuente 1990; Klein 1987; López Luján 1994:73, 75; Matos Moctezuma 1984a, 1984b; and Molina Montes 1987.

2. The manuscript was commissioned by Viceroy Mendoza around 1541–1550 (Robertson 1994:45).

3. Sons of wealthy parents were given better military training, and their parents were often able to pay one or more older soldiers to watch over their son on the battlefield. The young warrior sometimes caught his captive alone, but in cases in which he did receive help, it was important for the military community to decide who played the largest role in the capture and thus who deserved the most credit. To be fully considered a man, the young warrior needed to capture an enemy unaided (Hassig 1988:36, 45).

4. In his reconstruction of Teotihuacan warfare, Ross Hassig (1992) maintains that the city must have fielded very large armies, and that a meritocratic system like that of the Aztecs would explain the availability of so many soldiers.

5. The most comprehensive report of this appears in Sugiyama 1998, but also important are R. Millon 1992:397 and Sugiyama 1992:221.

6. It is important to note that the destruction and remodeling have been interpreted as corroborative evidence of a shift from a single despotic ruler to a collective form of governance (R. Millon 1988a, 1992; Pasztory 1992a). For a reflective discussion of the Ciudadela and the Street of the Dead Complex, see Cowgill 1983, 1996:280, and 1997:151–152.

7. Cowgill (1997:147–148) suggests a slightly different explanation, positing that feathered rattlesnake imagery and symbolism dominated in the early years of Teotihuacan until the mid-200s. After that, imagery of the various military orders—including birds, canines, and jaguars—may have gained in popularity and power.

8. The excavations of the White and Painted Patios were undertaken by Margáin, but he himself makes no note of the plaques. The only report of these plaques comes from Armillas (1950:57), who states that Margáin found them during excavations. Naturally, this secondhand information is less than desirable, and the plaques themselves have not been identified among Teotihuacan's archaeological materials.

9. Commenting on my earlier work (Headrick 1996b), Cowgill (1997:146, 2003a:43) agreed that military sodalities may have crosscut kinship ties to integrate Teotihuacan society.

10. Portico 2 of the White Patio also includes net jaguars in its imagery, which might suggest a strong affinity with this military order as well. However, the absence of net jaguars in the other two porticos indicates this order was less prominent.

CHAPTER 6

1. No clear report on the ceramics or stratigraphy of Atetelco has ever been published. The comments on construction sequence are based solely on observation and personal discussions with Rubén Cabrera.

2. Cowgill (personal communication 1996) related that recent ceramic analysis by Annick Daneels in the Group 5-prime three-temple complex suggests that these complexes may be no earlier than Miccaotli (A.D. 150–225).

3. I first noted this emphasis on western orientation in my dissertation (Headrick 1996b), and Pasztory (1997:96–97) has also recognized this tendency.

4. Cowgill (2000a:359) has also noted that the westward-facing Sun Pyramid and Feathered Serpent Pyramid and the East and West Avenues indicate the importance of an east-west axis for the city.

5. The explanation of the cave's role in the city's orientation was argued by R. Millon (1992:387–388, 1993:35), and Pasztory (1997:96–97) concurred with his analysis in her comprehensive account of Teotihuacan. For a discussion of the importance of zenith passage, see Aveni and Hartung 1981:51.

6. Cowgill's (1977) study of developments in Teotihuacan's early settlement patterns concurs with Heyden's (1981) belief that religious symbolism played a forceful role in the location of the city. He noted that the Cuanalan (500–100 B.C.) settlement was concentrated near prime agricultural lands. This materialist incentive seemed to matter little in the subsequent Patlachique phase (100 B.C.–50 A.D.), when settlement shifted away from agricultural areas to locations near the present northern portion of the Avenue of the Dead. He summed up the implications of this data,

I think that proximity to important shrines is the most reasonable explanation for the location of Patlachique settlement. This is not to say that irrigation agriculture was not, in all probability, an important food source for the Patlachique population. But it does look as if a considerable proportion of the Patlachique Phase inhabitants of Teotihuacán were willing to be 2 or 3 kilometers further from the irrigated land, in order to be close to important temples. (Cowgill 1977:188)

Apparently, religion contributed much to decisions made at Teotihuacan.

7. In a similar fashion, Taube (1986) connected such small altars to the Pyramid of the Sun by arguing that all fall into a category of wind temples.

8. I am indebted to Rubén Cabrera (personal communication 1993) for bringing the presence of the door in the west structure of the Painted Patio to my attention.

9. An earlier and reduced version of these ideas appears in Headrick 2001.

10. This account of creation is largely based on the work

of Freidel et al. (1993), who reconstructed the creation story in a masterful example of scholarship.

11. Mention of the Old Fire God in relationship to the creation story raises the specter of the Old Fire God braziers commonly found at Teotihuacan (see, for example, Berrin and Pasztory 1993:cat. nos. 9–10). Their presence at the site may indicate that a version of the Aztec myth existed at Teotihuacan and that the braziers are just one more indication that Teotihuacan promoted itself as the place of creation. One wonders if they were used in reenactments of creation that celebrated the placement of the three stones.

12. The Maya version of this sequence appears in Freidel et al. 1993:59–107.

13. Freidel et al. (1993:80) documented that the Maya recognized the stars of Alnitak (a star in the constellation of Orion's belt), Saiph, and Rigel as the three hearthstones, and that they also connected this constellation with contemporary Maya hearthstones (Freidel et al. 1993:66–67).

14. Using a masterful ethnographic approach, Allen Christenson (2001) explored continuity and personal creativity in Santiago Atitlan. While thoroughly explaining the iconography of the community's altarpiece, he discusses triadic mountains (73–82) and the role of supernaturals (143).

15. For a full discussion of the Maya concept of living at the center, see Vogt 1976.

16. Tempering this interpretation is the fact that other numerical clusters of mountains also appear within the corpus of Teotihuacan art. Although not nearly as common as the triad of mountains, these groupings cannot be ignored and demand interpretation.

17. Freidel et al. (1993:139–140) and Schele and Guernsey (2001) include discussions of cleft mountains and the Mountain of Sustenance. For a fascinating interpretation of the role of volcanic activity in Teotihuacan's history, see Pasztory 1997. Her hypothesis that volcanic activity shaped the religion of Teotihuacan is borne out by the archaeological remains of Tetimpa, where a patio altar was decorated with a miniature volcano (Plunket and Uruñuela 1998).

18. During the 1993–1994 excavations at the Pyramid of the Sun, archaeologists found evidence of a canal around it, which may afford this temple similar meaning as Sustenance Mountain (Matos 1995).

19. Further suggestion of the Moon Pyramid's association with water is included in Pasztory's argument that the pyramid represented the Storm God (Pasztory 1997:95–107).

20. Batres began his explorations in 1905 in preparation for a centennial celebration of Mexican independence in 1910. Various accounts of Batres' work appear in Bastien 1967; Batres 1906; Millon et al. 1965; and Serra Puche 1993.

21. Both Aveni's (1980:222–226) research and Millon's (1993:35) discussion of Aveni's work should be consulted.

22. The pecked crosses may explain the circles frequently found on the three-mountain motif. For more discussion of this, see Headrick 2001:178–179.

23. In his argument, Aveni (1980:222–228) demonstrated that a pecked cross in the plaster floor of a structure near the Sun Pyramid creates a sightline at 15°21′ with the pecked cross on Cerro Colorado. He then went on to connect this

with the first appearance of the Pleiades on the first day of zenith passage and with the orientation of the city. I find this association with the zenith passage very compelling, but since Aveni did his research, many more pecked crosses have been found near the Sun Pyramid (Matos 1995). Until a thorough study of all the pecked crosses has been conducted, it is ultimately unclear as to what their role was in shaping Teotihuacan site planning.

24. This quote was the title of a fine synthesis of Teotihuacan history (Millon 1993).

25. The archaeological evidence appears in Berrin and Pasztory 1993:174–175; Manzanilla 1991:9; Múnera 1985:88; Sánchez S. 1982b:252; and Widmer 1987:332.

26. Splendid reproductions of these murals are in Stuart 1992.

27. Both Sahagún and Durán have numerous references to the military orders. See Chapter 5 of this text for some of the more interesting examples.

28. This account of creation is based on Sahagún 1950–1982:VII:3–9.

CHAPTER 7

1. For a discussion of Tetimpa, see Plunket and Uruñuela 1998. Cowgill (2003b) also comments that Tetimpa demonstrates that talud-tablero architecture appeared in central Mexico before Teotihuacan.

2. See Coe 1972; Coggins 1983:55; Fash and Fash 2000:446; Laporte and Fialko 1995; and McCafferty 2000. Also see Sanders and Michels 1977 for a discussion of talud-tablero as an indication of contact between Kaminaljuyu and Teotihuacan. Among others, Juan Pedro Laporte (2003) reports that talud-tablero architecture at Tikal predates direct Teotihuacan intrusions and exhibits more variety at Tikal than at Teotihuacan. He cautions against models with unidirectional influence, instead urging consideration of models wherein there was a mutual exchange of ideas between several sites or regions. Further discussion of the nature of Teotihuacan and Maya interaction appears in the numerous articles contained in Braswell 2003a.

3. Von Winning (1947b) was the first to recognize the visual connection between butterfly imagery and Teotihuacan architecture. I am also deeply indebted to Marguerite Mayhall for her keen insights into the association of butterflies with architecture in a paper she wrote for a graduate seminar (Mayhall 1991).

4. Identifications of the butterfly noseplaque should not be confused with two other types of noseplaques that have been found archaeologically (see Cowgill 1996:Figure 6.8). One, dubbed the "Tlaloc" type, has a rectangular upper portion and a bifurcated tongue for a lower section. The other is more rounded on the upper portion and has two out-flaring, curled volutes at the bottom. Oralia Cabrera (1995) correctly identified this type as the terminal end of a rattlesnake rattle. In my opinion, neither of these archaeologically recovered noseplaques should be identified as the butterfly noseplaque seen in ceramic and mural depictions.

Unlike these noseplaques, the butterfly noseplaque has a rigidly rectangular upper portion and a definitively triangular base with sharply pointed corners, as opposed to the rounded forms seen on the terminus of the rattlesnake rattle noseplaque.

5. Von Winning (1987:I:111–124) included the butterfly within a fire complex, an association that I do not find as compelling. Nevertheless, Taube (2000a:301–302) provided a rationale for the butterfly's association with fire that has much merit.

6. Credit for the identification of the rubber-splattered paper belongs to Khristaan Villela (1990).

7. Information connecting the year sign and warfare is in Schele and Freidel 1990:146–147.

8. For an image with similar iconography, see the looted mural fragment published by Miller (1973:Figure 360). This Tlaloc also has a water lily gripped in his mouth, a Tlaloc jar flowing with water, and a lightning staff.

9. Similar Tlaloc mouths appear, for instance, on Tlaloc vessels and a molded plaque illustrated by von Winning (1987:I:72–73).

10. Sahagún (1950–1982:II:175) included one such account, but for a thorough history of research on the Templo Mayor, read Boone 1987.

11. Schele and Freidel (1990) followed an "internalist" view that the Maya appropriated foreign symbolism, but it is becoming ever more clear that the early "externalist" ideas of Coggins (1975, 1979a, 1979b, 1983), Proskouriakoff (1993), and Stuart (2000) are more accurate. In this view, Teotihuacan's presence was more direct and invasive in the Maya area. Nevertheless, Schele and Freidel's suggestion that some Maya adopted a form of warfare from the Teotihuacanos is not incompatible with the externalist viewpoint.

12. Karl Taube's (2000b) keen insight that many of the large assemblages seen in Teotihuacan's mural art may be hieroglyphs may temper this interpretation. An alternative way to view this mural is that it reads "Atlatl-Butterfly," a phrase suggestively similar to the proposed Teotihuacano "Atlatl-Owl" mentioned in the Tikal texts (Stuart 2000). In other words, it is possible that "Atlatl-Butterfly" was the name of a prominent historical personage at Teotihuacan.

13. Von Winning's interpretation of this symbol as a military title has also been adopted to explain the "Spearthrower-Owl" that appears in the Tikal texts (Schele and Freidel 1990:156–157; Freidel et al. 1993:300–303).

14. For other discussions of the butterfly's connection with warfare, see Headrick 2003a and Taube 2000a.

15. Von Winning's ideas were further expanded upon by Mayhall (1991) in a brilliant graduate seminar paper.

16. Von Winning (1947b, 1987:II:60) deserves credit for recognizing this conflation.

17. The pairing of birds and butterflies in this passage may offer another reason for the frequent conflation of birds and butterflies in Teotihuacan art.

18. See, for example, Berlo 1983b, 1984; Beyer 1965b; Kubler 1972:81; Pasztory 1976:157–159; Taube 2000a; Toscano 1954:33; and von Winning 1987:I:111–124.

19. Berlo (1983b, 1984:30–31, 63–65), Kubler (1972:81),

Taube (2000a), and von Winning (1987:I:121–122) suggest various funerary associations for censers.

20. Also see López Luján et al. 2000:236 and Cowgill 1997:142.

21. Discussion of the burials is in Berlo 1984:30–33; Linné 1942:125–132; Manzanilla 1993a, 1993b:96; Manzanilla and Carreón 1989; and Sejourné 1959:667.

22. For another example of the noseplaque doubling as the year sign, see Seler 1990–1998:VI:Plate LXVI, 1.

23. In the aftermath of the events of September 11, 2001, this comparison seems particularly compelling and suspect at the same time. I formulated most of my thoughts on this subject during the years preceding 2001, when citizens of the United States more often felt like spectators to these events than their most engaged participants (Headrick 1996a, 1996b). I have persisted with this comparison because it seems to reveal issues that are fundamentally human rather than culturally specific. Although the image that emerges may not be a positive one, it is nonetheless something that each of us may carry inside.

24. The most thorough discussion of this image is in Pasztory 1976.

25. In a seminar paper, Marguerite Mayhall (1991) emphasized the balanced nature of these two branches and argued for their equal treatment in analyzing the central figure of the Tepantitla murals.

26. Some caution is warranted in fully accepting an economic role for weaving at Teotihuacan. Citing work done by Oralia Cabrera, Cowgill (2003a:52) noted that evidence for textile production at the city is quite small. However, in the same article, Cowgill (2003a:49) reasoned that farming implements are also rare in the archaeological record, despite the fact that much of the population must have engaged in farming at least part-time. Sampling issues or other factors may account for the absence of such materials.

27. Cowgill (1997:133, 2003a:50) offered a cautionary note to Storey's analysis by pointing out that it is unclear whether generalization from one low-status compound accurately reflects mortality rates elsewhere at Teotihuacan. Furthermore, he suggested that because mortality rates were higher throughout Precolumbian Mesoamerica, people living at Teotihuacan may not have perceived Teotihuacan as particularly unhealthful.

28. Jill Furst (1977) wrote the most important analysis of this and other Mixtec ancestor trees.

29. The theme of ancestor emergence may appear in the Tepantitla murals as well. On one wall a mountain with water flowing from its base sits directly below the personified mountain, securing the identification of the upper image as a mountain (Figure 2.7). Like the Apoala tree, human figures emerge from openings in the mountain. The fact that the Teotihuacan ancestors emerge from a mountain rather than a tree is particularly interesting because the Mixtec seem to have believed that earlier civilizations, such as the Zapotec, had their origins in the earth, whereas the Mixtec came from trees. Thus, the earthly origins of the Teotihuacanos may tap into a greater Classic period paradigm.

30. Discussion of these tombs may be found in López and Ramos 1998 and Pickering and Cabrero 1998.

CHAPTER 8

1. As discussed in Chapter 2, the owl headdresses of the human figures may identify them as the ruler or rulers instead of priests.

2. For an elaborate account of the world tree in Meso-american symbolism, see Freidel et al. 1993:59–122. The specific interpretation of the San Martín Pajapan figure appears in Reilly 1994; Freidel et al. 1993:152–139; and Schele 1995.

3. The primary texts relied on by Freidel et al. (1993) are Quirigua Stela C and Palenque's Tablet of the Cross.

4. All of the information on the Tota tree comes from the account of the sixteenth-century friar Diego Durán (1971:160–167).

5. The identification of this bundle as Painal comes from Sahagún's (1950–1982:II:115) later account in the Florentine Codex. In that Painal is a human representative of Huitzilopochtli, the bundle seen in the *Primeros Memoriales* could be that of Huitzilopochtli.

6. The notched butterfly ornaments also appear in an image of the *xocotl* in the Codex Borbonicus.

7. Franke Neumann (1988) made this identification, and both he and Betty Brown (1988) argued that the Aztecs of Tenochtitlan historicized this ritual by shaping it to celebrate an important military victory over the Otomi. They suggested that the dough figure represented the patron deity of the Otomi, Otontecuhtli, and each time a warrior tore the dough into pieces, he symbolically reenacted this conquest. Although the paper ornaments on the dough figure may be an attribute of Otontecuhtli, their butterfly associations also tap into the much more widespread symbolism of the warrior cult.

8. A number of ceramic models from the west Mexican tradition also display evidence of tree raising and *voladores* rituals in this region. Christopher Beekman (2003:8–10) offered a recent discussion of the pertinent sources on this matter.

9. The gender of this figure is somewhat indeterminate, but his bare chest shows no indication of breasts, and most if not all of the other figures in the scene wear male loincloths.

10. See Taube 2000b for the most current discussion of Teotihuacan glyphs.

11. Karl Taube (2000b) is credited with the identification of the centipede dance.

12. For a full description of the Ballgame Talud mural, see Pasztory 1976:200–214. The appearance of a ballgame in the Tepantitla mural is particularly intriguing because the ballgame has a prominent role in Maya versions of the creation story. In the *Popol Vuh* the protagonists Hunahpu and Xbalanque play ball with the gods before sacrificing themselves and readying the world for creation (Tedlock 1985). This suggests that the ball playing in the Tepantitla murals may reenact a paradigmatic game in the creation cycle.

13. Earlier comparisons of the Tepantitla tree to these images can be seen in Pasztory 1976:146–156 and Heyden 2000:179–181. They also made the perfectly appropriate comparison of this tree to those seen on several Palenque panels.

14. See Pasztory 1974 and 1997. By means of clarification, I do not object to a female or goddess identification for this mountain, but I am uncomfortable with identifying it with a monolithic, all-encompassing goddess, as has typically appeared in the literature on the subject.

15. When I argued that the figure in the Tepantitla murals possibly depicted the damaged sculpture in the Moon Plaza (Headrick 2002), I founded much of my reasoning on the general consensus that the Museo Nacional sculpture also came from this plaza. Furthermore, I was convinced by Pasztory's (1997:99) argument that these two sculptures were quite similar and perhaps paired. However, upon finding that the Museo Nacional sculpture came from a different space (see Chapter 2 of this text), I am less inclined to view these as close replicas, which calls into question the iconography of the heavily mutilated sculpture.

16. For a recent compelling account of this Aztec belief, see Boone 2000:372–374.

17. Much of the following information concerning the astronomical rationale for Teotihuacan's view of creation comes from Millon 1993:35–36.

18. As documented by Doris Heyden (1981:14) in her thorough analysis of caves, Herrera (1944:I:308) stated that the sun and moon came from a cave, while Mendieta (1945:I:87) specified that a god transformed himself into the moon inside a cave.

19. David Drucker (1977) first recognized that the sun set on these two days at the same location. As for the day of creation, the Maya Long Count marks time since the zero-date of August 13, 3114 B.C. (Cowgill 2000a:361; Malmström 1978; Freidel et al. 1993:63).

20. R. Millon (1992:387) also notes that the summer solstice falls in the middle of the 105-day interval. Thus, it can be viewed as two counts of 52 days on either side of the solstice (52 + 1 + 52), and the number 52 is significant because there were 52 years in the Calendar Round.

21. See Cowgill 2000a for his commentary on the strong north-south symbolism of the city plan, and the Avenue of the Dead's function as an *axis mundi*. He also presented interesting ideas about the integrated symbolism of the Sun and Moon Pyramids.

22. René Millon (1993) titled his fine synthesis of Teotihuacan history "The Place Where Time Began," thus codifying this concept for Teotihuacan scholars.

23. Schondube (1975) was the first to argue that the western altars should be conceived of as one altar, making the total number of altars nine.

24. Schondube (1975:241) noted the accentuation of the eastern altar. I would further suggest that in its configuration, this interior room is reminiscent of the small rooms found within the temples in the Cross Group at Palenque. Schele and Freidel (1990:239) identified these by the Mayan term *pib na,* which refers to underground cooking pits and

sweat baths, both of which are conceptually places of transformation. These concepts are also thoroughly explored in
Houston 1996.

25. Schondube (1975) deserves full credit for this
connection.

26. The Codex Féjérvary-Mayer is believed to be Mixtec
and probably dates to the fifteenth century. For a full discussion of how this image links time and space, see Aveni
1980:154–158.

27. In addition to Brotherston 1976:45 and Aveni
1980:156, also see Paxton 2001:33, which connects calendars
like the Féjérvary-Mayer to observations Villa Rojas (1988)
made about modern Yucatec Maya concepts of space.

28. This interpretation of the text is based on Freidel
et al. 1993:71–73.

29. The cosmic monster was another manifestation of
the Milky Way canoe (Freidel et al. 1993:90–91).

30. In the later years of Teotihuacan, this may have been
an approximation because the sightline seems to have been
established in the first century A.D. Due to precession, the
sun would not have set on this spot on the day of creation
throughout Teotihuacan's history, so tradition may have
eclipsed observable reality when determining the proper day
for ritual.

CHAPTER 9

1. Two examples of creation texts that incorporate
instructions for gender roles are found among the Hopi
(Mullett 1979:1–6; Nequatewa 1967:7–23) and the Navajo
(Griffin-Pierce 1992).

BIBLIOGRAPHY

ACOSTA, JORGE R.

1962a   El Palacio de las Mariposas de Teotihuacán. *Boletín de INAH* 9:5–7.

1962b   Ultimos trabajos arqueológicos en Teotihuacán. *Boletín de INAH* 10:8–10.

1964   *El Palacio del Quetzalpapálotl.* Mexico, D.F.: INAH.

1972   El epílogo de Teotihuacan. In *Teotihuacan: XI Mesa Redonda,* pp. 149–156. Mexico, D.F.: Sociedad Mexicana de Antropología.

ADAMS, E. CHARLES

1991   *The Origin and Development of the Pueblo Katsina Cult.* Tucson: University of Arizona Press.

ALMARAZ, RAMÓN

1865   Apuntas sobre las pirámides de San Juan Teotihuacán. In *Memorias y trabajos ejecutados por la Comisión Científica de Pachuca en el año de 1864,* pp. 349–358. Mexico, D.F.: J. M. Andrade y F. Escalante.

ALTSCHUL, JEFFREY H.

1987   Social Districts of Teotihuacan. In *Teotihuacan: Nuevos datos, nuevas síntesis, nuevos problemas,* edited by Emily McClung de Tapia and Evelyn Childs Rattray, pp. 191–218. Mexico, D.F.: UNAM.

ANAWALT, PATRICIA REIFF

1981   *Indian Clothing Before Cortés: Mesoamerican Costumes from the Codices.* Norman: University of Oklahoma Press.

ANDREWS, J. RICHARD

2003   *Introduction to Classical Nahuatl.* Revised edition. Norman: University of Oklahoma Press.

ANGULO VILLASEÑOR, JORGE

1972   Reconstrucción etnográfica a traves de la pintura. In *Teotihuacan: XI Mesa Redonda,* pp. 43–68. Mexico, D.F.: Sociedad Mexicana de Antropología.

1987a   El sistema *otli-apantli* dentro del área urbana. In *Teotihuacan: Nuevos datos, nuevas síntesis, nuevos problemas,* edited by Emily McClung de Tapia and Evelyn Childs Rattray, pp. 399–415. Mexico, D.F.: UNAM.

1987b   Nuevas consideraciones sobre Tetitla y los llamados conjuntos departamentales. In *Teotihuacán: Nuevos datos, nuevas síntesis, nuevos problemas,* edited by Emily McClung de Tapia and Evelyn Childs Rattray, pp. 275–315. Mexico, D.F.: UNAM.

ARMILLAS, PEDRO

1944   Exploraciones recientes en Teotihuacan, México. *Cuadernos Americanos* 16:121–136.

1945   Los dioses de Teotihuacan. *Anales del Instituto de Etnografica Americana* 6:35–61.

1947   La serpiente emplumada: Quetzalcoatl y Tlaloc. *Cuadernos Americanos* 31:161–178.

1950   Teotihuacan, Tula y los Toltecas. *RUNA* 3:37–70.

1964   Northern Mesoamerica. In *Prehistoric Man in the New World,* edited by Jesse Jennings and Edward Norbeck, pp. 291–329. Chicago and London: University of Chicago Press.

AVELEYRA ARROYO DE ANDA, LUIS

1963   *La estela Teotihuacan de La Ventilla.* Mexico, D.F.: Museo Nacional de Antropología, INAH.

AVENI, ANTHONY F.

1980   *Skywatchers of Ancient Mexico.* Austin: University of Texas Press.

AVENI, ANTHONY F., AND HORST HARTUNG

1981   The Observation of the Sun at the Time of Passage through the Zenith in Mesoamerica. *Archaeoastronomy* 3:51–70.

1982   New Observations of the Pecked Cross Petroglyph. In *Space and Time in the Cosmovision of Mesoamerica,* edited by Franz Tichy. Lateinamerika Studien (10), pp. 25–41. Munich: Wilhelm Fink Verlag.

BAIRD, ELLEN T.

1993   *The Drawings of Sahagún's Primeros Memoriales: Structure and Style.* Norman and London: University of Oklahoma Press.

BAQUEDANO, ELIZABETH

1993   *Aztec, Inca, Maya.* New York: Alfred A. Knopf.

BARBA, LUIS ALBERTO

1986   La química en el estudio de areas de actividad. In *Unidades habitacionales mesoamericanas y sus áreas de actividad,* edited by Linda Manzanilla, pp. 21–39. Mexico, D.F.: UNAM.

BARBA, LUIS, AND LINDA MANZANILLA

1987   Superficie/excavación: Un esayo de predicción de rasgos arqueológicos en Oztoyohualco. *Antropológicas* 1:19–46.

BARBA, LUIS, BEATRIZ LUDLOW, LINDA MANZANILLA, AND RAÚL VALADEZ

1987   La vida doméstica en Teotihuacán. *Ciencia y desarrollo* 13(77):21–32.

BARBOUR, WARREN

1975   The Figurines and Figurine Chronology of Ancient Teotihuacán. Ph.D. dissertation, University of Rochester, New York.

BASTIEN, RÉMY

1967   The Pyramid of the Sun in Teotihuacan: A New Interpretation. In *The Civilizations of Ancient America: Selected Papers of the XXIXth International Congress of Americanists,* edited by Sol Tax, pp. 62–67. New York: Cooper Square Publishers.

BATRES, LEOPOLDO

1906   *Teotihuacan.* Mexico, D.F.: Fidencio S. Soria.

BEEKMAN, CHRISTOPHER S.

2003   Fruitful Symmetry: Corn and Cosmology in the Public Architecture of Late Formative and Early Classic Jalisco. *Mesoamerican Voices* 1:5–22.

BERLO, JANET C.

1983a   Conceptual Categories for the Study of Texts and Images in Mesoamerica. In *Text and Image in Pre-Columbian Art,* edited by Janet Berlo, pp. 1–39. Oxford: BAR.

1983b   The Warrior and the Butterfly: Central Mexican Ideologies of Sacred Warfare and Teotihuacan Iconography. In *Text and Image in Pre-Columbian Art,* edited by Janet Berlo, pp. 79–117. Oxford: BAR.

1984   *Teotihuacan Art Abroad: A Study of Metropolitan Style and Provincial Transformation in Incensario Workshops.* Oxford: BAR.

1989   Early Writing in Central Mexico: *In Tlilli, In Tlapalli* before A.D. 1000. In *Mesoamerica After the Decline of Teotihuacan,* edited by Richard A. Diehl and Janet Catherine Berlo, pp. 19–48. Washington, D.C.: Dumbarton Oaks Research Library and Collection.

1992   Icons and Ideologies at Teotihuacan: The Great Goddess Reconsidered. In *Art, Ideology, and the City of Teotihuacan,* edited by Janet Catherine Berlo, pp. 129–168. Washington, D.C.: Dumbarton Oaks Research Library and Collection.

BERNAL, IGNACIO

1948–1949   Exploraciones en Coixtlahuaca, Oaxaca. *Revista Mexicana de Estudios Antropológicos* 10:5–76.

1963   *Teotihuacan: Descubrimientos, reconstrucciones.* Mexico, D.F.: Instituto Nacional de Antropología.

1965   Posible imperio teotihuacano. *Estudios de Cultura Náhuatl* 5:31–38.

1966   Teotihuacan ¿Capital de imperio? *Revista Mexicana de Estudios Antropológicos* 20:95–110.

BERRIN, KATHLEEN

1993   Unknown Treasures: The Unexpected in Teotihuacan Art. In *Teotihuacan: Art from the City of the Gods,* edited by Kathleen Berrin and Esther Pasztory, pp. 75–87. San Francisco: Thames and Hudson and the Fine Arts Museums of San Francisco.

BERRIN, KATHLEEN, AND ESTHER PASZTORY (EDITORS)

1993   *Teotihuacan: Art from the City of the Gods.* San Francisco: Thames and Hudson and the Fine Arts Museums of San Francisco.

BEYER, HERMANN

1922   Sobre una plaqueta con una deidad Teotihuacana. *Société Scientifique "Antonio Alzate" Mémoires* 40:549–558.

1965a   La Gigantesca Diosa de Teotihuacan. *El Mexico Antiguo* X:419–423.

1965b   La mariposa en el simbolismo azteca. *El México Antiguo* X:465–469.

1969a   El temalacatl. *El México Antiguo* XI:310–315.

1969b   La diadema de los reyes aztecas. *El México Anti-guo* XI:406–410.

1969c   Estudio interpretativo de algunas grandes esculturas. *El Mexico Antiguo* XI:297–309.

1969d   Una excursion a las ruinas de Teotihuacan. *El México Antiguo* XI:238–244.

1969e   Relaciones entre la civilizacion Teotihuacana y la azteca. *El México Antiguo* XI:245–272.

BLANTON, RICHARD E.

1978   *Monte Alban: Settlement Patterns at the Ancient Zapotec Capital.* New York: Academic Press.

1983   Monte Alban During Period III. In *The Cloud People: Divergent Evolution of the Zapotec and Mixtec Civilizations,* edited by Kent V. Flannery and Joyce Marcus, pp. 128–131. New York: Academic Press.

BOONE, ELIZABETH H.

1987   Templo Mayor Research, pp. 1521–1978. In *The Aztec Templo Mayor,* edited by Elizabeth Hill Boone, pp. 5–69. Washington, D.C.: Dumbarton Oaks Research Library and Collection.

1989   *Incarnations of the Aztec Supernatural: The Image of Huitzilopochtli in Mexico and Europe.* Transactions of the American Philosophical Society, vol. 79, pt. 2. Philadelphia: American Philosophical Society.

2000   Venerable Place of Beginnings: The Aztec Understanding of Teotihuacan. In *Mesoamerica's Classic Heritage: From Teotihuacan to the Aztecs,* edited by Davíd Carrasco, Lindsay Jones, and Scott Sessions, pp. 371–395. Boulder: University of Colorado Press.

BRAMBILA, ROSA

1992   La arqueología de Teotihuacan en los años cuarenta. *Antropológicas* 1:3–10.

BRASWELL, GEOFFREY (EDITOR)

2003a   *The Maya and Teotihuacan: Reinterpreting Early Classic Interaction.* Austin: University of Texas Press.

BRASWELL, GEOFFREY

2003b   Introduction: Reinterpreting Early Classic Interaction. In *The Maya and Teotihuacan: Reinterpreting Early Classic Interaction,* edited by Geoffrey Braswell, pp. 1–43. Austin: University of Texas Press.

BRICKER, VICTORIA REIFLER

1981   *The Indian Christ, the Indian King: The Historical Substrate of Maya Myth and Ritual.* Austin: University of Texas Press.

BROTHERSTON, GORDON

1974   Huitzilopochtli and What Was Made of Him. In *Mesoamerican Archaeology: New Approaches,* edited by Norman Hammond, pp. 155–166. Austin: University of Texas Press.

1976   Mesoamerican Description of Space II: Signs for Direction. *Ibero-amerikanisches Archiv* 2(1):39–62.

BROWN, BETTY ANN

1988   All Around the Xocotl Pole: Reexamination of an Aztec Sacrificial Ceremony. In *Smoke and Mist: Mesoamerican Studies in Memory of Thelma D. Sullivan,* edited by Kathryn Josserand and Karen Dakin, pp. 173–189. Oxford: BAR.

BROWN, DAVID

1988   The Linguistic Affiliation and Phoneticism of Teotihuacan Iconography. Ph.D. dissertation, University of New Mexico, Albuquerque.

BUNZEL, RUTH L.

1932   Zuni Katcinas. *Annual Report* no. 47, pp. 837–1108. Washington, D.C.: Bureau of American Ethnology.

BURGOA, FRANCISCO DE

1989   *Geográfica descripción.* Vol. I. Mexico, D.F.: Editorial Porrúa.

BURKHART, LOUISE M.

1989   *The Slippery Earth: Nahua-Christian Moral Dialogue in Sixteenth-Century Mexico.* Tucson: University of Arizona Press.

BYLAND, BRUCE E., AND JOHN M. D. POHL

1994   *In the Realm of 8 Deer.* Norman: University of Oklahoma Press.

CABALLERO BARNARD, JOSÉ

1975   "*De Teotihuacan a Tollocan*": *Un viaje a traves del tiempo y del color.* Mexico, D.F.: Gobierno del Estado de Mexico.

CABRERA C., ORALIA

1995   *La Lapidaria del Proyecto Templo de Quetzalcoatl 1988–1989.* Thesis, Escuela Nacional de Antropología e Historia, México, D.F.

CABRERA CASTRO, RUBÉN

1982a   La excavacion de la estructura 1B' en la interior de la Ciudadela. In *Memoria de Proyecto Arqueológico Teotihuacán 80–82,* edited by Rubén Cabrera Castro, Ignacio Rodríguez G., and Noel Morelos G., pp. 75–87. Mexico, D.F.: INAH.

1982b   La excavación del conjunto 1C', en el interior del gran cuadrángulo del Templo de Quetzalcoatl. In *Memoria de Proyecto Arqueológico Teotihuacán 80–82,* edited by Rubén Cabrera Castro, Ignacio Rodríguez G., and Noel Morelos G., pp. 143–155. Mexico, D.F.: INAH.

1982c   El proyecto Teotihuacán. In *Teotihuacán 80–82: Primeros resultados,* edited by Rubén Cabrera, Ignacio Rodríguez G., and Noel Morelos, pp. 7–40. Mexico, D.F.: INAH.

1987a   La sequencia arquitectónica de edificio de los Animales Mitológicos en Teotihuacan. In *Homenaje a Roman Piña Chan,* edited by Barbro Dahlgren, Carlos Navarrete, Lorenzo Ochoa, Mari Carmen Serra, and Yoko Sugiura, pp. 349–371. Mexico, D.F.: UNAM.

1987b   Resumen y comentarios de los trabajos presentados en el simposio, por el proyecto arqueológico Teotihuacán 80–82. In *Teotihuacán: Nuevos datos, nuevas síntesis, nuevos problemas,* edited by Emily McClung de Tapia and Evelyn Childs Rattray, pp. 489–525. Mexico, D.F.: UNAM.

1988   Horno cerámico posteotihuacano en el Palacio de Atetelco. *Arqueología* 4:47–76.

1990a   El proyecto arqueológico Teotihuacán 80–82. Resumen general de sus resultados en la ciudad.

In *La Epoca Clásica: Nuevos hallazgos, nuevas ideas,* edited by Amalia Cardos de Mendez, pp. 73–80. Mexico, D.F.: Museo Nacional de Antropología, INAH.

1990b   The Metropolis of Teotihuacan. In *Mexico: Splendors of Thirty Centuries,* edited by John P. O'Neill, pp. 87–114. New York: Metropolitan Museum of Art.

1991   Una plataforma en "U" dentro del complejo Calle de los Muertos en Teotihuacan. *Cuadernos de Arquitectura Mesoamericana* 13:15–21.

1992   A Survey of Recently Excavated Murals at Teotihuacan. In *Art, Ideology, and the City of Teotihuacan,* edited by Janet Catherine Berlo, pp. 113–128. Washington, D.C.: Dumbarton Oaks Research Library and Collection.

1993   Human Sacrifice at the Temple of the Feathered Serpent: Recent Discoveries at Teotihuacan. In *Teotihuacan: Art from the City of the Gods,* edited by Kathleen Berrin and Esther Pasztory, pp. 101–107. San Francisco: Thames and Hudson and the Fine Arts Museums of San Francisco.

1995   Atetelco. In *La pintura mural prehispánica en Mexico,* tomo I, edited by Beatriz de la Fuente, pp. 203–256. Mexico, D.F.: Instituto de Investigaciones Estéticas, UNAM.

1996   Caracteres glíficos Teotihuacanos en el piso de La Ventilla. In *La pintura mural prehispánica en Mexico,* tomo II, edited by Beatriz de la Fuente, pp. 400–427. Mexico, D.F.: Instituto de Investigaciones Estéticas, UNAM.

CABRERA CASTRO, RUBÉN, AND ORALIA CABRERA C.

1993   El significado calendárico de los entierros del Templo de Quetzalcoatl. In *II Coloquio Pedro Bosch-Gimpera,* edited by María Teresa Cabrero G., pp. 277–297. Mexico, D.F.: Instituto de Investigaciones Antropológicas, UNAM.

CABRERA CASTRO, RUBÉN, AND GEORGE COWGILL

1990   Proyecto Templo de Quetzalcóatl: Historia, política e ideología. *Boletín: Consejo de Arqueología* 2:44–49.

CABRERA CASTRO, RUBÉN, GEORGE COWGILL, AND SABURO SUGIYAMA

1990   El proyecto Templo de Quetzalcoatl y la practica a gran escala del sacrificio humano. In *La Epoca Clásica: Nuevos hallazgos, nuevas ideas,* edited by Amalia Cardos de Mendez, pp. 123–146. Mexico, D.F.: Museo Nacional de Antropología, INAH.

CABRERA CASTRO, RUBÉN, GEORGE COWGILL, SABURO SUGIYAMA, AND CARLOS SERRANO

1989   El proyecto Templo de Quetzalcoatl. *Arqueología* 5:51–79.

CABRERA CASTRO, RUBÉN, AND J. RODOLFO CID B.

1990   Proyecto asentamientos humanos en la periferia del Valle de Teotihuacán. *Boletín: Consejo de Arqueología* 2:40–43.

CABRERA CASTRO, RUBÉN, AND ENRIQUE SORUCO

1982   Pequeños basamentos habitacionales en la Calle de los Muertos. In *Memoria de Proyecto Arqueológico Teotihuacán 80–82,* edited by Rubén Cabrera Castro, Ignacio Rodríguez G., and Noel Morelos G., pp. 217–224. Mexico, D.F.: INAH.

CABRERA CASTRO, RUBÉN, AND SABURO SUGIYAMA

1999   El proyecto arqueológico de la Pirámide de la Lúna. *Arqueología* 21:19–33.

CAMPOS REBOLLO, MARIO

1988   Análisis e interpretación de la vasija en forma de ave encontrada en el entierro 66 del palacio B de la Ventilla, Teotihuacan. *Revista Mexicana de Estudios Antropológicos* 34(1):53–73.

CARMACK, ROBERT M.

1973   *Quichean Civilization: The Ethnohistoric, Ethnographic, and Archaeological Sources.* Berkeley: University of California Press.

CARMICHAEL, ELIZABETH, AND CHLOË SAYER

1991   *The Skeleton at the Feast: The Day of the Dead in Mexico.* Austin: University of Texas Press.

CARRASCO, DAVÍD

1990   *Religions of Mesoamerica.* San Francisco: Harper and Row.

CARRASCO, PEDRO

1971   Social Organization of Ancient Mexico. In *Handbook of Middle American Indians,* vol. 10, edited by Robert Wauchope, Gordon Ekholm, and Ignacio Bernal, pp. 349–375. Austin: University of Texas Press.

CASO, ALFONSO

1937   Tenían los teotihuacanos conocimiento del Tonalpohualli? *El México Antiguo* 4:131–143.

1942a   El paraíso terrenal en Teotihuacan. *Cuadernos Americanos* 6:127–136.

1942b   Informe sobre las exploraciones verificadas en Teotihuacan, Mexico, Republica Mexicana, en el año 1942. INAH Archive 467.13; t. LXV.

1949   Una urna con el dios mariposa. *El México Antiguo* 7:78–95.

1966   Dioses y signos Teotihuacanos. *Teotihuacan: Onceava Mesa Redonda,* pp. 249–275. Mexico, D.F.: Sociedad Mexicana de Antropología.

CASTAÑEDA, FRANCISCO DE

1926   *Official Reports on the Towns of Tequizistlan, Tepechpan, Acolman, and San Juan Teotihuacan Sent by Francisco de Castañeda to His Majesty, Philip II, and the Council of the Indies in 1580.* Translated by Zelia Nuttall. Papers of the Peabody Museum of American Archaeology and Ethnology, Harvard University, vol. XI, no. 2. Cambridge: Peabody Museum of American Archaeology and Ethnology.

CHADWICK, ROBERT E. L.

1966   The "Olmeca-Xicallanca" of Teotihuacan: A Preliminary Study. *Mesoamerican Notes* 7–8:1–24.

CHANG, K. C.

1976   *Early Chinese Civilization: Anthropological Perspectives.* Cambridge: Harvard University Press.

1983   *Art, Myth, and Ritual: The Path to Political Authority in Ancient China.* Cambridge: Harvard University Press.

CHARLTON, THOMAS, RAÚL GARCÍA CHÁVEZ, AND
CYNTHIA OTIS CHARLTON

2003   East of Eden: Teotihuacan Non-urban Settle-
       ments. Paper delivered at the 68th Annual Meet-
       ing of the Society for American Archaeology,
       Milwaukee, Wisconsin.

CHASE, ARLEN F., AND DIANE Z. CHASE

1992   Mesoamerican Elites: Assumptions, Definitions,
       and Models. In *Mesoamerican Elites: An Archaeo-
       logical Assessment,* edited by Diane Z. and Arlen F.
       Chase, pp. 3–17. Norman and London: University
       of Oklahoma Press.

CHRISTENSON, ALLEN J.

2001   *Art and Society in a Highand Maya Community: The
       Altarpiece of Santiago Atitlán.* Austin: University of
       Texas Press.

CLAVIGERO, ABBÉ D. FRANCESCO SAVERIO

1979   *The History of Mexico,* vol. I. New York and Lon-
       don: Garland Publishing, Inc.

CODEX BODLEY

1960   *Interpretation of the Codex Bodley 2858.* Commen-
       tary by Alfonso Caso, translated by Ruth Morales
       and John Paddock. Mexico, D.F.: Sociedad Mexi-
       cana de Antropología.

CODEX CHIMALPOPOCA

1975   *Codex Chimalpopoca: Anales de Cuauhtitlán y leyenda
       de los soles.* Translated and edited by P. F. Veláz-
       quez. Mexico, D.F.: UNAM.

CODEX SELDEN

1964   *Interpretation of the Codex Selden 3135 (A. 2).* Com-
       mentary by Alfonso Caso, translated by Jacinto
       Quirarte and John Paddock. Mexico, D.F.: Socie-
       dad Mexicana de Antropología.

CODEX VINDOBONENSIS

1963   *Codex Vindobonensis Mexicanus I.* Commentary by
       O. Adelhofer. Graz, Austria: Academische Druck-
       u. Verlagsanstalt.

COE, MICHAEL

1975   Death and the Ancient Maya. In *Death and the
       Afterlife in Pre-Columbian America,* edited by Eliza-
       beth Benson, pp. 87–104. Washington, D.C.:
       Dumbarton Oaks Research Library and Collec-
       tion.

COE, MICHAEL D., AND RICHARD A. DIEHL

1980   *In the Land of the Olmec: The Archaeology of San
       Lorenzo Tenochtitlán.* Austin: University of Texas
       Press.

COE, WILLIAM R.

1972   Cultural Contact Between the Lowland Maya and
       Teotihuacan as Seen from Tikal, Peten, Guate-
       mala. In *Teotihuacan: XI Mesa Redonda,* pp. 257–271.
       Mexico, D.F.: Sociedad Mexicana de Antropo-
       logía.

COGGINS, CLEMENCY CHASE

1975   Painting and Drawing Styles at Tikal: An His-
       torical and Iconographic Reconstruction. Ph.D.
       dissertation, Department of Fine Arts, Harvard
       University, Cambridge, Massachusetts.

1979a A New Order and the Role of the Calendar: Some
       Characteristics of the Middle Classic Period at
       Tikal. In *Maya Archaeology and Ethnohistory,* edited
       by Norman Hammond and Gordon Willey, pp.
       38–50. Austin: University of Texas Press.

1979b Teotihuacan and Tikal in the Early Classic Period.
       *42nd International Congress of Americanists, Paris,
       1976,* 8:251–269. Paris: Société des Americanistes.

1983   An Instrument of Expansion: Monte Alban,
       Teotihuacan, and Tikal. In *Highland-Lowland Inter-
       action in Mesoamerica: Interdisciplinary Approaches,*
       edited by Arthur Miller, pp. 49–68. Washington,
       D.C.: Dumbarton Oaks Research Library and
       Collection.

1993   The Age of Teotihuacan and Its Mission Abroad.
       In *Teotihuacan: Art from the City of the Gods,* edited
       by Kathleen Berrin and Esther Pasztory, pp. 141–
       155. San Francisco: Thames and Hudson and the
       Fine Arts Museums of San Francisco.

COOK DE LEONARD, CARMEN

1956   Dos atlatl de la época teotihuacana. *Estudios Antro-
       pológicos: Publicados en Homenaje al Doctor Manuel
       Gamio.* Mexico, D.F.: UNAM.

1957   Proyecto del CIAM en Teotihuacan: Excavaciones
       en La Plaza #1, "Tres Palos," Teotihuacan. *Boletín
       del Centro de Investigaciones Antropológicas de México,*
       no. 4.

1971   Minor Arts of the Classic Period in Central
       Mexico. In *Handbook of Middle American Indians,*
       vol. 10, edited by Robert Wauchope, Gordon
       Ekholm, and Ignacio Bernal, pp. 206–227. Austin:
       University of Texas Press.

COOK, CARMEN, AND DON LEONARD

1949   Costumbres mortuorias de los indios huaves: Un
       viaje. *El México Antiguo* 7:439–496.

CORONA NÚÑEZ, JOSÉ

1960   *Arqueología: Occidente de México.* Mexico, D.F.:
       Jalisco en el Arte.

1972   Una tumba en Acatlan, Jalisco. *Estudios antropoló-
       gicos en el occidente de Mexico, Memoria de la Escuela
       de Antropología,* no. 1:52–62. Veracruz: Universidad
       Veracruzana.

COUCH, N. C. CHRISTOPHER

1985   *The Festival Cycle of the Aztec Codex Borbonicus.*
       Oxford: BAR.

COWGILL, GEORGE L.

1974   Quantitative Studies of Urbanization at Teotihua-
       can. In *Mesoamerican Archaeology: New Approaches,*
       edited by Norman Hammond, pp. 363–396.
       Austin: University of Texas Press.

1977   Processes of Growth and Decline at Teotihuacan:
       The City and the State. In *Los procesos de cambio
       en Mesoamérica y áreas circunvecinas,* XV Mesa Re-
       donda, vol. I, pp. 183–193. Mexico, D.F.: Sociedad
       Mexicana de Antropología.

1979   Teotihuacán, Internal Militaristic Competition,
       and the Fall of the Classic Maya. In *Maya Archae-
       ology and Ethnohistory,* edited by Norman Ham-

mond and Gordon R. Willey, pp. 51–62. Austin and London: University of Texas Press.

1983 Rulership and the Ciudadela: Political Inferences from Teotihuacan Architecture. In *Civilization in the Ancient Americas: Essays in Honor of Gordon R. Willey,* edited by Richard Leventhal and Alan Kolata, pp. 313–343. Cambridge: University of New Mexico Press and Peabody Museum of Archaeology and Ethnology.

1987 Métodos para el estudio de relaciones espaciales en los datos de la superficie de Teotihuacán. In *Teotihuacán: Nuevos datos, nuevas síntesis, nuevos problemas,* edited by Emily McClung de Tapia and Evelyn Childs Rattray, pp. 161–190. Mexico, D.F.: UNAM.

1992a Social Differentiation at Teotihuacan. In *Meso-american Elites: An Archaeological Assessment,* edited by Diane Z. and Arlen F. Chase, pp. 206–220. Norman and London: University of Oklahoma Press.

1992b Teotihuacan Glyphs and Imagery in the Light of Some Early Colonial Texts. In *Art, Ideology, and the City of Teotihuacan,* edited by Janet Catherine Berlo, pp. 231–246. Washington, D.C.: Dumbarton Oaks Research Library and Collection.

1992c Toward a Political History of Teotihuacan. In *Ideology and Pre-Columbian Civilizations,* edited by Arthur A. Demarest and Geoffrey W. Conrad, pp. 87–114. Santa Fe: School of American Research Press.

1993a Distinguished Lecture in Archaeology: Beyond Criticizing New Archaeology. In *American Anthro-pologist* 95(3):551–573.

1993b What We Still Don't Know about Teotihuacan. In *Teotihuacan: Art from the City of the Gods,* edited by Kathleen Berrin and Esther Pasztory, pp. 117–125. San Francisco: Thames and Hudson and the Fine Arts Museums of San Francisco.

1996 The Central Mexican Highlands from the Rise of Teotihuacan to the Decline of Tula. In *Meso-america,* edited by R. E. W. Adams and M. J. MacLeod, pp. 250–317. The Cambridge History of the Native Peoples of the Americas, vol. II, pt. 1. Cambridge: Cambridge University Press.

1997 State and Society at Teotihuacan, Mexico. *Annual Review of Anthropology* 26: 129–161.

2000a Intentionality and Meaning in the Layout of Teotihuacan, Mexico. *Cambridge Archaeological Journal* 10(2):358–361.

2000b "Rationality" and Contexts in Agency Theory. In *Agency in Archaeology,* edited by Marcia-Anne Dobres and John E. Robb, pp. 51–59. London and New York: Routledge.

2003a Teotihuacan: Cosmic Glories and Mundane Needs. In *The Social Construction of Ancient Cities,* edited by Monica L. Smith, pp. 37–55. Washington and London: Smithsonian Books.

2003b Teotihuacan and Early Classic Interaction: A Perspective from Outside the Maya Region. In *The*

Maya and Teotihuacan: Reinterpreting Early Classic Interaction, edited by Geoffrey Braswell, pp. 315–335. Austin: University of Texas Press.

DAHLGREN DE JORDAN, BARBRO

1954 Las pinturas rupestres de la Baja California. *Artes de México* 3:22–28.

DE BORHEGYI, STEPHAN F.

1966 Shell Offerings and the Use of Shell Motifs at Lake Amatitlan, Guatemala, and Teotihuacan, Mexico. *XXXVI Congreso Internacional de Ameri-canistas,* vol. 1, 355–371. Sevilla: ECESA.

DEFFEBACH, NANCY

1991 Atetelco: The Iconography of Warfare at the White Patio and the Painted Patio. Art history graduate seminar paper, University of Texas at Austin.

DELGADILLO, EUGENIA LARA

1991 Máscaras rituales: El otro yo. In *Teotihuacan 1980–1982: Nuevas interpretaciones,* edited by Rubén Cabrera Castro, Ignacio Rodríguez García, and Noel Morelos García, pp. 203–209. Mexico, D.F.: INAH.

DEW, THOMAS RODERRICK

1976 *The Masks of the Arroyo Pesquero.* M.A. thesis, Graduate School of the Arts and Sciences, University of Denver.

DIEHL, RICHARD A.

1972 Contemporary Settlement and Social Organization. In *Teotihuacan: XI Mesa Redonda,* pp. 353–362. Mexico, D.F.: Sociedad Mexicana de Antropología.

1990 The Olmec at La Venta. In *Mexico: Splendors of Thirty Centuries,* edited by John P. O'Neill, pp. 51–71. New York: Metropolitan Museum of Art.

DIEHL, RICHARD A., AND JANET C. BERLO (EDITORS)

1989 *Mesoamerica After the Decline of Teotihuacan, A.D. 700–900.* Washington, D.C.: Dumbarton Oaks Research Library and Collection.

DOSAL, PEDRO J.

1925 Descubrimientos arqueológicos en el Templo de Quetzalcoatl (Teotihuacan). *Anales del Museo Nacional de Arqueología, Historia y Etnografía* 3:216–219.

DRUCKER, R. DAVID

1977 A Solar Orientation Framework for Teotihuacan. In *Los procesos de cambio en Mesoamérica y áreas circunvecinas.* XV Mesa Redonda, vol. II, pp. 277–284. Mexico, D.F.: Sociedad Mexicana de Antropología and Universidad de Guanajuato.

DURÁN, FRAY DIEGO

1964 *The Aztecs: The History of the Indies of New Spain.* Translated by Doris Heyden and Fernando Hor-casitas. New York: Orion Press.

1971 *Book of the Gods and Rites and the Ancient Calendar.* Translated by Fernando Horcasitas and Doris Heyden. Norman: University of Oklahoma Press.

1994 *The History of the Indies of New Spain.* Translated by

Doris Heyden. Norman and London: University of Oklahoma Press.

EVANS, SUSAN T., AND JANET CATHERINE BERLO

1992   Teotihuacan: An Introduction. In *Art, Ideology, and the City of Teotihuacan,* edited by Janet Catherine Berlo, pp. 1–26. Washington, D.C.: Dumbarton Oaks Research Library and Collection.

FASH, WILLIAM L.

1991   *Scribes, Warriors, and Kings: The City of Copán and the Ancient Maya.* London: Thames and Hudson.

FASH, WILLIAM, AND BARBARA FASH

2000   Teotihuacan and the Maya: A Classic Heritage. In *Mesoamerica's Classic Heritage: From Teotihuacan to the Aztecs,* edited by Davíd Carrasco, Lindsay Jones, and Scott Sessions, pp. 433–463. Boulder: University of Colorado Press.

FIELDS, VIRGINIA M.

1989   The Origins of Divine Kingship Among the Lowland Maya. Ph.D. dissertation, University of Texas at Austin.

1991   The Iconographic Heritage of the Maya Jester God. In *Sixth Palenque Round Table, 1986,* general editor Merle Greene Robertson, volume editor Virginia M. Fields, pp. 167–174. Norman: University of Oklahoma Press.

FLANNERY, KENT V.

1976a   Contextual Analysis of Ritual Paraphernalia from Formative Oaxaca. In *The Early Mesoamerican Village,* edited by Kent V. Flannery, pp. 333–345. New York: Academic Press.

1976b   Research Strategy and Formative Mesoamerica. In *The Early Mesoamerican Village,* edited by Kent V. Flannery, pp. 1–11. New York: Academic Press.

1983   The Legacy of the Early Urban Period: An Ethnohistorical Approach to Monte Alban's Temples, Residences, and Royal Tombs. In *The Cloud People: Divergent Evolution of the Zapotec and Mixtec Civilizations,* edited by Kent V. Flannery and Joyce Marcus, pp. 132–136. New York: Academic Press.

FLANNERY, KENT V., AND JOYCE MARCUS

1983a   The Earliest Public Buildings, Tombs, and Monuments at Monte Albán, with Notes on the Internal Chronology of Period I. In *The Cloud People: Divergent Evolution of the Zapotec and Mixtec Civilizations,* edited by Kent V. Flannery and Joyce Marcus, pp. 87–91. New York: Academic Press.

1983b   Monte Albán and Teotihuacán: Editor's Introduction. In *The Cloud People: Divergent Evolution of the Zapotec and Mixtec Civilizations,* edited by Kent V. Flannery and Joyce Marcus, pp. 161–166. New York: Academic Press.

1983c   Preface. In *The Cloud People: Divergent Evolution of the Zapotec and Mixtec Civilizations,* edited by Kent V. Flannery and Joyce Marcus, xix–xxi. New York: Academic Press.

1983d   San Martín Huamelulpan, Periods I and II. In *The Cloud People: Divergent Evolution of the Zapotec and Mixtec Civilizations,* edited by Kent V. Flan-

nery and Joyce Marcus, pp. 123–124. New York: Academic Press.

FOLAN, WILLIAM, JOYCE MARCUS, SOPHIA PINCEMIN, MARIA DEL ROSARIO DOMÍNGUEZ CARRASCO, LARAINE FLETCHER, AND ABEL MORALES LÓPEZ

1995   Calakmul: New Data from an Ancient Maya Capital in Campeche, Mexico. *Latin American Antiquity* 6(4):310–334.

FOSTER, GEORGE M.

1944   Nagualism in Mexico and Guatemala. In *Acta Americana* 2:85–103.

1948   *Empire's Children: The People of Tzintzuntzan.* Smithsonian Institution, Institute of Social Anthropology, pub. no. 6.

FOX, JOHN W.

1987   *Maya Postclassic State Formation.* Cambridge: Cambridge University Press.

FRANKS, PAM

1991   Bloodletting and Sacrifice at Teotihuacan: The Non-Atetelco Murals. Art history graduate seminar paper, University of Texas at Austin.

FREIDEL, DAVID A., AND LINDA SCHELE

1988a   Kingship in the Late Preclassic Maya Lowlands: The Instruments and Places of Ritual Power. *American Anthropologist* 90:547–567.

1988b   Symbol and Power: A History of the Lowland Maya Cosmogram. In *Maya Iconography,* edited by Elizabeth P. Benson and Gillett G. Griffin, pp. 44–93. Princeton: Princeton University Press.

FREIDEL, DAVID A., LINDA SCHELE, AND JOY PARKER

1993   *Maya Cosmos: Three Thousand Years on the Shaman's Path.* New York: William Morrow and Company.

FUENTE, BEATRIZ DE LA

1990   Escultura en el tiempo: Retorno al pasado tolteca. *Artes de Mexico,* new series 7:36–53.

FURST, JILL

1977   The Tree Birth Tradition in the Mixteca, Mexico. *Journal of Latin American Lore* 3 (2):183–226.

FURST, PETER T.

1968   The Olmec Were-Jaguar Motif in the Light of Ethnographic Reality. In *Dumbarton Oaks Conference on the Olmec,* edited by E. P. Benson, pp. 143–174. Washington, D.C.: Dumbarton Oaks Research Library and Collection.

1974   Morning Glory and Mother Goddess at Tepantitla, Teotihuacan. In *Mesoamerican Archaeology: New Approaches,* edited by Norman Hammond, pp. 187–216. Austin: University of Texas Press.

GAMIO, MANUEL

1920   Los últimos descubrimientos arqueológicos en Teotihuacan. *Ethnos* 1:7–14.

1922   *Introducción, síntesis y conclusiones de la obra la población del Valle de Teotihuacan.* Mexico, D.F.: Secretaria de Agricultura y Fomento.

1979   *La población del Valle de Teotihuacan.* Mexico, D.F.: Instituto Nacional Indigenista.

GEMELLI CARRERI, JUAN FRANCISCO

1995   De los cúes o pirámides de San Juan Teotihua-can. In *La Pirámide del Sol, Teotihuacan,* edited by Eduardo Matos, pp.46–48. Mexico, D.F.: INAH.

GENDROP, PAUL

1970   Murales prehispánicos. *Artes de Mexico* 18(144).

GILLESPIE, SUSAN D.

1989   *The Aztec Kings: The Construction of Rulership in Mexica History.* Tucson and London: University of Arizona Press.

2000   Rethinking Ancient Maya Social Organization: Replacing "Lineage" with "House." *American Anthropologist* 102(3):467–484.

2002   Body and Soul among the Maya: Keeping the Spirits in Place. *Archeological Papers of the American Anthropological Association* 11(1):67–78.

GOMEZ CHAVEZ, SERGIO

1990   La función social del sacrificio humano en Teoti-huacan: Un intento para formalizar su estudio e interpretación. In *La Epoca Clásica: Nuevos hallazgos, nuevas ideas,* edited by Amalia Cardos de Mendez, pp. 147–161. Mexico, D.F.: Museo Nacional de Antropología, INAH.

GONZÁLEZ, ARNOLDO

1993   El Templo de la Cruz. *Arqueología Mexicana* 1(2):39–41.

GONZÁLEZ CASANOVA, P.

1920   Pictografos de Teotihuacan. *Ethnos* 1:14–17.

GONZÁLEZ DE LESUR, YOLOTL

1967   El dios Huitzilopochtli en la peregrinación mexica, de Aztlán a Tula. *Anales del Museo Nacional de Antropología,* ép. 6, 19:175–190.

GONZÁLEZ M., LUIS ALFONSO, AND DAVID FUENTES GONZÁLEZ

1982   Informe preliminar acerca de los enterramientos prehispánicos en la zona arqueológica de Teoti-huacan, Mexico. In *Teotihuacán 80–82, primeros resultados,* pp. 7–40. Mexico, D.F.: INAH.

GRAHAM, IAN, AND ERIC VON EUW

1977   *Corpus of Maya Hieroglyphic Inscriptions,* vol. 3, pt. 1, *Yaxchilan.* Cambridge: Peabody Museum of Archaeology and Ethnology, Harvard University.

GRIFFIN-PIERCE, TRUDY

1992   The Hooghan and the Stars. In *Visions of the Cos-mos in Native American Folklore,* edited by Ray Williamson and Claire Farrer, pp. 110–130. Albu-querque: University of New Mexico Press.

GROVE, DAVID C.

1968   Chalcatzingo, Morelos, Mexico: A Reappraisal of the Olmec Rock Carvings. *American Antiquity* 33(4):486–491.

1973   Olmec Altars and Myths. *Archaeology* 26(2):128–135.

1984   *Chalcatzingo: Excavations on the Olmec Frontier.* London: Thames and Hudson.

1987   *Ancient Chalcatzingo.* Austin: University of Texas Press.

GRUBE, NIKOLAI, AND WERNER NAHM

1994   A Census of Xibalba: A Complete Inventory of *Way* Characters on Maya Ceramics. In *The Maya Vase Book: A Corpus of Rollout Photographs of Maya Vases,* vol. 4. edited by Barbara and Justin Kerr, pp. 686–715. New York: Kerr Associates.

GRUZINSKI, SERGE

1992   *Painting the Conquest: The Mexican Indians and the European Renaissance.* Paris: Flammarion.

HARTUNG, HORST

1977   Relaciones urbanísticas lineales-visuales en Teoti-huacan y su zona de influencia. *Los procesos de cambio en Mesoamérica y áreas circunvecinas,* XV Mesa Redonda, vol. II, pp. 267–275. Mexico, D.F.: Sociedad Mexicana de Antropología.

1979   El ordenamiento espacial en los conjuntos arqui-tectónicos mesoamericanos: El ejemplo de Teoti-huacán. In *Comunicaciones 16/1979: Proyecto Puebla-Tlaxcala,* edited by Wilhelm Lauer and Konrad Tyrakowski, pp. 89–103. Puebla: Fundación Ale-mana para la Investigación Científica.

HARTUNG, HORST, AND ANTHONY F. AVENI

1991   Observaciones sobre el planeamiento de Teo-tihuacán: El llamado trazo cuadricular y las orientaciones a los puntos cardinales. *Cuadernos de Arquitectura Mesoamericana* 13:23–36.

HASSIG, ROSS

1988   *Aztec Warfare: Imperial Expansion and Political Control.* Norman and London: University of Oklahoma Press.

1992   *War and Society in Ancient Mesoamerica.* Berkeley: University of California Press.

HEADRICK, ANNABETH

1991   The *Chicomoztoc* of Chichen Itza. M.A. thesis, University of Texas at Austin.

1994   Eagles and Jaguars Caught in the Net: The Case for Nagualism at Teotihuacan. Paper presented at the 59th Annual Meeting of the Society for American Archaeology, Anaheim, California.

1996a   Teotihuacan Jihad: The Propaganda of Butterfly War. Paper presented at the 60th Annual Meeting of the Society for American Archaeology, New Orleans, April 14.

1996b   The Teotihuacan Trinity: UnMASKing the Po-litical Structure. Ph.D. dissertation, University of Texas at Austin.

1999   The Street of the Dead . . . It Really Was: Mor-tuary Bundles at Teotihuacan. *Ancient Mesoamerica* 10:69–85.

2001   Merging Myth and Politics: The Three Temple Complex at Teotihuacan. In *Landscape and Power in Ancient Mesoamerica,* edited by Rex Koontz, Kathryn Reese-Taylor, and Annabeth Headrick, pp. 169–195. Boulder: Westview Press.

2002   Gardening with the Great Goddess at Teoti-huacan. In *Heart of Creation: The Mesoamerican World and the Legacy of Linda Schele,* edited by Andrea Stone, pp. 83–100. Tuscaloosa and London: University of Alabama Press.

2003a   Butterfly War at Teotihuacan. In *Ancient Meso-*

american Warfare, edited by M. Kathryn Brown and Travis W. Stanton, pp. 149–170. Walnut Creek, Calif.: AltaMira Press.

2003b Seeing through Sahagún: Observations on a Mesoamerican Staff of Office. *Mesoamerican Voices* 1:23–40.

HENDON, JULIA A.

1991 Status and Power in Classic Maya Society: An Archaeological Study. In *American Anthropologist* 93(4):894–918.

HERRERA, ANTONIO DE

1944 *Historia general de los hechos de los Castellanos en las islas, y tierra-firme de el Mar Oceano.* Tomo I. Asunción del Paraguay: Editorial Especiales.

HEYDEN, DORIS

1973 La supervivencia del uso magico de las figurillas y miniaturas arqueológicas. In *Historia, religión, escuelas,* XIII Mesa Redonda, pp. 341–349. Mexico, D.F.: Sociedad Mexicana de Antropología.

1975 An Interpretation of the Cave Underneath the Pyramid of the Sun in Teotihuacan, Mexico. *American Antiquity* 40(2):131–147.

1976 Interpretación de algunas figurillas de Teotihuacan y su posible significado social. In *Las fronteras de Mesoamérica,* XIV Mesa Redonda, vol. 2, pp. 1–10. Mexico, D.F.: Sociedad Mexicana de Antropología.

1977a Economía y religión de Teotihuacan. *Cuadernos de Trabajo* no. 19. Mexico, D.F.: Departamento de Etnología y Antropología Social, INAH.

1977b El culto a los ancestros: Su posible presencia en Teotihuacan. In *Los procesos de cambio en Mesoamérica y áreas circunvecinas,* XV Mesa Redonda, vol. 2, pp. 247–257. Mexico, D.F.: Sociedad Mexicana de Antropología and Universidad de Guanajuato.

1978 Pintura mural y mitología en Teotihuacan. *Anales del instituto de investigaciones estéticas* 12(48):19–33.

1981 Caves, Gods, and Myths: World-View and Planning in Teotihuacan. In *Mesoamerican Sites and World-Views,* edited by Elizabeth P. Benson, pp. 1–39. Washington, D.C.: Dumbarton Oaks Research Library and Collection.

1988 La culebra del agua un mito de Tlacolulita, Oaxaca. *Revista Mexicana de Estudios Antropológicos* 34(1):7–11.

1989 *The Eagle, the Cactus, the Rock: The Roots of Mexico—Tenochtitlan's Foundation Myth and Symbol.* Oxford: BAR.

2000 From Teotihuacan to Tenochtitlan: City Planning, Caves, and Streams of Red and Blue Waters. In *Mesoamerica's Classic Heritage: From Teotihuacan to the Aztecs,* edited by Davíd Carrasco, Lindsay Jones, and Scott Sessions, pp. 165–184. Boulder: University Press of Colorado.

HIRTH, KENNETH G., AND WILLIAM SWEZEY

1976 The Changing Nature of the Teotihuacan Classic: A Regional Perspective from Manzanilla, Puebla. In *Las Fronteras de Mesoamérica,* XIV Mesa Re-

donda, vol. 2, pp. 1–10. Mexico, D.F.: Sociedad Mexicana de Antropología.

HOLLAND, WILLIAM R.

1964 Contemporary Tzotzil Cosmological Concepts as a Basis for Interpreting Prehistoric Maya Civilization. In *American Antiquity* 29(3):301–306.

HOLMES, WILLIAM H.

1885 The Monoliths of San Juan Teotihuacan, Mexico. *Journal of Archaeology and of the History of the Fine Arts* I:361–371.

1897 *Archaeological Studies among the Ancient Cities of Mexico.* Field Columbian Museum Publication 16, Anthropological Series, vol. 1, no. 1, pt. II. Chicago: Field Columbian Museum.

HOPKINS, MARY R.

1987 An Explication of the Plans of Some Teotihuacan Apartment Compounds. In *Teotihuacan: Nuevos datos, nuevas síntesis, nuevos problemas,* edited by Emily McClung de Tapia and Evelyn Childs Rattray, pp. 369–388. Mexico, D.F.: UNAM.

HOUSTON, STEPHEN D.

n.d. Deciphering Maya Politics: Archaeological and Epigraphic Perspectives on the Segmentary State Concept. To be included in *Segmentary States and the Maya,* edited by Peter Dunham.

1996 Symbolic Sweatbaths of the Maya: Architectural Meaning in the Cross Group at Palenque, Mexico. *Latin American Antiquity* 7:132–151.

HOUSTON, STEPHEN D., AND DAVID STUART

1989 The *Way* Glyph: Evidence for "Co-essences" Among the Classic Maya. *Research Reports on Ancient Maya Writing* 30. Washington, D.C.: Center for Maya Research.

HRDLICKA, ALES

1912 An Ancient Sepulchre at San Juan Teotihuacan, with Anthropological Notes on the Teotihuacan People. *Reseña de la segunda sesión del XVII Congreso Internacional de americanistas efectuada en la ciudad de México durante el mes septiembre de 1910,* Appendix, pp. 3–7. Mexico: Imprenta del Museo Nacional de Arqueología, Historia, y Etnología.

JARQUÍN PACHECO, ANA MARÍA, AND MARTÍNEZ VARGAS

1982a Exploración en el lado este de la Ciudadela-Estructuras: 1G, 1R, 1Q, y 1P. In *Memoria de Proyecto Arqueológico Teotihuacán 80–82,* edited by Rubén Cabrera Castro, Ignacio Rodriguez G., and Noel Morelos G., pp. 19–48. Mexico, D.F.: INAH.

1982b Las excavaciones en el conjunto 1D. In *Memoria de Proyecto Arqueológico Teotihuacán 80–82,* edited by Rubén Cabrera Castro, Ignacio Rodríguez G., and Noel Morelos G., pp. 89–126. Mexico, D.F.: INAH.

JILOTE, KIM C.

1991 The Clay Figurines of Teotihuacan, Mexico: A Guide to Identification. MS provided to author.

JOHNSON, JAMES

1997 *The Holy War Idea in Western and Islamic Traditions.* University Park: Pennsylvania State University Press.

JONGHE, M. EDOUARD DE (EDITOR)

1905   Histoyre du Méchique. In *Journal de la Société des Américainistes de Paris* 2:1–41.

JORALEMON, PETER DAVID

1971   A Study of Olmec Iconography. In *Studies in Pre-Columbian Art and Archaeology*, no. 7, edited by Elizabeth P. Benson. Washington, D.C.: Dumbarton Oaks Research Library and Collection.

JOYCE, ROSEMARY

1992   Images of Gender and Labor Organization in Classic Maya Society. In *Exploring Gender Through Archaeology: Selected Papers from the 1991 Boone Conference*, edited by Cheryl Claassen, pp. 63–70. Monographs in World Archaeology, no. 11. Madison: Prehistory Press.

KAMPEN, MICHAEL EDWIN

1972   *The Sculptures of El Tajin, Veracruz, Mexico.* Gainesville: University of Florida Press.

KARTTUNEN, FRANCES

1983   *An Analytical Dictionary of Nahuatl.* Austin: University of Texas Press.

KELLEY, DAVID H.

1983   The Maya Calendar Correlation Problem. In *Civilizations in the Ancient Americas: Essays in Honor of Gordon R. Willey*, edited by Richard M. Leventhal and Alan L. Kolata, pp. 157–208. Albuquerque: University of New Mexico Press.

KERR, JUSTIN

1990   *The Maya Vase Book*, vol. 2. New York: Kerr Associates.

1992   *The Maya Vase Book*, vol. 3. New York: Kerr Associates.

KIDDER, ALFRED, JESSE D. JENNINGS, AND EDWIN M. SHOOK

1946   *Excavations at Kaminaljuyu, Guatemala.* Carnegie Institution of Washington, no. 561, Washington, D.C.

KIRCHOFF, PAUL

1946   La cultura del occidente de Mexico. In *Arte precolombino del occidente de Mexico*, pp. 49–69. Mexico, D.F.: Secretaria de Educación Público.

KLEIN, CECELIA F.

1982   Woven Heaven, Tangled Earth: A Weaver's Paradigm of the Mesoamerican Cosmos. In *Ethnoastronomy and Archaeoastronmy in the American Tropics*, edited by Anthony Aveni and Gary Urton, pp. 1–36. New York: New York Academy of Sciences.

1987   The Ideology of Autosacrifice at the Templo Mayor. In *The Aztec Templo Mayor*, edited by Elizabeth Hill Boone, pp. 293–370. Washington, D.C.: Dumbarton Oaks Research Library and Collection.

1988   Rethinking Cihuacoatl: Aztec Political Imagery of the Conquered Woman. In *Smoke and Mist: Mesoamerican Studies in Memory of Thelma D. Sullivan*, edited by J. Kathryn Josserand and Karen Dakin, Part I, pp. 237–277. Oxford: BAR.

1990–1991   Snares and Entrails: Mesoamerican Symbols of Sin and Punishment. *RES* 19/20:81–104.

KLEIN, CECELIA F., EULOGIO GUZMÁN, ELISA C. MANDELL, AND MAYA STANFIELD-MAZZI

2002   The Role of Shamanism in Mesoamerican Art: A Reassessment. *Current Anthropology* 43(3):383–419.

KNAB, T. J., AND THELMA D. SULLIVAN

1994   *A Scattering of Jades: Stories, Poems, and Prayers of the Aztecs.* New York: Simon and Schuster.

KOWALEWSKI, STEPHEN A.

1990   Merits of Full-Coverage Survey: Examples from the Valley of Oaxaca, Mexico. In *The Archaeology of Regions: A Case for Full Coverage Survey*, edited by Suzanne K. Fish and Stephen A Kowalewski, pp. 33–86. Washington, D.C.: Smithsonian Institution Press.

KOWALSKI, JEFF KARL

1987   *The House of the Governor: A Maya Palace at Uxmal, Yucatan, Mexico.* Norman and London: University of Oklahoma Press.

KROTSER, PAULA, AND EVELYN RATTRAY

1980   Manufactura y distribución de tres grupos cerámicos de Teotihuacan. *Anales de Antropología* 17(1):91–104.

KUBLER, GEORGE

1948   *Mexican Architecture of the Sixteenth Century.* New Haven: Yale University Press.

1961   On the Colonial Extinction of the Motifs of Pre-Columbian Art. In *Essays in Pre-Columbian Art and Archaeology*, edited by Samuel K. Lothrop, pp. 14–34. Cambridge: Harvard University Press.

1962   *The Art and Architecture of Ancient America: The Mexican, Maya, and Andean Peoples.* Baltimore: Penguin Books.

1967   *The Iconography of the Art of Teotihuacan.* Washington, D.C.: Dumbarton Oaks Research Library and Collection.

1970   Period, Style and Meaning in Ancient American Art. *New Literary History* 1(2):127–144.

1972   La iconografía del arte Teotihuacan: Ensayo de análisis configurativo. In *Teotihuacan: XI Mesa Redonda*, pp. 69–85. Mexico, D.F.: Sociedad Mexicana de Antropología.

1973   Science and Humanism Among Americanists. In *The Iconography of Middle American Sculpture*, pp. 163–167. New York: Metropolitan Museum of Art.

1975   *The Art and Architecture of Ancient America.* Middlesex: Penguin Books.

LAGAMMA, ALISA

1991   A Visual Sonata at Teotihuacan. *Ancient Mesoamerica* 2:275–284.

LANDA, DIEGO DE

1966   *Landa's Relación de las Cosas de Yucatan, a Translation.* Translated and edited by Alfred Tozzer. Papers of the Peabody Museum of American Archaeology and Ethnology 18. New York: Kraus Reprint Corporation.

LANGLEY, JAMES C.

1986   *Symbolic Notation of Teotihuacan.* Oxford: BAR.

1992   Teotihuacan Sign Clusters: Emblem or Articulation? In *Art, Ideology, and the City of Teotihuacan,* edited by Janet Catherine Berlo, pp. 247–280. Washington, D.C.: Dumbarton Oaks Research Library and Collection.

1993　Symbols, Signs, and Writing Systems. In *Teotihuacan: Art from the City of the Gods,* edited by Kathleen Berrin and Esther Pasztory, pp. 129–139. San Francisco: Thames and Hudson and the Fine Arts Museums of San Francisco.

LAPORTE, JUAN PEDRO

2003　Architectural Aspects of Interaction between Tikal and Teotihuacan during the Early Classic Period. In *The Maya and Teotihuacan: Reinterpreting Early Classic Interaction,* edited by Geoffrey Braswell, pp. 199–216. Austin: University of Texas Press.

LAPORTE, JUAN PEDRO, AND VILMA FIALKO

1995　Un reencuentro con Mundo Perdido, Tikal. *Ancient Mesoamerica* 6:41–94.

LAUNEY, MICHEL

1992　*Introducción a la lengua y a la literatura Náhuatl.* Mexico, D.F.: Instituto de Investigaciones Antropológicas.

LE GLAY, MARCEL, JEAN-LOUIS VOISIN, AND YANN LE BOHEC

2001　*A History of Rome.* 2nd ed. Oxford and Malden: Blackwell Publishers.

LÉVI-STRAUSS, CLAUDE

1962　*Totemism.* Translated by Rodney Needham. Boston: Beacon Press.

1982　*The Way of the Masks.* Translated by Sylvia Modelski. Seattle: University of Washington Press.

1987　*Anthropology and Myth: Lectures, 1951–1982.* Translated by Roy Willis. Oxford: Basil Blackwell.

LEWIS-WILLIAMS, J. DAVID

1984　Ideological Continuities in Prehistoric Southern Africa: The Evidence of Rock Art. In *Past and Present in Hunter Gatherer Studies,* edited by Carmel Schrire, pp. 225–252. Orlando: Academic Press.

LEWIS-WILLIAMS, J. D., AND T. A. DOWSON

1988　The Signs of All Times: Entoptic Phenomena in Upper Paleolithic Art. *Current Anthropology* 29(2):201–245.

1993　On Vision and Power in the Neolithic: Evidence from the Decorated Monuments. In *Current Anthropology* 34(1):55–65.

LEWIS-WILLIAMS, DAVID, THOMAS A. DOWSON, AND JANETTE DEACON

1973　Rock Art and Changing Perceptions of Southern Africa's Past: Ezeljagdspoort Reviewed. In *Antiquity* 67:273–291.

LINNÉ, S.

1934　*Archaeological Researches at Teotihuacan, Mexico.* Stockholm: Ethnographical Museum of Sweden.

1942　*Mexican Highland Cultures: Archaeological Researches at Teotihuacan, Calpulalpan and Chalchicomula in 1934/35.* New series, pub. no. 7. Stockholm: Ethnographical Museum of Sweden.

LÓPEZ LUJÁN, LEONARDO

1989　*La recuperación mexica del pasado teotihuacano.* Mexico, D.F.: INAH.

1993　*Las ofrendas del Templo Mayor de Tenochtitlan.* Mexico, D.F.: INAH.

1994　*The Offerings of the Templo Mayor of Tenochtitlan.* Translated by Bernard R. Ortiz de Montellano and Thelma Ortiz de Montellano. Niwot: University Press of Colorado.

LÓPEZ LUJÁN, LEONARDO, HECTOR NEFF, AND SABURO SUGIYAMA

2000　The *9-Xi* Vase: A Classic Thin Orange Vessel Found at Tenochtitlan. In *Mesoamerica's Classic Heritage: From Teotihuacan to the Aztecs,* edited by Davíd Carrasco, Lindsay Jones, and Scott Sessions, pp. 219–249. Boulder: University of Colorado Press.

LÓPEZ MESTAS CAMBEROS, LORENZA, AND JORGE RAMOS DE LA VEGA

1998　Excavating the Tomb at Huitzilapa. In *Ancient West Mexico: Art and Archaeology of the Unknown Past,* edited by Richard Townsend, pp. 52–69. London and Chicago: Thames and Hudson and the Art Institute of Chicago.

L'ORANGE, H. P.

1965　*Art Forms and Civic Life in the Late Roman Empire.* Princeton, N.J.: Princeton University Press.

LUMHOLTZ, CARL

1902　*Unknown Mexico.* New York: Scribner's Sons.

MACÍAS GOYTIA, ANGELINA, AND KATINA VACKIMES SERRET

1989　Las turquesas de un lago. In *Homenaje a Román Piña Chán,* edited by Roberto García Moll and Angel García Cook, pp. 41–71. Mexico, D.F.: UNAM.

1990　Proyecto cuenca de Cuitzeo. In *Boletín: Consejo de Arqueología:* 71–81. Mexico, D.F.: INAH.

MALMSTRÖM, VINCENT H.

1978　A Reconstruction of the Chronology of Mesoamerican Calendrical Systems. *Journal for the History of Astronomy* 9:105–116.

MANZANILLA, LINDA

1986　Introducción. In *Unidades habitacionales mesoamericanas y sus áreas de actividad,* edited by Linda Manzanilla, pp. 9–18. Mexico, D.F.: UNAM.

1990　Sector noroeste de Teotihuacan: Estudio de un conjunto residencial y rastreo de tuneles y cuevas. In *La Epoca Clásica: Nuevos hallazgos, nuevas ideas,* edited by Amalia Cardos de Mendez, pp. 81–88. Mexico, D.F.: Museo Nacional de Antropología, INAH. .

1991　Arquitectura doméstica y actividades en Teotihuacán. *Cuadernos de Arquitectura Mesoamericana* 13:7–10.

1993a　*Anatomía de un conjunto residencial Teotihuacano en Oztoyahualco.* Mexico, D.F.: UNAM and INAH.

1993b　Daily Life in the Teotihuacan Apartment Compounds. In *Teotihuacan: Art from the City of the Gods,* edited by Kathleen Berrin and Esther Pasztory, pp. 91–99. San Francisco: Thames and Hudson and the Fine Arts Museums of San Francisco.

2000 The Construction of the Underworld in Central Mexico: Transformations from the Classic to the Postclassic. In *Mesoamerica's Classic Heritage: From Teotihuacan to the Aztecs,* edited by Davíd Carrasco, Lindsay Jones, and Scott Sessions, pp. 87–116. Boulder: University Press of Colorado.

MANZANILLA, LINDA, LUIS BARBA, RENÉ CHÁVEZ, JORGE ARZATE, AND LETICIA FLORES

1989 El inframundo de Teotihuacan: Geofísica y arqueología. *Ciencia y Desarrollo* 15(85):21–35.

MANZANILLA, LINDA, AND EMILIE CARREÓN

1989 Un incensario teotihuacano en contexto doméstico: Restauración e interpretación. *Antropológicas* 4:5–18.

MANZANILLA, LINDA, AND AUGUSTÍN ORTÍZ

1991 Los altares domésticos en Teotihuacan: Hallazgo de dos fragmentos de maqueta. *Cuadernos de Arquitectura Mesoamericana* 13:11–13.

MARCUS, JOYCE

1983a Stone Monuments and Tomb Murals of Monte Albán IIIa. In *The Cloud People: Divergent Evolution of the Zapotec and Mixtec Civilizations,* edited by Kent V. Flannery and Joyce Marcus, pp. 137–143. New York: Academic Press.

1983b Teotihuacán Visitors on Monte Albán Monuments and Murals. In *The Cloud People: Divergent Evolution of the Zapotec and Mixtec Civilizations,* edited by Kent V. Flannery and Joyce Marcus, pp. 175–181. New York: Academic Press.

MARCUS, JOYCE, AND KENT FLANNERY

1996 *Zapotec Civilization: How Urban Society Evolved in Mexico's Oaxaca Valley.* London: Thames and Hudson.

MARGÁIN, CARLOS R.

1951 Funcionalismo arquitectónico del Mexico prehispánico: Un ejemplo: Atetelco—Teotihuacan. Thesis, Escuela Nacional de Antropología e Historia, Mexico.

1966 Sobre sistemas y materiales de construcción en Teotihuacan. In *Teotihuacan: Onceava Mesa Redonda,* pp. 157–212. Mexico, D.F.: Sociedad Mexicana de Antropología.

MARTIN, RICHARD

1991 The Religious Foundations of War, Peace, and Statecraft in Islam. In *Just War and Jihad: Historical and Theoretical Perspectives on War and Peace in Western and Islamic Traditions,* edited by J. Kelsay and J. T. Johnson, pp. 91–117. Westport, Conn.: Greenwood Press.

MARTIN, SIMON, AND NIKOLAI GRUBE

2000 *Chronicle of the Maya Kings and Queens.* London: Thames and Hudson.

MARTÍNEZ VARGAS, ENRIQUE

1991 La Herradura: Análisis preliminar de la unidad arquitectónica de la zona metropolitana de Teotihuacán. *Boletín: Consejo de Arqueología* 3:190–195.

MATOS MOCTEZUMA, EDUARDO

1980 Teotihuacan: Excavaciones en la Calle de los Muertos. *Anales de Antropología* 17:69–90.

1984a *Guía Oficial: Templo Mayor.* 2nd revised edition. Mexico, D.F.: INAH/Salvat.

1984b Los edificios aledaños al Templo Mayor. *Estudios de Cultura Nahuatl* 17:15–21.

1987 The Templo Mayor of Tenochtitlan: History and Interpretation. In *The Great Temple of Tenochtitlan: Center and Periphery in the Aztec World,* pp. 15–60. Berkeley, Los Angeles, and London: University of California Press.

1988 *The Great Temple of the Aztecs.* London: Thames and Hudson.

1993 La estrategia del Proyecto Teotihuacán. In *Arqueología Mexicana* 1(2):73–75.

1995 Excavaciones recientes en la Pirámide del Sol, 1993-1994. In *La Pirámide del Sol Teotihuacan,* edited by Eduardo Matos, pp. 312–329. Mexico, D.F.: INAH and Instituto Cultural Domecq.

2000 From Teotihuacan to Tenochtitlan: Their Great Temples. In *Mesoamerica's Classic Heritage: From Teotihuacan to the Aztecs,* edited by Davíd Carrasco, Lindsay Jones, and Scott Sessions, pp. 185–194. Boulder: University Press of Colorado.

MATOS MOCTEZUMA, EDUARDO, AND LEONARDO LÓPEZ LUJÁN

1993 Teotihuacan and Its Mexica Legacy. In *Teotihuacan: Art from the City of the Gods,* edited by Kathleen Berrin and Esther Pasztory, pp. 156–165. San Francisco: Thames and Hudson and the Fine Arts Museums of San Francisco.

MAYER, BRANTZ

1844 *Mexico as It Was and as It Is.* London and Paris: Wiley and Putnam.

1852 *Mexico, Aztec, Spanish, and Republican: A Historical, Geographical, Political, Statistical, and Social Account of that Country from the Period of the Invasion by the Spaniards to the Present Time.* Hartford: S. Drake and Company.

MAYHALL, MARGUERITE

1991 The Butterfly Complex at Teotihuacan: Blood, War, and Transformation. Art history graduate seminar paper, University of Texas at Austin.

MCANANY, PATRICIA A.

1995 *Living with the Ancestors: Kinship and Kingship.* Austin: University of Texas Press.

MCBRIDE, HAROLD W.

1969 Teotihuacan Style Pottery and Figurines from Colima. *Katunob* 7(3):86–91.

MCCAFFERTY, GEOFFREY G.

2000 Tollan Chollollan and the Legacy of Legitimacy During the Classic-Postclassic Transition. In *Mesoamerica's Classic Heritage: From Teotihuacan to the Aztecs,* edited by Davíd Carrasco, Lindsay Jones, and Scott Sessions, pp. 341–367. Boulder: University Press of Colorado.

MCCAFFERTY, SHARISSE D., AND GEOFFREY G. MCCAFFERTY

1994a Conquered Women of Cacaxtla: Gender Identity or Gender Ideology? *Ancient Mesoamerica* 5(2):159–172.

1994b Engendering Tomb 7 at Monte Alban. *Current Anthropology* 35(2):143–166.

MCGUIRE, RANDALL H.

1986 Economies and Modes of Production in the Prehistoric Southwestern Periphery. In *Ripples in the Chichimec Sea,* edited by F. J. Mathien and R. H. McGuire, pp. 243–269. Carbondale: Southern Illinois University Press.

MENDIETA, FRAY GERONIMO DE

1945 *Historia eclesiástica indiana.* 4 vols. Mexico, D.F.: Editorial Salvador Chávez Hayhoe.

MILLER, ARTHUR G.

1967 The Birds of Quetzalpapalotl. *Ethnos* 32:5–17.

1972a A Lost Teotihuacan Mural. *B.B.A.A.* 35:61–83.

1972b Los pájaros de Quetzalpapalotl. In *Teotihuacan: XI Mesa Redonda,* pp. 87–101. Mexico, D.F.: Sociedad Mexicana de Antropología.

1973 *The Mural Painting of Teotihuacán.* Washington, D.C.: Dumbarton Oaks Research Library and Collection.

1974 The Iconography of the Painting in the Temple of the Diving God, Tulum, Quintana Roo, Mexico: The Twisted Cords. In *Mesoamerican Archaeology: New Approaches,* edited by Norman Hammond, pp. 167–186. Austin: University of Texas Press.

1991 The Carved Stela in Tomb 5, Suchilquitongo, Oaxaca, Mexico. *Ancient Mesoamerica* 2:215–224.

MILLON, CLARA

1972a A Commentary about a Lost Teotihuacan Mural. *B.B.A.A.* 35:85–89.

1972b The History of Mural Art at Teotihuacan. In *Teotihuacan: XI Mesa Redonda,* pp. 1–16. Mexico, D.F.: Sociedad Mexicana de Antropología.

1973 Painting, Writing, and Polity in Teotihuacan, Mexico. *American Antiquity* 38(3):294–314.

1988a Coyote with Sacrificial Knife. In *Feathered Serpents and Flowering Trees: Reconstructing the Murals of Teotihuacan,* edited by Kathleen Berrin, pp. 207–223. San Francisco: The Fine Arts Museums of San Francisco.

1988b Maguey Bloodletting Ritual. In *Feathered Serpents and Flowering Trees: Reconstructing the Murals of Teotihuacan,* edited by Kathleen Berrin, pp. 195–205. San Francisco: The Fine Arts Museums of San Francisco.

1988c A Reexamination of the Teotihuacan Tassel Headdress Insignia. In *Feathered Serpents and Flowering Trees: Reconstructing the Murals of Teotihuacan,* edited by Kathleen Berrin, pp. 14–134. San Franciso: The Fine Arts Museums of San Francisco.

MILLON, RENÉ

1960 The Beginnings of Teotihuacan. *American Antiquity* 26(1):1–10.

1966a Cronología y periodificación: Datos estratigráficos sobre períodos cerámicos y sus relaciones con la pintura mural. In *Teotihuacan: Onceava Mesa Redonda,* pp. 1–18. Mexico, D.F.: Sociedad Mexicana de Antropología.

1966b Extensión y población de la ciudad de Teotihuacan en sus differentes períodos: Un cálculo provisional. XI Mesa Redonda, manuscript at Instituto de Investigaciones Antropológicas, UNAM.

1966c El problema de integración en la sociedad teotihuacana. XI Mesa Redonda, manuscript at Instituto de Investigaciones Antropologías, UNAM.

1970 Teotihuacán: Completion of Map of Giant Ancient City in the Valley of Mexico. *Science* 170(3962):1077–1082.

1972 El Valle de Teotihuacan y su contorno. In *Teotihuacan: XI Mesa Redonda,* pp. 329–337. Mexico, D.F.: Sociedad Mexicana de Antropología.

1973 *Urbanization at Teotihuacan, Mexico: The Teotihuacan Map,* vol. 1, pt. 1. Austin: University of Texas Press.

1974 The Study of Urbanism at Teotihuacan, Mexico. In *Mesoamerican Archaeology: New Approaches,* edited by Norman Hammond, pp. 335–362. Austin: University of Texas Press.

1976 Social Relations in Ancient Teotihuacán. In *The Valley of Mexico: Studies in Pre-Hispanic Ecology and Society,* edited by Eric R. Wolf, pp. 205–248. Albuquerque: University of New Mexico Press.

1981 Teotihuacan: City, State, and Civilization. In *Handbook of Middle American Indians,* Supplement, vol. 1, edited by Victoria R. Bricker, pp. 198–243. Austin: University of Texas Press.

1988a The Last Years of Teotihuacan Dominance. In *The Collapse of Ancient States and Civilizations,* edited by Norman Yoffee and George Cowgill, pp. 102–164. Tucson: University of Arizona Press.

1988b Where Do They All Come From? The Provenance of the Wagner Murals from Teotihuacan. In *Feathered Serpents and Flowering Trees: Reconstructing the Murals of Teotihuacan,* edited by Kathleen Berrin, pp. 78–113. San Francisco: The Fine Arts Museums of San Francisco.

1991a Concentración de pinturas murales en el Conjunto Arquitectónico Grande, al este de la Plaza de la Luna. In *Teotihuacan 1980–1982: Nuevas interpretaciones,* edited by Rubén Cabrera Castro, Ignacio Rodríguez García, and Noel Morelos García, pp. 211–231. Mexico, D.F.: INAH.

1991b Descubrimiento de la procedencia de las pinturas murales saqueadas con representaciones de personajes que llevan el Tocado de Borlas. In *Teotihuacan 1980–1982: Nuevas interpretaciones,* edited by Rubén Cabrera Castro, Ignacio Rodríguez García, and Noel Morelos García, pp. 185–192. Mexico, D.F.: INAH.

1992 Teotihuacan Studies: From 1950 to 1990 and Beyond. In *Art, Ideology, and the City of Teotihuacan,* edited by Janet Catherine Berlo, pp. 339–419.

Washington, D.C.: Dumbarton Oaks Research Library and Collection.

1993   The Place Where Time Began: An Archaeologist's Interpretation of What Happened in Teotihuacan History. In *Teotihuacan: Art from the City of the Gods,* edited by Kathleen Berrin and Esther Pasztory, pp. 17–43. San Francisco: Thames and Hudson and the Fine Arts Museums of San Francisco.

MILLON, RENÉ, AND BRUCE DREWITT

1995   Estructuras tempranas en la Pirámide de Sol en Teotihuacan. In *La Pirámide del Sol Teotihuacan,* edited by Eduardo Matos, pp. 268–285. Mexico, D.F.: Instituto Cultural Domecq and INAH.

MILLON, RENÉ, BRUCE DREWITT, AND JAMES A. BENNYHOFF

1965   *The Pyramid of the Sun at Teotihuacan: 1959 Excavations.* Transactions of the American Philosophical Society (Philadelphia), vol. 55, pt. 6.

MINNAERT, P.

1940   Une oeuvre capitale de l'arte de Teotihuacan. *Bulletin de la Société des Américanistes de Belgique* 31:42–45.

MOLINA MONTES, AUGUSTO F.

1987   Templo Mayor Architecture: So What's New? In *The Aztec Templo Mayor,* edited by Elizabeth Hill Boone, pp. 97–108. Washington, D.C.: Dumbarton Oaks Research Library and Collection.

MONZÓN FLORES, MARTHA

1987   Dos casas habitación prehispánicas en Teotihuacán: Ome Calle Ipan Teotihuacan. Thesis, Escuela Nacional de Antropología e Historia. Mexico: INAH and SEP.

MOORE, FRANK W.

1966   An Excavation at Tetitla, Teotihuacan. *Mesoamerican Notes* 7–8:69–85.

MORELOS GARCÍA, NOEL

1982   Exploraciones en el area central de la Calzada de los Muertos al norte del Río San Juan, dentro del llamado Complejo Calle de los Muertos. In *Memoria de Proyecto Arqueológico Teotihuacán 80–82,* edited by Ruben Cabrera Castro, Ignacio Rodríguez G., and Noel Morelos G., pp. 271–317. Mexico, D.F.: INAH.

1986   El concepto de unidad habitacional en el Altiplano. In *Unidades habitacionales mesoamericanas y sus áreas de actividad,* edited by Linda Manzanilla, pp. 193–220. Mexico: UNAM.

1990   Proceso de formación de una urbe mesoamericana: El caso del Complejo Calle de los Muertos en Teotihuacan. In *La Epoca Clásica: Nuevos hallazgos, nuevas ideas,* edited by Amalia Cardos de Mendez, pp. 115–121. Mexico, D.F.: Museo Nacional de Antropología, INAH.

1991a   Adoratorios de la Calle de los Muertos: El sistema constructivo del volumen. In *Teotihuacan 1980–1982: Nuevas interpretaciones,* edited by Rubén Cabrera Castro, Ignacio Rodríguez García, and

Noel Morelos García, pp. 93–111. Mexico, D.F.: INAH.

1991b   Esculturas y arquitectura en un conjunto teotihuacano. In *Teotihuacan 1980–1982: Nuevas interpretaciones,* edited by Rubén Cabrera Castro, Ignacio Rodríguez García, and Noel Morelos García, pp. 193–201. Mexico, D.F.: INAH.

1993   Proceso de producción de espacios y estructuras en Teotihuacán: Conjunto Plaza Oeste y Complejo Calle de los Muertos. Mexico: INAH.

MOSER, CHRISTOPHER

1975   Cueva de Ejutla: Una cueva funeraria Postclásica? *Boletín del Instituto Nacional de Antropología e Historia* 14:25–36.

1983   A Postclassic Burial Cave in the Southern Cañada. In *The Cloud People: Divergent Evolution of the Zapotec and Mixtec Civilizations,* edited by Kent Flannery and Joyce Marcus, pp. 270–272. New York: Academic Press.

MULLETT, G. M.

1979   *Spider Woman Stories: Legends of the Hopi Indians.* Tucson: University of Arizona Press.

MÚNERA BERMUDEZ, LUIS CARLOS

1985   Un taller de cerámica ritual en la Ciudadela: Teotihuacan. Thesis, Escuela Nacional de Antropología e Historia, Mexico.

1991   Una representación de bulto mortuorio. In *Teotihuacan 1980–1982: Nuevas interpretaciones,* edited by Rubén Cabrera Castro, Ignacio Rodríguez García, and Noel Morelos García, pp. 335–341. Mexico, D.F.: INAH.

MÚNERA BERMUDEZ, LUIS CARLOS, AND SABURO SUGIYAMA

n.d.   Cerámica ritual de un taller en la Ciudadela, Teotihuacan: Catalogo. Manuscript provided to author.

NEQUATEWA, EDMUND

1967   *Truth of a Hopi: Stories Relating to the Origin, Myths, and Clan Histories of the Hopi.* Flagstaff: Northland Press.

NEUMANN, FRANKE J.

1988   The Otomí Otontecuhtli and the Mummy Bundle. In *Smoke and Mist: Mesoamerican Studies in Memory of Thelma D. Sullivan,* edited by Kathryn Josserand and Karen Dakin, pp. 173–189. Oxford: BAR.

NEYS, H., AND HASSO VON WINNING

1946   The Treble Scroll Symbol in the Teotihuacan and Zapotec Cultures. *Notes on Middle American Archaeology and Ethnology* 3:82–89.

NICHOLSON, HENRY B.

1983   *Art of Ancient Mexico.* Washington, D.C.: National Gallery of Art.

NOGUERA, EDUARDO

1925   Las representaciones del buho en la cultura teotihuacana. *Anales del Museo Nacional de Arqueología, Historia y Etnografía* 3:444–453.

1935   Antecedentes y relaciones de la cultura teotihuacana. *El Mexico Antiguo* 3(5/8):3–9.

1961   Exploraciones en Yayahuala, Teotihuacán. *Boletín del INAH* 5:5.

1962   Nueva clasificación de figurillas del horizonte clásico. *Cuadernos Americanos* 124:127–136.

NUTINI, HUGO G.

1988   *Todos Santos in Rural Tlaxcala: A Syncretic, Expressive, and Symbolic Analysis of the Cult of the Dead.* Princeton, N.J.: Princeton University Press.

NUTTALL, ZELIA

1903   *The Book of the Life of the Ancient Mexicans.* Berkeley: University of California.

1926   *Official Reports on the Towns of Tequizistlan, Tepechpan, Acolman, and San Juan Teotihuacan Sent by Francisco de Castaneda to His Majesty, Philip II, and the Council of the Indies in 1580.* Papers of the Peabody Museum of Archaeology and Ethnology, vol. 11–12. Cambridge: Harvard University.

1975   *The Codex Nuttall.* New York: Dover Publications.

OAKLAND, AMY

1982   Teotihuacan: The Blood Complex at Atetelco. Art history graduate seminar paper, University of Texas at Austin.

OLIVER VEGA, BEATRIZ M.

1975   Día de Muertos en un poblado otomí. *Ceremonias de días de Muertos,* pp. 12–23. Mexico, D.F.: INAH.

OROPEZA, MANUEL

1968   *Teotihuacan escultura.* Colección Breve 3. Mexico, D.F.: INAH and SEP.

PADDOCK, JOHN

1972   Distribución de rasgos teotihuacanos en Mesoamerica. In *Teotihuacan: XI Mesa Redonda,* pp. 223–239. Mexico, D.F.: Sociedad Mexicana de Antropología.

PANOFSKY, ERWIN

1960   *Renaissance and Renascences in Western Art.* New York: Harper and Row.

PARSONS, MARK L.

1985   Three Thematic Complexes in the Art of Teotihuacan. Art history graduate seminar paper, University of Texas at Austin.

1988   The Iconography of Blood Sacrifice in the Murals of the White Patio, Atetelco, Teotihuacan. M.A. thesis, University of Texas at Austin.

PASZTORY, ESTHER

1972   The Gods of Teotihuacan: A Synthetic Approach in Teotihuacan Iconography. In *Atti del XL Congreso Internazionale degli Americanisti* (Rome), vol. 1, pp. 147–159.

1974   *The Iconography of the Teotihuacan Tlaloc.* Washington, D.C.: Dumbarton Oaks Research Library and Collection.

1976   *The Murals of Tepantitla, Teotihuacan.* New York and London: Garland Publishing.

1988   A Reinterpretation of Teotihuacan and Its Mural Painting Tradition. In *Feathered Serpents and Flowering Trees: Reconstructing the Murals of Teotihuacan,* edited by Kathleen Berrin, pp. 45–77. San Francisco: The Fine Arts Museums of San Francisco.

1990   El poder militar como realidad y retórica en

Teotihuacan. In *La Epoca Clásica: Nuevos hallazgos, nuevas ideas,* edited by Amalia Cardos de Mendez, pp. 181–204. Mexico, D.F.: Museo Nacional de Antropología, INAH.

1990–1991   Still Invisible: The Problem of the Aesthetics of Abstraction for Pre-Columbian Art and its Implications for Other Cultures. *RES* 19/20:105–136.

1991   Strategies of Organization in Teotihuacan Art. *Ancient Mesoamerica* 2:247–248.

1992a   Abstraction and the rise of a Utopian State at Teotihuacan. In *Art, Ideology, and the City of Teotihuacan,* edited by Janet Catherine Berlo, pp. 281–320. Washington, D.C.: Dumbarton Oaks Research Library and Collection.

1992b   The Natural World as Civic Metaphor at Teotihuacan. In *The Ancient Americas: Art from Sacred Landscapes,* edited by Richard F. Townsend, pp. 135–145. Chicago: The Art Institute of Chicago.

1993   Teotihuacan Unmasked: A View Through Art. In *Teotihuacan: Art from the City of the Gods,* edited by Kathleen Berrin and Esther Pasztory, pp. 45–63. San Francisco: Thames and Hudson and The Fine Arts Museums of San Francisco.

1997   *Teotihuacan: An Experiment in Living.* Norman: University of Oklahoma Press.

PAULINYI, ZOLTAN

2006   The "Great Goddess" of Teotihuacan: Fiction or Reality? *Ancient Mesoamerica* 17:1–15.

PAXTON, MERIDETH

2001   *The Cosmos of the Yucatec Maya: Cycles and Steps from the Madrid Codex.* Albuquerque: University of New Mexico Press.

PELLICER, CARLOS, RUTH RIVERA, AND DOLORES OLMEDO DE OLVERA

1969   *Artes de México* 64/65.

PEÑAFIEL, ANTONIO

1890   *Monumento del Arte Mexicano Antiguo,* vol. 1. Berlin: A. Ashers and Co.

PENNEY, DAVID W.

1996   *Native American Art Masterpieces.* New York: Hugh Lauter Levin and Associates.

PENNEY, DAVID W., AND GEORGE C. LONGFISH

1994   *Native American Art.* New York: Hugh Lauter Levin and Associates.

PETERS, RUDOLPH

1977   *Jihad in Medieval and Modern Islam.* Leiden, Netherlands: E. J. Brill.

1979   *Islam and Colonialism: The Doctrine of Jihad in Modern History.* Paris: Mouton.

1996   *Jihad in Classical and Modern Islam.* Princeton: Markus Wiener Publishers.

PETERSON, FREDRICK A.

1952   Tlaloc en soportes de vasijas teotihuacanas. *Tlatoani* vol. 1, no. 1, 13.

PICKERING, ROBERT B., AND MARIA TERESA CABRERO

1998   Mortuary Practices in the Shaft-Tomb Region. In *Ancient West Mexico: Art and Archaeology of the Unknown Past,* edited by Richard Townsend, pp.

70–87. London and Chicago: Thames and Hudson and the Art Institute of Chicago.

PIÑA CHAN, ROMAN

1971   Preclassic Formative Pottery and Minor Arts of the Valley of Mexico. In *Handbook of Middle American Indians,* vol. 10, edited by Robert Wauchope, Gordon Ekholm and Ignacio Bernal, pp. 157–178. Austin: University of Texas Press.

PLOG, STEPHEN, AND JULIE SOLOMETO

n.d.   Alternative pathways in the Evolution of Western Pueblo Ritual. Paper Presented at the Chacmool Conference, November 1993, Calgary, Canada.

1997   The Never-Changing and the Ever-Changing: The Evolution of Western Pueblo Ritual. *Cambridge Archaeological Journal* 7(2):161–182.

PLUNKET, PATRICIA, AND GABRIELA URUÑUELA

1998   Preclassic Household Patterns Preserved Under Volcanic Ash at Tetimpa, Puebla, Mexico. *Latin American Antiquity* 9(4):287–309.

POHL, JOHN M. D.

1994   *The Politics of Symbolism in the Mixtec Codices.* Nashville: Vanderbilt University Publications in Anthropology.

POHL, MARY, AND LAWRENCE H. FELDMAN

1982   The Traditional Role of Women and Animals in Lowland Maya Economy. In *Maya Subsistence: Studies in Memory of Denis E. Puleston,* edited by Kent V. Flannery, pp. 295–311. New York: Academic Press.

POZAS A., RICARDO

1969   The Chulel and Their Soul in the Life of the Chamulas. *Artes de México* 124:80–83.

PROSKOURIAKOFF, TATIANA

1963   *An Album of Maya Architecture.* Norman: University of Oklahoma Press.

1993   *Maya History.* Edited by Rosemary Joyce. Austin: University of Texas Press.

PRICE, BARBARA

1986   Teotihuacan as World-System: Concerning the Applicability of Wallerstein's Model. In *Origen y formación del estado en mesoamerica,* edited by Andres Medina, Alfredo Lopez Austin, and Mari Carmen Serra, pp. 169–194. Mexico: UNAM.

PUBLICACIONES DEL ARCHIVO GENERAL DE LA NACIÓN

1912   *Procesos de indios idólatras y hechiceros,* vol. III, 115–124. Mexico.

RATTRAY, EVELYN CHILDS

1972   El Complejo Cultural Coyotlatelco. In *Teotihuacan: XI Mesa Redonda,* pp. 201–209. Mexico, D.F.: Sociedad Mexicana de Antropología.

1987a   Introducción. In *Teotihuacán: Nuevos datos, nuevas síntesis, nuevos problemas,* edited by Emily McClung de Tapia and Evelyn Childs Rattray, pp. 9–55. Mexico, D.F.: Universidad Nacional Autónoma de México.

1987b   Los barrios foráneos de Teotihuacan. In *Teotihuacán: Nuevos datos, nuevas síntesis, nuevos problemas,* edited by Emily McClung de Tapia and Evelyn

Childs Rattray, pp. 243–273. Mexico, D.F.: Universidad Nacional Autónoma de México.

1989   El barrio de los comerciantes y el conjunto Tlamimilolpa: un estudio comparativo. *Arqueología* 5:105–129.

1990   Nuevos hallazgos sobre los origenes de la cerámica anaranjado delgado. In *La Epoca Clásica: Nuevos hallazgos, nuevas ideas,* edited by Amalia Cardos de Mendez, pp. 89–106. Mexico, D.F.: Museo Nacional de Antropología, INAH.

1991   Fechamientos por radiocarbono en Teotihuacan. *Arqueología* 6:3–18.

1992   *The Teotihuacan Burials and Offerings: A Commentary and Inventory.* Nashville: Vanderbilt University Publications in Anthropology.

RATTRAY, EVELYN C., AND MARÍA ELENA RUIZ A.

1980   Interpretaciones culturales de la Ventilla, Teotihuacan. *Anales de Antropología* 17(1):105–114.

RECINOS, ADRIÁN

1957   Títulos de la casa Ixquín-Nehaib, señora del territorio de Otzoya. In *Crónicas indígenas de Guatemala,* edited by Adrián Recinos, pp. 71–94. Guatemala City: Editorial Universitaria.

REDFIELD, ROBERT, AND ALFONSO VILLA ROJAS

1934   *Chan Kom: A Maya Village.* Chicago and London: University of Chicago Press.

REDMOND, ELSA M.

1983   *A Fuego y Sangre: Early Zapotec Imperialism in the Cuicatlán Cañada, Oaxaca.* Memoirs, Museum of Anthropology, no. 16. Ann Arbor: University of Michigan.

REENTS-BUDET, DORIE

1982   Pre-Classic Development in the Valley of Teotihuacan and Teotihuacan and Maya Contacts as Evidenced in the Maya Iconographic Programs. Art history graduate seminar paper, University of Texas at Austin.

REICHEL-DOLMATOFF, GERARDO

1971   *Amazonian Cosmos: The Sexual and Religious Symbolism of the Tukano Indians.* Chicago: University of Chicago Press.

1972   The Cultural Context of an Aboriginal Hallucinogen: *Banisteriopsis Caapi.* In *Flesh of the Gods: The Ritual Use of Hallucinogens,* edited by Peter T. Furst, pp. 84–113. New York and Washington: Praeger Publishers.

1975   *The Shaman and the Jaguar.* Philadelphia: Temple University Press.

1978   *Beyond the Milky Way: Hallucinatory Imagery of the Tukano Indians.* Los Angeles: UCLA Latin American Center Publications.

REILLY, F. KENT

1989   The Shaman in Transformation Pose: A Study of the Theme of Rulership in Olmec Art. In *Record of the Art Museum* (Princeton University) 48(2):4–21.

1994   Visions to Another World: Art, Shamanism, and Political Power in Middle Formative Mesoamerica. Ph.D. dissertation, University of Texas at Austin.

RELACIÓN DE MICHOACÁN

1989   *Relación de Michoacán: Edición de Leoncio Cabrero.* Madrid: Historia 16.

ROBERTSON, DONALD

1994   *Mexican Manuscript Painting of the Early Colonial Period: The Metropolitan Schools.* Norman and London: University of Oklahoma Press.

ROBERTSON, IAN G.

2007   *Mapping the Social Landscape of an Early City: Teotihuacan, Mexico.* Tucson: University of Arizona Press, in press.

RODRIGUEZ MANZO, VERONICA

1992   Patrón de enterramiento en Teotihuacan durante el periodo clásico: Estudio de 814 entierros. Thesis, Escuela Nacional de Antropología e Historia, INAH, Mexico, D.F.

ROMERO NOGUERÓN, MANUEL

1982   Conjunto 1E. In *Memoria de Proyecto Arqueológico Teotihuacán 80-82,* edited by Rubén Cabrera Castro, Ignacio Rodríguez G., and Noel Morelos G., pp. 157–162. Mexico, D.F.: INAH.

ROSS, KURT

1978   *Codex Mendoza: Manuscrit Azteque.* CH-Fribourg: Seghers.

RUBÍN DE LA BORBOLLA, DANIEL F.

1947   Teotihuacán: Ofrendas de los Templos de Quetzalcoatl. *Anales del Instituto Nacional de Antropología e Historia* 2:61–72.

RUZ LHUILLIER, ALBERTO

1952   Exploraciones en Palenque: 1951. *Anales del INAH* 5:47–66.

SAHAGÚN, FRAY BERNARDINO DE

1950–1982 *Florentine Codex: General History of the Things of New Spain.* Translated by Charles E. Dibble and Arthur J. O. Anderson. Books 1–13. Monographs of the School of American Research and the Museum of New Mexico. Santa Fe: School of American Research and University of Utah.

1993   *Primeros memoriales: Facsimile Edition.* Norman: University of Oklahoma Press.

1997   *Primeros memoriales.* Translated by Thelma D. Sullivan. Norman: University of Oklahoma Press.

SAHLINS, MARSHALL

1958   *Social Stratification in Polynesia.* Seattle: University of Washington Press.

1981   *Historical Metaphors and Mythical Realities: Structure in the Early History of the Sandwich Islands Kingdom.* Ann Arbor: University of Michigan Press.

1985   *Islands of History.* Chicago and London: University of Chicago Press.

SALAZAR ORTEGÓN, PONCIANO

1952   El Tzompantli de Chichen Itza, Yucatan. *Tlatoani* 1(5–6):37–41.

1966a   Maqueta prehispánica teotihuacana. *Boletín del INAH* 23:4–11.

1966b   Interpretación del altar central de Tetitla, Teotihuacán. *Boletín del INAH* 24:41–47.

SALOMON, FRANK

1991   Introductory Essay: The Huarochirí Manuscript. In *The Huarochirí Manuscript: A Testament of Ancient and Colonial Andean Religion,* translated by Frank Salomon and George L. Urioste, pp. 1–38. Austin: University of Texas Press.

SÁNCHEZ ALANIZ, JOSE IGNACIO

1989   Las unidades habitacionales de Teotihuacan: El caso de Bidasoa. Thesis, Escuela Nacional de Antropología e Historia. Mexico, D.F.: INAH and SEP.

1991   Unidades habitacionales del periodo clásico. In *Teotihuacán 1980–1982: Nuevas interpretaciones,* edited by Rubén Cabrera Castro, Ignacio Rodríguez García, and Noel Morelos García, pp. 171–182. Mexico, D.F.: INAH.

SÁNCHEZ BONILLA, JUAN

1993   Similitudes entre las pinturas de Las Higueras y las obras plásticas del Tajín. In *Tajín,* Juergen Brueggemann, Sara Ladrón de Guevara, and Juan Sánchez Bonilla, pp. 133–160. Mexico, D.F.: Citibank.

SÁNCHEZ SÁNCHEZ, JESÚS E.

1982a   El Conjunto NW del Río San Juan. In *Memoria de Proyecto Arqueológico Teotihuacán 80-82,* edited by Rubén Cabrera Castro, Ignacio Rodríguez G., and Noel Morelos G., pp. 227–246. Mexico, D.F.: INAH.

1982b   Exploraciones en el area SW del Complejo Calle de los Muertos. In *Memoria de Proyecto Arqueológico Teotihuacán 80-82,* edited by Rubén Cabrera Castro, Ignacio Rodríguez G., and Noel Morelos G., pp. 249–270. Mexico, D.F.: INAH.

1991   El conjunto arquitectónico de los edificios superpuestos: Implicaciones sobre su functionamiento. In *Teotihuacán 1980–1982: Nuevas interpretaciones,* edited by Rubén Cabrera Castro, Ignacio Rodríguez García, and Noel Morelos García, pp. 61–93. Mexico, D.F.: INAH.

SANDERS, WILLIAM T.

1970   The Population of the Teotihuacan Valley, the Basin of Mexico and the Central Mexican Symbiotic Region in the Sixteenth Century. In *The Teotihuacan Valley Project—Final Report,* vol. 1, pp. 385–457. University Park: Pennsylvania State University.

1989   Household, Lineage, and State at Eighth-Century Copan, Honduras. In *The House of the Bacabs, Copan, Honduras,* edited by David Webster, pp. 89–105. Studies in Pre-Columbian Art and Archaeology 29. Washington, D.C.: Dumbarton Oaks Research Library and Collection.

SANDERS, WILLIAM T., AND JOSEPH W. MICHELS (EDITORS)

1977   *Teotihuacan and Kaminaljuyu: A Study in Prehistoric Culture Contact.* University Park: Pennsylvania State University Press.

SANDERS, WILLIAM T., AND DAVID WEBSTER

1988   The Mesoamerican Urban Tradition. *American Anthropologist* 90:521–546.

SARRO, PATRICIA JOAN

1991   The Role of Architectural Sculpture in Ritual

Space at Teotihuacan, Mexico. *Ancient Mesoamerica* 2:249–262.

SCHÁVELZON, DANIEL

1979   Maquetas seccionales de Teotihuacan. In *Las representaciones de arquitectura en la arqueología de America,* vol. I, *Mesoamerica,* edited by Daniel Schávelzon, pp. 332–342. Mexico, D.F.: UNAM.

SCHEFFLER, LILIAN

1976   La celebración del Día de Muertos en San Juan Tocolac, Tlaxcala. *Boletín del Departamento de Investigación de las Tradiciones Populares* 3:91–103.

SCHELE, LINDA

1986   *The Tlaloc Complex in the Classic Period: War and the Interaction between the Lowland Maya and Teotihuacan.* Paper presented at the Symposium on the New Dynamics, Fort Worth: Kimbell Art Museum.

1988   The Xibalba Shuffle: A Dance After Death. In *Maya Iconography,* edited by Elizabeth Benson and Gillett Griffin, pp. 294–317. Princeton: Princeton University Press.

1995   The Olmec Mountain and the Tree of Creation in Mesoamerican Cosmology. In *The Olmec World: Ritual and Rulership,* pp. 105–117. Princeton: The Art Museum, Princeton University, and Harry N. Abrams, Inc.

1999   Sprouts and the Early Symbolism of Rulers in Mesoamerica. In *The Emergence of Lowland Maya Civilization: The Transition from the Preclassic to Early Classic,* edited by Nikolai Grube, pp. 117–135. Acta Mesoamericana, vol. 8. Möckmühl, Germany: A. Saurwein.

SCHELE, LINDA, AND DAVID FREIDEL

1990   *A Forest of Kings: The Untold Story of the Ancient Maya.* New York: William Morrow and Company.

SCHELE, LINDA, AND JULIA GUERNSEY

2001   What the Heck's Coatepec? In *Landscape and Power in Mesoamerica,* edited by Rex Koontz, Kathryn Reese-Taylor, and Annabeth Headrick, pp. 29–53. Boulder: Westview Press.

SCHELE, LINDA, AND MATTHEW LOOPER

1996   *Notebook for the Twentieth Maya Hieroglyphic Forum at Texas.* Austin: University of Texas at Austin.

SCHELE, LINDA, AND MARY MILLER

1986   *The Blood of Kings: Dynasty and Ritual in Maya Art.* New York and Fort Worth: George Braziller and the Kimball Art Museum.

SCHONDUBE, OTTO

1975   Interpretación de la estructura ubicada al pie de la Pirámide de la Luna. In *XIII Mesa Redonda,* tomo 2, pp. 239–246. Mexico, D.F.: Sociedad Mexicana de Antropología.

SCHUSTER, ANGELA

1998   New Tomb Found at Teotihuacan. *Archaeology.* Electronic document. http://www.archaeology .org/online/features/mexico/index.html, accessed November 13, 2005.

SCOTT, SUE

1982   Figurines from Hacienda Metepec, Teotihua-

can, Mexico: A Stylistic Analysis. M.A. thesis, Universidad de las Américas.

SÉJOURNÉ, LAURETTE

1956   *Burning Water: Thought and Religion in Ancient Mexico.* New York: Vanguard Press.

1956–1957   Estudio del material arqueológico de Atetelco, Teotihuacan. *Revista Mexicana de Estudios Antropológicos* 14:15–23.

1959   *Un palacio en la ciudad de los dioses: Teotihuacan.* Mexico, D.F.: INAH.

1962   Interpretación de un jeroglífico teotihuacano. *Cuadernos Americanos* 124:137–158.

1963   Exploración de Tetitla. In *Teotihuacan: Descubrimientos, reconstrucciones.* Mexico, D.F.: Instituto Nacional de Antropología.

1964   La Simbólica del Fuego. *Cuadernos Americanos* 23(4):149–178.

1966a   *Arqueología de Teotihuacan: La Cerámica.* Mexico, D.F.: Fondo de Cultura Económica.

1966b   *Arquitectura y pintura en Teotihuacan.* Mexico, D.F.: Siglo XXI.

1966c   *El lenguaje de las formas en Teotihuacan.* Mexico, D.F.: Siglo XXI.

SÉJOURNÉ, LAURETTE, AND MANUEL ROMERO NOGUERÓN

1982   Exploraciones en Atetelco. In *Memoria de Proyecto Arqueológico Teotihuacán 80–82,* edited by Rubén Cabrera Castro, Ignacio Rodríguez G., and Noel Morelos G., pp. 397–399. Mexico, D.F.: INAH.

SELER, EDUARD

1915   Die Teotihuacan Kultur des Hochlands von Mexiko. In *Gesammelte Abhandlungen zur Amerikanischen Sprach- und Altertumskunde,* vol. 5, pp. 405–585. Berlin: Behrend.

1917   *Die Ruinen von Uxmal.* Königlich Preussischen Akademie der Wissenschaften. Philhist. Klasse No. 3, Berlin.

1990–1998   *Collected Works in Mesoamerican Linguistics and Archaeology.* 6 vols. Edited by J. Eric S. Thompson and Francis B. Richardson; Frank E. Comparato, general editor. Culver City, California: Labyrinthos.

SEMPOWSKI, MARTHA L.

1987   Differential Mortuary Treatment: Its Implications for Social Status at Three Residential Compounds in Teotihuacan, Mexico. In *Teotihuacan: Nuevos datos, nuevas síntesis, nuevos problemas,* edited by Emily McClung de Tapia and Evelyn Childs Rattray, pp. 115–131. Mexico, D.F.: UNAM.

1992   Economic and Social Implications of Variations in Mortuary Practices at Teotihuacan. In *Art, Ideology, and the City of Teotihuacan,* edited by Janet Catherine Berlo, pp. 27–58. Washington, D.C.: Dumbarton Oaks Research Library and Collection.

SERRA PUCHE, MARI CARMEN

1993   The Role of Teotihuacan in Mesoamerican Archaeology. In *Teotihuacan: Art from the City of the Gods,* edited by Kathleen Berrin and Esther

Pasztory, pp. 65–73. San Francisco: Thames and Hudson and the Fine Arts Museums of San Francisco.

2001   The Concept of Feminine Places in Mesoamerica. In *Gender in Pre-Hispanic America,* edited by Cecelia Klein, pp. 255–283. Washington, D.C.: Dumbarton Oaks Research Library and Collection.

SERRANO, CARLOS, AND ZAID LAGUNAS

1975   Sistema de enterramiento y notas sobre el material osteológico de La Ventilla Teotihuacán, México. *Anales del INAH* (1972–1973).

SERRANO SÁNCHEZ, CARLOS

1993   Funerary Practices and Human Sacrifice in Teotihuacan Burials. In *Teotihuacan: Art from the City of the Gods,* edited by Kathleen Berrin and Esther Pasztory, pp. 109–115. San Francisco: Thames and Hudson and the Fine Arts Museums of San Francisco.

SERRANO SÁNCHEZ, CARLOS, MARTHA PIMIENTA MERLIN, AND ALFONSO GALLARDO VELÁZQUEZ

1993   Mutilación dentaria y filiación étnica en los entierros del Templo de Quetzalcoatl, Teotihuacan. In *II Coloquio Pedro Bosch-Gimpera,* edited by María Teresa Cabrero G., pp. 263–276. Mexico, D.F.: Instituto de Investigaciones Antropológicas, UNAM.

SHARER, ROBERT

2003   Founding Events and Teotihuacan Connections at Copan, Honduras. In *The Maya and Teotihuacan: Reinterpreting Early Classic Interaction,* edited by Geoffrey Braswell, pp. 143–165. Austin: University of Texas Press.

SILICEO PAUER, PAUL

1925   Representaciones prehispánicas de dientes humanos hechas en concha. *Anales del Museo Nacional de Arqueología, Historia y Etnografía* 3:220–222.

SIMÉON, RÉMI

1977   *Diccionario de la lengua Nahuatl o Mexicana.* Mexico, D.F.: Siglo Veintiuno.

SMITH, A. LEDYARD

1950   *Uaxactun, Guatemala: Excavations of 1931–1937.* Pub. no. 588. Washington, D.C.: Carnegie Institution of Washington.

SNOW, DEAN R.

1972   Classic Teotihuacan Influences in North Central Tlaxcala. In *Teotihuacan: XI Mesa Redonda,* pp. 245–251. Mexico, D.F.: Sociedad Mexicana de Antropología.

SOTO SORIA, ALFONSO

1969   The Huichols and Their Magic World. *Artes de México* 124:64–67.

SPENCE, LEWIS

1923   *The Gods of Mexico.* London: T.F. Unwin, Ltd.

SPENCE, MICHAEL W.

1974   Residential Practices and the Distribution of Skeletal Traits in Teotihuacan, Mexico. *Man* 9:262–273.

1977   Teotihuacan y el intercambio de obsidiana en Mesoamerica. *Los procesos de cambio en Mesoamérica y áreas circunvecinas,* XV Mesa Redonda, vol. II, pp. 293–299. Mexico, D.F.: Sociedad Mexicana de Antropología.

1989   Excavaciones recientes en Tlailotlacan: El barrio oaxaqueño de Teotihuacan. *Arqueología* 5:81–104.

1992   Tlailotlacan, Zapotec Enclave at Teotihuacan. In *Art, Ideology, and the City of Teotihuacan,* edited by Janet C. Berlo, pp. 59–88. Washington, D.C.: Dumbarton Oaks Research Library and Collection.

SPENCE, MICHAEL W., CHRISTINE D. WHITE, FRED J. LONGSTAFFE, AND KIMBERLY R. LAW

2004   Victims of the Victims: Human Trophies Worn by Sacrificed Soldiers from the Feathered Serpent Pyramid, Teotihuacan. *Ancient Mesoamerica* 15:1–15.

SPINDEN, HERBERT J.

1935   *Indian Manuscripts of Ancient Southern Mexico.* Annual report (1933) of the Smithsonian Instution, pp. 429–451. Washington, D.C.: Smithsonian Institution.

SPORES, RONALD

1983a   Ramos Phase Urbanization in the Mixteca Alta. In *The Cloud People: Divergent Evolution of the Zapotec and Mixtec Civilizations,* edited by Kent V. Flannery and Joyce Marcus, pp. 120–123. New York: Academic Press.

1983b   Yucuñudahui. In *The Cloud People: Divergent Evolution of the Zapotec and Mixtec Civilizations,* edited by Kent V. Flannery and Joyce Marcus, pp. 155–158. New York: Academic Press.

STADEN, HANS

1928   *The True History of His Captivity.* Translated and edited by Malcolm Letts. London: George Routledge and Sons, Ltd.

STENZEL, WERNER

1970   The Sacred Bundles in Mesoamerican Religion. In *Verhandlungen des XXXVIII Internationalen Amerikanistenkongresses,* Stuttgart 1968, vol. II, 347–352. Munich: Kommissionsverlag Klaus Renner.

STOCKER, TERRANCE L., AND MICHAEL W. SPENCE

1973   Trilobal Eccentrics at Teotihuacan and Tula. *American Antiquity* 38:195–199.

STONE, ANDREA J.

2002   Spirals, Ropes, and Feathers: The Iconography of Rubber Balls in Mesoamerican Art. *Ancient Mesoamerica* 13(1):21–39.

STOREY, REBECCA

1985   An Estimate of Mortality in a Pre-Columbian Urban Population. *American Anthropologist* 87:519–535.

1987   A First Look at the Paleodemography of the Ancient City of Teotihuacan. In *Teotihuacan: Nuevos datos, nuevas síntesis, nuevos problemas,* edited by Emily McClung de Tapia and Evelyn Childs Rattray, pp. 91–114. Mexico, D.F.: UNAM.

1992   *Life and Death in the Ancient City of Teotihuacan: A*

Modern Paleodemographic Synthesis. Tuscaloosa and London: University of Alabama Press.

STUART, DAVID

1987   Ten Phonetic Syllables. *Research Reports on Ancient Maya Writing* 14. Washington, D.C.: Center for Maya Research.

2000   "The Arrival of Strangers": Teotihuacan and Tollan in Classic Maya History. In *Mesoamerica's Classic Heritage: From Teotihuacan to the Aztecs,* edited by Davíd Carrasco, Lindsay Jones, and Scott Sessions, pp. 465–513. Boulder: University of Colorado Press.

2005   A Foreign Past: The Writing and Representation of History on a Royal Ancestral Shrine at Copan. In *Copan: the History of an Ancient Maya City,* edited by E. Wyllys Andrews and William Fash, pp. 373–394. Santa Fe: School of American Research Press.

STUART, GEORGE E.

1992   Mural Masterpieces of Ancient Cacaxtla. *National Geographic* 182(3):120–136.

SUGIYAMA, SABURO

1982   Los trabajos efectuados por la sección de topografía. In *Memoria del Proyecto Arqueológico Teotihuacán 80–82,* edited by Rubén Cabrera Castro, Ignacio Rodríguez G., and Noel Morelos G., pp. 467–475. Mexico, D.F.: INAH.

1988   Los animales en la iconografía Teotihuacan. *Revista Mexicana de Estudios Antropológicos* 34(1):13–52.

1989a   Burials Dedicated to the Old Temple of Quetzalcoatl at Teotihuacan, Mexico. *American Antiquity* 54:85–106.

1989b   Iconographic Interpretation of the Temple of Quetzalcoatl at Teotihuacan. *Mexicon* 11(4):68–74.

1991   Descubrimientos de entierros y ofrendas dedicadas al Templo Viejo de Quetzalcóatl. In *Teotihuacán, 1980–1982: Nuevas interpretaciones,* edited by Rubén Cabrera Castro, Ignacio Rodríguez García, and Noel Morelos García, pp. 275–326. Mexico, D.F.: INAH.

1992   Rulership, Warfare, and Human Sacrifice at the Ciudadela: An Iconographic Study of Feathered Serpent Representations. In *Art, Ideology, and the City of Teotihuacan,* edited by Janet Catherine Berlo, pp. 205–230. Washington, D.C.: Dumbarton Oaks Research Library and Collection.

1998   Termination Programs and Prehispanic Looting at the Feathered Serpent Pyramid in Teotihuacan, Mexico. In *The Sowing and the Dawning,* edited by Shirley Boteler Mock, pp. 147–164. Albuquerque: University of New Mexico Press.

2005   *Human Sacrifice, Militarism, and Rulership: Materialization of State Ideology at the Feathered Serpent Pyramid, Teotihuacan.* Cambridge: Cambridge University Press.

SUGIYAMA, SABURO, AND RUBÉN CABRERA C.

2000   El proyecto Pirámide de la Luna: Algunos resultados de la segunda temporada, 1999. *Arqueología,* 2nd ep., 23:161–172.

SUTRO, LIVINGSTON D., AND THEODORE E. DOWNING

1988   A Step Toward a Grammar of Space: Domestic Space Use In Zapotec Villages. In *Household and Community in the Mesoamerican Past,* edited by Richard R. Wilk and Wendy Ashmore, pp. 29–50. Albuquerque: University of New Mexico Press.

TAUBE, KARL A.

1983   The Teotihuacan Spider Woman. *Journal of Latin American Lore* 9(2):107–189.

1985   The Classic Maya Maize God: A Reappraisal. In *Fifth Palenque Round Table, 1983,* edited by Merle Greene Robertson, pp. 171–181. San Francisco: Pre-Columbian Art Research Institute.

1986   The Teotihuacan Cave of Origin. *RES* 12:51–82.

1988   A Study of Classic Maya Scaffold Sacrifice. In *Maya Iconography,* edited by Elizabeth P. Benson and Gillett G. Griffin, pp. 330–351. Princeton, N.J.: Princeton University Press.

1992a   The Iconography of Mirrors at Teotihuacan. In *Art, Ideology, and the City of Teotihuacan,* edited by Janet Catherine Berlo, pp. 169–204. Washington, D.C.: Dumbarton Oaks Research Library and Collection.

1992b   *The Major Gods of Ancient Yucatan.* Washington, D.C.: Dumbarton Oaks Research Library and Collection.

1992c   The Temple of Quetzalcoatl and the Cult of Sacred War at Teotihuacan. *RES* 21:53–87.

1994   The Birth Vase: Natal Imagery in Ancient Maya Myth and Ritual. In *The Maya Vase Book,* edited by Justin Kerr, vol. 4, pp. 652–685. New York: Kerr Associates.

1995   The Rain Makers: The Olmec and Their Contribution to Mesoamerican Belief and Ritual. In *The Olmec World: Ritual and Rulership,* pp. 83–103. Princeton, N.J.: The Art Museum, Princeton University, and Harry N. Abrams, Inc.

2000a   The Turquoise Hearth: Fire, Self Sacrifice, and the Central Mexican Cult of War. In *Mesoamerica's Classic Heritage: From Teotihuacan to the Aztecs,* edited by Davíd Carrasco, Lindsay Jones, and Scott Sessions, pp. 269–340. Boulder: University of Colorado Press.

2000b   The Writing System of Ancient Teotihuacan. *Ancient America,* vol. I. Barnardsville, N.C.: Center for Ancient American Studies.

2003   Tetitla and the Maya Presence at Teotihuacan. In *The Maya and Teotihuacan: Reinterpreting Early Classic Interaction,* edited by Geoffrey Braswell, pp. 273–314. Austin: University of Texas Press.

TEDLOCK, DENNIS

1985   *Popol Vuh.* New York: Simon and Schuster.

TEOTIHUACAN

1952   In *Tlatoani,* vol. 1, nos. 3 and 4, mayo–agosto, Mexico, D.F.: INAH.

THOMPSON, J. ERIC S.

1970   *Maya History and Religion.* Norman: University of Oklahoma Press.

THOMPSON, WADDY
1847   *Recollections of Mexico.* New York and London: Wiley and Putnam.

TITIEV, MISCHA
1944   *Old Oraibi: A Study of the Hopi Indians of Third Mesa.* Papers of the Peabody Museum of American Archaeology and Ethnology, vol. 22. Cambridge: Harvard University.

TOBRINER, STEPHEN
1972   The Fertile Ground: An Investigation of Cerro Gordo's Importance to the Town Plan and Iconography of Teotihuacan. In *Teotihuacan: XI Mesa Redonda,* pp. 103–115. Mexico, D.F.: Sociedad Mexicana de Antropología.

TOLSTOY, PAUL
1971   Utilitarian Artifacts of Central Mexico. In *Handbook of Middle American Indians,* vol. 10, edited by Robert Wauchope, Gordon Ekholm, and Ignacio Bernal, pp. 270–296. Austin: University of Texas Press.

TOOR, FRANCES
1947   *A Treasury of Mexican Folkways.* New York: Crown Publishers.

TORQUEMADA, FRAY JUAN DE
1977   *Monarquía indiana.* Vol. IV. Mexico, D.F.: UNAM.

TORRES MONTES, LUIS
1972   Materiales y technicas de la pintura mural de Teotihuacan. In *Teotihuacan: XI Mesa Redonda,* pp. 17–42. Mexico, D.F.: Sociedad Mexicana de Antropología.

TOSCANO, SALVADOR
1954   Los murales prehispanicos. *Artes de México* 3:30–38.

TOURTELLOT, GAIR
1988   Developmental Cycles of Households and Houses at Seibal. In *Household and Community in the Mesoamerican Past,* edited by Richard R. Wilk and Wendy Ashmore, pp. 97–120. Albuquerque: University of New Mexico Press.

TOWNSEND, RICHARD F.
1992a   *The Aztecs.* London: Thames and Hudson.
1992b   Landscape and Symbol. In *The Ancient Americas: Art from Sacred Landscapes,* edited by Richard F. Townsend, pp. 29–47. Chicago: Art Institute of Chicago.

TOZZER, ALFRED M.
1907   *A Comparative Study of the Mayas and the Lacandones.* New York: Archaeological Institute of America, Macmillan Co.
1957   Chichen Itza and Its Cenote of Sacrifice. In *Memoirs of the Peabody Museum of Archaeology and Ethnology,* XI and XII. Cambridge: Harvard University.

TUGGLE, H. DAVID
1968   The Columns of El Tajín, Veracruz, México. *Ethnos* 33:40–70.

TURNER, MARGARET H.
1992   Style in Lapidary Technology: Identifying the Teotihuacan Lapidary Industry. In *Art, Ideology, and the City of Teotihuacan,* edited by Janet Catherine Berlo, pp. 89–112. Washington, D.C.: Dumbarton Oaks Research Library and Collection.

EL UNIVERSAL
1995   Calakmul: Discovery of a Mummy Bundle in a Tomb. *Mexicon* 17(1):6.

VALADEZ, RAÚL, AND LINDA MANZANILLA
1988   Restos faunísticos y áreas de actividad en una unidad habitacional de la antigua ciudad de Teotihuacan. *Revista Mexicana de Estudios Antropológicos* 34(1):147–168.

VALLE, PERLA
1988   Papalotl: Del mito y de la realidad. *Revista Mexicana de Estudios Antropológicos* 34(1):112–121.

VARGAS, LUIS ALBERTO
1971   Conception of Death in Mexico Today. *Artes de México* 18(145):91–93.

VIDARTE DE LINARES, JUAN
1964   Exploraciones arqueológicas en el rancho "La Ventilla." Informe al INAH del Proyecto Teotihuacan. Mexico, D.F.: INAH.
1968   Teotihuacan, la ciudad del quinto sol. *Cuadernos Americanos* 158:133–145.

VILLA ROJAS, ALFONSO
1988   The Concepts of Space and Time among the Contemporary Maya. In *Time and Reality in the Thought of the Maya,* Miguel León-Portilla, pp. 113–159. Norman: University of Oklahoma Press.

VILLAGRA CALETI, AGUSTÍN
1951   Las pinturas de Atetelco en Teotihuacan. *Cuadernos Americanos* 10(55):153–162.
1952   Teotihuacan, sus pinturas murales. *Anales del INAH* 5:67–74. México.
1954a   Las pinturas de Tetitla, Atetelco, e Ixtapontongo. *Artes de Mexico* 3:39–43.
1954b   Trabajos realizados en Teotihuacán. *Anales del INAH* 6:69–78.
1956–1957 Las pinturas murales de Atetelco, Teotihuacán. *Revista Mexicana de Estudios Antropológicos* 14:9–13.
1961   Los murales de Atetelco, Teotihuacan. *Boletín INAH* 4:1–3.
1965   La conservación de los murales prehispánicos. *Anales del INAH* 8:109–116.
1971   Mural Painting in Central Mexico. In *Handbook of Middle American Indians,* vol. 10, edited by Robert Wauchope, Gordon Ekholm, and Ignacio Bernal, pp. 135–156. Austin: University of Texas Press.

VILLELA, KHRISTAAN D.
1990   The Iconography of Auto-sacrifice at Teotihuacan. Honors thesis, Yale University.

VOGT, EVON Z.
1965   Zinacanteco "Souls." *Man* 29:33–35.
1976   *Tortillas for the Gods: A Symbolic Analysis of Zinacanteco Rituals.* Norman and London: University of Oklahoma Press.

VON WINNING, HASO
1947a   A symbol for dripping water in the Teotihuacan culture. *El Mexico Antiguo* 6:333–341.

1947b Representations of Temple Buildings as Decorative Patterns on Teotihuacan Pottery and Figurines. *Notes on Middle American Archaeology and Ethnology* 83:170–177. Washington, D.C.: Carnegie Institution.

1948 The Teotihuacan Owl-and-Weapon Symbol and Its Association with "Serpent Head X" at Kaminaljuyu. *American Antiquity* 14:129–132.

1949 Shell Designs on Teotihuacan Pottery. *El Mexico Antiguo* 7:126–153.

1974 *The Shaft Tomb Figures of West Mexico.* Southwest Museum Papers, no. 24. Los Angeles: Southwest Museum.

1979 Representaciones de fachadas de templos en cerámica de Teotihuacan. In *Las representaciones de arquitectura en la arqueología de America,* vol. I, Mesoamerica, edited by Daniel Schávelzon, pp. 319–327. México: UNAM.

1987 *La iconografía de Teotihuacan: Los dioses y los signos.* 2 vols. Mexico, D.F.: UNAM.

WALLRATH, MATTHEW
1966 The Calle de los Muertos Complex: A Possible Macrocomplex of Structures near the Center of Teotihuacan. In *Teotihuacan: Onceava Mesa Redonda,* pp. 113–122. Mexico, D.F.: Sociedad Mexicana de Antropología.

WEBSTER, DAVID
1975 Warfare and the Evolution of the State: A Reconstruction. *American Antiquity* 40(4):464–470.

WESTHEIM, PAUL
1965 *The Art of Ancient Mexico.* New York: Doubleday and Company.

WHITE, CHRISTINE D., MICHAEL W. SPENCE, FRED J. LONGSTAFFE, HILARY STEWART-WILLIAMS, AND KIMBERLY R. LAW
2002 Geographical Identities of the Sacrificial Victims from the Feathered Serpent Pyramid, Teotihuacan: Implications for the Nature of State Power. *Latin American Antiquity* 13:217–236.

WICKE, CHARLES R.
1954 Los murales de Tepantitla y el arte campesino. *Anales del INAH* 8(37):117–122.

WIDMER, RANDOLPH J.
1987 The Evolution of Form and Function in a Teotihuacan Apartment Compound: The Case of Tlajinga 33. In *Teotihuacán: Nuevos datos, nuevas síntesis, nuevos problemas,* edited by Emily McClung de Tapia and Evelyn Childs Rattray, pp. 317–368. Mexico, D.F.: UNAM.

WILKERSON, S. JEFFREY K.
1990 El Tajín: Great Center of the Northeast. In *Mexico: Splendors of Thirty Centuries,* edited by John P. O'Neill, pp. 155–181. New York: Metropolitan Museum of Art.

WINTER, MARCUS
1990 Monte Albán: Hilltop Capital in Oaxaca. In *Mexico: Splendors of Thirty Centuries,* edited by John P. O'Neill, pp. 115–134. New York: Metropolitan Museum of Art.

WORSLEY, PETER
1967 Groote Eylandt Totemism and *Le Totémisme aujourd'hui. The Structural Study of Myth and Totemism,* edited by Michael Banton, pp. 141–160. London: Tavistock Publications.

YOFFEE, NORMAN
1991 Maya Elite Interaction: Through a Glass, Sideways. In *Classic Maya Political History: Hieroglyphic and Archaeological Evidence,* edited by T. Patrick Culbert, pp. 285–310. Cambridge: School of American Research and Cambridge University Press.

ZINGG, ROBERT MOWRY
1938 *The Huichols: Primitive Artists.* New York: G. E. Stechert and Company.

INDEX

2 of the White Patio, 13, 28, 30–32, 41, 78, 80–81, 84, 86, 96, 101–103, 176n10; Portico 3 of the White Patio, 73, 78–80, 82–87; White Patio, 27–28, 30–32, 41, 78–80, 87, 96, 99–100, 102–104, 106, 109–110, 118–123, 126, 130, 166, 169, 172n5, 176n8

Atlatl-Owl, 38, 178n12. *See also* Spearthrower Owl

altatls, 37, 72–74, 78, 80, 87–88, 121, 126–130, 133, 143, 178n12

atl caualo, 46

Aveni, Anthony, 116, 161, 176n5, 177n21, 177n23, 180n26, 180n27

Avenue of the Dead, 1–7, 10, 32, 55, 65, 70, 87, 95, 99, 105, 107–109, 113, 125, 127, 135, 138, 145, 158–160, 168, 172n16, 173n22, 179n21; and association with Milky Way, 174n19; and derivation of the name, 62–64, 174n18, 174 n21; ritual on 163–164

axis mundi, 28, 30–31, 33, 38, 147–149, 151, 154, 157, 163–164, 168, 179n21. *See also under* Maya

Aztec, 16, 19–21, 24, 31, 36, 38, 42, 46–49, 58–59, 62–64, 73–79, 83, 86–87, 91–93, 96–102, 112–114, 117–119, 121–123, 126–127, 136–143, 150–151, 154–158, 163–164, 167–168, 171n2, 172n23, 173n3, 174n11, 175n18, 175n21, 176n4, 177n11, 179n7, 179n16; Templo Mayor, 24, 36–37, 127, 178n10. *See also under* ancestors; headdresses; military; mortuary bundles; plazas; priests; ritual; rulers; sun; temples

Aztlan, 75

backracks, 77, 152, 154, 175n8

ballgame, 26, 155, 179n12

Barba, Luis, 105

Barbour, Warren, xii

Barrio of the Looted Murals, 83

barrios, 45, 69, 106–107, 120

Bastien, Rémy, 115, 177n20

Batres, Leopoldo, 115, 177n20

bears, 105

Beekman, Christopher, 179n8

Berlo, Janet, 20, 32–33, 39, 126, 133, 138, 140, 142, 144, 172n21, 172n7, 173n14, 173n16, 178n18, 178n19, 178n21

Bernal, Ignacio, 8, 51, 54, 17, 174n7, 174n8

Berrin, Kathleen, 55, 68, 144, 173n21, 174n10, 175n13, 177n11, 177n25

Beyer, Hermann, 36, 137–138, 178n18

bifaces, 88, 175n13

birds, 28–33, 42, 57, 64, 74–89, 93, 96–102, 119–123, 131–133, 136, 140, 151–157, 166, 173n13, 176n7, 178n17; eagles, 74, 76, 88; falcons, 88; hummingbirds, 59, 136; owls, 21, 37, 73, 88, 131, 133, 179n1; quetzals, 21. *See also under* butterflies; headdresses; sacrifice

Blanton, Richard, 69

blood, 78–79, 82–84, 137, 151, 172n6

bloodletters, 82, 86

Boone, Elizabeth, 178n10, 179n16

Braswell, Geoffrey, 8, 171n4, 172n10, 177n2

Bricker, Victoria, 75–76, 172n7, 175n6

Brotherston, Gordon, 161, 180n27

Brown, Betty, 179n7

Building of the Altars, 159–164, 168, 179n23, 179n24

Bunzel, Ruth, 100

Burgoa, Francisco de, 62

burials, 9, 10, 19, 23–26, 51, 55, 62, 66, 172n2; in apartment compounds, 45–46, 49, 171n6, 171n8, 173n5; associated with altars, 45–47; associated with patios, 45–46, 66, 173n5; and censers, 138, 178n21; Cerro de la Campana, 52; Coixtlahuaca, 51, 54; cremation, 54–57, 66; disarticulated, 57; in Feathered Serpent Pyramid, 9, 10, 24, 87–88, 95, 167, 172n12, 172n13, 175n20, 176n22; female, 45, 67, 143; fetal, infant and child, 46, 174n6; flexed, 57; Maya, 24, 51, 52, 67, 174n9; in Moon Pyramid, 88–89, 172n4, 174n16, 175n2; Tlaxcala, 47–48; United States, 165–166; West Mexican, 143, 173n9, 179n30; Zapotec, 31, 69, 98. *See also* mortuary bundles; sacrifice. *See also under* rulers

Burkhart, Louise, 75

butterflies, 21, 125–145, 152–154, 164, 168, 177n3, 178n5, 178n12, 178n14, 179n6, 179n7; and architecture, 134–136; association with atlatl, 129; and bird conflation, 130–133, 178n17; and souls of dead warriors, 136–145. *See also* headdresses; noseplaques

Byland, Bruce, 59–62, 68, 174n15

Cabrera, Oralia, xii, 9–10, 24, 177n3, 178n26

Cabrera, Rubén, xii, 2, 9–10, 24–25, 58, 66, 88–89, 93, 120, 171n7, 172n4, 172n5, 172n15, 172n17, 174n16, 175n2, 175n21, 176n1, 176n8, 176n22

Cacaxtla, 41, 120–123. *See also under* murals; patios

cacti, 157; barrel, 136; biznaga, 80, 82

Calakmul, 51, 54, 174n9

calendars, 25, 150–151, 153, 158, 160–163, 179n20, 180n27

calmecac, 100

calpolli, 100

canines, 74, 80–88, 93, 96, 99–102, 119–123, 166, 175n2, 175n19, 176n7; wolf, 88, 166, 175n2

cannibalism, 84–86

Carmack, Robert, 175n6

Carmichael, Elizabeth, 47, 173n4

Carrasco, Davíd, 174n21

Caso, Alfonso, 9, 133, 140, 147–148

caves, 9–10, 14, 19, 28–30, 49, 64, 70, 148, 179n18; and Huichol, 62; and Mixtec, 59, 61–62; under the Sun Pyramid, 9–10, 62–63, 107–108, 114, 117, 158, 162–164, 168, 171n3. *See also under* astronomy

censers, 38, 72, 125, 132–133, 137–138, 144–145, 168, 178n19; as effigy mortuary bundles, 138; and portraiture, 144–145

Central Highlands, 6

ceramics, 10–11, 18, 31, 36–37, 46, 55–58, 63, 74, 104, 114, 125–126, 129–135, 138, 144, 146, 168, 171n8, 172n5, 172n16, 174n11, 176n1, 176n2, 177n4, 179n8; workshop, 55–56, 73–74, 144–145. *See also* censers; figurines

Cerro Colorado, 116–117, 177n23

Cerro de la Campana, 52–53

Cerro Gordo, 1–2, 4, 30, 35, 38, 113–115, 117, 159, 163, 173n31; name of, 114

Cerro Malinalco, 113, 116–117

Cerro Patlachique, 113–115, 117

Chac, 11–12

Chalcatongo, 59–62

Chang, K. C., 66, 69, 79

Charlton, Thomas, 66

Chichen Itza, 73
ch'iebal, 48–49
childbirth, 141–143, 168
chimalcoatl, 98
China. *See under* ancestors; ritual; rulers; shamanism
Cholula, 125
Christenson, Allen, 177n14
cihuacoatl, 41–42
Ciudadela, 2, 4, 10, 55, 73, 95, 144–145, 178
Clark, John, xii
class, 59, 70, 91–93, 122, 133
Classic period, 19–20, 38, 46, 51–52, 111–112, 123, 125, 137, 143, 154, 158, 162, 171n8, 172n23, 178n29
Clavigero, Abbé D., 37–38
Coatepec, 75, 117
codices, 16, 52, 55, 57–59, 64; Bodley, 62, 64–65; Borbonicus, 179n6; Borgia, 98, 156–157; Boturini, 59, 61, 65–66; Chimalpopoca, 112, 118, 158; Féjévary-Mayer, 160–162, 180n26; Florentine, 97, 122, 141, 152, 158, 179n5; Madrid, 111; Magliabecchiano, 153; Mendoza, 91–92, 122; Nuttall, 17, 59–60, 174n15; *Primeros Memoriales,* 152–153, 179n5; Selden, 52, 111–112; Vindobonesis, 142–143
Coe, Michael, 24, 84, 172n1, 177n2
Coggins, Clemency, 138, 177n2, 178n11
Coixtlahuaca, 51, 54
Colonial period, 19, 25, 51, 62, 75–76, 91, 98, 157
colossal sculptures: Colossus of Coatlinchan, 39–41; Moon Plaza sculpture, 38–39; Museo Nacional sculpture, 33–39, 157, 173n18, 179n15
confederacy model, 69
Conides, Cynthia, xii
continuity, 19–22
Cook de Leonard, Carmen, 173n4
Copan, 8, 174n27
corn. *See* maize
cotton, 72, 91
Cowgill, George, xii, 2, 5–6, 9–10, 20, 24–25, 35, 39, 41, 45, 51, 67, 70, 93, 104–107, 114, 120, 140, 164, 171n2, 171n4, 171n6, 172n9, 172n10, 172n11, 172n20, 172n21, 173n1, 173n7, 173n8, 173n11, 173n13, 173n14, 173n16, 174n22, 174n24, 174n28, 174n29, 175n15, 175n17, 176n2, 176n4, 176n6, 176n7, 176n9, 177n1, 177n4, 178n20, 178n26, 178n27, 179n19, 179n21
craft production, 6, 141, 174n24
Cuanalan period, 176n6
Cuauhcalli, 91
Cuauhipalli, 98

dance, 78–79, 83, 86, 101, 150–155, 164, 179n11
Days of the Dead, 47, 173n4
deities, 6, 12, 15, 19, 21, 26, 28–29, 31–33, 38–39, 47–49, 59, 64, 69, 80, 84, 95–97, 112, 114, 117–119, 122–123, 126–127, 129, 133, 139–142, 147–148, 150, 152, 155–158, 168, 172n21, 172n23, 174n11, 174n21, 179n7, 179n14, 179n18. *See also names of individual deities. See also under* sacrifice
Delgadillo, Eugenia, 55
divination, 80, 82
Dosal, Pedro, 9
Dos Pilas, 11

Doutriaux, Miriam, xii
Drucker, David, 179n19
Durán, Fray Diego, 75–76, 86, 91, 97–98, 122, 150–157, 175n12, 177n27, 179n4

eagle and jaguar knights, 79, 87, 91–93, 96–102, 119, 121–122
earflares, 29, 33, 57, 73, 133
eight-partitioned house, 162, 164, 168
Epiclassic period, 41
Esquintla, 125–126, 133
Evans, Susan Toby, xii, 174n8

factionalism, 19, 68–69, 100, 167
Fash, William and Barbara, 8, 177n2
Feast of the Waters, 150
feathered eye, 130–131, 133, 175n19, 175n21
Feathered Serpent Pyramid, 2, 8–10, 24, 27, 41, 70, 85, 88–89, 93–96, 101, 105, 120, 144, 167–168, 173n13, 176n4. *See also under* burials
feathered serpents, 24, 25, 73, 121, 176n7; warriors, 87
feathers, 31–32, 54, 73, 76, 80, 87, 97–98, 121–122, 131, 156
Fields, Virginia, 148
figurines, 36–38, 56–58, 61, 77–80, 88, 134–135, 174n12, 174n13
Fischer, Edward, xii
Flannery, Kent, xii, 8, 31, 69, 85
Folan, William, 174n7, 174n9
food, 46, 57, 105, 114, 141, 150, 176n6; preparation, 6
Formative period, 20, 111, 148
Foster, George, 47, 175n4, 175n7
Freidel, David, xii, 20–21, 80, 111, 114, 127, 129, 137–138, 148–149, 158, 162–163, 174n19, 175n7, 176n5, 176n10, 177n12, 177n13, 177n17, 178n7, 178n11, 178n13, 179n2, 179n3, 179n19, 179n24, 180n28, 180n29
Fuente, Beatriz de la, 176n1
Furst, Jill, 178n28
Furst, Peter, 77, 140, 147, 175n4

Gamio, Manuel, 9, 113, 174n18
Gemelli Carreri, Juan, 37–38, 173n23
gender roles, 139–145, 180n1
Gillespie, Susan, 42, 67–69, 172n1, 174n6, 174n25
gods. *See* deities
graves. *See* burials
Gray Knights, 91
Great Compound, 2, 7
Great Feast of the Dead, 47, 151, 153–154
Great Goddess, 29, 33, 39, 140–141, 147, 172n21, 172n7, 173n13, 173n14, 173n16, 173n17. *See also* mountain-tree
Great Seeing ceremony, 79
greenstone, 27, 29, 36, 51, 54, 76–78, 80, 88, 98, 111–112
Griffin-Pierce, Trudy, 180n1
Grube, Nikolai, 80, 175n5, 175n7
Guernsey, Julia, xii, 177n17

hallucinatory trance, 14, 175n16
Hammon, Byron, 174n20
Hassig, Ross, 31, 91, 100, 122, 175n8, 176n3, 176n4
headdresses, 15, 18, 26–30, 33, 35, 38, 45, 54, 57, 73–74, 79–80, 82, 84, 87, 126, 130–131, 134–135, 140, 147–148, 156; Aztec,

91, 153; bird, 29–30, 32, 42, 173n13, 179n1; butterfly, 153–153; canine, 87, 175n19; hummingbird, 59, 64; Maya, 127; Olmec, 35; tassel, 87, 175n18; vertebral column, 32, 79, 126; year sign, 78, 138

Headrick, Annabeth, 142, 172n5, 173n10, 173n18, 174n16, 174n17, 175n11, 176n3, 176n9, 177n22, 178n14, 178n23, 179n15

hearts, 32–33, 36, 79, 82–87, 101, 126, 153, 155

Hendon, Julia, 174n27

Heyden, Doris, 10, 20, 62, 108, 114, 171n3, 176n6, 179n13, 179n18

hieroglyphic writing, 11, 16–18, 20, 25–27, 37, 39, 56, 87, 127, 133, 155, 167, 172n17, 172n22, 175n14, 178n12, 179n10. *See also under* Maya; Mixtec; rulers

Hirth, Kenneth, 8

Hodges, Kirvin, xii

Holland, William, 48, 175n4

Holmes, W. H., 35, 115, 173n19

Houston, Stephen, 175n5, 175n7, 179n24

Huehueteotl. *See* Old Fire God

Huichol, 62, 118

Huitzilapa, 143, 173n9, 179n30

Huitzilopochtli, 59, 61, 64–65, 127, 174n17, 179n5

Huixachtecatl, 150

Humboldt Celt, 111

iconographic clusters, 21, 137

infant and child mortality, 46, 141–142

Islam, 139–140

jade. *See* greenstone

Jaguar Paddler, 111

jaguars, 31, 51, 75, 77–78, 80, 85, 97–98, 105, 121, 148, 175n4, 175n16, 176n7; net, 80, 84–86, 176n10. *See also* eagle and jaguar knights

Janusek, John, xii

jihad, 124, 139–140

Jilote, Kim, xii

Johnson, James, 139

Joyce, Arthur, xii

Joyce, Rosemary, 33n4

Kaminaljuyu, 8, 126

katsina societies, 100–101

Kerr, Justin, 173n12

K'ichee', 75–77, 175n6, 175n7

Kidder, Alfred, 8

kings. *See* rulers

K'inich Janaab' Pakal I, 28–29, 54, 149, 174n19

K'inich Kan B'alam II, 11, 23

Klein, Cecelia, 142, 174n11, 175n5, 176n1

Knab, T. J., 112

Knights of the Sun, 91

Koontz, Rex, xii

Kowalewski, Jeff, 69

Kubler, George, 10, 19–21, 26, 137–138, 178n18, 178n19

Lady 6 Monkey, 41, 59–60

Lady Six Sky, 41

Lady 9 Grass, 59–60, 62, 70

Lady Xoc, 137

lakes, 112, 155; Lake Texcoco, 151, 154

Landa, Diego de, 56, 174n11

landscape, 1, 2, 151, 154. *See also under* architecture

Langley, James, 25

Laporte, Juan Pedro, 177n2

Las Colinas vessel, 17–18, 87, 93, 120

Las Higueras, 54–55

La Ventilla 1992–1993 (apartment compounds), 25, 66, 171n7, 172n17

La Ventilla B (apartment compound), 46

Lévi-Strauss, Claude, 67

Lewis-Williams, David, 14

Leyenda de los soles, 158

lineage, 19; and apartment compounds, 45–51, 64–72, 90, 93, 98, 100–101, 105, 145, 166–167, 174n28; and clans, 67, 69, 100, 174n28; and dynasties, 10, 14, 21, 24–25, 37, 68–70; Mixtec, 59–61, 142; opposed to house model, 67–68

Linné, S., 45, 66, 144, 138, 178n21

Little Feast of the Dead, 47, 151, 153–154

Looper, Matthew, xii, 111

looting, 9, 24, 26, 55, 62–63, 83, 95, 172n13, 172n14, 178n8

López Luján, Leonardo, 176n1, 178n20

López Mestas, Lorenza, 173n9, 179n30

Lord 8 Deer, 17, 59–60, 62

Luin, L. F., xii

Lumholtz, Carl, 62

maize, 28, 35, 86, 98, 114

Malinalco, 98

Malström, Vincent, 179n19

Manzanilla, Linda, 5, 6, 105, 171n6, 177n25, 178n21

Marcus, Joyce, 8, 31, 85

Margáin, Carlos, 174n23, 176n8

markets, 2, 6–7. *See also* Great Compound

Martin, Richard, 139–140

Martin, Simon, 41

masks, 38, 133, 137–138, 144, 146, 173n21, 174n8, 174n9. *See also under* mortuary bundles

Masson, Marilyn, xii

Matos, Eduardo, 36, 114, 125, 127, 176n1, 177n18, 177n23

Maya, 7–8, 21, 29, 31, 37, 46, 48, 79, 125–127, 137, 141, 143, 172n8, 172n10, 174n6, 177n15, 179n24, 180n27; calendar, 160; concepts of mountains, 114, 117; creation story, 111–113, 150, 158, 162–163, 177n12, 177n13, 179n12, 179n19; hieroglyphic writing, 14, 21, 25, 37, 75, 117, 149, 158, 175n5; kin-based models, 67–68; mortuary bundles, 51, 54; mortuary practices, 56, 67, 174n57; nagualism, 75–76, 80, 91, 175n4; north house, 162; portraiture, 14, 20; royal burial patterns, 24; rulers, 8, 10–11, 14, 23, 25, 28, 30, 33, 54; and Teotihuacan art compared, 10, 14–16, 20, 23, 25, 41, 83–84, 175n15; and Teotihuacan interaction, 177n2, 178n11; tree raising, 149, 153, 158; *Wakah-Chan* (world tree), 149–150, 162–163. *See also under* ancestors; burials; headdresses; palaces; plazas; public art and architecture; ritual; sun; temples

Mayer, Brantz, 35

Mayhall, Marguerite, 131, 177n3, 178n15, 178n25
McAnany, Patricia, xii, 174n11
McBride, Harold, 174n12
McCafferty, Geoffrey, 41, 141, 177n2
McCafferty, Sharisse, 41, 141
McGuire, Randall, 100
Merchant Marines, 166
merchants, 7, 19, 169
Merchants' Barrio, 45, 171n8
Mesoamerica, 7–8, 14, 16, 20–21, 23–24, 29, 31, 33, 42, 51, 54, 58, 75, 79, 125, 137, 141, 157, 163, 168–169, 175n5
metates, 143
Metepec period, 5, 63
Mexico City, 6, 33, 35, 39
mica, 37–38, 133, 173n22
Miccaotli period, 5, 62, 176n2
midwives, 142
military, 33, 72, 90–91, 93, 123–125, 129–130, 133, 138, 140–141, 168, 175n8, 176n4, 178n13; Aztec, 31, 42, 91–93, 96–100, 121–122, 127, 136, 139, 153–154, 167, 176n3, 177n27, 179n7; costume of, 72–74, 86, 122, 125–126, 135; and kinship, 98–102, 176n9; Maya, 25, 129; Mixtec, 59; and nagualism, 75–83; orders, 18–19, 86–90, 93–102, 119, 122–123, 166–169, 175n17, 176n7, 176n9, 176n10; Roman, 42; and rulers, 32–33, 71, 96–99, 119, 122, 145, 166–167; and social mobility, 91–93, 101–102, 122, 167, 176n4; and state formation, 98–99; United States, 74, 101, 145, 165–166; and women, 142; Zapotec, 98–99. *See also* warriors. *See also under* sodalities
Milky Way, 149, 163–164, 174n19, 180n29
Miller, Arthur, 12, 53, 57, 172n19, 175n19, 178n8
Miller, Mary, 137, 172n18, 175n15
Millon, Clara, 18, 25, 84, 87, 172n17, 173n16, 175n18, 175n19
Millon, René, 5–8, 10, 16, 19, 24, 45, 62, 66, 70, 83, 95, 106–107, 117–118, 158, 171n1, 171n4, 171n6, 171n8, 172n2, 172n3, 172n9, 172n14, 172n16, 174n18, 174n21, 174n29, 176n5, 176n6, 177n20, 177n21, 177n24, 179n17, 179n20, 179n22
mirrors, 10, 31–32, 36–38, 56, 73–74, 76, 78, 80, 82, 88, 133, 173n20, 175n1
Mixtec, 16, 59–62, 64–65, 68–69, 112, 141–143, 178n28, 178n29, 180n26, hieroglyphic writing, 16, 53. *See also under* ancestors; caves; lineage; military; mortuary bundles; priests; rulers; temples
mociuaquetzque, 142
Molina, Augusto, 176n1
mollusks, 105
Monte Albán, 8, 31, 69
Monzón, Martha, 45, 67
moon, 96, 179n18
Moon Pyramid, 2, 4–5, 7, 10, 24–25, 30, 35, 45, 88–89, 93, 106–107, 110, 159–160, 163, 171n2, 172n15, 177n19, 179n21; and Cerro Gordo, 114–115, 117, 122, 124; offerings in, 88, 101, 120, 146, 166, 168, 175n2. *See also under* burials; sacrifice
Morelos, Noel, 95
mortuary bundles, 51–71, 167, 174n19; Aztec, 59, 64, 174n17; burning of, 57–58, 60, 174n15; and caves, 59, 61–64, 70; effigies of, 55–56; images of, 52–58, 60–65, 174n12,

174n13; and masks, 51, 54–56, 58–59, 61–63, 66, 68, 138, 146, 167; Maya, 51, 54; Mixtec, 51–54, 59–65, 68, 70, 174n15; as oracles, 59, 62, 64, 70; Tarascan, 54; Veracruz, 54. *See also under* altars; censers
Moser, Christopher, 62
Motecuhzoma I, 42, 75
mountains, 1–2, 15–16, 21, 28–30, 35, 38, 48–49, 125, 163, 172n7, 173n17, 177n14, 177n17, 179n14; and ancestors, 48–49, 178n29; and creation story, 112–117, 123, 164, 168; Huixachtecatl, 150–151; and sacrifice, 48, 155; San Martín Pajapán, 148; Sustenance Mountain, 114, 179n17; and temples, 117–118; three mountain motif, 113, 117, 155, 177n16, 177n22; volcanic, 1, 30, 35, 48, 112, 114, 148, 177n17. *See also* Cerro Colorado; Cerro Gordo; Cerro Malinalco; Cerro Patlachique, Coatepec
mountain-tree, 15–16, 28–30, 32–33, 35, 42, 49, 57, 140–141, 143, 147–148, 154–157, 172n21, 173n15. *See also* Great Goddess
Mullett, G. M., 180n1
Múnera Bermúdez, Carlos, 55–58, 144, 177n25
murals, 6, 11–13, 15–18, 20, 25–33, 41–42, 49–50, 57–58, 64, 66, 73–74, 78–88, 91, 93, 95–97, 99–103, 109, 119–121, 123, 125–130, 140–142, 144, 146–148, 154–157, 163–164, 166, 168–169, 171n7, 172n21, 172n5, 173n8, 173n13, 175n13, 175n14, 177n4, 178n8, 178n12, 178n25, 178n29, 179n15; at Cacaxtla, 120–121, 123, 177n26; cropping of images in, 12; on mud, 6, 66, 171n7; production techniques, 12; Veracruz, 54–55

nagualism, 48, 75–89, 175n3, 175n4, 175n7. *See also* shamanism. *See also under* Maya; military
Nahuatl, 20, 25, 62, 64, 75, 133, 174n18, 175n3
Nanahuatzin, 96–97, 122
necklaces, 27, 33, 36, 39, 54, 57, 73; of teeth, 88
Nequatewa, Edmund, 180n1
Neumann, Franke, 179n7
Noguera tunnel, 24, 172n3
Northwest Compound, 108–109
noseplaques, 33, 39, 41, 178n22; butterfly, 125, 133–135, 138, 145–146, 168, 177n4; fanged, 29–30, 32–33, 57, 173n13; rattlesnake, 177n4; "Tlaloc," 177n4
Nutini, Hugo, 46–49, 173n4
Nuttall, Zelia, 114

Oaxaca, 31, 51–52, 54, 62, 84, 98, 125, 142, 171n8
Oaxaca Barrio, 8, 171n8
obsidian, 6, 37, 51, 79–80, 82–83, 87–88, 126, 175n13
Old Fire God, 112, 118, 177n11
Olmec, 11, 14, 28–32, 35, 37, 77–78, 80, 84, 111–112, 148, 153, 163, 175n4. *See also under* headdresses; ritual; rulers
Orr, Heather, xii
Otomi, 179n7
Oztoyahualco (apartment compound), 105

Paddock, John, 8
Painal, 152, 179n5
Palace of Quetzalpapalotl, 82
palaces, 5, 32, 55, 64, 66, 70, 82, 85, 95, 105, 144, 158, 175n13; Maya, 110

Palenque, 11, 23, 29, 54, 80, 149, 162, 174n19, 174n23, 179n3, 179n13, 179n24

palo volador, 150–152, 156

Panofsky, Erwin, 20

Pantitlan, 151

paper, 12, 46, 54, 73, 126, 136, 152–153, 157, 178n6, 179n7

Parsons, Mark, 131, 172n6

Pasztory, Esther, xii, 2, 14–16, 18–19, 24, 26, 29, 32, 35, 39, 42, 55, 61, 63, 70, 84, 106, 140–141, 144, 147–148, 157, 172n3, 172n7, 172n20, 172n21, 172n23, 173n14, 173n15, 173n16, 173n21, 174n10, 174n29, 175n13, 176n3, 176n5, 176n6, 177n11, 177n17, 177n19, 177n25, 178n18, 178n24, 179n12, 179n13, 179n14, 179n15

Patio of the Jaguars, 105

patios, 6, 45, 96, 103, 120, 173n22; at Cacaxtla, 121; orientation of, 103–104, 107–110, 176n3; principal patios, 6, 27, 38, 45, 48–49, 66, 95, 104–110, 118–119, 125, 138, 144–145; at Tetimpa, 104–105, 177n17. *See also names of individual apartment compounds. See also under* burials; temples

Patlachique period, 176n6

patriline, 48, 67, 74

Paulinyi, Zoltan, 140, 172n7, 172n21, 173n14, 173n16

Paxton, Meredith, 180n27

pecked crosses, 116–117, 177n22, 177n23

Penney, David, 74

Period I (Monte Albán), 31

Period II (Monte Albán), 85, 98

Period III (Monte Albán), 98

Peters, Rudolph, 139–140

Pickering, Robert, 179n30

Piedras Negras, 51–53

pilgrimage, 4, 7, 10, 38, 59, 108

plaster, 6, 12, 64, 66, 116, 162, 171n7, 174n23, 177n23

plazas, 2, 5, 106, 169; Aztec, 151; Maya, 110; Oaxaca, 69; Plaza of the Glyphs, 25–26; Plaza of the Moon, 5, 35, 38–39, 107, 114, 157, 159–164, 166, 168, 173n18, 173n23, 175n13, 179n15; Plaza of the Sun, 116; Plaza One, 106. *See also under* altars

Pleiades, 117, 177n23. *See also* astronomy

Plog, Stephen, 100–101

Plunket, Patricia, 104–105, 177n1, 177n17

pochteca, 126, 175n18

Pohl, John, 51, 59–62, 68, 174n15

Pohl, Mary, 141

Popol Vuh, 179n12

population, 6–7, 46, 68, 100, 142, 171n6, 176n6

porticos, 6, 17, 27, 78, 96, 99. *See also* Atetelco; Tepantitla; Tetitla

portraiture. *See* censers; Maya; rulers; Teotihuacan

Postclassic period, 19–20, 47–48, 51, 59, 61, 85, 96–98, 111–112, 122–123, 143, 153–155, 160, 162, 174n11

priests, 10, 15, 19, 32, 42, 70, 147–148, 157, 162, 164, 169, 173n15, 179n1; Aztec, 151, 156; Colonial, 51; Mixtec, 59, 62

primogeniture, 60, 66, 93

private art, 10, 36

private space, 6–7, 38–39, 72, 106–107, 145, 158; Tlaxcala, 49

propaganda, 19, 119, 124, 139–145, 168–169; for men, 139–140; for women, 141–143

Proskouriakoff, Tatiana, 8, 110, 138, 181

public art and architecture, 10, 23, 33, 36, 39, 41, 44, 89, 135; Maya, 67; Zapotec, 99. *See also* architecture

public space, 5, 7, 10, 85, 99, 101, 120, 145, 163; and ritual, 98; San Martín Huamelulpan, 85; Tlaxcala, 49

Pueblo Perdido, 63

pumas, 82, 88, 166, 175n14

pyrite, 38, 51, 55, 73, 88, 173n21

quechquemitl, 33–35, 38, 42, 53, 157, 173n15

Quetzalcoatl, 114

Quirigua, 111, 149, 179n3

rain, 6, 21, 48, 100, 114, 117, 126–127, 155. *See also* water

Ramos Phase, 84

Rattray, Evelyn, 8, 45–46, 56, 63, 66, 104, 171n8

Reagan, Ronald, 165–166

Redmond, Elsa, 98–99

Reents-Budet, Dorie, xii

Reese-Taylor, Kathryn, xii

Reichel-Dolmatoff, Gerardo, 175n16

Reilly, F. Kent, xii, 31, 77, 111, 149, 175n9, 175n10, 179n2

Relación de Michoacán, 54

Relación geográfica, 62

residences, 5, 7, 64, 99, 174n22; San Martín Huamelulpan, 85. *See also* apartment compounds; Ciudadela; *and names of individual apartment compounds*

ritual, 6–7, 15, 19, 32, 47, 57–58, 61–62, 78–80, 82, 84–88, 99, 101, 108, 110, 120, 135, 144, 146, 166, 168–169, 180n30; and architecture, 5–6, 104, 110, 117–118; Aztec, 46–49, 75, 78–79, 91, 97, 150–154, 179n7; Chinese, 79; and fire, 118; katsina, 100–101; Maya, 46, 52, 110–112, 149–150; Olmec, 77–78, 148–149; private, 7, 38, 45, 48–49, 72, 106–107; public, 7, 25, 49, 85, 98, 101, 105–107, 146–147, 159, 163, 166; and rubber, 174n14; space, 6, 109–110, 119, 124; tree-raising, 148–157, 162–164, 179n8

Robertson, Donald, 176n99

Robertson, Ian, xii, 174n21

rulers, 8–11, 15–16, 18, 23–25, 37, 44, 68–72, 90–91, 96, 98–99, 101, 103, 119, 122–123, 145, 147, 166–167, 169, 172n2, 176n6; Aztec, 24, 31, 36, 42, 66, 75, 91, 97–100, 102, 122–123; burial of, 9, 24, 172n2, 172n4, 172n12, 172n13, 174n11; Chinese, 79; female, 41; joint rulership, 42–43; limiting power of, 10, 24, 43, 70, 176n6; Maya, 8, 12, 14, 23, 25, 28, 30, 33, 54, 68, 175n15; Mixtec, 54, 59, 61, 68–69; names in hieroglyphs, 17, 26, 37, 133; Olmec, 28, 30–32, 35, 77, 148–149, 163; portraiture of, 15, 27–44, 70–71, 78, 80, 96, 119, 157, 173n13, 173n17, 179n1; residence of, 2, 10, 95, 144; Roman, 42; staff of, 9, 24, 31–32, 172n12; Tarascan, 54, 57–58; Tupinamba, 85; Zapotec, 8, 31

sacrifice, 82–86, 103; of animals, 88; auto-sacrifice, 82, 97, 179n12; of birds, 78–79, 82, 86; of children or infants, 46, 48, 155; of deities, 96, 122; gladiator, 97, 136; heart, 36, 82, 84, 155; human sacrifice, 9, 16, 24–25, 32–33, 79–80, 82, 84, 86–87, 89, 135, 154–155; in Moon Pyramid, 88; of warriors, 123, 136, 139–140, 145, 153–154, 169. *See also* Feathered Serpent Pyramid. *See also under* mountains

Sahagún, Bernardino de, 31, 46, 48, 75, 78–79, 85, 97–98, 122,

127, 136–139, 142, 144, 150–158, 173n3, 175n21, 177n27, 177n28, 178n10, 179n5

Sahlins, Marshall, 20–22

Sánchez Alaniz, Jose, 45–46

Sánchez Sánchez, Jesús, 177n25

Sanders, William, 174n27, 177n2

San Martín Huamelulpan, 85

San Martín Pajapán, 148, 179n2

Santiago Atitlan, 112–113, 177n14

Sarabia, Alejandro, xii

Sattler, Mareike, xii

scepters, 9, 24, 172n12

Scheffler, Lilian, 47, 173n4

Schele, Linda, xii, 20–21, 27–28, 32, 111, 127, 129, 137–138, 148–149, 163, 172n7, 172n18, 173n9, 175n15, 177n17, 178n7, 178n11, 178n13, 179n2, 179n24

Schondube, Otto, 160–162, 179n23, 179n24, 180n25

Schuster, Angela, 88

sculpture, 32–42, 56, 64, 95, 118, 120, 148, 156–157, 160, 163, 173n13, 173n18, 173n19, 173n23, 174n11, 179n15. *See also* colossal sculptures

Séjourné, Laurette, 58, 80, 84, 118, 133, 171n5

Seler, Eduard, 19–20, 136–138, 178n22

Sempowski, Martha, 45

Serrano, Carlos, 46, 58, 85

Serra Puche, Mari Carmen, 41, 177n20

shamanism, 32–33, 37, 75, 77–80, 86, 175n4, 175n5, 175n16; in China, 79. *See also* nagualism

Sharer, Robert, 8

shell, 21, 27, 45, 54–55, 73, 88; trumpets, 31, 33, 173n9

shields, 36–37, 56, 74, 77–78, 82, 91, 98, 129–135, 142, 152, 175n14

snakes, 9, 24, 32, 45, 75, 84, 88, 93, 95, 98, 101, 111, 120–121, 137, 175n19, 177n4; on balustrades, 105; warriors, 93. *See also* Coatepec; Feathered Serpent Pyramid; feathered serpents

sodalities, 19, 100–101, 166, 176n9. *See also* military: orders

solstice, 161–162

souls, 47–49, 79–80, 136–137, 141, 147, 153–155

spears, 31, 37, 73, 77, 173n12

Spearthrower Owl, 37, 178n12, 178n13. *See also* Atlatl-Owl

speech scrolls, 25–26, 31, 59, 61, 80, 131, 140, 155

Spence, Michael, 8, 44–45, 171n8, 174n26, 175n21, 176n22

spiders, 141–142, 168

spindle whorls, 143

Spores, Ronald, 84–85

stelae, 10–12, 23, 25, 31, 41, 51–53, 84, 111, 127–129, 150, 175n15, 179n3

Stone, Andrea, xii, 174n14

Storey, Rebecca, xii, 45–46, 66, 84, 141–142, 174n13, 178n27

Street of the Dead Complex, 10, 176n6

streets, 6, 7, 171n7. *See also* Avenue of the Dead

Stuart, David, 8, 37, 127, 133, 138, 175n5, 175n7, 178n11, 178n12

Stuart, George, 177n26

Sugiyama, Saburo, xii, 9–10, 24–25, 73, 88–89, 95, 120, 144, 172n4, 172n12, 172n13, 172n15, 172n23, 174n16, 175n2, 175n19, 175n21, 176n5, 176n22

sun, 96, 107, 117, 158–159, 160–161, 163–164, 168, 179n19, 180n30; in Aztec myth, 79, 96–97, 102, 122, 136, 139–140, 142, 150, 158, 179n18; in Aztec ritual, 150–151; in Maya myth, 158. *See also* astronomy

Sun Pyramid, 2–4, 7, 9–10, 24, 37, 106–110, 115–116, 118–119, 122, 129, 158–160, 163–164, 171n2, 172n3, 173n22, 176n4, 176n7, 177n18, 177n23, 179n21; cave underneath, 9–10, 62, 70, 108, 117, 158, 162, 171n3; and Cerro Patlachique, 114–115, 117; possible tomb, 24; size of, 7. *See also under* astronomy; caves

Superimposed Buildings Compound, 108–109

talud-tablero, 4, 124–125, 138, 168; as compositional element, 147; outside of Teotihuacan, 125, 177n2; at Tetimpa, 105, 177n1; symbolism of, 125, 134–135, 145

Taube, Karl, xii, 10–11, 20, 25–26, 31–32, 38, 46, 80, 82, 97–98, 114, 133, 138, 141, 144, 172n22, 173n16, 173n20, 174n16, 175n1, 176n7, 178n5, 178n12, 178n14, 178n18, 178n19, 179n10, 179n11

Techinantitla (apartment compound), 17–18, 25, 172n17

Tecuciztecatl, 96–97, 122

Tecum Umam, 76, 175n7

Tedlock, Denis, 179n12

telpochcalli, 100

Temple of Agriculture, 57–58

temples, 1, 2, 5, 35–36, 39, 51, 63–64, 70, 125, 134–135, 160; Aztec, 24, 64, 91, 117, 127, 150, 153; in triads, 23, 104–111, 113, 117–119, 176n2, 176n6, 176n7; Maya, 24, 110, 179n24; miniature in apartment compound patios, 6, 118; Mixtec, 59, 64; in quadratic arrangements, 108–110. *See also* three-temple complexes; *names of individual temples. See also under* mountains

Tenan, 114

Tenochtitlan, 24, 77, 91, 117, 122–123, 127, 151, 156–157, 175n12, 179n7

Teocalli, 156–157

teomamas, 59, 61

Teopancaxco (apartment compound), 15–16

Teotihuacan: art style, 10–16, 19, 26–28, 155–156; corporate model for, 14–16; derivation of the name, 64, 174n21; foreign contacts, 7, 8, 14, 125, 167–168, 178n11; foreigners residing at, 19, 87, 171n8; location of, 7; map, 5; Mapping Project, 66, 105; orientation of, 1; portraiture, 14, 26–27; size of, 7–8

Teotihuacan Valley, 1, 7, 113–114, 117, 155, 168

tepache, 150

Tepantitla (apartment compound), 11, 15–16, 25–30, 32–33, 35, 42, 49–50, 87, 140–143, 147–148, 154–157, 163–164, 168, 172n21, 173n8, 173n13, 173n15, 175n19, 178n25, 178n29, 179n13, 179n15; Portico 2, 147, 154

tepetate, 25, 88, 105

Terminal Classic period, 52, 54, 121, 123

Teteoinnan, 152

Tetimpa, 104–105, 125, 177n1, 177n17

Tetitla (apartment compound), 5, 12, 17, 32–33, 45, 78, 80, 96–97, 100–101, 108–110, 118, 120, 123, 126–127, 129, 133, 173n17

Teuchtitlan. *See* Huitzilapa

Thin Orange ceramics, 7, 72, 84, 169

Thompson, J. Eric, 141